PENGUIN MOD

MY APPRE

Beatrice Webb was born, as Beatrice Potter, in 1858 near Gloucester. She investigated working-class conditions in London with Charles Booth and studied co-operative theory and practice. She wrote *The Co-operative Movement in Great Britain* in 1891. A year later she married Sidney Webb, with whom she served on many royal commissions, on poor law, trade-union law and coal-mines. They helped to found the London School of Economics and Political Science (1895) and the *New Statesman* (1913), set up a socialist *salon* in London and produced jointly a series of detailed studies in social history, including their *History of Trade Unionism* (1894), *Industrial Democracy* (1897), *English Local Government* (10 vols., 1906–29) and the politically important minority report of the Poor Law Commission (1909). In 1932 the Webbs visited Russia in order to study the Soviet system, and in 1935 published *Soviet Communism: A New Civilization?* Beatrice died in 1943, having written *My Apprenticeship* in 1926. *Our Partnership*, the beginnings of a book about her life with Sidney, was published posthumously in 1948, and two volumes of selections from the *Diaries*, edited by Margaret Cole, in 1952 and 1956.

BEATRICE WEBB

*My Apprenticeship*

WITH AN INTRODUCTION
BY BRIAN JACKSON

*Penguin Books*

Penguin Books Ltd, Harmondsworth, Middlesex, England
Penguin Books Inc., 7110 Ambassador Road, Baltimore, Maryland 21207, U.S.A.
Penguin Books, Australia Ltd, Ringwood, Victoria, Australia

—

First published by Longmans, Green & Co 1926
Published in Penguin Books 1971

—

Made and printed in Great Britain by
Cox and Wyman Ltd, London Reading and Fakenham
Set in Linotype Georgian

# Contents

was faintly familiar: but who was Beatrice Webb, I wondered?

'Beatrice' said her mother 'is the only one of my children who is below the average in intelligence.' But Herbert Spencer, the dominant Victorian philosopher who was her friend and tutor in the strange, prosperous relationship between 'the child and the thinker' said that she 'reminded him of George Eliot'. She was born on 2 January 1858 at Standish House near Gloucester as Beatrice Potter. Her parents were members of the idle rich until they lost much of their wealth in the financial crash of 1847. 'A stroke of good luck,' said Beatrice later, for it turned them into a family of the active, working rich. She grew up in a household where great speculators and industrialists dined with her father, lingering round the table to drink his madeira and smoke his havanas, while they toyed with the latest prospect of putting their capital to work by sinking a mine or charting out a railway or planning a new chain of mills ('water plentiful and labour docile'). Meanwhile their women, groomed for suitable marriage-bed and child-bed were otherwise condemned to a life of elaborate pleasure: 'a tiresome undertaking', said the awkward Beatrice and one 'entailing expensive plant'.

During Beatrice's childhood, England was at the very tip of her powers. Europe was exhausted by the Napoleonic wars, and scarred by the succeeding decades of revolution. America was isolated, split, uncertain of what she yet was to be. And the old civilizations of the Orient seemed frozen or dying. The map was being painted red. Every year up to a quarter of a million people left Britain to form the new stock of the Dominions, and the ruling class of that fantastic spread of British Colonies. Canada began to unify in 1840; New Zealand federated in 1854 and Australia and Cape Colony followed after. Other nations faced civil war, *coups d'état*, revolution in the streets; Britain passed her great Reform Bills, and prospered. She was a unified state: America and Germany were not. The power-balance was tipped heavily in her favour. She was an industrial nation, buying cheap and selling dear: she had no rival. The Royal Navy of this tiny island swept the oceans, and 'the world-wide power of the City of London' in David Thomson's phrase[2] 'was as discretely veiled from public view as the legs of a mid-Victorian piano'.

It seemed to many that most human problems on these islands could be solved simply by expansion, enterprise, and the incredible increase in national wealth. 'For the history of our country during the last hundred and sixty years is eminently the history of physical, of moral, and of intellectual improvement,' writes Macaulay opening his *History of England* in the very year in which Karl Marx is penning the Communist Manifesto. But of the moral improvement there may be some question: for the immense economic success of mid-Victorian England had been subtly transformed into a style of life, a way of valuing people. Because – for the moment – industry and trade flourished best without state protection, it came to be assumed that men's and women's best interests were also well served if they were compelled to rely entirely on their own resources. And the wisdom of Jeremy Bentham ('the greatest happiness of the greatest number') was misread, and used as the philosophic *imprimatur* on a 'free-for-all-and-devil-take-the-hindmost' society. It was Beatrice's own tutor, Herbert Spencer, who coined the phrase 'the survival of the fittest'.[3] Behind all stood the oppressive ghosts of Adam Smith and Charles Darwin.

*My Apprenticeship* gives us glimpses of a child and young woman growing up in this world of belief. At 15 she is travelling with her father in the United States (where he has added the presidency of the Great Trunk Railway of Canada to his chairmanship of the Great Western Railway in Britain). Taken round the schools in Chicago, she is surprised to note that 'boys and girls, of all classes, are educated here. It was so funny to see a common little Negro girl sitting between two

2. See *England in the Nineteenth Century* by David Thomson (Harmondsworth), for an excellent overview of the age.
3. There is an unusual essay on Spencer in *The Art of the Soluble* by Peter Medawar (Harmondsworth), and a suggestive reassessment in *The Origins of British Sociology* by Philip Abrams (Chicago).

well-dressed banker's daughters, and learning the same thing!' And in San Francisco she can make nothing of the Chinese theatre: 'There was no attempt at scenery, and the actors had the most unceremonious way of laughing and joking with their friends in the audience.' Besides, 'being in such close quarters with John Chinaman was not exactly pleasant'.

But ten years later Beatrice begins to break through the narrow moralities, the self-contained culture of her background. Sitting by firelight she listens to Da, her old nurse, telling her once again of her working-class relatives, who come from one or two generations back when her grandfather was an ambitious lad in the cotton mills round Rossendale and Bacup. ' "Da", said I, as I watched a narrow bridge of black coal give way, tumble into the red-hot mass below and burst into flame; "I should dearly love to go to Bacup next time you go." ' So begins the marvellous account of her first stay with the weavers. 'I felt as if I were living through a page of puritan history.' Once drab words – co-op, chapel, union, overtime – vibrate with new meaning; and in these unforgettable pages you feel that in some deep way, she has chosen her path.

At this point she could perhaps have decided to be a novelist, paid her tribute to Bacup with her own *Mill on the Floss* or criticized the savage, fundamentally financial morality of the big city with her own successor to *Our Mutual Friend*. As Dr Leavis hinted, you have to make sense of Beatrice Webb by relating her to the great novelists. But in some way from the 1880s onwards, the novel gradually lost some of its territory to emergent sociology. Before that, the whole social landscape belonged to the novelist. But gradually we see the social scientists – Beatrice Webb, Charles Booth, Seebohm Rowntree – claiming more and more of that land, and prospecting it in quite different ways, while slowly the novel (with great exceptions) curls back into the exploration of essentially small groups and private lives.

After Bacup, Beatrice joins Octavia Hill and the Barnetts in the work of the Charity Organization Society (C.O.S.), and later manages Katharine Buildings, near St Katharine Dock – a working-class tenement block erected by philanthropists. But now one notes how quickly she sizes up, and then rejects the C.O.S. Their purpose is not to be charitable at all, but to prevent 'indiscriminate' charity and advise people to stand on their own feet. 'The belief – it may almost be called an obsession – that the mass-misery of great cities arose mainly, if not entirely, from spasmodic, indiscriminate and unconditional doles, whether in the form of alms or in that of Poor Law relief, was, in the sixties and seventies, the common opinion of such enlightened members of the governing class as were interested in the problems of poverty.' With that eye for detail and incident which makes *My Apprenticeship* such a vivid social theatre she recalls how one old gentleman on the C.O.S. committee secretly pushed a sixpence underneath a poor woman's hand, just as Octavia Hill 'was pointing out to her the reasons why we could not give her money, and offering her the soundest advice'. Poor old man: he was seen and driven tearfully back to the party line.

Katharine Buildings ('block dwellings in the style known as the *Later Desolate*' said the Liberal C. F. S. Masterman) was Beatrice Webb's base for two years. Again and again we see in this extraordinary woman how she differed from her family or her colleagues by finding out for herself and trusting the evidence of her eyes. This is very true of her later research into the past documentation or present nature of local government, the unions or the co-ops. But in *My Apprenticeship* it is strikingly true of people. When she gives evidence to the House of Lords Committee into the abominable sweating system in the spring of 1888 she is the only investigator who has actually been a trouser-hand. And been sacked: 'for my sewing, they said, was too good for the trade.' But at Katharine Buildings she had worked herself to exhaustion, and – in the eyes of the 'enlightened members of the governing class' pulled off a great success. Yet it was all, she wrote in her diary, an 'utter failure'. By itself it did not, and could not, make any significant difference to the lot of the millions blown around the spirals of poverty. Where was the lever which would multiply her strength?

That too was the question which the other pioneer social investigators were asking. And one of them was her cousin, the Liverpool shipping magnate, Charles Booth. In 1887 she joined him in his colossal seventeen-year survey of *The Life and Labour of the People of London*: the 'map of poverty' which, now that the tidal wave it sent through late Victorian society has died down, remains one of the founding works of the empirical school of British sociology. 'Prior to this inquiry, neither the individualist nor the socialist could state with any approach to accuracy what exactly was the condition of the people of Great Britain.'

This vast inquiry standing midway between the world of the great Victorian social novel and the world of demographic statistics, gave us a new voice: 'a subtle combination of quantative and qualitive analysis' which has since been the very pith of British social science. In a paragraph in the first volume of the survey which has not had perhaps the fame it deserves, Charles Booth writes:

To judge rightly we need to bear both in mind, never to forget the numbers when thinking of the percentages, nor the percentages when thinking of the numbers. This last is difficult to those whose daily experience or whose imagination brings vividly before them the trials and sorrows of individual lives. They refuse to set off and balance the happy hours of the same class, or even of the same people, against these miseries; much less can they consent to bring the lot of other classes into the account, add up the opposing figures, and contentedly carry forward a credit balance. In the arithmetic of woe they can only add or multiply, they cannot subtract or divide. In intensity of feeling such as this, and not in statistics, lies the power to love the world. But by statistics must this power be guided if it would move the world aright.

And yet the social survey as Booth developed it was not quite the lever. It yielded facts in place of supposition, but it didn't always yield illumination. 'It is the sense of helplessness that tries everyone,' said Booth, 'the wage earners, as

I have said, are helpless to negotiate or obtain the value of their work; the manufacturer or dealer can only work within the limits of competition; the rich are helpless to relieve want without stimulating its sources; the legislature is helpless because limits of successful interference by change of law are closely circumscribed.' Later, reflecting on the vast and noble task he set himself, Booth noted 'I have at times doubted whether the prolongation of this work has had any other basis than an inability on my part to come to a conclusion.'

The trouble was that sociology in its infancy – struggling to break away from ideas about the survival of the fittest and limited by its often crude, home-hewn tools of inquiry and analysis – didn't, in this country at least, sufficiently explain those questions of poverty and inequality which dominated people's concern. On the other hand the rising socialist movement offered very black and white explanations indeed, and the prospect of socialist experiment – and ultimately a socialist administration – attracted Beatrice quite as powerfully, as the hope of advance through a more developed social science.

So Beatrice Webb served her 'apprenticeship'. Later in 1889 when she begins her serious study of the Co-operative Movement we get pages of wonderful documentary writing, and lovely vignettes in the footnotes such as the touching picture of J. T. W. Mitchell the illegitimate boy who became chairman of the Co-op and who – wherever he was – would travel back third class and all night in order to take his weekly Sunday School at Rochdale Chapel. But we get a new intellectual rigour, and that clarity of mind which leads her to discover (what we all now accept) that the Co-operative Movement was not, as it thought it was and said it was, a co-operative of workers, but 'a democracy of customers of the store, and thus of the consumers, not of the producers of the commodities'. Her subsequent studies of trade unions share the same central clarity of analysis – seeing them to be, in contradiction to their picture of themselves – as associations to limit the supply of labour. It is a measure of how much

Beatrice Webb helped to create our thinking about society that these analyses, so outrageous to many in the working-class movements of the past, are now the norm and staple of our thinking. Her mind has been so engrained in ours that (to repoint T. S. Eliot's tribute to Aristotle) 'she is what we know'.

*My Apprenticeship* is Beatrice's book. But by the final pages the great partner of her life ('the little man with the big head who was to become the man of my destiny') is elusively there. And the next book is to be *Our Partnership*. It is a lovely individual tale of courtship and joint work. All the more moving for the grainy, unfashionable honesty with which she relates it. Sidney Webb is a very great man who has never had his due – except from Beatrice. Apparently it was always so for him. On their engagement, Beatrice went along to see Herbert Spencer. 'We met yesterday at The Athenaeum by appointment. He was affectionate and cordial to me personally. "I cannot congratulate you – that would be insincere." Then there was a short pause. "My family have taken it benevolently," I remarked, and then observed that there was after all nothing against Mr Webb, he had proved himself to be a man of capacity and determination. "You see that he has succeeded in marrying me, Mr Spencer; that shows he has a will." ' No couple can pull off such incredible achievements as the Webbs did, without some germ of envy stirring within us. Sidney Webb was usually the one who attracted the defensive ridicule which this led to. It was hard to accept that he knew as much as he did, worked as hard as he did, and was as successful as he was – and all done with quiet modesty, and without the aids of blue blood, wealth or even a public school. Beatrice had known the opposite kind of man when she had fallen in love with Joseph Chamberlain – *there* was the prima donna to whom society bowed down, who in his meteoric career had the unique distinction of joining both parties and splitting them both. And still the poor were poor.

Sidney Webb was a man of rarer metal. In after years Bernard Shaw remembered his first meeting. Sidney Webb was then a young civil servant by day and a lecturer at the Working Men's College by night. Shaw encountered him at a debate: 'He knew all about the subject of the debate; he knew more than the lecturer; knew more than anybody present; had read everything that had ever been written on the subject; and remembered all the facts that bore upon it.'

Shaw and Webb were two of that tiny band of left-wing thinkers who had founded the Fabian Society. Beatrice first heard of him in the autumn of 1889 when that thin pamphlet which was to help change so much – *Fabian Essays* – was first published. She noted: 'by far the most significant and interesting essay is the one by Sidney Webb; he has the historic sense.' This was the paper in which he spelled out the strong thinking behind the later motto-phrase 'the inevitability of gradualness' – or 'Sidney Webbicalism' as his critics put it. By a lovely coincidence, earlier in the same year Sidney had reviewed the first volume of Charles Booth's great survey, and noted 'the only contributor with any literary talent is Miss Beatrice Potter.'

Now they met; soon Sidney was sitting at Beatrice's feet among the 'relays of working men' as she travelled third class to the Glasgow Co-operative conference. Two months later she is lying in Epping Forest, while Sidney reads her Rossetti, and in the summer of 1892 they are married.

It is hard to think of the Webbs and their achievements apart. Yet marvellous as their union was, their talents and works were different. Sidney's is perhaps the harder to estimate, partly because of his modesty. 'No personalities please,' he said when Beatrice told him her plans to write *My Apprenticeship* and *Our Partnership*. But it was Sidney Webb, more than any other man, who built up and generalled the Fabian Society. Under his discreet leadership they focused their wealth of ideas and proposals on to the London County Council, and when in 1889 a Progressive Majority was returned, the great experiment began. London is the laboratory of Britain. If the Fabians – and particularly Sidney Webb – could bring in 'municipal socialism' there, and make it credible, then tomorrow it could be done for the whole country. It is easy to forget the hostile climate in which Sidney Webb pulled off this revolutionary feat. This was a period when the leader writer of *The Times* could still maintain that any suggestion that a man had 'a right to work or eat' was 'a wild proposition'. And one in which even the ladies who worked with Beatrice in the Charity Organization Society could express horror at the idea of 'ill-considered and wholesale feeding of school children' or at evil talk of 'rate-paid and State-subsidized medical treatment'.

Apart from marrying Beatrice, Sidney Webb's first great achievement was to transform the city state of London – a declining, but still incredibly powerful centre of world capitalism – into an experiment in socialism. An experiment which worked, and which multiplied. A brilliant array of practical ideas, backed by a thousand hours in committee, and many more drafting and lobbying, gave London 'municipal socialism'. With characteristic humour, he described the result:

The individualist town councillor will walk along the municipal pavement, lit by municipal gas and cleansed by municipal brooms with municipal water and – seeing by the municipal clock in the municipal market, that he is too early to meet his children coming from the municipal school, hard by the county lunatic asylum and the municipal hospital, will use the national telegraph system to tell them not to walk through the municipal park, but to come by the municipal tramway to meet him in the municipal reading-room, by the municipal museum, art-gallery, and library, where he intends ... to prepare his next speech in the municipal town hall in favour of the nationalization of canals and the increase of Government control over the railway system. 'Socialism, Sir,' he will say, 'don't waste the time of a practical man by your fantastic absurdities. Self-help, Sir, individual self-help, that's what has made our city what it is.'

His second great achievement, and one in which Beatrice hardly played the lesser role, was to extend the ambience of the Fabian Society so that its essential influence rippled over the generations and into nooks and crannies of power where its presence was hardly suspected. He did this in two particular ways; by founding the London School of Economics, and by setting up the *New Statesman*. In the late nineties, there were only a score of undergraduates studying economics in London: quite sufficient, claimed the authorities. But a splendid windfall came the way of the Fabian Society: a little known but quarrelsome old member, startled them by bequeathing £10,000 in his will. Sidney was appointed a Trustee. He decided that what was needed was not more 'nondescript socialists' in Parliament, but to found 'slowly and quietly a London School of Economics and Political Science'. 'We want,' he said, 'the ordinary citizen to feel that reforming society is no light matter, and must be undertaken by experts specially trained for the purpose.' There was infinite lobbying to be done, and fund-raising too ('extracted by Beatrice Webb' wrote Shaw across his own cheque). And there was a shade of doubt about whether Sidney could rightfully use the money in this way. He sought legal advice from R. B. Haldane. Haldane studied the deed, and asked whether Sidney remained a convinced socialist:

'Yes.'

'Do you then believe that the more social conditions are studied scientifically and impartially, the stronger does the case for socialism become?'

'Yes.'

'Very well, if you believe that, you are entitled to use the bequest for the starting of a school for scientific, impartial study, and teaching.'

In 1898, the Webbs rented two rooms in the Adelphi, and the L.S.E. was born. The *New Statesman and Nation* ('*Damnation*' as the critics called it) was an equally adroit operation. In 1912, the Webbs saw that the Fabian influence would be better advanced by a public paper, quite independent of the little society. They collected a thousand pounds from the ironically generous Shaw, topped it up with other donations, and ignoring the pessimistic advice of the professionals they compiled a mailing list of 20,000 names and addresses, made a pre-publication cut-price offer, and with 2,500 subscribers in the day before the first issue was printed, they were away. Later, the paper gobbled up the *Nation* and became far and away the most influential socialist platform in the country, and, at several critical moments, in the world.

Sidney Webb's third major achievement was the colouring he gave to the British Labour Party. The Labour Party has always been a strange coalition of interests – Methodist, trade union, socialist, cooperative. And the socialist group has always been a minority, if a powerful one, in the party. Again it was the same story: good ideas backed by thousands of hours of quiet, intelligent and infinitely painstaking work. But the result was that in a dozen different ways he stamped a gradualist, socialist marking on the party – and it proved to be a temper that the electorate would eventually accept. He was the man who took the trouble to draft its basically socialist constitution in 1918. He gave it, as did Beatrice, so much of its vocabulary ('the inevitability of gradualness' 'collective bargaining'). And together they built a perpetual pump-primer in the Labour Research Department.

Beatrice's part in this plentiful partnership is, with time, a little easier to assess. The Webbs of course would not have agreed. They would have claimed that such importance as they had, lay in their joint work, and especially in their major volumes of historical and social research stretching from the *History of Trade Unionism* in 1894 (which Lenin himself translated into Russian) to *Soviet Communism: A New Civilization?* in 1935. And in *My Apprenticeship* Beatrice writes ruefully: 'And if by any chance the book that I am now writing should prove a "better seller" than the most intellectually distinguished of our works – *Statutory Authorities for Special Purposes, 1698–1835* (which, I regret to say, has had but a small sale) – I shall see rising up before me the striking presence of my old friend, and hear her reiterate in ghostly but sarcastic tones, *"Mais que le public Anglais est bête!"*'

For once she was wrong. Though it has its peers, no autobiography in English is as intellectually distinguished as *My Apprenticeship*. And her prime achievements are probably her volumes of autobiography and diary, and her immense fight against the old Poor Law which led, as Nazi Germany collapsed and a Labour Government returned to power in Great Britain, to the creation of the Welfare State.

No one who has read the history of the nineteenth century, or the novels of Dickens, can forget that the shadow of the 1834 Poor Law hovered continually over the lives of the working population. Even today, the old, the sick, and the poor still encounter patches of the Poor Law attitudes in some social security offices or the most backward institutions for the old. Beatrice Webb gave her blood to end it. The principles of 1834 were that a man's poverty and destitution were basically his own fault, and very frequently the result of fecklessness and idleness. To subsidize him at all meant taking money away from the pockets of other working men who by their industry and character had avoided destitution. To subsidize him to any serious extent meant making destitution tolerable, and even profitable – and by offering this support reducing the individual's self-reliance and ultimately increasing the number of feckless people in society. The result was that the country maintained a system of workhouses – each 'Union' governed by its local board of guardians. No relief whatsoever was to be offered to able-bodied persons and their families except in the workhouse. And the workhouse itself was to be deliberately made so unpleasant that any person would do his utmost to avoid being sent there. For in the Poor Law workhouse, children were to be separated from parents, wives from husbands, old married couples split apart. Food was to be of the meanest, work of the dreariest, discipline of the strictest.

It was to inquire into this hated system that the Balfour Government in 1905 set up a Royal Commission, amongst whose members was Beatrice Webb. So began the finest, and most prolonged, campaign of her life. Despite a brilliant Webb attack – lobbying, dinners, facts, research, pressure – they did not succeed in getting their programme through, and the Commission's Report in 1909 recommended only modest changes. But they had succeeded in splitting the

Commission, and Beatrice led three others into signing a *Minority Report* (drafted by Sidney). The *Minority Report* argued a complete end of the Poor Law. It pointed out, and offered evidence that poverty was the result of many causes – old age, illness, accident, mental problems, ill-luck. It claimed that the only humane and efficient way was to tackle these problems at source. And as examples of what it meant it proposed a system of old-age pensions, medical care provided by the state, a policy of public works to maintain full employment, a national minimum wage, and local Assistance offices where money could be given to those in need, and the other social services coordinated. For once a *Minority Report* attracted more attention and sold more copies than the main report. It took the Webbs thirty-five years of campaigning, research and propaganda, before this great Report led, via the Beveridge Report, to the Welfare State in 1945. It was a noble achievement.

Like so many other social scientists in Britain, she had always only had one eye on research – and the other on the Government of the day. Had she (and Rowntree and Beveridge and their successors) stuck to their books, we may well have had that flourishing tradition of university sociology which the Webbs themselves had hoped for in helping found the first British chair in the subject at L.S.E. in 1907. As it is, we have had (and few did more than the Webbs to stamp its character) a freelancing, extramural, line of inquiry and proposal – which, though but a part of the whole, gave us the Welfare State – and at least half an answer to the questions which so vexed the Victorians.

But back in 1924 the first precarious Labour Government was formed, with four Fabians as Cabinet Ministers. Amongst them was Sidney Webb as President of the Board of Trade. For the first time for many years Beatrice was left on her own. Throughout her life she had kept a packed diary, had always felt the need – solitary at her desk in the evenings or sitting quietly in the coolness of St Paul's – to reflect, retire in upon herself and away from the perpetual pressures of those battlefields where she so excelled. Often she had felt a yearning that perhaps she had taken a wrong course, and should instead have followed George Eliot as a novelist: 'I should have become, not a worker in the field of sociology, but a descriptive psychologist.' She often speaks of being 'tempted' or 'haunted' by the attractions of novel writing, as if it were some dark angel beckoning her away from more useful work. 'The whole multitude of novels I have read pass before me; the genius, the talent, the clever mechanism or the popularity-hunting of mediocrities – what have the whole lot of them, from the work of genius to the penny-a-liner, accomplished for the advancement of society on the one and only basis that can bring with it virtue and happiness – the scientific method?'

Her answer was too narrow, and she knew it. For the diaries are the journal and commonplace book of a fine creative artist. She never used them as the fibre of the novels that sometimes filled her fantasies. But now that Sidney was involved night and day in the tormented life of the first Labour Government, she planned to turn the diaries into an autobiography. It was to have four volumes, of which *My Apprenticeship* would be the first, and *Our Partnership* would title the last three. The work was harder than she anticipated. It took two years to prepare *My Apprenticeship*, which was first published in 1926. Meanwhile a second precarious Labour Government had been returned, and Sidney became Lord Passfield, and took over the Colonial Office. Beatrice refused to be Lady Passfield, and continued with *Our Partnership*. It went ever more slowly. Throughout the thirties, the Webbs were absorbed by Soviet Russia, and as perpetual hosts at Passfield Corner to the new generation of Labour party intellectuals. And still she kept her marvellously rich diary. She died on 30 April 1943, having had the satisfaction of knowing that the Soviets had beaten the Nazis at the battle of Stalingrad, and that the feared counter-revolution all over Europe was mastered. Sidney saw the war out, and the triumphant return of a strong Labour Government, which counted 230 Fabians on its benches. He died in 1947, and in December of that year their ashes were

*Note to the Penguin Edition*

This edition differs from the edition of
1926 in omitting the Introductory Note, and the
methodological appendices.

# CHAPTER I

─────── ❈❖❈ ───────

## *Character and Circumstance*

IN the following pages I describe the craft of a social investigator as I have practised it. I give some account of my early and crude observation and clumsy attempts at reasoning, and then of the more elaborated technique of note-taking, of listening to and recording the spoken word and of observing and even experimenting in the life of existing institutions. Though for the purpose of describing my craft I quote pages from my MS. diary, I have neither the desire nor the intention of writing an autobiography yet the very subject-matter of my science is society; its main instrument is social intercourse; thus I can hardly leave out of the picture the experience I have gathered, not deliberately as a scientific worker, but casually as child, unmarried woman, wife and citizen. For the sociologist, unlike the physicist, chemist and biologist, is in a quite unique manner the creature of his environment. Birth and parentage, the mental atmosphere of class and creed in which he is bred, the characteristics and attainments of the men and women who have been his guides and associates, come first and foremost of all the raw material upon which he works, alike in order of time and in intimacy of contact. It is his own social and economic circumstance that determines the special opportunities, the peculiar disabilities, the particular standpoints for observation and reasoning – in short, the inevitable bias with which he is started on his way to discovery, a bias which ought to be known to the student of his work so that it may be adequately discounted. Moreover, in the formative years of childhood and youth, the passionate search for a creed by which to live precedes the acquisition of a craft; the craft, in fact, growing out of the creed, or maybe out of the loss of a creed. Hence, if in describing my apprenticeship I tell too long and too egotistical a tale, the student can skip what appears to him irrelevant.

The family in which I was born and bred was curiously typical of the industrial development of the nineteenth century. My paternal grandfather, Richard Potter, was the son of a Yorkshire tenant farmer who increased the profits of farming by keeping a general provision shop at Tadcaster; my maternal grandfather, Lawrence Heyworth, belonged to a family of 'domestic manufacturers' in Rossendale in Lancashire, the majority of whom became, in the last decades of the eighteenth century, 'hands' in the new cotton mills. Evidently my grandfathers were men of initiative and energy, for they rose rapidly to affluence and industrial power, one as a Manchester cotton warehouseman, the other as a Liverpool merchant trading with South America. Nonconformists in religion and Radicals in politics, they both became, after the 1832 Reform Act, Members of Parliament, intimate friends of Cobden and Bright, and enthusiastic supporters of the Anti-Corn Law League.[1]

My father graduated in the New London University, of which my grandfather, as a leading Unitarian, was one of the founders. He was called to the Bar, but without intending to practise. For a few years he divided his time between nursing his father, who was in failing health, and amusing himself in London political society. On the death of his father, being young, attractive and with sufficient means, he took to a life of leisure. It was at Rome, in the course of making the grand tour with a young sister, that he met my mother, likewise enjoying herself with a young brother. They fell in love amid the sights of Rome, married and settled as mere *rentiers* in Herefordshire, intending to take an active part in the work and pleasures of the county. But a stroke of good luck saved my parents and their children from

1. Richard Potter, who had contested the borough of Wigan when it was still a close corporation, was returned as its member in the 1832 Parliament. Lawrence Heyworth became member for Derby in 1847. For details about the Potters of Tadcaster see *From Ploughshare to Parliament*, by my sister Georgina Meinertzhagen.

this deadening environment. The financial crisis of 1847–8 swept away the major part of his moderate inheritance; and, with a rapidly increasing family, he had, at the age of thirty, to find some way of earning a sufficient livelihood. His father-in-law, Lawrence Heyworth, at that time a leading promoter of the new railways, made him a director of the Great Western Railway, whilst a schoolfellow, W. E. Price,[2] offered him a partnership in an old-established timber merchant's business at Gloucester. From this position of vantage my father became a capitalist at large.

The family income was mainly drawn from the timber yards of Gloucester, Grimsby and Barrow; but the mere routine of money-making did not satisfy my father. Daily attendance at an office, at work each day on the same range of facts, seemed to him as much the badge of an underling as manual work in factory or in mine. Once engaged in business he quickly developed a taste for adventurous enterprise and a talent for industrial diplomacy. For the first two years of business life he worked assiduously at the Gloucester office, mastering the technique of the timber market. The horrors of winter fighting in the Crimean War yielded the first opportunity for big enterprise. He persuaded the English War Office, and afterwards the French Emperor, to save the soldiers' lives during the winter weather, by using the timber merchant's brains, together with the depreciated stock in the timber yard, for the output of wooden huts: an operation which was worth a profit of £60,000 to the firm.[3]

2. Mr Price remained my father's greatest friend till death parted them. Ugly, shrewd, silent and kindly, he was for many years chairman of the Midland Railway and Liberal member for Gloucester. His grandson, Philips Price, famous for his adventures in and sympathy for Soviet Russia, contested Gloucester in the 1923 and 1924 elections as a Labour candidate of the Left Wing.

3. From an entry dated 7 February 1855, in the unpublished journals of N. W. Senior, quoted in *Many Memories of Many People*, by M. C. M. Simpson (daughter of Nassau Senior), pp. 170–71, I gather that my father found the French Government more efficient than the British Government in respect of the handling of the wooden huts.

'Jeune told me that Potter told him that for three weeks after he had made his proposal to the Duke of Newcastle he got no answer;

From that time onwards he spent the bulk of his energy and all his intellectual keenness in the administration of public

---

that he wrote to ask what was to be done, and was told that the paper had been mislaid, and that they wished for a copy of it; that at length the War Department having, after a great delay, resolved to have them, they were made and sent by rail to Southampton, but that the contract entered into by the Ordnance ended when they reached the railway terminus; that, after some delay, another contract was entered into for putting them on board of steamers, but that this contract merely heaped them on deck; that a further contract and a further delay was necessary to get them down into the hold; and he does not believe that at this instant they have got beyond Balaklava. Louis Napoleon sent for Potter to Saint-Cloud to consult about their being supplied to the French army. In a couple of hours the whole matter was arranged between Louis Napoleon and himself. The question then was how soon the execution of it could be begun. This was Saturday. A letter could not get to Gloucester before Monday. Louis Napoleon rang for a courier, gave him fifteen napoleons, and ordered him to be in Gloucester in twenty-four hours. Potter proposed to go to his hotel, write out the contract and specification, and return with them. Louis Napoleon said no, they must be written out immediately; that he was going out for a couple of hours, and hoped on his return to find all ready. Potter was thus left two hours alone in Louis Napoleon's cabinet, with all his private papers about. The contract, etc., was ready in two hours, was in Gloucester on Sunday, and the workmen were employed in executing it by six o'clock on Monday morning.'

When it came to settling the account, my father's experience was reversed. The British Government paid up at once. After making many applications to the French Government, my father betook himself to Paris, but utterly failed to get access to the minister concerned. With a large overdraft at the bank the financial position became intolerable. Presently his friend Tom Brassey appeared on a like quest but with greater experience of foreign governments. 'My dear Potter, what an innocent you are! Go to the Bank of France and cash a cheque for a thousand pounds; give the porter at the ministry twenty francs, and pay your way handsomely until you get to the minister; then put down five hundred pounds and you will get your money all right. Otherwise you will never get it: Great Britain will not go to war with France to get you paid!' My father took the advice. When he was admitted into the minister's presence he put down the equivalent of five hundred pounds. The minister put it in his pocket, said pleasant things about my father's stay in Paris, and signed the requisite papers authorizing immediate payment. My father used frequently to ask the more scrupulous of his business associates what they would have done under the circumstances.

companies and in financial speculations. For some years he was chairman of the Great Western Railway of England; for ten years, just the years of my girlhood, he was president of the Grand Trunk Railway of Canada. Memory recalls a maze of capitalist undertakings of which he was director or promoter; undertakings of every degree of rank and permanence, of success or failure – from high-grade concerns like the Hudson's Bay Company and the Dutch Rhenish railways, to humble establishments for the manufacture of railway wagons and signals. The most far-fetched and risky projects were not excluded from his vision. I remember a concession from the Turkish Government, obtained by him and a group of friends – among them Tom Brassey, the great contractor – to make a Grand Canal through Syria to compete with the Suez Canal; an enterprise abandoned on the report of the engineers that such a canal would not only submerge the Holy places – a small matter – but take forty years to fill. 'We are not going to wait forty years for our money to make Potter's fortune,' said Brassey to Perks and Watkin. There was another scheme for a live-cattle trade between Barrow-in-Furness and the United States, balked by Privy Council orders against cattle disease, or, as my father complained, against free trade in food. Some issues were moral rather than financial. I recollect anxious discussions as to whether he ought to 'cover' certain misdoings of the financiers who dominated the board of a great trans-continental railway, by remaining a director, which was settled in the negative; and there was a conscientious refusal to accept the presidency of another Canadian railway because he suspected queer transactions in land on the part of its promoters. But the purest commercial ethics did not always prevail. The German, like the British Government, could not be bribed, but in the transactions with most other foreign governments legislators and officials were paid 'for services rendered' without scruple. There were similar ups and downs with regard to the speculative investments: he lost heavily in Welsh coal-mines by buying and selling at the wrong time; he gained considerably by taking up the shares of the Barry

Docks before the investing public had become aware of their value. His not infrequent losses were due to an over-sanguine temperament, a too easy-going way with subordinates, and, above all, to a rooted distaste for the work of inspection and control. His successes as a money-maker arose from his talent for negotiating new agreements; his genius was, in fact, for planning and not for executing. He had a winning personality, a pleasant voice, a strong will, a clearly conceived aim, and a remarkable faculty for finding the exact form of words which would give him all he wanted without seeming to deny the aims of the other parties. Moreover, he believed in the Jewish maxim – a maxim he often cited – that a bargain is not a good bargain unless it pays both sides.

When I was myself searching for a social creed I used to ponder over the ethics of capitalist enterprise as represented by my father's acts and axioms. He was an honourable and loyal colleague; he retained throughout his life the close friendship of his partners; his cooperation was always being sought for by other capitalists; he never left a colleague in a tight place; he was generous in giving credit to subordinates; he was forgiving to an old enemy who had fallen on evil times. But he thought, felt and acted in terms of personal relationship and not in terms of general principles; he had no clear vision of the public good. 'A friend', he would assert, 'is a person who would back you up when you were in the wrong, who would give your son a place which he could not have won on his own merits.' Any other conduct he scoffed at as moral pedantry. Hence he tended to prefer the welfare of his family and personal friends to the interests of the companies over which he presided, the profits of these companies to the prosperity of his country, the dominance of his own race to the peace of the world. These graded obligations were, of course, adjusted to the law of the land and to the conventions of the circle in which he was at the time moving. His conception of right conduct was a spacious one, of loose texture, easily penetrated by the surrounding moral atmosphere. What he did in the United States he would not do in the United Kingdom. For the circumstances of mid-Victorian capitalist enterprise were hostile to any fixed standard of morality. The presidents of American railways, international financiers, company promoters and contractors, were forceful men, frequently of magnetic personality and witty conversation; but the common ideal which bound them in a close fraternity was a stimulating mixture of personal power and personal luxury; their common recreation was high living. Uniquely typical was the life on board a president's car on an American railway: the elaborate accommodation and fittings; the French chef; the over-abundant food; the extravagantly choice wines and liqueurs; above all, the consciousness of personal prestige and power; the precedence of the president's car over all other traffic; the obsequious attentions of ubiquitous officials; the contemptuous bargaining with political 'bosses' for land concessions and for the passage of bills through legislatures – altogether a low moral temperature. My father struggled against this adverse moral environment; he submitted, with childlike docility, and, be it added, with childish delight in evasion, to the dietetic rules imposed on him by his women-kind and the family physician; his insistence on his daughters' company whenever he went abroad was, I think, partly due to a subconscious intention to keep out of less desirable associations. In his struggle with the sins of the world and the flesh (he was never tempted by the devil of pride, cruelty or malice) he had two powerful aids – his wife and his God. His wife was puritan and ascetic, and he adored her. He had been brought up in the arid creed of Unitarianism and he had lived with intellectual iconoclasts; but unlike his wife and some of his daughters, he was never troubled with doubts as to the divine government of the world, or as to the reality of communion with an outside spiritual force. He attended church regularly, took the sacrament and prayed night and morning. It seems incredible, but I know that, as a man, he repeated the prayer taught him at his mother's lap – 'Gentle Jesus, meek and mild, look upon a little child', etc.

As a citizen of the British Empire my father bred true to

the typical political development of Victorian capitalism. His grandfather, the Tadcaster farmer and shopkeeper, had had his windows broken by the Tory mob for refusing to illuminate at the reported victory of the British troops over the Americans in their War of Independence; his father, the Manchester cotton warehouseman, was a leading rebel in the days of Peterloo and, as a member of the reformed House of Commons of 1832, he belonged to the Free Trade and pacifist Radical group which made matters lively for the Whig Government. But I doubt whether my father was ever a convinced Radical; and some time in the sixties he left the Reform Club and joined the Carlton. Fervent and long-enduring therefore was his indignation at Disraeli's 'treacherous' Reform Act of 1867; from first to last he objected to any extension of the suffrage below the £10 householder, in which class he wished to include women householders, women being, as he thought, more intuitively Conservative than men. The central article of his political faith was, indeed, a direct denial of democracy: an instinctive conviction, confirmed as he thought by his experience of American institutions, that the rulers of the country, whether Cabinet Ministers or judges, permanent heads of Government Departments or Members of Parliament, ought in the main to be drawn from a leisured class – all the better if the property upon which the leisure depended was inherited property. The political and municipal corruption of the United States of America was, he maintained, due to the absence of an hereditary caste of leisured persons standing, as trustees for the permanent prosperity of the country, above the struggle for existence, whether of wage-earners or profit-makers. Even more disastrous was the replacing of this caste by political bosses elected by a mob of propertyless persons, but drawing their incomes from particular financial and industrial corporations. 'The American boss', he said, 'combines the ignorance of the labourer with the graft of the company promoter.' But he was always ready to compromise with new forces and to adjust his political programme to social circumstances. When once the suffrage had been lowered he became enthusiastic about working-class education. 'We must educate our masters,' he was never tired of asserting. 'If necessary we must send our daughters to educate the masses,' was an indiscreet remark at a political meeting, which shocked the Conservatives and infuriated the Radicals. Unlike my mother, he had no use for the abstract principles of political economy; his father's old friends Cobden and Bright he regarded as fanatics deceiving themselves and others with wire-drawn logic and moral platitudes. Some sliding-scale tax on corn ought to have been maintained so as to preserve and stabilize an agricultural population. As for 'peace at any price', any experienced businessman knew that, broadly speaking, 'trade followed the flag!'

Notwithstanding frequent absence, my father was the central figure of the family life – the light and warmth of the home. How well I remember how we girls raced to the front door when we heard the wheels on the carriage drive: the eager questions, the cheery replies, however tired he might be. He worshipped his wife, he admired and loved his daughters; he was the only man I ever knew who genuinely believed that women were superior to men, and acted as if he did; the paradoxical result being that all his nine daughters started life as anti-feminists! He made his wife and daughters his confidantes in all his undertakings, or at any rate he seemed to do so. In spite of his business preoccupations he had retained a love of poetry, of the drama, of history and of idealistic philosophy; he was a devout student of Dante (in the original), of Shakespeare and of Plato; he taught us to appreciate the eighteenth-century humorists and the French encyclopaedists and the novels of Jane Austen and Thackeray; he was a fanatical admirer of Burke and Carlyle and John Henry Newman – an oddly assorted trio, proving, I think, that his preferences were inspired by emotional thought rather than by pure reason. He always talked to us as equals; he would discuss with his daughters, even when they were young girls, not only his business affairs, but also religion, politics and the problems of sex, with frankness and freedom. I remember asking him at the age of thirteen whether he advised me to read *Tom Jones*. 'By all means read it, if it interests you; it will give you a good idea of the manners and customs of the eighteenth century, and Fielding wrote splendidly virile English'; to which he added, as if thinking aloud, 'If you were a boy I should hesitate to recommend *Tom Jones*, but a nice-minded girl can read anything; and the more she knows about human nature the better for her and for all the men connected with her.' Perhaps as a consequence of this policy of the 'open door' I recollect no curiosity about sex: my knowledge of the facts always outrunning my interest in the subject. He delighted in the beauty of moor and mountain, in wild winds and the changing hues of cloud and sea. But his peculiar charm lay in his appreciation – his over-appreciation – of the intellect and character of those with whom he lived. We girls thought him far too long-suffering of Mother's arbitrary moods; she thought him far too acquiescent in his daughters' unconventional habits. Yet in spite of this habitual self-subordination to those he loved, notwithstanding his 'noble-amiability', to use an epithet of Herbert Spencer's, he controlled the family destinies. My mother lived where it suited him to live, and he came and went as he chose; his daughters married the sort of men he approved, notwithstanding many temptations to the contrary.

My mother was nearing forty years of age when I became aware of her existence, and it was not until the last years of her life, when I was the only grown-up daughter remaining in the home, that I became intimate with her. The birth of an only brother when I was four, and his death when I was seven years of age, the crowning joy and devastating sorrow of my mother's life, had separated me from her care and attention; and the coming of my youngest sister, a few months after my brother's death, a partial outlet for my mother's wounded feelings, completed our separation. 'Beatrice,' she wrote in a diary when I was yet a child, 'is the only one of my children who is below the average in intelligence,' which may explain her attitude of indifference. Throughout my childhood and youth she seemed to me a remote personage discussing business with my father or poring over books in her boudoir; a source of arbitrary authority whose rare interventions in my life I silently resented. I regarded her as an obstacle to be turned, as a person from whom one withheld facts and whose temper one watched and humoured so that she should not interfere with one's own little plans. This absence of affection between us was all the more pitiful because, as we eventually discovered, we had the same tastes, we were puzzling over the same problems; and she had harboured, deep down in her heart, right up to middle life, the very ambition that I was secretly developing, the ambition to become a publicist.

My mother's pilgrimage through life was a much harder one than my father's. She had started life heavily handicapped by the unqualified indulgence and adoration of a wealthy widowed father, who insisted on her brothers regarding her as a paragon of virtue, beauty and learning – a perilous ordeal even for a selfless nature. Fortunately for her happiness, and I think also for her character, she found the same unqualified adoration in marriage; and she and my father remained lovers to the day of her death. In all other aspects her life had been one long series of disappointments. She had visualized a home life of close intellectual comradeship with my father, possibly of intellectual achievement, surrounded by distinguished friends, of whom she had many as a girl and young married woman (among them I recollect the names of Sir George Cornewall Lewis and Dr Jeune). The vision of a life of learned leisure was rudely swept on one side by the loss of the unearned income. When wealth returned it found her an invalid, with a nursery full of children, and a husband who was preoccupied and constantly away.

But her great disillusionment was in her children. She had been reared by and with men, and she disliked women. She was destined to have nine daughters and to lose her only son. Moreover, her daughters were not the sort of women she admired or approved. She had been brought up 'a scholar and a gentlewoman': her daughters refused to be educated and defied caste conventions. For the most part they were unmistakably Potters, the descendants of the tall dark woman of Jewish type who read Hebrew and loved music – my father's mother, whose confinement in a lunatic asylum during the latter years of my grandfather Potter's life (she was obsessed by the mania of leading the Jews back to Jerusalem and actually got as far as Paris, alas! poor lady, alone and without her fancied following) was always referred to as a slur on our birth. But besides these untoward circumstances, my mother was cursed with a divided personality; she was not at peace in herself. The discords in her nature were reflected in her physiognomy. In profile, she was, if not ugly, lacking grace: a prominent nose with an aggressive bridge, a long straight upper lip, a thin-lipped and compressed mouth, a powerful chin and jaw, altogether a hard outline, not redeemed by a well-shaped but large head. Looked at thus, she was obviously a managing woman, unrelenting, probably domineering, possibly fanatical. But her full face showed any such interpretation of her character to be a ludicrous libel. Here the central feature, the soul of the personality, were the eyes, soft hazel brown, large but deeply set, veiled by overhanging lids and long eyelashes set off by delicately curved and pencilled eyebrows; eyes uniting in their light and shade the caress of sympathy with the quest of knowledge. To this outstanding beauty were added fine flossy hair, an easily flushed fair skin, small flashing teeth, a low musical voice, pretty gestures and long delicate hands: clearly a woman to charm, perhaps to inspire. 'I think you knew my grandfather Lawrence Heyworth,' said I to John Bright when I met him at a political demonstration at Birmingham in 1884 – three years after my mother's death. 'Lawrence Heyworth, yes. Then you are the daughter of Laurencina Heyworth?' And after a pause he added – 'One of the two or three women a man remembers to the end of life as beautiful in expression and form.' (MS. diary, 16 March 1884).

As I discovered during the few years of intimacy, the divided personality reflected in the diverse testimony of profile and full face was manifested in consciousness by a never-ending controversy relating, not only to man's relation to the universe, but also to the right conduct of life. Her soul longed for the mystical consolations and moral discipline of religious orthodoxy. She spent hours studying the Greek Testament and the Fathers of the Church; and she practised religious rites with exemplary regularity. But she had inherited from her father an iconoclastic intellect. I remember as a wee child being startled by my grandfather Heyworth's assertion that Adam and Eve, so long as they lingered in the Garden of Eden, were roaming pigs, and that it was only by eating the forbidden fruit of the tree of knowledge that their descendants became something more than beasts of the field. What troubled my mother was the doubt whether men and women *had* become, or were becoming, more than pigs, however much they buried their snouts in the heaped-up apples of the tree of knowledge; whether seeking pleasure and avoiding pain did not sum up all human instincts, impulses and motives, and thus constitute the whole duty of man. An ardent student of Adam Smith, Malthus, and particularly of Nassau Senior, she had been brought up in the strictest sect of Utilitarian economists. In middle life she had translated some of the essays of her friend Michel Chevalier, who represented the French variant of orthodox political economy, a variant which caricatured the dogmatic faith in a beneficent self-interest.[4] And my mother practised what she preached. Tested by economy in money and time she was an admirable expenditor of the family income: she never visited the servants' quarters and seldom spoke to any servant other than her own maid. She acted by deputy, training each daughter to carry out a carefully thought-out plan of the most economical supply of the best regulated demand. Her intellect told her that to pay more than the market rate, to exact fewer than the customary hours or insist on less than the usual strain – even if it could be proved that these conditions

4. The following description of my mother, given by her friend Michel Chevalier to his friend Taine, the historian, appears in *Notes on England*, by H. Taine, trans. by W. F. Rae, 1872 (p. 93): 'M. ——,

were injurious to the health and happiness of the persons concerned – was an act of self-indulgence, a defiance of nature's laws which would bring disaster on the individual and the community. Similarly, it was the bounden duty of every citizen to better his social status; to ignore those beneath him, and to aim steadily at the top rung of the social ladder. Only by this persistent pursuit by each individual of his own and his family's interest would the highest general level of civilization be attained. It was on this issue that she and Herbert Spencer found themselves in happy accord. No one of the present generation realizes with what sincerity and fervour these doctrines were held by the representative men and women of the mid-Victorian middle class. 'The man who sells his cow too cheap goes to Hell' still epitomizes, according to John Butler Yeats, 'the greater part of the religion of Belfast'[5] – that last backwater of the sanctimonious commercialism of the nineteenth century. My mother's distinction was that she was free of the taint of hypocrisy; she realized the hopeless inconsistency of this theory of human nature and human conduct with her mystical cravings, either with the Sermon on the Mount or with the *Imitation of Christ*, which she read night and morning. In the latter years of her life she withdrew from social intercourse, and left her daughters free to make their own way in London Society and to entertain their own friends in the country home; merely asking to be told the names of the guests, and to be provided with clues enabling her to carry

---

being invited to the country, discovered that the mistress of the house knew much more Greek than himself, apologized, and retired from the field; then, out of pleasantry, she wrote down his English sentence in Greek. Note that this female Hellenist is a woman of the world, and even stylish. Moreover, she has nine daughters, two nurses, two governesses, servants in proportion, a large, well-appointed house, frequent and numerous visitors; throughout all this, perfect order; never noise or fuss; the machine appears to move of its own accord. These are gatherings of faculties and of contrasts which might make us reflect. In France we believe too readily that if a woman ceases to be a doll she ceases to be a woman.'

5. *Early Memories*, by John Butler Yeats, p. 48.

out the formal duties of hostess with intelligent courtesy. As age crept on, even the desire to impose her will on the rest of the household fell from her, and she became pathetically eager to subordinate her claims to those of the growing nurseries of grandchildren. More and more absorbed in her lonely studies and despairing of solving the problems which troubled her, her restless intellect fastened on the acquisition of languages, more especially their grammars. Of these grammars she made a curious and extensive collection, preferring the grammar of one foreign language in that of another; a Greek grammar in French, a Latin grammar in Italian, a Hebrew grammar in German, and a Spanish grammar in some Scandinavian language, and so on; according to the principle, I imagine, that it is economical to acquire two things with one unit of energy. It was in this day-to-day, routine mental activity, one day exactly like another, that she attained a certain peaceful understanding of life, nay more, a zest in living, which left her at the age of sixty amazingly young alike in body and mind. 'I shall know twelve languages before I die,' said she to me with a triumphant smile, as, a few months before her sudden and unexpected death in the spring of 1882, we paced up and down the measured span of gravel walk for an hour. This self-congratulation was quickly followed by a caressing glance and a sympathetic suggestion that I might succeed where she had failed, and become a writer of books.

Whether it was the result of this new and unexpected sympathy with my secret ambition, or whether it was due to some subtly potent quality in her personality, she exercised a far greater influence over my life after her death than while she was living.

I never knew how much she had done for me [I wrote remorsefully in my diary a few months after her death], how many of my best habits I had taken from her, how strong would be the influence of her personality when pressure had gone – a pressure wholesome and in the right direction, but applied without tact. Tact – that quality which gains for people more affection and consideration than any other, and yet in itself not one necessarily belonging to the noblest group of moral and intellectual qualities. . . . When I work with many odds against me, for a far distant and perhaps unattainable end, I think of her and her intellectual strivings which we were too ready to call useless, and which yet will be the originating impulse of all my ambition, urging me onward towards something better in action and thought. [MS. diary, 13 August 1882.]

Six years afterwards, when my life was divided between nursing my father and contributing chapters to Charles Booth's *Life and Labour of the People in London*, I find the following entry in my diary, showing how closely my intellectual effort had become associated with the memory of my mother.

These latter days [I] constantly think of mother: sometimes the feeling of her presence is so strong that I am tempted into a kind of communion with her. We knew each other so little in her lifetime. Strangely enough I love her better now, I feel that she at last knows me, tries to cheer my loneliness and to encourage my effort. She seems now to belong more to me than to the others; the others have their husbands and their children: I have nothing but my work and the fitful warmth of friendship. So mother seems to stand by my side, to be watching me, anxious to reach out to me a helping hand; at any rate to bless me. . . . I can fight through the rest of the battle of life with courage. And perhaps when it is over, I shall know that she has been by my side. [MS. diary, 1888.]

Inseparably associated with my mother, and in many respects her complement, was Martha Jackson (afterwards Mills), my mother's lifelong companion and attendant. Engaged by my grandfather to accompany his daughter on her travels, she had witnessed the love-making in Rome; she had followed my mother into married life, and she had acted as nurse to my elder sisters, thus acquiring the nick-name of 'Dada'. Now Dada was a saint, the one and only saint I ever knew. She mothered all the members of the large household, whether children or servants, whether good or naughty; she nursed them when they were ill, comforted them when they were in trouble, and spoke for them when they were in dis-

42

grace. It was Martha who was called into counsel by my father in hours of friction and stress; it was she alone who dared, unasked but unreproved, to counsel my mother whenever she – Martha – thought fit. 'I would not do that, Mrs Potter, it will only cause more trouble,' she would say in her low impersonal tone, as she went about her business carrying out my mother's orders, apparently unconcerned with the result even if she disapproved the decision. And when my mother vehemently reasserted her will, and argued hotly that she was in the right, Martha would remain blandly silent as if half convinced, presently making a soothing reference to the frailty or helplessness of the other party to the dispute, or some shrewd suggestion as to how the practical problem could be solved to the advantage of everybody. But in spite of this all-inclusive benevolence it was difficult to deceive her. Cut deep in my memory is a scene of sixty years ago: a small child telling a cowardly lie, a moment of silence and then, as the sole response, a flash in her grey eyes of mingled amusement and love: the small child resolving not to tell another lie if only she could wriggle out of this one without confessing the double sin!

Though Martha was a saint she was a very human one, capable of taking a false step so far as her own happiness was concerned. In middle life, weary perhaps of continuously giving and never receiving solicitous affection, she got married. By profession a railway guard who became a butler, by preference a local preacher among the Baptists, Mills was a portly figure of a man, honest and domesticated. For some years he preferred to remain with an old and wealthy master, and acquiesced in his wife staying with us, being greatly concerned to accumulate an independence. When the old master died a disastrous break in our household seemed inevitable. My mother and Martha rose to the occasion. Mills became our butler; he would have become the butt of the household if it had not been for the quiet dignity of his wife, who mothered and protected him, as she mothered and protected all the other members of the household. But she knew she had made a big mistake, the mistake of her life, and shrewd and sharp were her warnings to the younger servants when they consulted her about 'getting married'. For Mills was a ludicrously pompous person, preposterously pleased with the sound of his own voice. If one rang the bell for another scuttle of coal, Mills appeared in the middle of the room and stood and delivered a set speech, repeating your request and adding his comments in grandiloquent language. In the misuse of pedantic words and phrases he travestied Mrs Malaprop; whilst the rhetorical paraphrase of Biblical texts, out of which he compiled his amateur sermons, seemed heart-stirring eloquence or mere muddle-mindedness, according to the degree of literacy in the listener. 'Mills would be all right if he would keep his mouth shut,' muttered the disillusioned but devoted wife on the occasion of a Christmas dinner.

Eventually the couple retired on savings and pensions to the lodge of our Monmouthshire farmhouse, where my father and I spent the summer months during the last years of his life. On this lonely hill-top Mills found his vocation in attracting, by his ornate oratory, little groups of bemused labourers to deserted Baptist chapels, whilst Martha washed, mended and cooked for him, read her Bible, opened and closed the gate, and awaited with patient eagerness the arrival of one or other of the beloved family. Meanwhile, as luck would have it, and as I shall tell in another chapter, Martha had become my guide and 'cover' in my first attempt at observation and experiment. It was she who, after my mother's death, introduced me as her 'young friend Miss Jones, a farmer's daughter from Wales', into the homes of my cousins, the Bacup cotton operatives; and it was incidentally during this visit that I discovered that she, also, was a relative.

The most far-reaching and influential of Martha's gifts was her revelation of the meaning of the religious spirit. Fresh from listening to my mother's interminable arguments with Herbert Spencer concerning the origin of religion, Martha's formal creed, that of a Particular Baptist, seemed to me primitive if not barbaric. But she held the dogmas of the atonement, predestination, eternal pun-

44

ishment and of the literal infallibility of the Old and New Testament, not to mention the Protestant assumption that the Roman Catholic Church was the 'Scarlet Woman' of Revelation, humbly and without question, as an act of loyalty to the faith in which she had been reared. Religion meant to her from beginning to end a state of mind, a state of mind which she believed reflected the state of mind of her Saviour Jesus of Nazareth, an overpowering consciousness of love. It was a strangely impersonal love; if I may so phrase it, it was an equalitarian beneficence without respect for persons or even for the characteristics of persons: it was manifested quite indifferently to all human beings, whether they were attractive or hideous, of high or low degree, geniuses or mental defectives, nobly self-sacrificing or meanly egotistical. Instinctively she gave her sympathy and care not according to merits, but according to needs. Faults in character and faults in circumstances were inevitable incidents in the pilgrim's way through this life to the next, only to be overcome or smoothed out by a patient and persistent charity to all human beings, tempered by what she called 'facing the facts'. For she never gushed or sentimentalized over those she helped through physical or mental trouble: her sympathy was always tempered by a sense of humour and a sense of proportion, by an appreciation of the equities of the case. 'There are other people's needs and claims besides yours,' her smile and flashing eye would seem to say. She seldom spoke of her religious experiences, and she never tried to convert us to her particular brand of Protestant Christianity. Yet it was evident to all who knew her intimately that she held, with radiant conviction, that the state of mind which was to her religion could only be created and maintained by communion with an outside spiritual force, itself a manifestation of the spirit of love at work in the universe.

At the other end of the scale of human values, and in significant contrast with the household saint – in intellect towering above her, but in emotional insight depths below her – stood the oldest and most intimate friend of the family, the incessantly ratiocinating philosopher. From Herbert Spencer's *Autobiography* I take the following description of his first meeting with my parents at my grandfather Heyworth's house near Liverpool, not for the flattering family portraits, but because this extract proves that the future thinker was, in his youth, as modest about his own gifts as he was enthusiastically appreciative of those of his friends.

Mr Heyworth and I had a great deal of conversation, and on the whole agreed remarkably well in our sentiments. He is a particularly liberal-minded and thinking man, and, though nominally a Churchman, is practically no more one than I am myself. ... I was, however, most highly pleased with his daughter, and her husband – Mr and Mrs Potter. They have been lately married, and appear to me the most admirable pair I have ever seen. I don't know whether you have ever heard me mention Miss Heyworth as being somewhat of a notability. I have, however, been for some time past curious to see her, partly in consequence of the very high terms in which my uncle Thomas has always spoken of her, and partly because I have once or twice seen her name mentioned in the papers as one who was very zealous in the anti-corn law agitation, engaging herself in distributing tracts and conversing with persons on the subject.

It would never be inferred from her manner and general appearance that she possessed so independent a character. She is perfectly feminine and has an unusually graceful and refined manner. To a phrenologist, however, the singularity of the character is very obvious. [Here follow a profile outline of her head and a set of inferences.]

Mr Potter, however, commanded my highest admiration. He is, I think, the most lovable being I have yet seen. He is evidently genuine. His amiability is not that of manner but that of reality. He has a noble head – a democratic one of course, but one so beautifully balanced in other respects that one can quite delight in contemplating it. The perfect agreement between his head and face is remarkable: the features are Grecian and their expression is exactly what a phrenologist would anticipate.

He is, I believe, very poetical – admires Shelley enthusiastically and conceives him by far the finest poet of his era, in which I quite coincide with him. In fact we sympathized in our sentiments on all subjects on which we conversed, and although I might feel somewhat flattered by this, I must say I felt so strongly the beauty of his disposition as contrasted with my own, that I felt more dissatisfied with myself than I have done for a long time past.[6]

From that day Herbert Spencer remained my father's ardent admirer and my mother's intellectual associate. That the man of twenty-four should have enjoyed talking for hours together with an attractive woman a few years older than himself is not to be wondered at. What is surprising is that Herbert Spencer's admiration, I might almost say ador- ation, of my father, should have survived the latter's com- plete indifference to the working of the philosopher's intellect, whether expressed in the spoken or the written word. Always cheerfully beneficent, my father had a genuine if somewhat pitying affection for the philosopher on the hearth; he would walk with him, he would fish with him, he would travel with him, he would give him sound advice and tell him tales from business life which illustrated the work- ing of this or that economic 'law' in which they both be- lieved; but argue with him or read his books he would not. 'Won't work, my dear Spencer, won't work,' my father would say good-humouredly, when the professional doubter

6. *Autobiography*, Herbert Spencer, 1904, vol. i. pp. 260–61. Herbert Spencer adds: 'The friendship thus initiated lasted until the deaths of both. It influenced to a considerable extent the current of my life; and, through their children and grandchildren, influences it still.' And here is one among many entries in my diary descriptive of my father, written two years after my mother's death:

'The grand simplicity of his nature, his motives transparent and uncomplicated – all resolvable indeed into one – desire to make those belonging to him happy. Read to me yesterday some of his journal in Rome when he was courting mother. Just the same mind as now: uncritical reverence for what was beautiful and good: no trace of cynicism or desire to analyse or qualify. Perhaps in his business career, in business matters, he has developed a shrewdness and sharp- ness of thought and action, and with it a cynical depreciation of men and their ways. But this is foreign to his nature, has been acquired in the struggle for existence, and never enters into his intimate rela- tionships. With him the instinctive feelings are paramount. He would sacrifice all, to some extent even his self-respect, if he thought the happiness of some loved one were at stake. He is far away the most unselfish nature and most unself-conscious nature I know.' [MS. diary, 16 May 1883.]

defiantly proclaimed his practice on a Sunday morning of deliberately walking against the tide of church-goers. This distaste for Herbert Spencer's peculiar type of reasoning was all the more noteworthy because my father enjoyed intellectual society; he delighted in talks with Huxley, Tyndall and James Martineau, and when his friend James Anthony Froude asked him on one or two occasions to join the afternoon walk with Thomas Carlyle he did so in the spirit of reverential awe, repeating to us afterwards the very words of the master. But Herbert Spencer's 'synthetic philosophy', whether it concerned the knowable or the unknowable, bored him past endurance; he saw no sense in it. When I tried to interest him in the 'law of increasing heterogeneity and definiteness in structure and function' at work – so the philosopher demonstrated – throughout the universe, my father answered in this wise: 'Words, my dear, mere words. Experience tells me that some businesses grow diverse and complicated, others get simpler and more uniform, others again go into the Bankruptcy Court. In the long run and over the whole field there is no more reason for expecting one process rather than the other. Spencer's intellect is like a machine racing along without raw material: it is wearing out his body. Poor Spencer, he lacks instinct, my dear, he lacks instinct – you will discover that instinct is as important as intellect.' And then, taking out his engagement book, he added, in a more sympathetic tone, 'I must see whether I can't arrange another day's fishing with him – poor man.' Nor was my father's indifference to his reasoning power unnoticed by Herbert Spencer. 'Mrs Potter was scarcely less argumentative than I was,' he recounts after a visit to the young couple, 'and occasionally our evening debates were carried on so long that Mr Potter, often playing chiefly the role of listener, gave up in despair and went to bed; leaving us to continue our unsettleable controversies.'[7]

Memory recalls a finely sculptured head, prematurely bald, long stiff upper lip and powerful chin, obstinately compressed mouth, small sparkling grey eyes, set close together,

7. *Autobiography*, Herbert Spencer, 1904, vol. i. p. 311 (æt. 26, 1846).

with a prominent Roman nose – altogether a remarkable headpiece dominating a tall, spare, well-articulated figure, tapering off into diminutive and well-formed hands and feet. Always clad in primly neat but quaintly unconventional garments, there was distinction, even a certain elegance, in the philosopher's punctilious manners and precise and lucid speech. And if his elaborate explanations, couched in pedantic terms, of commonplace occurrences as exemplifications of the recondite principles of the synthetic philosophy, seemed to the philistine listener just a trifle absurd, to the enthusiastic novice in scientific reasoning his ingenious intertwining of elementary observations with abstruse ratiocination was immensely impressive. But the sharpest imprint on my youthful mind was the transformation scene from the placid beneficence of an unwrinkled brow, an aspect habitual towards children and all weak things, to an attitude of tremulous exasperation, angry eyes and voice almost shrewish in its shrillness – when he 'opined' that his or any one else's personal rights were being infringed. To the children of the household the philosopher always appeared in the guise of a liberator. His delightful axiom 'submission not desirable' was adorned and pointed by detailed criticism of the ways of governesses and other teachers: 'stupid persons who taught irrelevant facts in an unintelligible way', a criticism which made even my mother uneasy, and which infuriated the old-fashioned dame who presided for many years over the activities of the schoolroom. 'You can go out this morning, my dears, with Mr Spencer,' said the governess to her pupils, after listening with pursed up lips to one of the philosopher's breakfast tirades against discipline, 'and mind you follow his teaching and do exactly what you have a mind to.' Whether due to an 'undesirable submissiveness' to the governess or to a ready acquiescence in the doctrine of revolt, the philosopher found himself presently in a neighbouring beech-wood pinned down in a leaf-filled hollow by little demons, all legs, arms, grins and dancing dark eyes, whilst the elder and more discreet tormentors pelted him with decaying beech leaves. 'Your children are r-r-r-rude children,' exclaimed the *Man versus the State* as he stalked into my mother's boudoir. But for the most part he and we were firm friends: we agreed with his denunciation of the 'current curriculum', history, foreign languages, music and drawing, and his preference for 'science' – a term which meant, in practice, scouring the countryside in his company for fossils, flowers and water-beasties which, alive, mutilated or dead, found their way into hastily improvised aquariums, cabinets and scrap-books – all alike discarded when his visit was over. Speaking for myself, I was never interested in these collections of animate and inanimate things, even when looked at through his microscope or pulled to pieces by teasers. What fascinated me, long before I began to study his writings, was watching him collect illustrations for his theories. I do not suggest that 'some direct observations of facts or some fact met with in reading' did not precede the formulation of his principles: though it appears from an interesting account given in the *Autobiography*, that only those facts were noted and contemplated which had to him some 'general meaning', *i.e.* directly or indirectly helped towards the building up of 'a coherent and organized theory' of the universe. But by the time I became his companion these 'First Principles' had ceased to be hypotheses; they had become a highly developed dogmatic creed with regard to the evolution of life. What remained to be done was to prove by innumerable illustrations how these principles or 'laws' explained the whole of the processes of nature, from the formation of a crystal to the working of the party system within a democratic state. Herbert Spencer was, in fact, engaged in the art of casuistry, and it was in this art that for a time I became his apprentice, or was it his accomplice? Partly in order to gain his approbation and partly out of sheer curiosity about the working of his mind, I started out to discover, and where observation failed, to invent, illustrations of such scraps of theory as I understood. What I learnt from this game with his intellect was not, it is needless to remark, how to observe – for he was the most gullible of mortals and never scrutinized the accuracy of my tales – but whether the sample facts I brought him came within the 'law' he wished to illustrate. It was indeed the training required for an English lawyer dealing with cases, rather than that of a scientific worker seeking to discover and describe new forms of life. What he taught me to discern was not the truth, but the relevance of facts; a gift said to be rare in a woman and of untold importance to the social investigator confronted with masses of data, whether in documents or in the observed behaviour of men – ascertained facts significant and insignificant, relevant and irrelevant. And it so happens that I find in my diary an authoritative confirmation of this appreciation of Herbert Spencer's intellectual processes in a conversation with Professor Huxley in 1887, when I was considering my old friend's request that I should act as his literary executor.

I ventured to put forward the idea [I record], that Herbert Spencer had worked out the theory of evolution by grasping the disjointed theories of his time and welding them into one. 'No,' said Huxley, 'Spencer never knew them: he elaborated his theory from his inner consciousness. He is the most original of thinkers, though he has never invented a new thought. He never reads: merely picks up what will help him to illustrate his theories. He is a great constructor: the form he has given to his gigantic system is entirely original: not one of the component factors is new, but he has not borrowed them.' And we disagreed on another point. I suggested that as I had known Herbert Spencer he was personally humble. Both the Huxleys exclaimed: they had always found him pre-eminently just; ready to listen to adverse criticism and adverse facts from those he respected or had affection for. But most men were to him the common herd. Perhaps there is truth in this. I asked Huxley whether he thought it was a mistake for me to undertake the literary executorship. 'Oh no,' said the great man benignly, 'all a man wants in a literary executor is a sympathetic friend.' Herbert Spencer's biography tells its own story: it is intensely characteristic of the man.[8]

8. MS. diary, 6 May 1887. The remainder of the entry may be of interest to the reader, though as I was only slightly acquainted with the great scientist my casual observation is of little value.
'Throughout the interview, what interested me was not Huxley's

In the next chapter I shall refer to the part played in the development of my craft and creed by Herbert Spencer's *Synthetic Philosophy*. Here I express the debt I owe to the loyal friendship and mutual helpfulness which grew up between the child and the thinker; and which endured, undimmed by growing divergence in opinion, to the day of his death in 1903. It was the philosopher on the hearth who, alone among my elders, was concerned about my chronic ill-health, and was constantly suggesting this or that remedy for my ailments; who encouraged me in my lonely studies; who heard patiently and criticized kindly my untutored scribblings about Greek and German philosophers; who delighted and stimulated me with the remark that I was a 'born metaphysician', and that I 'reminded him of George Eliot'; who was always pressing me to become a scientific worker, and who eventually arranged with Knowles of the *Nine-*

---

opinion of Spencer, but Huxley's account of himself. ... How as a young man, though he had no definite purpose in life, he felt power; was convinced that in his own line he would be a leader. That expresses Huxley: he is a leader of men. I doubt whether science was pre-eminently the bent of his mind. He is truth-loving, his love of truth finding more satisfaction in demolition than in construction. He throws the full weight of thought, feeling, will, into anything that he takes up. He does not register his thoughts and his feelings: his early life was supremely sad, and he controlled the tendency to look back on the past and forward into the future. When he talks to man, woman or child he seems all attention and he has, or rather had, the power of throwing himself into the thoughts and feelings of others and responding to them. And yet they are all shadows to him: he thinks no more of them and drops back into the ideal world he lives in. For Huxley, when not working, dreams strange things: carries on lengthy conversations between unknown persons living within his brain. There is a strain of madness in him; melancholy has haunted his whole life. "I always knew that success was so much dust and ashes. I have never been satisfied with achievement." None of the enthusiasm for what is, or the silent persistency in discovering facts; more the eager rush of the conquering mind, loving the fact of conquest more than the land conquered. And consequently his achievement has fallen far short of his capacity. Huxley is greater as a man than as a scientific thinker. The exact opposite might be said of Herbert Spencer.'

*teenth Century* for the immediate publication of my first essay in social investigation.

Even more important for the young student than these acts of personal kindness was the example of continuous concentrated effort in carrying out, with an heroic disregard of material prosperity and physical comfort, a task which he believed would further human progress. There is indeed no limit to what I owe to my thirty or forty years' intimacy with this unique life: unique, as I came to see, no less as a warning than as a model. Here I can do no more than add by way of illustration one or two of the many entries in my diary descriptive of my friendship with Herbert Spencer.

Mr Spencer's visits always interest me and leave me with new ideas and the clearing up of old ones. Also with due realization of the poverty of my intellect, and its incapacity for tackling the problems which are constantly cropping up – the comparative uselessness of all my miserable little studies. [MS. diary, September 1881.]

Spent the whole day with Herbert Spencer at private view. He worked out, poor man, a sad destiny for one whose whole life has been his work. There is something pathetic in the isolation of his mind, a sort of spider-like existence; sitting alone in the centre of his theoretical web, catching facts, and weaving them again into theory. It is sorrowful when the individual is lost in the work – when he has been set apart to fulfil some function, and then when working days are past left as the husk, the living kernel of which has been given to the world. On looking around and watching men and women, one sees how important a part 'instinct' plays in their lives, how all-important it becomes in old age, when the purely intellectual faculties grow dim; and one appreciates the barrenness of an old age where the instinctive feelings are undeveloped and the subject-matter for them absent. There is a look of sad resignation on Herbert Spencer's face, as if he fully realized his position and waited patiently for the end, to him absolutely final. To me there is a comic pathos in his elaborate search after pleasurable 'sensations', as if sensations can *ever* take the place of emotion; and alas! in his consciousness there hardly exists an 'exciting cause' for emotional feeling. And yet there is a capacity for deep feeling, a capacity which has lain dormant and is now covered up with crotchety ideas presenting a hedgehog's coat to the outer world, a surface hardly inviting contact! I see what it is in him which is repulsive to some persons. It is the mental deformity which results from the extraordinary development of the intellectual faculties joined with the very imperfect development of the sympathetic and emotional qualities, a deformity which, when it does not excite pity, excites dislike. There is no life of which I have a really intimate knowledge which seems to me so inexpressibly sad as the inarticulate life of Herbert Spencer, inarticulate in all that concerns his happiness. [MS. diary, 5 May 1884.]

Herbert Spencer deliciously conscious about the 'Miss Evans' episode – asked me seriously what was my impression of their relationship on reading those passages referring to him. Had wished John Cross to insert contradiction that there had ever been aught between them. Shows his small-mindedness in the extreme concern. But as George Eliot says, his friendship will always endure because of his truthfulness. Told me that he never talked or wrote differently to different people; he was only anxious to correct what *he* thought – quite independently of the way in which it would best be understood by others.[9] [MS. diary, January 1885.]

Poor Herbert Spencer. On reading the proof of his *Autobiography* I often think of that life given up to feeling his pulse and analysing his sensations, with no near friends to be all and all to him, to give him the tenderness and brightness that father gets in these his last days. Strange that he should never have felt the sacrifice he was making.... 'I was never in love,' he answered, when I put the question straight: 'Were you never conscious of the wholesale sacrifice you were making, did you never long for those other forms of thought, feeling, action you were shut out from?' Strange – a nature with so perfect an intellect and little else – save friendliness and the uprightness of a truth-loving mind. He has sometimes told me sadly that he has wondered at the weakness of his feelings, even of friendship, and towards old friends and relations; that he thought it came from his mind being constantly busied with the perfection of this one idea – never once doubting the value of it. [MS. diary, 9 June 1886.]

9. It was an open secret that it was George Eliot who was in love with the philosopher, and when, on her death, newspaper paragraphs appeared implying that he had been one of her suitors he consulted my father about publishing the truth, the whole truth and nothing but the truth. 'My dear Spencer, you will be eternally damned if you do it,' replied my father.

'In November 1887,' he writes in his *Autobiography*, 'I was induced by Miss Beatrice Potter to take rooms in the same house with them at Bournemouth, where they were fixed for the winter (my friend Potter having also now become an invalid).'

'Outward circumstances are sad enough at the present time,' I write on this Christmas Day of 1887, 'Father sweet as ever, but his mind failing rapidly, his companionship nought but answering disjointed questions. . . . The old philosopher downstairs to whom I am tied by pity and reverential gratitude, the victim of a strange disease of mind and body, sits in his chair not daring to move body or mind; one day passes like another and yet no improvement; he waiting with despondent patience for returning strength, pursued by the desire to finish his *System* of *Philosophy*. I can give him no help. I sit in his room writing or reading, now and again saying some kind word – a bright anecdote or a stray reflection. Yesterday as I sat there I heard a sudden moan as if he were in pain. "Are you suffering?" "No," groaned the poor old man, "a momentary fit of impatience. Why suffer more todays?" a question I could not answer.' [MS. diary, December 1887.]

'The change of scene, and still more the presence close at hand of those about whom I cared, produced a great effect'; he continues in his *Autobiography*,[10] 'and at the end of January 1888 I returned to town, frequented the Athenaeum daily for a month, and even got so far as playing a game of billiards. Then, as usual, came a catastrophe,' [and so on].

But the episode of my literary executorship is perhaps the most characteristic of these entries.

Paid Herbert Spencer a visit. Found him in a pitiable condition: hopeless: thinks he can neither eat, work nor talk. Sent me away after I had spoken to him for a short time, and told me to return to him in an hour's time as he wished to discuss an important business matter. When I returned I found him in a nervous state with a good deal of suppressed excitement. He asked me whether I should recommend A. C. or C. B. as a trustee for the continuance of his sociological research. Advised A. C. He then said he wanted to consult me as to another appointment: that of 'Beatrice Potter as literary executor'. I was taken aback, but it was evident that he had set his heart on it and longed, poor old man, that some one who cared for him should write his life. I

10. *Autobiography*, Herbert Spencer, 1904, vol. ii. p. 412.

was very much touched by his confidence, though I suggested he might find a fitter person from a literary point of view. I quite understand his feeling. He instinctively feels that his life seems lonely and deserted, and that the world will look back on him as a thinking machine and not as a man with a man's need for a woman's devotion and love, and the living affection of children. Poor old man, he is paying the penalty of genius: his whole nature is twisted by excessive development of one faculty. [MS. diary, 22 April 1887.]

Dear B. – What admirable promptness, he writes on 24 April 1887. I expected several days at least to elapse before getting a reply, and here I get letters settling the matter in little more than 24 hours after naming it to you. I give you hearty thanks for having so quickly and well negotiated.

Pray do not entertain any qualms respecting what you have undertaken. I am perfectly content, and can say with literal truth that with no choice could I have been more content. With the exception of my friend Lott, I cannot think of any one who has had better opportunities of knowing me, and I do not think that even he would have been able to make as good a portrait. For though he had sincerity and catholicity in equal degrees with you, he had not as much perspicacity. Moreover, your criticisms have shown me that you have the instincts of an artist, to which I add the faculty of being lively on fit occasion.

Before I leave off, which I must do now because my amanuensis wishes to go and see his sick mother, let me express my concern about your health. Losing bulk in the way you have done is a serious symptom. Pray cut off a large part of your work, *and do not dream of doing any work before a substantial breakfast*. Only strong people can do that with impunity. – Ever affectionately yours,

HERBERT SPENCER

My appointment as his literary executor was, however, cancelled early in 1892 on the announcement of my engagement to marry the leading Fabian Socialist.

We met yesterday at The Athenaeum by appointment. He was affectionate and cordial to me personally. 'I cannot congratulate you – that would be insincere.' Then there was a short pause. 'My family have taken it benevolently,' I remarked, and then observed that there was after all nothing against Mr Webb, he had proved himself to be a man of capacity and determination. 'You see that he has succeeded in marrying me, Mr Spencer – that shows he has a will.' 'Undoubtedly,' groaned the philosopher, 'that is exactly what I fear – you both have Wills, and they *must* clash.' 'He has a sweet temper and has been an excellent brother and son,' I urged quietly, and gave a vivid description of his good domestic qualities. But presently the real source of anxiety was disclosed.

'I feel I am in a fix about the personal matter to which you alluded in your letter – the literary executorship. It would not do for my reputation that I should be openly connected with an avowed and prominent Socialist – that is impossible. Inferences would be drawn however much I protested that the relationship was purely personal with you.'

'I quite agree with you, Mr Spencer,' I answered sympathetically. 'I fully realized that I should have to give up the literary executorship.'

'But what can *I* do,' he said plaintively. 'Grant Allen, whom I thought of before, has become a Fabian. There is no one who possesses at once the literary gift, the personal intimacy with my past life and the right opinions, to undertake the task.'

'What about Howard Collins?' I said, thinking of the grim irony of the poor old man thrown back on the mechanically minded Timothy. 'He is sound; would he not do?'

'He would be the proper person – but then he has no gift like you have of making his subject interesting.'

'But I should be delighted to help him in any way you like to propose, either acknowledged or not.'

The Philosopher lay back in his chair with a sigh of relief. 'That arrangement would be admirable – that is exactly what I should desire – the Life would appear under his name and you would add reminiscences and arrange the material. That would quite satisfy me,' he repeated with a very visible access of cheerfulness.

'Well, Mr Spencer, you can rely on my doing my utmost. Mr Collins and I are excellent friends; we should work together admirably.'

And so ended the interview; he satisfied about his reputation and I at ease with the dictates of filial piety. [MS. diary, February 1892.]

Our friendship was, however, in no way marred by the mishap of my marriage to a Socialist.

Second visit this year to the poor old man at Brighton. 'If I believed in Induction I should be forced to believe that I was being pursued by demons,' he laments: 'and who knows?' he adds in strangely humble tone, 'the veil may be lifted: it may be so.' And all this because one or two persons with whom he has been casually connected have misbehaved themselves with women, and thus imperilled his reputation! [MS. diary, 16 February 1899.]

And here are the final entries, prior to and immediately following his death:

A pathetic three days at Brighton just before we left London. A note from Herbert Spencer's secretary one morning, saying that the old man was very ill, made me take the train to Brighton – I did not like the thought that he should be nearing death without an old friend by his side. I found the devoted secretary and kindly girl housekeeper much upset; the doctor said he would not last long, and he was so self-willed about his treatment that it was almost impossible to keep him fairly comfortable. They could not tell whether or no he would like to see me. However, when the secretary told him I was there, he asked for me. The poor old man looked as if he were leaving this world: and what pained me was his look of weary discomfort and depression. I kissed him on the forehead and took his hand in mine. He seemed so glad of this mark of affection: 'It is goodbye, dear old, or is it young friend,' he said with a slight flicker of a smile; 'which word is the most appropriate?' And then he seemed anxious to talk. 'If pessimism means that you would rather not have lived, then I am a pessimist,' he said in tones of depression. 'Life will be happier and nobler for those who come after you, Mr Spencer, because of your work.' 'It is good of you to say so,' he answered in a grateful tone. 'Yes, humanity will develop – development is what we must look for,' his voice becoming more earnest. 'Come and see me before you go – that is enough at present.'

My visit had excited him; and he dictated to his secretary an almost passionate little note (which I unfortunately lost) imploring me to come and be by his side when I heard that there was no hope of recovery. The little outburst of human affection had carried him out of his querulous reserve. Thinking that he could only last a few days, I came back the next day and established myself at an hotel near by. I saw him once or twice again, and both times he talked about the future of society. Poor old man! Co-partnership and piecework seemed an adequate solution of all problems – inaugurating industrial peace and bringing about a decay of militarism! As he grew stronger, his desire to live, which had given way in his extreme weakness, returned; and again he became chary of seeing any one who excited him. Now he seems to be gaining strength, and it looks as if he might live for many a day. If he would only give up his self-preserving policy and be content to make the most of every hour without considering the cost, he might yet have a happy end before him. [MS. diary, June 1903.]

Melancholy letter from H. S. Ran down to see him. Again repeated that he and we agreed in essentials, differed only in form. Was extremely sensitive as to his reputation and influence, felt that he had dropped out and was no longer of much consideration. 'What you have thought and taught has become part of our mental atmosphere, Mr Spencer,' I said soothingly. 'And like the atmosphere we are not aware of it. When you cease to be our atmosphere, then we shall again become aware of you as a personality.' 'That is a pleasant way of putting it,' and he smiled. I tried to suggest that he should give up the struggle against ill fate and accept the rest of his existence. 'Why should I be resigned?' he retorted almost angrily. 'I have nothing to hope for in return for resignation. I look forward merely to extinction – that is a mere negative. No,' he added with intense depression, 'I have simply to vegetate between this and death, to suffer as little as I need, and, for that reason, I must not talk to you any more: it prevents me sleeping and upsets my digestion. Goodbye – come and see me again.'

It is tragic to look at the whole of man's life as a bargain in which man gets perpetually the worst of it. But the notion of contract – a *quid pro quo* – is so ingrained in the poor old man that even illness and death seem a nasty fraud perpetrated by nature. [MS. diary, 3 July 1903.]

My old friend passed away peacefully this morning (I write afterwards). Since I have been back in London this autumn I have been down to Brighton most weeks – last week I was there on Monday, Friday and Saturday, trying to soften these days of physical discomfort and mental depression by affectionate sympathy. 'My oldest and dearest friend,' he has called me these last visits. 'Let us break bread together,' he said on Monday, and insisted on a plate of grapes being set on the bed and both of us eating them. 'You and I have had the same ends,' he repeated again; 'it is only in methods we have differed.' On Saturday he was quite conscious and bade me an affectionate farewell – but he clearly wanted to be let alone to die and not troubled with further mental effort. Certainly these last months while he has been looking for death immediately – even longing for it – he has been benigner and less inclined to be querulous about his own miseries. But what with his dogmatic perversity in persisting in pernicious ways of living, his fretfulness towards and suspicion of his household, his pessimism about the world – it has been a sad ending. Indeed the last twenty years have been sad – poisoned by morphia and self-absorption, and contorted by that strangely crude vision of all human life as a series of hard bargains. ... Still if we strip Herbert Spencer's life of its irritation and superficial egotism – brought about, I believe, by poisonous food and drugs – and of its narrow philosophy of conduct, there remains the single-hearted persistent seeker after truth – the absolute faith that a measure of truth was attainable and would, if sought for earnestly, bring about consolation and reformation to mankind – the implicit assumption that he must live for the future of the human race, not for his own comfort, pleasure or success. If he had only not dogmatically denied that which he could not perceive or understand, if he had, with sincerity, admitted his own deficiencies of knowledge and perception – perhaps even of reasoning power – if he had had a ray of true humility – what a great and inspiring personality he might have been. As it was, he was a light to others in the *common places* of existence, but one that failed in the greater crises of life, and was quenched by sorrow or by temptation. Did the Light that was in him survive even for himself? To me he seemed in these last years to be stumbling in total darkness, hurting himself and then crying aloud in his lonely distress, clinging to his dogmas but without confident faith – with an almost despairing and defiant pride of intellect. Again, I assert that all these strange shortcomings and defects were like an ugly and distorted setting to a small but brilliant stone. This setting may drop from him as death and the everlasting brilliant of truth-seeking remain? He will be among the elect.

As I sat this morning arranging the papers for our next chapter my thoughts were perpetually drifting to the dear old man, trying to recall the details of my long debt of gratitude for his friendship. As a little child he was perhaps the only person who persistently cared for me – or rather who singled me out as one who was worthy of being trained and looked after. Intellectually he had no dominant influence until after the age of twenty, when I first began to study his works systematically. But though I had not until then grasped his philosophy, merely talking to him and listening to his long and pleasant discussions with Mother stimulated both my curiosity as to the facts and my desire to discover the principles or laws underlying these facts. He taught me to look on all social institutions exactly as if they were plants or animals – things that could be observed, classified and explained, and the action of which could to some extent be foretold if one knew enough about them.

It was after Mother's death – in the first years of mental vigour – that I read the *First Principles* and followed his generalizations through Biology, Psychology and Sociology. This generalization illuminated my mind; the importance of functional adaptation was, for instance, at the basis of a good deal of the faith in collective regulation that I afterwards developed. Once engaged in the application of the scientific method to the facts of social organization, in my observations of East End life, of co-operation, of factory acts, of trade unionism, I shook myself completely free from *laissez-faire* bias – in fact I suffered from a somewhat violent reaction from it. And in later years even the attitude towards religion and towards supernaturalism which I had accepted from him as the last word of enlightenment, have become replaced by another attitude – no less agnostic but with an inclination to doubt materialism more than I doubt spiritualism – to listen for voices in the great Unknown, to open my consciousness to the non-material world – to prayer. If I had to live my life over again, according to my present attitude I should, I think, remain a conforming member of the National Church. My case, I think, is typical of the rise and fall of Herbert Spencer's influence over the men and women of my own generation.

It is more difficult to unravel the effect of his *example* on the conduct of life. The amazing loyalty to a disinterested aim, the patience, endurance, the noble faith manifested in his daily life, sustained me through those dark years of discouragement, before success made continuous effort easy, and loving comradeship made it delightful. Contrariwise, the fitfulness, suspicion, petty irritations and antagonisms which have disfigured the later years have, perhaps unjustly (?), increased my distaste for all varieties of utilitarian ethics, all attempts to apply the scientific method to the *Purpose* as distinguished from the *Processes* of existence. His failure to attain to the higher levels of conduct and feeling has sealed my conviction in the bankruptcy of science when it attempts to realize the cause or the aim of human existence. [MS. diary, 8 and 9 December 1903.]

In any attempt to portray the father and the mother, the household saint and the philosopher on the hearth, I have drifted down the stream of time, far away from the circumstances surrounding childhood and youth. To these circumstances I now recur.

The leased house on the slope of the Cotswold Hills, nine miles from my father's main business – the timber yards and waggon works in the city of Gloucester – where I was born and mostly bred, was in all its domestic arrangements typical of the mid-Victorian capitalist. The building, a plain and formless structure, more like an institution than a home (it is now a county hospital), was sharply divided into front and back premises. The front region, with a south-western aspect, overlooked flower gardens and the beautiful vale of the Severn: the stairs and landings were heavily carpeted; the bedrooms and sitting-rooms were plainly but substantially furnished in mahogany and leather, the 'best' drawing-room and my mother's boudoir more ornately blossoming into reminiscences of the 1851 Exhibition. In this front portion of the house resided my father and mother and any honoured guests; the library and study were frequented by my elder sisters, and in the large and sunny dining-room all the family assembled for the mid-day meal. The back premises, with a predominantly northern aspect, overlooked laurel shrubberies, the servants' yard, the stables and extensive kitchen gardens. Bare stone steps led to long corridors of bedrooms, one apartment exactly like the other in shape and necessary furniture; stone-flagged passages connected the housekeeper's room of the upper servants with the larger servants' hall for the underlings, and a stone-paved yard separated the kitchen, scullery and larder from the laundries. In this back region of the house were the day and night nurseries, the large bare schoolroom overlooking the servants' yard and stables, the governesses' bedrooms, the one bathroom of the establishment, and, be it added, my father's billiard- and smoking-room. But Standish House and its surroundings had not the significance usually attached to a family home, seeing that, individually or collectively, the family was always on the move. For the restless spirit of big enterprise dominated our home life. In the early spring of most years we moved to a furnished house for the London season; from thence to Rusland Hall in Westmorland, a residence necessitated by timber yards at Barrow; whilst a small property encircling a ramshackle old manor house overhanging the Wye valley served as a playground for the younger members of the family, when the elders were entertaining 'house parties' in Gloucestershire. But the most upsetting factor were my father's frequent business tours, usually accompanied by two of his daughters, in Canada, the United States or Holland, as railway president and director of industrial companies.

The same note of perpetual change characterized our social relationships. We had no intercourse either in the country or in London with our nearest neighbours; nor did we belong to any organized profession or church; and my father, who had been brought up a Radical and had become a Conservative, took little part in local politics beyond subscribing handsomely to his party's funds. It is true that there was, somewhere in the background of our Gloucestershire life, a social entity called 'county society', consisting for the most part of a monotonous level of fox-hunting squires and the better-off incumbents; this plain of dull conventionality being broken here and there by the social peaks of peer or baronet, by the outstanding opulence of a retired manufacturer or trader, or, and this was the most invigorating variety, by the wider culture and more heterodox opinions of the Bishop and the Dean of Gloucester of the period. But the attachments of the family of the timber merchant of Glou-

cester to county society had always been loose and undefined; and as I grew up and the family became more
nomadic, these more stationary ties fell to the ground. The
world of human intercourse in which I was brought up was
in fact an endless series of human beings, unrelated one to
the other, and only casually connected with the family group
– a miscellaneous crowd who came into and went out of our
lives, rapidly and unexpectedly. Servants came and went;
governesses and tutors came and went; businessmen of all
sorts and degrees, from American railways presidents to
Scandinavian timber growers, from British Imperial company promoters to managers and technicians of local works,
came and went; perpetually changing circles of 'London
Society' acquaintances came and went; intellectuals of all
schools of thought, religious, scientific and literary, came and
went; my elder sisters' suitors, a series extensive and peculiar,
came and went, leaving it is true, in the course of my girlhood, a permanent residue of seven brothers-in-law, who
brought with them yet other business, professional and political affiliations, extending and diversifying the perpetually
shifting panorama of human nature in society which opened
to my view. Our social relations had no roots in neighbourhood, in vocation, in creed, or for that matter in race; they
likened a series of moving pictures – surface impressions
without depth – restlessly stimulating in their glittering
variety. How expressive of the circumstance of modern
profit-making machine enterprises is now its culminating
attempt to entertain the world – the ubiquitous cinema!

There was, however, one section of humanity wholly un-
represented in these moving pictures, the world of labour.
With the word labour I was, of course, familiar. Coupled
mysteriously with its mate capital, this abstract term was
always turning up in my father's conversation, and it occurred and reoccurred in the technical journals and reports
of companies which lay on the library table. 'Water plentiful
and labour docile', 'The wages of labour are falling to their
natural level', 'To raise artificially the wage of labour is like
forcing water up hill: when the pressure is removed the

wage, like the water, falls down hill', were phrases which puzzled me: the allusion to water and its ways giving a queer physico-mechanical twist to my conception of the labouring classes of the current history books. Indeed, I never visualized labour as separate men and women of different sorts and kinds. Right down to the time when I became interested in social science and began to train as a social investigator, labour was an abstraction, which seemed to denote an arithmetically calculable mass of human beings, each individual a repetition of the other, very much in the same way that the capital of my father's companies consisted, I imagined, of gold sovereigns identical with all other gold sovereigns in form, weight and colour, and also in value, except 'when the capital is watered' explained my father. Again this mysterious allusion to water! Was it because water was the most monotonous and most easily manipulated of the elements? I inquired.

This ignorance about the world of labour, did it imply class consciousness, the feeling of belonging to a superior caste? A frank answer seems worth giving. There was no consciousness of superior riches: on the contrary, owing to my mother's utilitarian expenditure (a discriminating penuriousness which I think was traditional in families rising to industrial power during the Napoleonic wars) the Potter girls were brought up to 'feel poor'. 'You girls', grumbled a brother-in-law, as he glanced from a not too luxurious breakfast table at the unexpectedly large credit in his bank-book, 'have neither the habit nor the desire for comfortable expenditure.' The consciousness that was present, I speak for my own analytic mind, was the consciousness of superior power. As life unfolded itself I became aware that I belonged to a class of persons who habitually gave orders, but who seldom, if ever, executed the orders of other people. My mother sat in her boudoir and gave orders – orders that brooked neither delay nor evasion. My father, by temperament the least autocratic and most accommodating of men, spent his whole life giving orders. He ordered his stockbroker to buy and sell shares, his solicitor to prepare contracts and undertake legal proceedings. In the running of the timber yards, his intervention took the form of final decisions with regard to the new developments in buying and selling, and new agreements with railway companies as to rates and transport facilities. When those maps of continents were unrolled before him I listened with fascinated interest to eager discussions, whether a line of railway should run through this section or that; at what exact point the station or junction should be placed; what land should be purchased for the contingent town; whether this patch or that, of forest, coalfield or mineral ore, should be opened up or left for future generations to exploit. And these manifold decisions seemed to me to be made without reference to any superior authority, without consideration of the desires or needs of the multitudes of lives which would, in fact, be governed by them; without, in short, any other consideration than that of the profit of the promoters. As for the shareholders' control (with what bewildered curiosity I watched the preparation for these meetings!), I knew it was a myth as far as human beings were concerned; it was patently the shares that were counted and not the holders; and share certificates, like all other forms of capital, could be easily manipulated. And when, one after the other, my sisters' husbands joined the family group, they also were giving orders: the country gentleman on his estate and at sessions; the manufacturer in his mill; the shipowner to his fleet of ships on the high seas; the city financier in the money market floating or refusing to float foreign government loans; the Member of Parliament as Financial Secretary of the Treasury; the surgeon and the barrister well on their way to leadership in their respective professions. It remains to be added, though this is forestalling my tale, that on the death of my mother I found myself giving orders and never executing them. Reared in this atmosphere of giving orders it was not altogether surprising that I apparently acquired the marks of the caste. When, in search of facts, I found myself working as a trouser hand in a low-grade Jewish shop, I overheard the wife of the sub-contractor, as she examined my bungled buttonholes, remark to her husband, 'She's no good at the sewing: if I keep her I will put her to look after the outworkers – she's got the voice and manner to deal with that bloody lot.' Alas! to be recognized – not as a scholar, not even as a 'r-e-e-l lidee' unaccustomed to earn her livelihood – but as a person particularly fitted by nature or nurture 'to give work out' and to 'take work in' in such a manner and in such a voice as to make the biggest profit, for (I say it as a justifiable retort) that bloody sweater!

The masculine world of big enterprise, with its passion for adventure and assumption of power, had its complement for its womenkind in the annual 'London season' and all that it implied. I do not know whether this peculiar and I imagine ephemeral type of social intercourse still survives; or whether, in so far as the daughters of business and professional men are concerned, it gradually faded away with the opening of university education and professional careers to women in the twentieth century. But in the seventies and eighties the London season, together with its derivative country-house visiting, was regarded by wealthy persons as the equivalent, for their daughters, of the university education and professional training afforded for their sons, the adequate reason being that marriage to a man of their own or a higher social grade was the only recognized vocation for women not compelled to earn their own livelihood. It was this society life which absorbed nearly half the time and more than half the vital energy of the daughters of the upper and upper middle class; it fixed their standards of personal expenditure; it formed their manners and, either by attraction or repulsion, it determined their social ideals. When I turned to social investigation as my craft in life, it was just my experience of London Society that started me with a personal bias effectually discounting, even if it did not wholly supersede, my father's faith in the social value of a leisured class.

Can I define, as a good sociologist should, the social entity I am about to criticize? For this purpose I do not know whether it is an advantage or disadvantage that I observed it, not from a position of privilege, but as one of the common herd of well-to-do folk who belonged or thought they belonged to London Society. From my particular point of observation London Society appeared as a shifting mass of miscellaneous and uncertain membership; it was essentially a body that could be defined, not by its circumference, which could not be traced, but by its centre or centres; centres of social circles representing or epitomizing certain dominant forces within the British governing class. There was the Court, representing national tradition and custom; there was the Cabinet and ex-Cabinet, representing political power; there was a mysterious group of millionaire financiers representing money; there was the racing set – or was it the Jockey Club? I am not versed in these matters – representing sport. All persons who habitually entertained and who were entertained by the members of any one of these key groups could claim to belong to London Society. These four inner circles crossed and recrossed each other owing to an element of common membership; this, in the seventies and eighties, happening to consist of striking personalities: such, for instance, as Edward, Prince of Wales, and the magnetically attractive Grand Seigneur who, as the tiresome tag tells, won the Derby, married a Rothschild and was destined to become Prime Minister of the British Empire at a time when there was still a British Empire. Surrounding and solidifying these four intersecting social circles was a curiously tough substance – the British aristocracy – an aristocracy, as a foreign diplomatist once remarked to me, 'the most talented, the most energetic and the most vulgar in the world'; characteristics which he attributed to a perpetual process of casting out and renewal, younger sons and daughters falling out of social rank to sink or swim among their fellow-commoners, whilst the new rich of the British Empire and the United States were assimilated by marriage, or by the sale of honours to persons of great riches but with mean minds and mediocre manners, in order to replenish the electoral funds of the 'ins' and 'outs'. But however diluted or enlarged the old landed aristocracy might be by marriage of the manufactured-for-money article, it did not surround or isolate the

Court; it was already a minor element in the Cabinet; and though it might still claim precedence on the race-course and the hunting field, it was barely represented in the ever-changing group of international financiers who ruled the money market. The bulk of the shifting mass of wealthy persons who were conscious of belonging to London Society, who practised its rites and followed its fashions, were, in the last quarter of the nineteenth century, professional profit-makers: the old-established families of bankers and brewers, often of Quaker descent, coming easily first in social precedence; then one or two great publishers and, at a distance, shipowners, the chairmen of railway and some other great corporations, the largest of the merchant bankers – but as yet no retailers. Scattered in this pudding-stone of men of rank and men of property were jewels of intellect and character, cultivated diplomatists from all the countries of the world, great lawyers, editors of powerful newspapers, scholarly ecclesiastics of the Anglican and Roman Catholic communions; the more 'stylish' of the permanent heads of Government departments, and here and there a star personage from the world of science, literature or art, who happened to combine delight in luxurious living and the company of great personages with social gifts and a fairly respectable character. To this strangely heterogeneous crowd were added from time to time topical 'lions', belonging to all races and all vocations, with strictly temporary tickets of admission for the season of their ephemeral notoriety.

Now the first and foremost characteristic of the London season and country-house life, a characteristic which distinguished it from the recreation and social intercourse of the rest of the community, was the fact that some of the men and practically all the women made the pursuit of pleasure their main occupation in life. I say advisedly *some* of the men, because the proportion of functionless males, I mean in the economic sense, varied according to whether the particular social circle frequented was dominated by the Cabinet and ex-Cabinet or by the racing and sporting set. Among my own acquaintances (I except mere partners at London and country-house dances, for dancing men in my time were mostly fools) there were very few men who were not active brain-workers in politics, administration, law, science or literature. In the racing set, which I knew only by repute, I gathered that the professional brain-workers, whether speculators or artists, book-makers, trainers or jockeys and the like, rarely belonged to 'society'; in their social and economic subordination these professional workers of the world of sport did not differ materially from other providers of entertainment – gamekeepers, gardeners, cooks and tradesmen. But about the women there was no such distinction. In the brilliant memoirs of Mrs Asquith – a document, owing to its frankness, of great value to the sociologist – this fact is brought out with startling emphasis and attractive vividness. Riding, dancing, flirting and dressing up – in short, entertaining and being entertained – all occupations which imply the consumption and not the production of commodities and services, were the very substance of her life before marriage and a large and important part of it after marriage. And my own experience as an unmarried woman was similar. How well I recollect those first days of my early London seasons: the pleasurable but somewhat feverish anticipation of endless distraction, a dissipation of mental and physical energy which filled up all the hours of the day and lasted far into the night; the ritual to be observed; the presentation at Court, the riding in the Row, the calls, the lunches and dinners, the dances and crushes, Hurlingham and Ascot, not to mention amateur theatricals and other sham philanthropic excrescences. There was of course a purpose in all this apparently futile activity, the business of getting married; a business carried on by parents and other promoters, sometimes with genteel surreptitiousness, sometimes with cynical effrontery. Meanwhile, as one form of entertainment was piled on another, the pace became fast and furious; a mania for reckless talking, for the experimental display of one's own personality, ousted all else from consciousness. Incidentally I discovered that personal vanity was an 'occupational disease' of London Society; and that anyone who suffered as I did from constitutional excitability in this direction, the symptoms being not only painful ups and downs of inflation and depression but also little lies and careless cruelties, should avoid it as the very devil. By the end of the season, indigestion and insomnia had undermined physical health; a distressing mental nausea, taking the form of cynicism about one's own and other people's character, had destroyed all faith in and capacity for steady work. And when these years of irresponsible girlhood were over, and I found myself my father's housekeeper and hostess, I realized that the pursuit of pleasure was not only an undertaking, but also an elaborate, and to me a tiresome undertaking, entailing extensive plant, a large number of employees and innumerable decisions on insignificant matters. There was the London house to be selected and occupied; there was the stable of horses and carriages to be transported; there was the elaborate stock of prescribed garments to be bought; there was all the commissariat and paraphernalia for dinners, dances, picnics and week-end parties to be provided. Among the wealthier of one's relatives and acquaintances there were the deer forests and the shooting-boxes, all entailing more machinery, the organization of which frequently devolved on the women of the household.

For good or evil, according to the social ideals of the student, this remarkable amalgam, London Society and country-house life, differed significantly from other social aristocracies. There were no fixed caste barriers; there seemed to be, in fact, no recognized types of exclusiveness based on birth or breeding, on personal riches or on personal charm; there was no fastidiousness about manners or morals or intellectual gifts. Like the British Empire, London Society had made itself what it was in a fit of absent-mindedness. To foreign observers it appeared all-embracing in its easy-going tolerance and superficial good nature. 'One never knows who one is going to sit next at a London dinner party,' ruefully remarked the aforementioned diplomatist. But deep down in the unconscious herd instinct of the British governing class there *was* a test of fitness for membership of this most gigantic of all social clubs, but a test which was seldom recognized by those who applied it, still less by those to whom it was applied, *the possession of some form of power over other people*. The most obvious form of power, and the most easily measurable, was the power of wealth. Hence any family of outstanding riches, if its members were not actually mentally deficient or legally disreputable, could hope to rise to the top, marry its daughters to Cabinet Ministers and noblemen, and even become in time itself ennobled. I once asked a multi-millionaire of foreign extraction, with a domestic circle not distinguished in intellect or character, why he had settled in England rather than in Paris, Berlin or Vienna. 'Because in England there is complete social equality,' was his rapid retort: an answer that was explained, perhaps verified, by a subsequent announcement that King Edward and his *entourage* had honoured by his presence the millionaire's palatial country residence. Personal wealth was, however, only one of the many different types of power accepted as a passport to good society; a great industrial administrator, not himself endowed with much capital, so long as he could provide remunerative posts for younger sons or free passes on transcontinental railways, could, if he chose, associate on terms of flattering personal intimacy with those members of the British aristocracy, and there were many of them, who desired these favours. And it must be admitted that there was no narrow view as to the type of power to be honoured with the personal intercourse of great personages. Thirty years before the Labour Party became His Majesty's Government there was a distinct desire, on the part of a select politico-social set, to welcome the leaders of the newly enfranchised trade-union democracy. And if the tiny group of Labour leaders had not been singularly refined and retiring, and, be it added, puritanical men, they also would have been caught up in the meshes of society to be immediately dropped when they ceased to represent their thousands of members. The same worship of power was shown in the supersession of one type of person by another. For instance, in the seventies the editors of great newspapers and other periodicals, men of broad culture and great experience of public affairs, were honoured guests; but even in my time the editors were beginning to be overshadowed by the millionaire newspaper proprietors, men who were not distinguished by wit, wisdom, technical skill or professional good manners. The more recent and more notorious instance of this driving out of the finer by the baser type was the social subserviency of quite well-bred and cultivated men and women to the South African millionaires, some of whom had neither manners nor morals; and all of whom were immeasurably inferior in charm and refinement, if not to the Rothschilds, most assuredly to the Barings and Glyns, the Lubbocks, Hoares and Buxtons, who had represented money power in the London Society of the seventies and eighties. What was even more demoralizing than this degraded and coarsening scale of values, because it bred a poisonous cynicism about human relations, was the making and breaking of personal friendships according to temporary and accidental circumstances in no way connected with personal merit: gracious appreciation and insistent intimacy being succeeded, when failure according to worldly standards occurred, by harsh criticism and cold avoidance. More especially was this the case in the relations between women. The rumour of an approaching marriage to a great political personage would be followed by a stream of invitations; if the rumour proved unfounded the shower stopped with almost ridiculous promptitude. A similar drying up of the effusive and appreciative friendship of leaders of Society was experienced by wives and daughters stripped by death of celebrated husbands and fathers. This sub-conscious pursuit of power was manifested in a more equivocal form. The conventional requirements with regard to personal morality, sexual or financial, were graded with almost meticulous exactitude to the degree of social, political or industrial power exercised by the person concerned. A duchess, especially if she came from a princely family, might exchange her insignificant duke for a powerful marquis as a habitual companion without causing the slightest dent in her social acceptability. But if Mrs Smith indulged in similar domestic waywardness the penalty was complete social ostracism. The same graded requirements were applied to financial misdemeanour. Past iniquities of a multi-millionaire, whose millions were secure, were discreetly forgotten; an honourable bankruptcy brought about by lack of knowledge or sheer ill luck led to ignoring not the sin but the sinner. There seemed in fact to be a sort of invisible stock exchange in constant communication with the leading hostesses in London and in the country; the stock being social reputations and the reason for appreciation or depreciation being worldly success or failure however obtained. Some stocks were gilt-edged, royal personages or persons who were at once outstandingly wealthy and genuinely aristocratic, their value could neither be 'bulled' nor 'beared' by current rumours; but the social value of the ruck of individuals who trooped to the political receptions or foregathered in the houses of the less well-known hostesses, went up and down as rapidly and unexpectedly as do the shares of the less well-known and more hazardous 'industrials' in the money market.[11] It was this continuous uncertainty as to social status that led to all the ugly methods of entertaining practised by the crowd who wanted 'to get into society'; the variety or 'menagerie' element in many entertainments so often caricatured by *Punch*; the competition in conspicuous expenditure on clothes, food, wine and flowers; above all, the practice of inviting persons with whom you had nothing in common because they would attract desired guests to your house. Nor did the manners of the most gifted and fastidious members of the governing groups remain unaffected by this com-

11. It appears from *Lord Randolph Churchill*, by Winston Churchill, 1906, vol. i. p. 74, that even the sons of a duke might suffer this swift change from caressing friendliness to cold neglect, if he had incurred the enmity of a sufficiently powerful person, say, for instance, Edward, Prince of Wales. 'But in the year 1876', recounts the son and biographer of Lord Randolph, 'an event happened which altered, darkened and strengthened his whole life and character. Engaging in his brother's quarrels with force and reckless partisanship, Lord Randolph incurred the deep displeasure of a great personage. The

petitive element in London Society, the push inwards by the crowd being inevitably followed, in order to rid themselves of unwelcome attentions, by a push outwards by the members of the inner circles. Now, it is the push that is vulgar, not its direction; and the fact that the push outwards was, by well-bred persons, usually manifested, not in words or acts, but by subtle forms of insolent expression, 'that distant look characteristic of people who do not wish to be agreeable, and who from suddenly receding depths of their eyes seem to have caught sight of you at the far end of an interminably straight road', to quote the inimitable Marcel Proust, did not make it less a breach of good-fellowship, and therefore of good manners, than the swear-words of Billingsgate. And yet who could blame socially distinguished men and women for developing in the course of a long life, spent in the midst of a mob of competing hostesses, this self-protective colouring of a detached but withering insolence of gesture and expression assumed at will towards this or that person whom they were compelled to recognize as social acquaintances, but whose company had always been or had become distasteful to them? There may be saints who can live untainted in such an environment, exactly as we know that there are men and women who retain their moral refinement in a one-room tenement, inhabited by persons of both sexes and all ages. But the true born saint, whether rich or poor, is an uncommon variety of the human species.

Such was the attitude of man towards man in the social environment in which I was reared. The dominant impulse was neither the greed of riches nor the enjoyment of luxurious living, though both these motives were present, but the

---

fashionable world no longer smiled. Powerful enemies were anxious to humiliate him. His own sensitiveness and pride magnified every coldness into an affront. London became odious to him. The breach was not repaired for more than eight years, and in the interval a nature originally genial and gay contracted a stern and bitter quality, a harsh contempt for what is called "Society," and an abiding antagonism to rank and authority.' How oddly old-fashioned this scale of values reads in these democratic days!

desire for power. The attitude of man towards the universe – that is to say, the metaphysical atmosphere – is more difficult to describe, partly, I deem, because the period was one of rapid transition from one metaphysic to another. For, looking back, it now seems to me that it was exactly in those last decades of the nineteenth century that we find the watershed between the metaphysic of the Christian Church, which had hitherto dominated British civilization, and the agnosticism, deeply coloured by scientific materialism, which was destined, during the first decades of the twentieth century, to submerge all religion based on tradition and revelation. Judging by my own experience among the organizers of big enterprise, with their 'business morality' and their international affiliations, the Christian tradition, already in the seventies and eighties, had grown thin and brittle, more easily broken than repaired. When staying in the country my parents were, it is true, regular churchgoers and communicants; and my father always enjoyed reading the lessons in the parish churches frequented by the household in Gloucestershire, Westmorland and Monmouthshire. Parenthetically I may remark that it was symptomatic of the general decline of orthodoxy that one who had been brought up as a Unitarian and had never been admitted to the Anglican Church by the rite of confirmation, should have been not only accepted as a communicant by Anglican clergymen who knew the facts, but also habitually invited, as the wealthy layman of the congregation, to take an active part in the service. Owing to personal religion, filial respect, or the joy of walking to and fro with the beloved father, one or two of the Potter girls would find themselves in the family pew each Sabbath day. But here conformity ended. No compulsion, even no pressure, was put on us to attend religious services. During the London season my father, accompanied by a bevy of daughters, would start out on a Sunday morning to discover the most exciting speaker on religious or metaphysical issues; and we would listen with equal zest to Monsignor Capel or Canon Liddon, Spurgeon or Voysey, James Martineau or Frederic Harrison; discussing on the walk back across the

London Parks the religious rhetoric or dialectical subtleties of preacher or lecturer. Except for this eclectic enjoyment of varieties of metaphysical experience, the atmosphere of the home was peculiarly free-thinking. There was no censorship whether of talk in the family, or of the stream of new books and current periodicals, or of the opinions of the crowd of heterogeneous guests. Any question which turned up in classical or modern literature, in law reports or technical journals, from the origin of species to the latest diplomatic despatch, from sexual perversion to the rates of exchange, would be freely and frankly discussed within the family circle. Perhaps the only expenditure unregulated and unrestricted by my mother, she herself being the leading spendthrift, was the purchase or subscription for books, periodicals and newspapers. And whether we girls took down from the well-filled library shelves the *Confessions of St Augustine* or those of Jean Jacques Rousseau, whether the parcel from Hatchett's contained the latest novels by Guy de Maupassant and Émile Zola or the learned tomes of Auguste Comte or Ernest Renan; whether we ordered from the London Library or from Mudie's a pile of books on Eastern religions, or a heterogeneous selection of what I will call 'yellow' literature, was determined by our own choice or by the suggestion of any casual friend or acquaintance. When we complained to my father that a book we wanted to read was banned by the libraries: 'Buy it, my dear', was his automatic answer. And if the whirl of society in which we lived undermined character by its amazing variety, it most assuredly disintegrated prejudices and destroyed dogma. My father had a weakness for ecclesiastics, and Dr Ellicott, the then Bishop of Gloucester, was his favourite associate in the county; whilst Cardinal Manning was an honoured visitor in London. But Herbert Spencer, who was far and away the most intimate of the family friends, was always arguing with my mother on the origin of religion, deriding and denouncing ecclesiasticism and all its works; and I think it was he who brought into our circle of acquaintances Francis Galton and Sir Joseph Hooker, Huxley and Tyndall, whilst to Spencer's

## CHAPTER 2

*In Search of a Creed*
1862–82

THE youngest but one of the nine daughters, creeping up in the shadow of my baby brother's birth and death, I spent my childhood in a quite special way among domestic servants, to whom as a class I have an undying gratitude. I was neither ill-treated nor oppressed: I was merely ignored. For good or for evil I was left free to live my own little life within the large and loose framework of family circumstance.

The first scene I remember was finding myself naked and astonished outside the nursery door, with my clothes flung after me, by the highly trained and prim woman who had been engaged as my brother's nurse. What exactly happened to me on that particular morning I do not recollect. The French and English governesses who presided over the education of my sisters decided I was too young for the schoolroom. Eventually I took refuge in the laundry, a spacious and well-lighted room, sunny in the summer and deliciously warm in the winter, under the voluntary but devoted care of the head laundry-maid, a kind and clever girl, skilful worker and pious chapel-goer, who, now over eighty years of age, is still my friend. On Monday, the washing day, when my chum and her assistants were immersed in soapsuds and enveloped in steam, I was warned off the premises, but from Tuesday afternoon I was welcome to come and go. Here, curled up amid rough-dried tablecloths and bedsheets, I dozed and daydreamed; or, sitting on the ironing-board swinging my legs, I chattered to an audience of admiring maids about my intention, when I was grown up, of becoming a nun. Another favoured place was the hayloft, up a ladder from the harness room, to which by a benevolent coachman I was admitted, with a big tabby cat, my adored follower and purring playmate. Out of doors there were 'secret' places in the shrubberies where I arranged and re-arranged stones and sticks; grottoes in the woods where I puddled leaky pools in trickling streams; all the time building castles in the air in which the picture of a neglected child enjoying her own melodramatically forgiving death-bed was succeeded by the more cheerful vision of courting lovers. How and when I learnt to read I do not remember. Long before I drifted into the schoolroom for spells of regular lessons, continuous reading, self-selected from the masses of books stacked in the library, study and schoolroom book-cases, or from the miscellaneous pamphlets, periodicals and newspapers scattered throughout the house, had become my main occupation; a wholesome alternative to castle-building but not conducive to robust health. Indeed, almost continuous illness, bouts of neuralgia, of indigestion, of inflammation of all sorts and kinds, from inflamed eyes to congested lungs, marred my happiness; and worse than physical pain was boredom, due to the incapacity of ill-health, the ever-recurring problem of getting rid of the time between the meals, and from getting up to going to bed; and worst of all, the sleepless hours between going to bed and getting up. I have a vivid memory of stealing and secreting a small bottle of chloroform from the family medicine-chest as a vaguely imagined alternative to the pains of life and the ennui of living; and of my consternation when one day I found the stopper loose and the contents evaporated.[1]

1. 'My childhood was not on the whole a happy one', I wrote in 1884; 'ill-health and starved affection, and the mental disorders which spring from these, ill-temper and resentment, marred it. Hours spent in secret places, under the shade of shrub and tree, in the leaf-filled hollows of the wood and in the crevices of the quarries, where I would sit and imagine love scenes and death-bed scenes and conjure up the intimacy and tenderness lacking in my life, made up the happy moments. But dreary times of brooding and resentfulness, sharp pains of mortified vanity and remorse for untruthfulness, constant physical discomfort and frequent pain absorbed the greater part of my existence; and its loneliness was absolute.' [MS. diary, 8 April 1884.]

Meanwhile the procession of governesses, English, French and German, did not trouble me. For the most part I liked them and they liked me. But after a few weeks or months of experimenting in regular schoolroom hours, and disagreeable tussles with arithmetic or grammar, I always took to my bed, the family doctor prescribing 'no lessons, more open-air exercise, if possible a complete change of scene'. When the last of my elder sisters 'came out', and my youngest sister had to be provided with a nursery governess, all pretence at formal education was abandoned.

But by this time I had invented a device of my own for self-culture – reading the books of my free choice, and in my private manuscript book extracting, abstracting and criticizing what I had read. To these immature reviews of books were added from time to time, as the spirit moved me, confessions of personal shortcomings or reflections on my own or other people's affairs.

I imagine that the majority of lonely but mentally alert children get into the habit of scribbling their thoughts and feelings, either to rid themselves of painful emotion or in order to enjoy the unwonted pleasure of self-expression. When this habit is combined with native wit, original observation and a quaint use of words, these scribblings may easily rise into literature. I have no such treasure to unlock. Unlike one or two of my sisters, I was born without artistic faculty, either for dancing or acting, for painting or music, for prose or poetry. The talents entrusted to my care were a tireless intellectual curiosity together with a double dose of will-power – all the more effective because it was largely subconscious, instinctively avoiding expression if insistence threatened to prevent fulfilment. It was the 'overcoming by yielding' type of will, inherited from my father, which, when I was living amid the Jews in East London, I thought I recognized as a racial characteristic. But however useful intellectual curiosity and concentrated purpose may be to the scientific worker, they are not attractive gifts in a child or in a marriageable young woman, and they are therefore apt to be hidden. Nor do they lead to facile literary expression.

Once I was started on the career of social investigator, the manuscript books became a record of other people's character and conversation; of their gestures and acts; in fact, of human behaviour; and, as such, these entries have an interest of their own. The diary becomes, in fact, one of the craftsman's tools; in a later chapter I call it synthetic note-taking, in order to distinguish it from the analytic note-taking upon which historical work is based. Hence, in describing the technique of a social investigator – for instance the use of the 'interview' and 'watching organizations at work' – I shall produce entries from my diary exactly as, in the Appendix, I give samples of analytic notes. But the scribblings of pre-craftsman years are records, not of objective facts but of subjective experiences; they represent the tracings on a sensitive brain, owing to family circumstances exposed to an unusually varied mental environment, of religious emotion and scientific thought, and of the business axioms and political theories characteristic of the last quarter of the nineteenth century. Seeing that my purpose in this chapter is to describe the search after a creed by which to live, I do not hesitate to quote, as the most trustworthy evidence, some of my crude and illiterate jottings, written not for publication, but in order to clear the child's thought and express her feelings.

I am quite confident [I wrote on a half-sheet of notepaper when I was about ten years old] that the education of girls is very much neglected in the way of their private reading. Take, for instance, a girl of nine or ten years old, she is either forbidden to read any but child's books, or she is let loose on a good library; Sir Walter Scott's novels recommended to her as charming and interesting stories, 'books that cannot do any possible harm', her adviser declares. But the object in reading is to gain knowledge. A novel now and then is a wise recreation to be offered to a crowing mind [sic, query 'growing'], it cultivates the imagination, but taken as the continual nourishment, it destroys many a young mind. . . . The whole of their thought (for a child of nine or ten spends little or no thought on her lessons) is wasted on making up love scenes, or building castles in the air, where she is always the charming heroine without a fault. I have found it a serious stumbling-block to myself; whenever I get alone I always find myself building castles in the air of some kind; it is a habit that is so thoroughly immured in me that I cannot make a good resolution without making a castle in the air about it.

This autumn unsatisfactory to me in many ways [I confess to myself in the autumn of 1872 at the more critical age of four-teen]. I have hardly learned anything in the way of lessons; honestly speaking, I have been extremely idle, especially during and after the company. But one thing I have learnt is, that I am exceedingly vain, to say the truth I am very disgusted with myself; whenever I am in the company of any gentleman, I cannot help wishing and doing all I possibly can to attract his attention and admiration; the whole time I am thinking how I look, which attitude becomes me, and contriving everything to make myself more liked and admired than my sisters. The question is, how can I conquer it, for it forwards every bad passion and suppresses every good one in my heart; the only thing I can think of, is to avoid gentlemen's society altogether. I feel I am not good enough to fight any temptation at present, I have not enough faith. Talking about faith, I don't know what to think about myself. I believe, and yet I am always acting contrary to my belief, when I am doing any silly action, when I am indulging my vanity, I hear a kind of voice saying within me, 'It doesn't matter at present what you say and do, if there is a God, which I very much doubt, it will be time to think of that when you are married or an old maid', and what is worse still I am constantly acting on that idea. Meanwhile I feel my faith slipping from me, Christ seems to have been separated from me by [a] huge mass of worldliness and vanity. I can no more pray to Him with the same earnest faith as I used to do, my prayers seem mockeries. I pray against temptations, which I run into of my own accord, and then I complain secretly that my prayers are not answered. And intellectual difficulties of faith make it impossible to believe. I am very very wicked; I feel [as] if Christ can never listen to me again.

Vanity, all is vanity. I feel that I have transgressed deeply, that I have trifled with the Lord. I feel that if I continue thus I shall become a frivolous, silly, unbelieving woman, and yet every morning when I wake I have the same giddy confident feeling and every night I am miserable. The only thing is to give up any pleasure rather [than] go into society; it may be hard, in fact I know it will, but it must be done, else I shall lose all the remaining sparks of faith, and with those all the chances of my becoming a good and useful woman in this world, and a companion of our Lord in the next. 23 December 1872.

BEATRICE POTTER.

May God help me to keep my resolution.

How far this pious resolution to keep 'out of society' led me in the following London season to concentrate on extracting tickets for the Ladies' Gallery of the House of Commons from my sisters' admirers I do not know.[2] But I recollect spendings hours listening to debates–loathing Gladstone and losing my heart to Disraeli; on one occasion (I think it was after one of the big debates on the Ballot Bill) returning in a hansom cab in the small hours of the morning, alone with my latchkey, to our house in Princes Gardens, an occasion stamped on my memory by ravenous hunger. The autumn and winter of that year found me travelling with my father and my sister Kate in the United States of America. It is during this exciting episode that I start the habit of writing regularly in a MS book, the first of an unbroken series of volumes extending now (1926) over half a century. The beauties and marvels of Niagara, the Yosemite Valley and the Californian geysers are duly recorded; but it is the human beings I meet and their attitude towards life which

2. We were brought up to be interested in politics and politicians, as is shown in the following description in a letter to my mother, when I was about eight, of the two Conservative candidates for Gloucester, I think at a by-election about 1866 – a letter intended, I suspect, to impress my mother with my learning, the long words ornamented with capitals having obviously been copied out of some newspaper. 'The two Conservative Candidates were here yesterday, one of them is very short and very finely dressed; he had his top coat trimmed with sealskin; he had also silver buckles on his boots and his hands were covered with rings, with a very stylish blue tye which covered his vastcoat; He also saied he spoke italian and french perfectly. He played on the piano and sung; he seemed not to (k)now what mony words ment, for he asked papa what was the meaning of Demonstration, and Major Lees asked the meaning of Hustings and Nomination. Major Lees is very tall and very fat, with a great beard mustache and whiskers, with an eye glass which he satisfied his curiosity in staring at everybody.'

really interests me, and the only city I describe in any detail
is Salt Lake City (Utah), where the state of mind of the
plural wife rouses my curiosity. In spite of the proverbial
dullness of journals of travel, particularly from inex-
perienced and untrained minds, I give a few entries illustrating the general outlook on men and affairs of the girl of
fifteen.

We left England on the 13th of September, two days after G.'s
marriage.[3] I only enjoyed our passage pretty well, the people not
being anything particular. The only nice people were, Mr Bradford, Dr Hall, Dr Sharp, Mr A. Pullman, Miss Holmes (I would
say Mr Knowles, but we hardly made his acquaintance on
board). Mr Bradford is an American artist – an Arctic traveller,
and a great friend of Dr Rae's.[4] He was one of those enthusiastic
little men who have not a spark of sarcasm or cynicism in them,
and see only the beauty and good in everybody. He was a general
favourite on board, from his extreme kindness to and thought-
fulness about everybody. Kate made great friends with him, and
they were to be seen constantly walking up and down the deck,
arm in arm, evidently liking each other immensely, and sym-
pathizing in their views of people and things. I often envy Kate
that way she has of drawing clever people out, and of making
them talk to her as if they were talking to their own equal. Mr
Hall is the popular Presbyterian minister of New York. He was
perhaps the man on board whom I saw most of, and took the
greatest fancy to, so I shall describe him somewhat at length both
physically and morally. He was a tall man, with a decided stoop,
large features and forehead, not handsome but very impressive-
looking. His face seemed to reflect his mind; when he was not
talking, he had a perfectly calm, simple expression of calm,
almost childish faith and love. But when he was preaching or
talking seriously to one, he looked quite a different man; his face
assumed a look of dignity and earnestness, and a strange smile
came over his mouth, a smile which always reminded me of Dr
Arnold – I do not think he would be half such a charming man
to live with as my favourite hero would have been, as he holds

3. My fourth sister, Georgina (married to Daniel Meinertzhagen,
September 1873).
4. The Arctic traveller with whom I had been friends during the
preceding London season of 1873.

stern uncompromising opinions which seemed to me to be sometimes devoid of charity and which would have been almost
offensive to people brought up broadly as ourselves if it had not
been for the extreme kindness and gentleness of his manner. We
went afterwards to hear him preach at New York; what I was
most struck with were his beautiful metaphors; he illustrated all
his religious views by nature . . .

*Tuesday, 7 October (Chicago)*. – Miss Owen came and called
for us in her carriage, and after a short drive round the town we
went to lunch at her Uncle's, Mr (illegible) agent for G.T.[5] They
were evidently people whose position in England would hardly
be among the gentry, and yet there was an elegance and gentility
about the girl's dress and manners which you would hardly find
among the corresponding class in England. After lunch we drove
to the public schools, which were very interesting. Both boys and
girls, of all classes, are educated here. It was so funny to see a
common little Negro girl sitting between two well-dressed
banker's daughters, and learning the same thing! There were
eleven hundred scholars in that particular school, divided into
classes, each having a girl as its teacher, all of whom looked
remarkably nice intelligent young women . . .

*Wednesday, 8*. – Left Chicago at ten in the morning. We were
very sad at leaving dear father, and when we saw the last of his
grey hat, as he stood waving it on the platform, I felt quite melancholy. The country that we passed through that day was
nothing very interesting, it was one great farm of Indian corn,
now and then interrupted by a mile or two of prairie wood. In the
evening we passed over the Mississippi. It was very fine, though
of course one would have liked to see it by day . . .

*Thursday, 9 (Omaha)*. – We saw nothing of interest between
this and Ogden, except the prairie fires and the prairie dogs. We
saw the fires best the evening after we left Omaha; they were most
beautiful, sometimes lighting up the horizon, as it were, with a
row of candles, and sometimes with a lurid blaze, as if a great
city were on fire . . .

*San Francisco, 24 October*. – In the afternoon I drove with
Richot[6] to Cliff House. We sat on the balcony watching the

5. The Grand Trunk Railway of Canada, of which my father was
then President.
6. The French-Canadian cook of the President's car who had been
sent with us by my father while he himself remained in Canada.

seals on the rocks. It was a very pretty sight, and I tried to make a sketch of it, which I afterwards re-did in the train. Talking about sketching, it makes me remember the violent fancy for really going in for that art, that the Yosemite inspired me with. I remember the same fancy seized me when at the Lakes, and I remember all the way coming down in the train from Lancashire I studied the different effects of light and shade, and built castles in the air of my future industry in art. It was the same on the road from the Yosemite, there was but one thought in my head – ambition to become a great artist – and belief that I could if I liked. It seemed to me then that if I could copy nature with some slight success, then, that I had had neither instruction nor any practice, that with an immense deal of patience and perseverance and time devoted to it I might really end by being successful. But now that the fever is cooled I see the difficulties, nay, the impossibilities of carrying out my resolutions. Even if I had the patience and perseverance, where could I find the time, and I have a very strong objection to dabble with art. Perhaps I shall find some day a solution to this great difficulty, of, how I ought to employ my time . . .

The same evening Arthur,[7] Mr Knowles and I, attended by Richot and Mr Cole, walked through the Chinese quarter to the Chinese theatre. Just before leaving Kitty had thought it more prudent to give it up, she was not at all well; indeed, she had not been that ever since we left the Yosemite. So we left her to go to bed and started off. We were very much amused by the Chinese acting. There was no attempt at scenery, and the actors had the most unceremonious way of laughing and joking with their friends in the audience, when not reciting their parts. Each actor was heralded by a tremendous clashing of gongs and kettles as he came on to the stage and the noise was carried on also while the actors sang, so as to deafen you. Altogether it was impossible for me to stay in the place for more than five or six minutes, the noise was so deafening, and then being in such close quarters with John Chinaman was not exactly pleasant. The theatre was crowded with Chinese; the only European face we saw was that of the collector of tickets. They say that the plays extend over centuries, being really the history of their different dynasties . . .

*Tuesday, 27 October (San Francisco).* – The morning was

7. My sister Mary's husband, Arthur Playne, who was travelling with us.

spent in getting photographs of the Yosemite. At four o'clock in the afternoon Mr Latham called to take Arthur and me down to his country place. I was so fearfully tired that I could not talk, and somehow or other I felt quite shy all the way down in the train. When we got there we were shown into the drawing-room where Mrs Latham and Miss Washington (a friend of hers) were sitting. Mrs Latham was an extremely pretty person, almost a beauty at first sight, but with uninteresting features when one came to pick them to pieces. She had a decidedly elegant figure, large handsome black eyes, a pretty complexion, and a good nose and mouth, but not one single feature showed any depth of intellect or character. From what she told me, I gathered that she had been kept very strictly 'in' by her parents, until seventeen, and then suddenly presented to the world as a *belle*. She married Mr Latham very young, a splendid match in way of money and position, and indeed a thoroughly nice and kind man, but old enough to be her father. I don't think it can be good for a young woman to be transported into the midst of luxury, and to be merely required to look pretty and graceful in her husband's drawing-room, without having any household duties or cares. Her friend, Miss Washington, was a different sort of girl. In appearance she was short and plump, with a pretty nose and nice soft intelligent eyes. She was an orphan (grandniece to the great Washington), and I fancy lived a great deal with Mrs Latham. She was a nice bright jolly little person, who took interest in everybody and thing. Altogether she was more the hostess at Menton Park than Mrs Latham herself. It was a splendid house, furnished with great taste, evidently without the least regard to expense. The garden was rather pretty, indeed very pretty for an American garden, but nothing to be compared to an English garden of any size. Mr Latham went away early next morning, and we stayed till the four o'clock train up to Frisco. The whole of that evening I spent in packing up, as Kitty was quite unequal to it.

*Salt Lake, Saturday 1 November.* – We arrived here about 12.30. We lost about one hour in deciding what we would do; that is the worst of having a party, with no one really to take the lead, and arrange anything. At last Kate and I called out for lunch, thinking, at any rate, we should be better tempered after it. Then we decided all to go to the photographer's, as Richot had told Mr Blackwall to call upon Arthur at 2.30. We had no introduction to this Mr Blackwall, except that Richot knew him to be the son of the manager of the G.T. before Mr Bridges was made Managing Director. However, he turned out to be a very nice young man, full of life and interest, and quite determined that we should enjoy ourselves. We drove first to his house, where there was a picture of Mr Munger's of Emma mine. Then we went to the Tabernacle and Temple; the latter is not nearly finished. It is built in granite and will be, as far as one can see, a very handsome building. The Tabernacle is, without exception, the most remarkable building I ever saw. It is entirely of wood, and the roof is covered with shingles (of wood). Inside, it is perfectly plain, without the least attempt at ornament. There is a raised platform at one end of the building, in the centre of which is Brigham's chair. Just below him sit the twelve apostles and the elders. Above him, sit his daughters and sons, forming the choir. His wives are scattered among the congregation, and have no particular seats of their own. The rest of the building is filled up with wooden seats, and there is a large gallery all round. The organ, said to be the second finest in America, was completely constructed at Utah. After seeing the Tabernacle, we drove up to the camp, where Mr Blackwall took us to call on General and Mrs Munro. They evidently lived on a small scale; Mrs Munro coming in with a servant's print on, apologized, as it was house-cleaning day. The General looked an extremely nice man, but I had no opportunity of talking to him. The camp is on a hill above Salt Lake, so you have a magnificent view of the whole city. The city lies in the middle of a vast plain, completely surrounded (except on the side of the Lake) by two beautiful ranges of mountains, tipped all the year round with snow. As each house has its orchard and garden, it gives the city and its suburbs, viewed from above, the appearance of a wood, just spotted with white villas.

Then the large roof of the Tabernacle stands out in strong relief from the trees and houses, forming the ruling spirit of the picture. Mr Blackwall came to dine, and took us to the theatre in the evening. The piece was *The Stranger*, with a farce called *The Blue-eyed Susan*. The acting was wretched, especially Mrs Haller and the Stranger. But in spite of this I enjoyed myself immensely. First, our companion, Mr Blackwall, made himself extremely pleasant, he was such a change from practical Mr Knowles and homesick Arthur. Poor Mr Knowles didn't half like it, being so completely put in the shade by this newcomer. Then it was very interesting to see the different Mormon ladies; some looked very pleasant, nice women, but most certainly had a dejected air, as if they felt they were degraded. The next morning we went a long walk through the streets. It was a beautiful day and everything looked lovely and bright.

Salt Lake City is not to be compared with any town in England or America; it is so utterly different from anything I have ever seen. The streets are very wide, and on both sides of them flow beautiful streams of crystal water brought from the mountains ten or twenty miles off. It is through this water that Brigham Young and his few followers transformed this sandy desert into a fertile farm; wherever it penetrates thither also does vegetation; wherever it ceases, grows nothing but the eternal sagebrush. The houses are for the most part low, built rather in the French style, and of wood whitewashed over, with green shutters and doors. This gives the city a fresh innocent appearance, especially as (as I have mentioned before) each house has its garden and orchard.

The Tabernacle is by far the most important building in Salt Lake City; then come Brigham's two houses, 'The Lion' and 'The Beehive', and a very pretty villa he is building for Mrs Amelia Young, his last and most beloved wife. Most of his other wives either live in one of his two houses, or else have small houses round them in his garden. The only one of his wives we saw was Mrs Eliza Young, No. 17, who separated from him, and is now lecturing on Mormonism all over America. She was staying at Walker's Hotel; she was rather a pretty woman at a distance, but decidedly coarse when you examined her near.

In the afternoon we went to hear Anson Pratt, an Apostle, and one of the original founders of the Mormon creed. During the summer the service is held in the Tabernacle, but as it is built of wood they are afraid of heating it, which of course makes it impossible to use it in winter. So each ward has its own meeting-house where they assemble on Sundays during the winter months. We went to the 13th ward. The congregation was mostly of the working-men's class. They seemed to be very attentive and earnest in their devotions. I noticed here particularly the dejected look of the women, as if they had continually on their mind their inferiority to their lords and masters. The service was begun by a hymn. Then a decidedly clever-looking man (a bishop) stood up and recited a prayer, in itself very good, but said more in a tone of 'we only demand what we have a right to', than of humble supplication. Then the sacrament was handed round and another hymn sung, after which Anson Pratt got up and began his discourse; which Kate wrote down the following day, so that I shall benefit by her memory and transcribe her letter into my diary . . .

And now that our party is breaking up, let us see in what relation they stand to each other. Arthur is a dear good affectionate creature, but he is not a good travelling companion. At times he would even be unpleasant, he would get so low-spirited and discontented about everything, and would not even allow you to take a pleasant and enthusiastic view of what you saw. Then he has no power of making himself and his party considered; he is too sensitive and fearful of giving anybody pain or trouble. He does not take that vivid interest in the country he passes through, which is so necessary in a travelling companion. But in spite of all these little faults I have a much more sisterly feeling towards Arthur than when we left England. I know his faults, therefore I like him. Kate and I can say that we have seen his worst side; I don't fancy he is often as irritable as he was sometimes with us, and irritability and indecision are his worst faults. Now for Mr Knowles. About as opposite a man to our sensitive aristocratic brother-in-law as you could find. A plain, good and pure-hearted man, with a practical way of looking at everything, totally devoid of any kind of sentiment or poetry. He has a simple kind way of looking after you when you are ill, and seeing that you do not overtire yourself. He is not what I should call an interesting man, because he has no conversation, except on his own particular subjects, such as coal-mining, etc., and both Kate and I found it impossible to engage him in any literary or political conversations. And then he does not seem to seize the most interesting facts with regard to the country he passes through, but only remarks the smaller mechanical things. But to make up for this, he has a perfect temper, and is most kind and accommodating in any arrangements, and is always ready to make the best of it. We got rather tired of him towards the end, and I was rather glad when he left us at Omaha.

Here the diary breaks off suddenly as did our delightful tour. At Chicago I have a dim remembrance of being carried out of the train in a state of semi-consciousness by my father and his friend Mr George Pullman, who had been summoned by my sister to meet us, and during the following six weeks my devoted sister nursed me single-handed through scarlet fever, rheumatic fever and, breaking out the day before we were to have started for New York, an untoward attack of measles. I give the concluding entry of the American diary of 1873.

*December*. The day before we leave New York! Kate and father have gone out to dinner, so I shall have a little time to have a chat to myself. It seems a long, long time since I passed through the hall at Standish, feverish with excitement and longing to see the world, with sisters kissing us, and giving us a tearful good-bye, and with a file of wedding guests on each side, looking on with amusement and interest. I wonder if I have altered? and if altered, whether for the better or the worse. I shall find my own level when I get home, that is one good thing in a large family.

One thing I want to do, when I get home, that is to make more a friend of Maggie. Hitherto I have lived a great deal too much apart from my sisters, partly from indolence, and partly from my unfrank disposition. Dear Kitty, I have got quite fond of her, she has been such a dear kind devoted sister. I can't imagine why she does not get on better at home.[8] Though we lived on the most intimate relationship for the last three months or more, I really have not found out one serious fault.

The American trip over, I start again on my career of self-culture; the MS. book becomes, in the main, extracts from and reviews of books read.

I am now busily engaged in studying. I am translating *Faust* and reading a novel of Tieck. *Faust* is wonderfully clever and often very beautiful. Putting the introduction piece out of the question, which is fearfully blasphemous, it might almost have been written by a good man, as a satire on the philosophers of the present day. *Faust* is supposed to have reached the zenith of human knowledge, and is shown how inadequate that knowledge is to make a man contented and happy. He first resolves to commit suicide, but is stopped by the feelings which the church bells and the songs of the choir on Easter morning awaken in him, by the sweet recollection of Easter-tide in his youth, with its

8. At that time my sister Kate, who had from childhood upwards been devoted to the poor and suffering, was claiming to be permitted to withdraw from 'society' and take service under Miss Octavia Hill as rent-collector in East London – a claim that was acceded to in 1875.

pleasures and religious impulses and sensations. As far as I have gone, I think it is far more powerful than Tasso, which I must say I neither admired nor liked. I have left off music almost entirely; I practise exercises and scales for half an hour, half because Mother wishes it, and half because I do not want to leave it off entirely. Drawing is what I should like to excel in, and now in the evenings, before I go and read Shakespeare to Miss Mitchell,[9] I make a point of copying one of the patterns in the School of Art book, and correcting it with compass and ruler . . .

. . . I am not thoroughly contented with the way that I have passed this week [I record a fortnight later]. I have been extremely irregular in all my duties. I have not worked as much as I ought to have done, I have been lazy about my religious duties, I have been lazy in getting up; altogether I have been totally devoid of any method. Now I must really try and be more regular, go to bed early, get up early; practise and not be lazy about my drawing, else I shall never get on. I don't think it hurts at all, now and then, to read some of St Paul's life instead of studying German, say twice a week. Father came home yesterday evening; it has been a very exciting week for him what with this Grand Trunk Meeting and the dissolution of Parliament. Poor G.T. has had another relapse: will it ever raise itself from this state of chronic disease? It is wearing Father out; he might have been able to go into Parliament and do some good for this country, except for G.T. I am in a complete muddle about politics. I think they are one of those things of which you cannot see the 'right' or the 'wrong'. I can't help having a sort of sympathy with the Radicals, they are so enthusiastic, but I don't think that their time is come yet. They require a much more perfect state [of] society than that at present. But it is ridiculous for me to waste my time in scribbling about politics when I am so ignorant on all those questions . . .

Sometimes I feel as if I must write, as if I must pour my poor crooked thoughts into somebody's heart, even if it be into my own. I am fascinated with that book of Joaquin Miller's, a lover of the wild, half-savage state, and a hater, because a stranger, of the civilized world. It's queer, after reading of nothing but the influence of civilization on this or that nation, of progress, to hear a man boldly stand up and declare that civilization often is degradation, that the savage is often better, wiser and 'nearer

9. My little sister's nursery governess, whose mind I was apparently intent on cultivating.

God' than the civilized man; and that too from an American. Dear me! my trip to America seems to have opened a new world to me, and into which I seemed to have had a glimpse, a glimpse long enough to make one wish for another. [MS. diary, 13 January 1874.]

The American trip, with its vision of human nature in the melting-pot, had in fact increased 'those intellectual difficulties of faith' already troubling me in the autumn of 1872.

I am really trying to gain a firm belief for myself [I write a few days before we leave Standish for London]. I think it is no good going to others to have your belief cut out for you; you must examine, study, both the Bible and the lives of those who follow the Bible and those who don't. It is no sin to doubt, but it is a sin, after you have doubted, not to find out to the best of your capability why you doubt, and whether you have reasons to doubt. It was because no one doubted, and because every one was too idle to examine and to prove, that Christianity became so corrupted in the middle ages. I must make a faith for myself, and I must work, work, until I have. [MS. diary, 4 April 1874.]

But my lonely studies are broken into by the London season – a break which is described when we are again settled in Gloucestershire.

It is a long time since I last wrote in my diary. 4 April is the last date. It was just then that the whirl of the London season was beginning, which included me, though a schoolroom girl, in its rush. I enjoyed it immensely. It is seldom I have had so much pleasure in so small a space of time. And yet at times one was hardly happy. One looked from day to day for some new excitement, and in the intervals between these excitements one hardly knew what to do with oneself. The theatricals were the climax of all the pleasure and excitement. The getting up of them was in itself great fun, though I was only a looker-on. And then that tremendous excitement the week before them, the thought of my having to act Kate Hardcastle before two audiences of 200 people! But, however, that never came to pass; Maggie got well in time and carried off the laurels. The dance, oh! how I did enjoy that. It was the first dance I had ever been at as a grown-up young lady, and I felt considerably satisfied with myself, as I had two or three partners for each dance. Ah, vanity! vanity! Unfortunately for me, my ruling passion. Now this is enough about myself for the present; in what way did the London season affect the rest of the Potter family. Blanche was the excitement in the beginning of the season, as Georgie had been last year. [MS. diary, 3 August 1874.]

There follows an affectionate but somewhat sarcastic account of the love affairs of my four unmarried sisters, ending in a critical estimate of the character and attainments of their various admirers. 'The gentleman himself turned grave and severe, and at the end of the season looked very gloomy and yellow', I remark of one of them.

The gay life in London had weakened body and mind; and the autumn of 1874, spent at Standish alone with my mother, an elder sister, and the little one (my father with two daughters travelling again in Canada), finds me in bad health and desperately unhappy.

Here we are alone, Mother, Blanche and myself. Poor Mother, she has two rather broken crutches to lean upon. Blanche is a dear girl but she is unpractical and rather inclined to bore you; and as for me, I am, as Mother says, too young, too uneducated, and, worst of all, too frivolous, to be a companion to her. But, however, I must take courage, and try to change, and above all I must guard against that self-satisfaction which I consider is one of my worst faults. If I give in to it, it will prevent my ever improving myself. And the only way to cure myself of it is to go heart and soul into religion. It is a pity I ever went off the path of orthodox religion; it was a misfortune that I was not brought up to believe that to doubt was a crime. But since I cannot accept the belief of my Church without inward questioning, let me try and find a firm belief of my own, and let me act up to it. That is the most important thing. God help me to do it! [MS. diary, September 1874.]

By December I am down in the depths of egotistical misery.

I think that the great benefit one receives from keeping a diary is that it often leads one to examine oneself and that it is a vent for one's feelings, for those feelings in particular that one cannot communicate to other people. Since I have been poorly this autumn I have been thinking of nothing but myself, and I am sure that it is the most unhealthy state of mind. I am suffering from an indisposition which is decidedly trying to one's health of mind as it prevents one from doing much, and that always makes one discontented and low-spirited. I have never felt so low-spirited as I have this autumn. I have felt for the first time in my life how much unhappiness there is in life. But one has not been given the choice of existing or not existing, and all one has to think of is how to live the best and mose useful and the happiest life. I have come to the conclusion that the only real happiness is devoting oneself to making other people happy. I feel that it is very discouraging to lose so much valuable time when I might be studying, but I believe that if I take this ill-health in a proper way, and bear it bravely and cheerfully, I shall improve my character more than I should have improved my mind in the same time. And character weighs more than intellect in the scales of life. [MS. diary, December 1874.]

The breakdown in health became serious, and before the next London season I am settled in Bournemouth as a 'parlour boarder' in a fashionable girls' school, free to spend my time in lonely study and religious meditation. It is here that I seek mental security in traditional Christianity, and decide to be confirmed and become a regular communicant. The 'high church' was attended by the school, but I preferred the 'low church' and the remarkably eloquent evangelical preacher, Mr Eliot (afterwards a canon of Windsor), became my spiritual director and prepared me for confirmation. The following entries describe my religious experiences during the next nine months. From these I gather that the doctrine of the Atonement remained a stumbling-block, not because it struck me as irrational, but because it seemed to me immoral.

*Easter Eve.* The day before I receive for the first time the Holy Sacrament. The last month or two has been a very solemn epoch in my life, and may God grant that I may never cease remembering the vows which I have made before God and man, that I intend to become a true Christian, that is, a true disciple and follower of Jesus Christ, making Him my sole aim in life. And now I am going to receive the great sacrament, which He Himself instituted as a perpetual means of remembering His visit on earth. God grant that it may really strengthen me. There are many things which remain still mysteries to me, like the doctrine of Atonement. The idea that God demanded that some innocent person should die for the sins of men, and that, by the voluntary death of that just man, wicked and damned men, who would not otherwise have been saved, are saved, is repugnant to me. I firmly believe that Jesus Christ has and will save the world, but not so particularly by His death as by His Word, which He came down to preach. His whole preaching seems to me to indicate that He never says that we shall be saved by His death but by belief in Him and in the word which He has preached. 'And this is life eternal, that they may know thee the only true God and Jesus Christ, whom thou hast sent.' 'He that believeth on me shall have eternal life.' 'It is the spirit that quickeneth, the flesh profiteth nothing; the words that I speak unto you they are spirit, they are life.' And this last was said after that long discourse about His flesh as the bread of life. And yet it is evident that every one of His disciples believed in the Atonement as a saving doctrine, and Christ Himself seems to set it forth once as a great truth in the institution of the Lord's Supper. [MS. diary, 27 March 1875.]

But the main struggle was with my own lack of morality.

It is very discouraging to find that after forming such high resolutions, after reading and studying and getting as one would have thought out of the world of vanity and vexation of spirit, that directly one gets into society one talks such confounded nonsense. Confounded, or rather confounding, in the literal sense of the term. It is such a dreadful thing to think that on the Sunday one has taken the Holy Sacrament, and by doing that renewed as it were the vow one made on the day of one's confirmation, that one should [be] guilty of talking frivolously. As it is, my Sunday is the most unholy day in the week. I cannot sympathize with the Sullivans[10] in their views of religion. Oh that I had more char-

10. Two old friends of my father were 'authorized' to take me out walks – Admiral Sullivan, a fanatical Protestant but jolly old Irishman, with whose family I spent Sundays, they being attendants at Mr Eliot's church; and Admiral Grey, whose courteous manners and broad culture remain a pleasant memory. But my particular friend at Stirling House was Oscar Beringer, who gave the girls music

ity, true charity, so that I might see and reverence and not sneer at and despise what I do not understand! God only can give me help. I am so weak, so vain, so liable to fall into self-confidence ... [MS. diary, July 1875.]

I must confess I am much more sorry to leave Standish [after the summer holiday] than I expected. The last fortnight I have enjoyed very much and have been blessed with good health. But I hope at Bournemouth to grow much stronger, and I must be resolved to allow no pleasure or interesting study to interfere with care of health; and I must be particularly careful of my diet. The two studies I have taken up, Jewish History and English Law, are both very interesting. I have chosen the latter because it is so thoroughly different from the former, and employs a different set of muscles. I must try and not become egotistical in my thoughts, for that is a great danger when one leads a solitary life, for my life with regard to thought is completely solitary at Stirling House. I propose every Sunday to write a short sketch of my work during the week, and whether I can conscientiously say that I have not transgressed the rules of health. I must also above everything endeavour not to think myself superior to the other inmates of Stirling House, because I have been brought out more by circumstances and encouraged to reason on subjects which other girls have mostly been told to take on faith. Both systems have their advantages and disadvantages. But perhaps the mistake I felt most was joining gossiping conversations. And this is certainly most difficult, because it in a great way necessitates keeping myself aloof from the girls' society. [MS. diary, 19 September 1875.]

I have this morning been disappointed in going to receive the Holy Sacrament. Somehow or other I feel I neither understand nor appreciate it, though I believe it helps me. I think it is the constant allusion to atonement in the English communion service which so distresses me. I cannot at present believe in that doctrine. It disgusts me. Probably I completely misunderstand it.

---

lessons and afterwards became famed as an accomplished pianist. Finding that I had 'musical feeling' but no musical faculty, he spent the time allotted to me in playing his favourite pieces and explaining to me their meaning – a type of 'music lesson' which I appreciated when a few years later I spent six months in Germany attending concerts and operas.

But I believe that the sacrament ought to be regarded, first as an earnest avowal of your belonging to the Church of Christ both to God, yourself and mankind; secondly, as a sign of your penitence and your desire to become better; and thirdly, the receiving of the sacrament ought to be stepping-stones in the path of Holiness. I wish I could become more truthful. It is such a dreadful fault, and yet I find myself constantly telling downright lies. God grant that I may earnestly strive to cure myself of this great sin. I do not know whether I am right in giving all the time I have to spare for the study of religion completely to the Old Testament. But it appears to me that by watching the Light glimmer through the minds of the prophets I shall be able to appreciate better the full glory and greatness of the Religion of God revealed through the words of Christ. [MS. diary, 3 October 1875.]

Lied again today. I will make a practice of noting these lies, by putting a cross for every one to the day of the month. I am quite convinced that it is a most dangerous habit. [MS. diary, 4 October 1875.]

Another week passed. I have read only pretty well. I suppose I cannot expect to do much in the way of quiet study. But let me devote my energy to becoming truthful and to guarding against that feeling of satisfaction and vanity, and to speaking not for effect but from conviction. Oh! that by the next time I take the sacrament I may be more truthful and less vain. [MS. diary, 10 October 1875.]

Have read very regularly last week: But I am afraid this week it will be impossible to do much in that way as I am already in bed with a headache, which feels decidedly bad. [MS. diary, 18 October, 1875.]

A beautiful sermon from Mr Eliot. It seemed to awaken me to the truth that I am rather inclined to rest on the slight improvements I have made. I must work harder, try and become more truthful both in my acts and in my conversation, less vain and admiration-seeking, and never let my thoughts rest with complacency on any little distinction I may have of body or mind. I seem to get on very slowly with my studies, and it is rather discouraging sometimes to get so little done. [MS. diary, 31 October 1875.]

The reason why I tell so many stories is pride and vanity. It is very often from the wish that people may think me or my people better in one way or another, that I exaggerate so fearfully. I see clearly if one wishes really to become truthful one must seek to be so in one's smallest actions and words. [MS. diary, 9 December 1875.]

I am going to see Mr Eliot tomorrow, and to tell the truth I rather dread it. Why I do not know. I suppose it is because I am not quite sure what I am going to say to him. It is a great want of courage, for of course it must be a great advantage for a young student of religion to be able to ask advice and explanation of a man who has spent all his life in the study and practice of it. [MS. diary, 16 December 1875.]

The dreadful interview is over. I felt decidedly nervous and was unable to say all that I wished. A girl is at a decided disadvantage sitting opposite to a clergyman and discussing religious doctrines. Mr Eliot said that the doctrine of atonement being found in the Scriptures we ought to believe in it, as it is only through them that we can gain any knowledge of God or his dealings with men. I answered that I did not see that the doctrine of the Atonement came prominently forward in the Gospels, and hardly at all in Christ's own words. He then asked me if I did not consider that the Epistles stood on the same footing in this claim to infallibility as the Gospels. I said I thought not, as I considered the latter to be the faithful record of Christ's own words, while the former were the writings of good men, many of whom had learnt at the feet of Christ, but who could hardly claim for their words the authority of their Master. (In studying St Paul's Epistles I must be careful to examine how much authority he *does* claim.) He finally lent me Dr Crawford's book on the doctrine of the Atonement. I hope when I return home I shall not lose the little earnestness I have gained; that I shall be diligent in the study of religion. I do not want to 'come out', and I hope I shall have enough determination and firmness to carry my point. The family does not really want another come out member; they are almost too many as it is. I wish my aim in life to be the understanding and acting up to religion. Before I can enter society with advantage I must conquer two great faults, love of admiration and untruth, and I must become a little more settled in my religious belief. [MS. diary, 18 December 1875.]

The determination not to 'come out' seems to have vanished after a series of house parties and dances in Gloucestershire; and at the conventional age of eighteen I joined my sisters in the customary pursuits of girls of our class, riding, dancing, flirting and dressing-up, an existence without settled occupation or personal responsibility, having for its end nothing more remote than elaborately expensive opportunities for getting married. It was during this round of gaiety that I became for the first time in my life intimate with one of my sisters. My sister Margaret, next in age to me and four years older, was in many ways the most intellectually gifted of the Potter girls. Warm-hearted and self-sacrificing towards her own family, a cynical *gamine* towards the rest of the world, an omnivorous reader and witty reflector of all that was racy in English, German and French literature, and all that was libertarian and iconoclastic in philosophy, ancient and modern, she proved to be the best of comrades in the hazards of the marriage-market, and the most stimulating companion in the long rides and walks, continuous reading and discussion with which we wiled away the dull months in Gloucestershire or Westmorland between bouts of London society, country-house visiting and foreign travel.

Some parts of this autumn have been very sweet [I note in the autumn of 1878]. We three sisters have seen much of each other; and Maggie and I particularly have had a perfect communion of pursuits and ideas. We had a delightful little trip among our sublime little hills; and read through the first two volumes of *Modern Painters* together; and this experience has inspired us with a wish to go sketching and reading tours together, should we remain lonely spinsters.

Maggie left this morning.[11] I feel her loss terribly. We are perfectly intimate and at one with each other and when I am with her I want no other society. We have had a very happy time here together – have read, talked, walked and slept together, and

11. During the winter of 1879-80 my sisters Margaret and Kate were travelling in Egypt with Canon and Mrs Barnett and Herbert Spencer. (There is an entertaining account of this trip in the *Life of Canon Barnett*, vol. i. pp. 226-56.)

now she is gone it is a dreary blank. I do hope the dear girl will enjoy herself and come back much happier and more contented with life *as she is likely to get it*. I must go plodding on – towards some goal that may never be reached. Ah me! Courage, *mon amie*, courage. [MS. diary, October 1879.]

The London season of 1876 came and went, and with it disappeared my feeble hold on orthodox Christianity. The restless and futile activities of society life, and the inevitable reaction in self-disgust and corresponding depreciation of other people's motives, did not constitute a fruitful soil for religious experience; and even if there had not been a sudden revolt of the intellect I doubt whether I should have remained a practising Christian. But it so happened that during these very months intellectual curiosity swept me into currents of thought at that time stirring the minds of those who frequented the outer, more unconventional and, be it added, the more cultivated circles of London society; movements which, though unconnected with and in some ways contradictory to each other, had the common characteristic of undermining belief in traditional Christianity. The most immediately subversive of these ferments, because it seemed to provide an alternative form of religious emotion, arose out of the opening up of the religions of the Far East; ancient cultures destined to be reflected during the twentieth century in the new and strange varieties of mysticism now current in Central Europe, the United States of America, and, to a lesser extent, in Scandinavia and Great Britain. More widely and deeply influential, because it was associated with the great discoveries of mid-Victorian science, and was, moreover, closely connected with the conduct of affairs, was the then-called 'religion of science': that is, an implicit faith that by the methods of physical science and by these methods alone, could be solved all the problems arising out of the relation of man to man and of man towards the universe.

I have indeed altered my religious belief this last six months to an extent I should never have thought possible a year ago. I see now that the year I spent at Bournemouth I was vainly trying to smother my instinct of truth in clinging to the old faith. And now that I have shaken off the chains of the beautiful old faith, shall I rise to something higher, or shall I stare about me like a newly liberated slave, unable to decide which way to go, and perhaps the worse for being freed from the service of a kind master? Do I look on death and trouble with less calmness than I used? [MS. diary, 16 August 1876.]

It was characteristic of the circle in which I grew up that ideas and literature, however metaphysical the generalization, or however classic the book, were inextricably mixed up in my mind with the affairs of yesterday and the problems of tomorrow. Thus, it was an ex-Indian civil servant, a pioneer in Sanscrit scholarship, who became my guide in a superficial study of Eastern thought. Brian Hodgson, a Gloucestershire neighbour, rode to hounds, and took his place in the County as one among many country gentlemen, rather than as a scholar of international reputation.[12] A delightful old man, then verging on eighty years of age, he was not overtly heterodox with regard to the supremacy of the Christian religion and the Anglo-Saxon race; he was, indeed, too modest to be explicitly a rebel. But, not without a touch of intellectual malice, he encouraged the young inquirer to

12. Brian Houghton Hodgson (1800–1894) was, in his day, one of the most distinguished scholars of Oriental languages, religions and customs, of a world-wide reputation very little appreciated in the country of his birth. Going to India from Haileybury College as a writer in 1816, he became Assistant Commissioner of Kumaon, adjoining Nepal, to which native state he was appointed in 1820; remaining there for twenty-three years, being confirmed as Resident in 1833. He was exceptionally successful in his difficult post, but at last incurred the displeasure of the most autocratic of Governor-Generals, Lord Ellenborough, who summarily, in 1843, deprived him of his appointment; whereupon Hodgson retired from the service. Besides endless papers in the proceedings of learned societies, his principal works were: *Illustrations of the Literature and Religion of the Buddhists*, 1841; *The Koch, Bodo and Dhimal People*, 1847; *Essays ... on Nepaul and Thibet*, 1874; *Miscellaneous Essays relating to Religious Subjects*, 1880. He was omitted from the *Dictionary of National Biography*, but died in time to be given a place in the First Supplement; and there is a short biography by Sir W. W. Hunter, 1896.

question the superiority of Western over Eastern civilization. For he had behind him a distinguished but officially unsuccessful career in the government of India. Political Resident in Nepal during the critical years 1823–43, he had spent his leisure in mastering the languages, literature and religions of the people he was supposed to serve, and in acquiring, at his own cost, a wonderful collection of ancient Buddhist scripts which attracted learned commentators in France and Germany, and eventually even in England. Meanwhile he had lost his foothold on the ladder of official promotion, largely through an unmeasured denunciation of the educational policy of the East India Company, endorsed by the Governor-General and the Board of Control, in deciding to use the English language as the sole medium of education, so far as Government subsidies were concerned, of all the races of British India. At that time the dominant intellectual influence at Calcutta was wielded by the greatest of our contemporary rhetoricians. To Macaulay's unscientific and slap-dash intellect, it seemed that there were only two alternatives open: on the one hand English, with its Shakespeare and its Bible, its utilitarian ethics and commercialized administration; and, on the other, the ancient Sanscrit Scriptures, reinforced with Persian poems and Arabic philosophy with their preposterous mythologies and their over-subtle, and therefore, to his mind, ridiculous metaphysics. As Macaulay put it, in his famous Minute:

The question now before us is simply whether, when it is in our power to teach this language [English], we shall teach languages in which, by universal confession, there are no books on any subject which deserve to be compared with our own; whether, when we can teach European science, we shall teach systems which by universal confession, whenever they differ from those of Europe, differ for the worse; when we can patronize sound philosophy and true history, we shall continue to teach at the public expense medical doctrines which would move to laughter the girls of an English boarding-school; history abounding in kings fifty feet high, and reigns thirty thousand years long; geography made up of seas of treacle and seas of butter.[13]

13. Trevelyan's *Life of Macaulay*, p. 402 of vol. ii.

'But why not the vernaculars?' insisted the wise and learned administrator at Katmandu: a question which insinuated that Macaulay had been guilty, in his vivid phrases, of the fallacy of the suppressed alternative. I recall, by the way, that it was Brian Hodgson, in his talks about India, who explained to me the peculiar liability of rulers belonging to an alien race and civilization to this particular lapse, alike in abstract logic and human sympathy: their habitual neglect to explore the many alternative ways of reaching the desired end, so as to discover the method of approach most in harmony with the deep-rooted tradition, habits and ideals of the people they governed. Unfortunately, the man learned in ancient lore and native custom was no rhetorician: he had not even a command of what ought to have been his own vernacular, as one British official addressing another, namely, sound 'blue-book English', never deviating, either in thought or expression, from the commonplace and the conventional. He unpacked his soul in a series of lengthy epistles to a local journal, which he got reissued as a slim octavo. I can now see that this queer book, *Pre-eminence of the Vernaculars, or the Anglicists answered, being four letters on the Education of the People of India*, is a mine of administrative wisdom and philosophic insight. But owing to its involved and pedantic phraseology,[14] and its far-fetched allusions to Indian

14. Since writing about Brian Hodgson I have come across the following account of him by Sir Joseph Hooker, from which I gather that this great scientist found him as hard to understand as I did. 'My friend, Brian Hodgson, was an arch-Buddhist scholar, and we spent many a long evening in the Himalaya over Buddhism; but his knowledge was too profound to be communicated intelligently to a novice. I have his works. I fancy he did more by the collection of materials, than by his dissertations, to advance the study.' (*Life and Letters of Sir Joseph Dalton Hooker, O.M., G.C.S.I.*, by Leonard Huxley, vol. ii. p. 433.)

And here is a description, by the same author, of Hodgson in 1848, which gives another version of his dismissal from the Residency of Nepal: 'Hodgson is a particularly gentlemanly and agreeable person, but he looks sickly; he is handsome, with a grand forehead and delicate, finely-cut features; when arrayed in his furs and wearing the Scotch bonnet and eagle feather, with which it is his pleasure to adorn himself, he would make a striking picture. He is a clever person and

and English classics, it was quite unreadable to my un-
cultured mind; and after glancing at its pages with
baffled curiosity, I turned with zest to the other books he lent
me, his own intricate but enlightening essays on the
languages, literature and religions of Nepal and Tibet; the
works of his French commentators, St Hilaire and Burnouf,
and, more fascinating to the immature student, Beal's translation of the *Chinese Scriptures* and Monier Williams's
many volumes on Indian thought and literature.

The immediate result of all this reading, illuminated by
talks with Brian Hodgson, was the sweeping away of my
belief in the Christian Church and its Bible as the sole or
even as the pre-eminent embodiment of the religious impulse in the mind of man; in fact, as the only alternative to
scientific materialism. Hinduism, with its poetical metaphors
and subtle reasoning, a mentality deeply rooted in an ancient
and enduring civilization of teeming millions, threw into the
shade for me the barbaric Jehovah of the Jews and the mean
doings of the kings, and even stretched beyond the fervid
eloquence, mostly about current events, of the prophets of
the tribes of Judah and Israel. Rightly or wrongly – and here
I am not defending a thesis, I am only describing the state of
mind of a Victorian girl in her teens – the Buddha and his
philosophy seemed logically and ethically superior to the
Christ and the teachings of the New Testament. The majes-
tic impersonality of Sakyamuni; his aloofness from the joys
and sorrows of mortal man; his very lack of what is called
humanity, attracted me. If there were any validity in as-
ceticism, in the deliberate denial of physical instinct and the
persistent abstention from worldly doings, then why not re-

can be wickedly sarcastic; he called Lord Ellenborough (the haughti-
est nobleman in all India) a 'knave and coxcomb' to his face (true
enough, though not exactly a fact to be *told* with impunity), and then
squibbed his lordship; you must know that Lord E. had previously
applied to Hodgson the sobriquet of an *Ornithological Humbug*, and
had turned him out of his Residentship at Nepal because he had
(by Lord Auckland's desire) clapped the Rajah into confinement. In
short, Lord Ellenborough and Mr Hodgson kept up a running fire till
his Lordship left the country' (ibid. vol. i. p. 262).

nounce, at once and for all time, the world and the flesh, and seek by prayer and meditation, possibly by the development of an incipient or arrested faculty, to become pure spirit? Was it because of the compromising attitude of Jesus of Nazareth (as interpreted by Paul) towards the world that the Christian Church, unlike the Buddhist monks or the Hindu Saddhus, had found itself entangled in temporal dynasties and national wars, and had grasped at secular as well as spiritual power? Further, Buddhist metaphysics had at least a superficial likeness to the philosophy of modern science. The agnosticism of Buddha as to an ultimate cause was even more complete than that of Herbert Spencer. Unlike the crude eternal bliss and eternal damnation of the Christian Church, the doctrine of Karma seemed in harmony with such assumptions of modern science as the universality of causation and the persistence of force. Even the transmigration of souls appeared as a far-off precursor of the doctrine of the evolution of the human species from other forms of life. Finally the mysterious Nirvana, and the attainment of this unconditional blessedness by ridding yourself of your own personality, fascinated my imagination. Living in a stronghold of capitalism, surrounded by the pleasure-grounds of London society, I distrusted human personality, whether I observed it at work in my own consciousness or in the behaviour of other people. And yet Buddhism and Hinduism found in me no convert. All that happened was my detachment from Christianity.

It is no longer a wonder to me [I jot down in my diary at the end of some hundreds of pages of extracts and abstracts] that Buddhism does not exercise much power over the nations professing it. The great doctrine it taught was false: that man's aim in life was to be mainly a selfish one, i.e. to rid himself of the evil of existence. Starting from the idea that life was an evil and would ever continue one, they proceeded to check every desire, good and bad; to run before death, so as not to be overtaken by that great Changer before they had plunged themselves into non-existence – or rather into the supreme impersonality of the universe. How could a religion which – though enjoining on man

every passive virtue – forbade the exercise of the faculties, re-
generate or advance the growth of man? The seed of selfishness
grounded in superstition is contained in all the ancient religions
of the world: and it is this seed, small at first and hidden by a
beautiful morality, which eventually overthrows one religion
after the other. Man as he progresses cannot shut his eyes to the
fact that he is but an insignificant part of the universe; that he
best fulfils the object of his existence in trying humbly to understand and, in so far as they relate to him, live in harmony with
the laws revealed by nature and his consciousness, without hope
or wish for supernatural reward.

But Buddhism, though based on falsehood, gathered round it,
as it grew, a most lovely morality and a breadth and poetry in its
theory of the origin of all things, which I do not think we find in
the more positive theology of Christianity. It guarded as sacred
the Great Mystery, and that is the reason, I believe, of its charm
to modern thinkers. [MS. diary, 13 September 1877.]

I have never been so struck with the truth that there is a great
mystery (I repeat a few days later) as when reading the metaphysical reasonings of these Eastern philosophers. They seem to
have had an intuitive feeling that each hypothesis advanced was
insufficient to account for the origin of all things; and they expressed, as far as it is possible to express in words, the idea of the
unconditioned which was according to them the absolutely real
underlying the relatively real. [MS. diary, 16 September 1877.]

This rejection of all traditional religion – of the underlying
philosophy of Buddhism as well as that of Christianity – was
made easier for me because it was during the autumn of 1876
that I thought I had reached a resting-place for the soul of
man, from which he could direct his life according to the
dictates of pure reason, without denying the impulse to
reverence the Power that controlled the Universe. This
resting-place was then termed, by its youngest and most uncompromising adherents, the Religion of Science. The God
was The Unknowable: the prophet was Herbert Spencer.
Prayer might have to go, but worship would remain. Looking
back on my intimacy with the philosopher, it is certainly surprising to me that I do not appear to have read any of his
books until I was eighteen years of age. Under date of Nov-

ember 1876 I find an extract from *Social Statics* – a passage which, oddly enough, I cannot now trace in any edition to which I have access, but which it is clear that I did not invent! I quote this eloquent expression of philosophic optimism with regard to the evolution of the universe because it convinced me at the time, although it failed me later on. Indeed, it is a favourite speculation of mine that Herbert Spencer himself eventually discovered that there was no evidence in the findings of physical science for any such assumption of essential beneficence in the working of natural forces; and that the mental misery of his later life was not altogether unconnected with the loss of the inspiring creed with which he began his *Synthetic Philosophy*.[15]

15. From Herbert Spencer's references, during the last years of his life, to current scientific controversy, I gathered that he was profoundly disturbed by some of the newer hypotheses of the physicists; but as I had neither knowledge of, nor interest in, these questions I failed to understand the cause of this unrest. In answer to my inquiry, my friend Bertrand Russell suggests the following explanation:

'I don't know whether he was ever made to realize the implications of the second law of thermodynamics; if so, he might well be upset. The law says that everything tends to uniformity and a dead level, diminishing (not increasing) heterogeneity. Energy is only useful when unevenly concentrated, and the law says that it tends to become evenly diffused. This law used to worry optimists about the time when Spencer was old. On the other hand, his optimism was always groundless, so his pessimism may have been equally so; perhaps the cause of both was physiological.' (Letter from Bertrand Russell to Beatrice Webb, 4 June 1923.)

It is interesting to note that Charles Darwin seems in his own range of subjects to have shared this strange optimism with regard to the correspondence of the nature of things with a human scale of values. In a letter to Sir Charles Lyell he writes:

'When you contrast natural selection and "improvement", you seem always to overlook (for I do not see how you can deny) that every step in the natural selection of each species implies improvement in that species in relation to its conditions of life. No modification can be selected without it be an improvement or advantage. Improvement implies, I suppose, each form obtaining many parts or organs, all excellently adapted for their functions. As each species is improved, and as the number of forms will have increased, if we look to the whole course of time, the organic condition of life for other forms will become more complex, and there will be a necessity for other

It is in truth a sad sight for anyone who has been, what Bacon recommends, 'a servant and interpreter of nature', to see these political schemers, with their clumsy mechanisms, trying to supersede the great laws of existence. Such a one, no longer regarding the mere outside of things, has learned to look for the secret forces by which they are upheld. After patient study this chaos of phenomena into the midst of which he was born has begun to generalize itself to him, and where there seemed nothing but confusion, he can now discern the dim outline of a gigantic plan. No accidents, no chance; but everywhere order and completeness.

Throughout he finds the same vital principles, ever in action, ever successful, and embracing the minutest details. Growth is unceasing; and though slow, all powerful; showing itself here in some rapidly developing outline, and there, where necessity is less, exhibiting only the fibrils of incipient organization. Irresistible as it is subtle, he sees, in the working of these changes, a power that bears onwards peoples and governments, regardless of their theories, and schemes, and prejudices – a power which sucks the life out of their landed institutions, shrivels up their state parchments with a breath, paralyses long venerated authorities, obliterates the most deeply graven laws, makes statesmen recant and puts prophets to the blush, buries cherished customs, shelves precedents, and which, before men are conscious of the fact, has wrought a revolution in all things, and filled the world with a higher life. Always towards perfection is the mighty movement – towards a complete development and more unmixed good; subordinating in its universality all petty irregularities and fallings back, as the curvature of the earth subordinates mountains and valleys. Even in evils, the student learns to recognize only a struggling beneficence. But above all, he is struck with the inherent sufficingness of things and with the complex simplicity of principles. Day by day he sees further beauty. Each new fact illustrates more clearly some recognized law, or discloses

forms to become improved, or they will be exterminated; and I can see no limit to this process of improvement, without the intervention of any other and direct principle of improvement. All this seems to me quite compatible with certain forms fitted for simple conditions, remaining unaltered, or being degraded.
'If I have a second edition, I will reiterate "Natural Selection and, as a general consequence, Natural Improvement"' (*The Life and Letters of Charles Darwin*, vol. ii. p. 177, 1887 edition).

some unconceived completeness; contemplation thus perpetually discovering to him a higher harmony, and cherishing in him a deeper faith.[16] 'Who could wish for a grander faith than this!' [I exclaim at the end of this extract].

There follows in my diary, evidently copied out at the same time, the well-known passage now standing at the end of Part I of *First Principles*, but originally appearing in *Social Statics*, where it is to be found only in the earlier editions.

Not as adventitious, therefore, will the wise man regard the faith that is in him – not as something which may be slighted, and made subordinate to calculations of policy; but as supreme authority to which all his actions should bend. The highest truth conceivable by him he will fearlessly utter; and will endeavour to get embodied in fact his purest idealisms: knowing that, let what may come of it, he is thus playing his appointed part in the world – knowing that, if he can get done the thing he aims at – well: if not - well also; though not *so* well. [MS. diary, November 1876.]

It was during the six years of irresponsible girlhood (1876–82) that I tried the religion of science and found it wanting. Memory is a risky guide in tracing the ups and downs of belief and unbelief; gaps in the argument are apt to be filled in, and the undulating line of feeling becomes artificially straightened. As being free from the fallacy of 'being wise after the event', I prefer the contemporary entries in the MS. diary. But this string of quotations from the subjective musings of a girl conveys its own false implications; inevitably these extracts emphasize the hidden over the outer life. Somewhere down in the depths the Ego that affirms and the Ego that denies were continuously wrangling over the duty and destiny of man; but it was only now and again that their voices were heard above the din of everyday life. For the most part consciousness was listening to the promptings of physical instinct and personal vanity, to the calls of family affection and casual comradeship – above all, to the exciting messages of the master-wave of

16. *Social Statics*, Herbert Spencer.

intellectual curiosity. Thus, during the spring and summer months of most years, riding, dancing, flirting and dressing-up absorbed current energy; six months out of these six years were spent in the Rhineland, reading German literature and listening to German music; another six months in Italy, in churches and galleries, revelling in Italian art. Nor were family events unexciting. My sister Kate, after an apprenticeship under Octavia Hill, had become a rent-collector in Whitechapel; and it was when staying with her in London that I first became aware of the meaning of the poverty of the poor. The three other elder sisters had found their mates; and with the marriage of my sister Margaret, though she remained an affectionate sister, I lost my one intimate friend. As against this loss there was the rapidly growing intellectual comradeship with my mother during the latter years of her life, which I have described in the last chapter.

Better reflected in the current diary than any of these episodes is the mass of miscellaneous reading, fiction, biography, history and politics, with which I occupied the lonely autumn and winter months spent in Westmorland and Gloucestershire. And here I think it well to note that, although as a girl I was an omnivorous reader, I had an unusually restricted literary taste. Owing to a mental defect, which I believe is not so uncommon as it is unrecognized and unrecorded, the whole realm of poetry was closed to me: I was poetry blind, as some persons are colour blind. Rhythm, rhyme, cadence, in fact the 'magic of words' in any of its forms, paralysed my intelligence; before I could understand the meaning of a poem I had laboriously to translate it into workaday prose, thereby challenging the accuracy of every term and the relevance of every metaphor. When that was done, the meaning had evaporated. 'That words have meanings is just the difficulty,' observes, with refreshing frankness, the great Hindu poet. 'That is why the poet has to turn and twist them in metre and verse, so that the meaning may be held somewhat in check, and the feeling allowed a chance to express itself,'[17] he adds by way of explanation. Thus,

17. I give the remainder of the extract, as it expresses exactly my

Racine and Corneille (insisted on by my mother because she thought they would improve our French style) brought to me no conviction that they knew anything about the men and affairs they portrayed; and their long rhymed couplets appeared to me to introduce an element of the ridiculous. Tennyson, the idol of the day, was even worse; his sentimental imageries seemed to me incomprehensible nonsense; and I have to confess that, in spite of the glamour with which my father enveloped Shakespeare, his plays and poems, except for some isolated passages, bored me. Of all the great authors whose works I tried to read, only Goethe dominated my mind. For many years I felt towards him as if he were an intimate friend, sharing out his wealth of experience and knowledge, and revealing to me an entirely new ideal of personal morality, of the relation of art to science, and of art and science to the conduct of life. After Goethe, in order of influence, came the translations of the Greek classics, to which I devoted the best part of a year; more particularly Thucydides and Plato. These certainly altered my mind. Of the translations of Latin authors I recall only Marcus Aurelius ['He wrote in Greek,' interjects The Other One! 'Pedant!' I retort], a book that superseded *The Imi-*

---

difficulty in appreciating poetry. 'But does one write poetry to explain any matter? What is felt within the heart tries to find outside shape as a poem. So when, after listening to a poem, anyone says he has not understood, I feel nonplussed. If someone smells a flower and says he does not understand, the reply to him is: there is nothing to understand, it is only a scent. If he persists, saying: *that* I know, but what does it all *mean*? Then one has either to change the subject, or make it more abstruse by saying that the scent is the shape which the universal joy takes in the flower' (Then follow the words quoted in the text) ... 'This utterance of feeling', he continues, 'is not the statement of a fundamental truth, or a scientific fact, or a useful moral precept. Like a tear or a smile it is but a picture of what is taking place within. If science or philosophy may gain anything from it they are welcome, but that is not the reason of its being. If while crossing a ferry you can catch a fish you are a lucky man, but that does not make the ferry-boat a fishing-boat, nor should you abuse the ferryman if he does not make fishing his business.' (*My Reminiscences*, by Rabindranath Tagore, 1917, p. 222).

*tation of Christ* as a manual of devotion; and Lucretius, whose cold wit and searching logic alternately attracted and repelled me. Of French authors, Diderot, Voltaire, Balzac, Flaubert and Zola stand out as teaching me what I wanted to know. Among English writers I had no favourites; it was always the particular subject-matter that I was after, and the personal outlook and literary style of the author seemed to me relatively unimportant. I may add that this cramped literary taste was afterwards accentuated by the craft of the researcher. There comes a time when a heap of illiterate MS. minutes, or bundles of local Acts relating to particular towns, are easier and more enticing reading, tested by the time one can stick at it, than sparkling wit, or the most original and most perfectly expressed wisdom, on subjects for the moment irrelevant. One of the unforeseen pleasures of old age is the faint beginning of a liking for exquisite literature irrespective of its subject-matter.

The following entries in the diary, scattered over five or six years and given in order of date, may be taken as notes of the controversy between the Ego that denies and the Ego that affirms the validity of religious mysticism.

This book, begun as a diary, ends in extracts and abstracts of books. One's interest in one's own character ceases to be so absorbing, as one grows in knowledge. Christianity certainly made one more egotistical, more desirous to secure one's own salvation. Whatever may be the faults, or rather the shortcomings, of the new religion, it accomplishes one thing: it removes the thoughts from that wee bit of the world called self to the great whole – the individual has no part in it; it is more than silent as to his future existence. Man sinks down to comparative insignificance; he is removed in degree but not in kind from the mere animal and vegetable. In truth, it requires a noble nature to profess with cheerfulness this religion; and the ideal it presents to us is far higher than any presented by the great religions of the world. [13 September 1877.]

Mr Spencer's *First Principles* has had certainly a very great influence on my feelings and thoughts. It has made me feel so happy and contented. ... I do admire that still, reverent consciousness of the great mystery; that fearless conviction that no advance in science can take away the beautiful and elevating consciousness of something greater than humanity. One has always feared that when the orthodox religion vanished, no beauty, no mystery would be left, but nothing but what could and would be explained and become commonplace – but instead of that each new discovery of science will increase our wonder at the Great Unknown and our appreciation of the Great Truth. [MS. diary, 15 December 1878.]

The religion of science has its dark side. It is bleak and dreary in sorrow and ill-health. And to those whose lives are one continual suffering it has but one word to say – suicide. If you cannot bear it any longer, and if no ties of duty turn you from extinguishing that little flame of your existence – depart in peace: cease to exist. It is a dreadful thought. It can never be the religion of a 'suffering humanity'. The time may come, and I believe will come, when human life will be sufficiently happy and full to be unselfish. But there are long ages yet to be passed, and generations of men will still cry in their misery for another life to compensate for their lifelong sorrow and suffering. [MS. diary, 8 March 1878.]

As it may be interesting in future years to know what my religious convictions were at nineteen, I might as well state roughly what are my vague beliefs. I do not see that there is sufficient evidence, either for believing in a future life or in a personal creator of the universe. I at present believe (by no means without inward fear at my audacity) that Christianity is in no way superior in kind, though in degree, to the other great religions; that it was a natural product of the human mind; that Christianity is not the highest religion conceivable; and that the idea of working out your own salvation, of doing good, and believing blindly, in order to arrive at eternal bliss, is, through its intense selfishness, an immoral doctrine. I believe also that, as soon as our religion becomes truly unselfish, the enormous interest in speculations as to the future existence of the individual will die out. But what seems to me clear is that we are at a very early period of man's existence, and that we have only just arrived at the true basis of knowledge: and that bright and glorious days are in store for our successors on this earth. [MS. diary, 31 March 1878.]

. . . One thing is clear, Goethe wishes to impress on his reader the advantages of liberty, of unrestrained liberty in thought and deed. I do not mean licentiousness, i.e. giving free scope to your passions: this involves an enslavement of the intellect, or rather the cessation of its rightful activity. But Goethe would go on the principle, both in education of children and in life, that it is better to develop the whole of your nature – looking upwards to a noble ideal, and allowing perhaps some ugly weeds to grow – than to repress the good with the bad. One often has felt in life that there are two courses open to one; an endeavour after nobler and purer living, i.e. an earnest attempt to silence and put down what is vile in you; or the alternative principle of fixing your eye steadfastly on all that is wise and noble, and developing with all your power your better self; not heeding the little slips, perhaps sometimes into very dirty places. I do not think that many have sufficient nervous power to do both; and Goethe tells you to choose freedom of development. In life you should seek a really congenial career, as a life-occupation, and then you should keep your heart and mind open to the outer world with various interests and activities.

Until you have found this career you should wander up and down regarding no place as too low and dirty, no society too licentious and frivolous – perhaps in lowest society you may light on some human soul who will impart to you some vital truth. [MS. diary, 14 December 1878.]

The one thought that I have been pondering over is – Does my want of happiness come from my want of belief in the old faith which has helped so many thousands along this weary way? Or is it simply physical melancholy which attaches itself to my pet grievance, and which, if I had been without education and culture, would have attached itself to some passing trifle? And when one looks around and sees good Christians fussing and fretting about little holes in their purses, little disappointments to their vanity and their greed, one begins to think that each human being has his share of 'distemper' – but perhaps the patient is on the whole happier who has it out in surface irritations than he who believes it to be a sign of an inward and incurable complaint, peculiar not only to himself alone but to the whole human race.

I cannot help having a half-conscious conviction that, if the human race is mortal, if its existence is without aim, if that exist-

ence is to end, at however remote a period, in a complete dissolution, like that which overcomes the individual, then life
indeed is not worth living – not worth living to the mass of
mankind. [MS. diary, 30 March 1879.]

I cannot write down what I felt on this Sunday morning –
watching the silent Mass in St Peter's. Perhaps there was a good
deal of mere emotion in it – but it made me look back with regret
on those days when I could pray, in all sincerity of spirit, to my
Father in Heaven. I tried afterwards to work out in my mind the
theory of the Roman Catholic faith as it might be accepted by
the agnostic.

Human nature is a circumstance, with which we have to deal.
It seems to be divided into two parts, the emotional and the
intellectual. My intellectual or logical faculty drives me to the
conclusion that, outside the knowledge of the relative or
phenomenal, I know nothing, except perhaps that there must be
an absolute, a something which is unknowable. But whether the
very fact that it is knowable does not prevent me from considering it, or thinking about it, or contemplating it, is a question
which Mr Spencer's logic has not set at rest. My *reason* forces me
to a purely negative conclusion; but I see very darkly before me,
and feel that my logical faculty is very insufficient for the task I
set it. Nor do I feel that its present decision is a final one. But I
possess another faculty – the emotional – which is the dominant
spirit in all my better and nobler moments. This spirit un-
ceasingly insists that there is something above and around us
which is worthy of absolute devotion and devout worship. Sometimes it presents this as the formula of 'the great mystery'; and
here it has attempted to join hands with my logical faculty, but
this last persists that the unknowable has no qualities, and
cannot be an object for feeling. Then it points to a great ideal,
Plato's idea of the beautiful or perfect; but this idea, though it
may be a subject for contemplation, cannot be an object of worship. Lastly, there is the great Father and Creator, the perfect
object for devotion. He is the God of Christianity, not a far-off
personality but united to man through His incarnation. This
God is worshipped by Protestant and Catholic alike.

The Protestant, however, declares virtually the supremacy of
his own reason. He asserts that his religion is rational and can be
defended by arguments. It is true that, originally, he declared the
infallibility of the Scriptures – but these, in their great variety,

can be shown to assert many contradictory dogmas, and when once his individual mind is regarded as arbitrator as to how these contradictory statements are to be reconciled so that a whole may be constructed, he cannot rest until he has made some examination into the different claims of the various authors of the Scriptures to divine inspiration. This he finds was decided by men whose infallibility he would not dare to assert. During this process, whatever may have been his conclusions on particular points, the Bible has lost its infallibility. He has sat in judgement over it and acknowledged that his reason, his sense of logical truth, is his real guide, the guide whom he is morally obliged to follow. If he comes now into contact with modern science and modern philosophy, and is sincere in his search after truth, he must arrive ultimately at a more or less sceptical conclusion.

But the Catholic Church deals differently with the question. True, our nature is divided into the intellectual and emotional. True, also, that your intellectual or logical faculty will force you to certain conclusions. These conclusions, however, are utterly repugnant to your emotional nature; there is a want of harmony in your life – you would be free from the little vanities and vexations of daily life, from all your own little petty struggles for self and its glory; you would rest in the worship and adoration of some being who is perfect in wisdom and beauty – and in that worship you would strengthen that ideal within you, which should leaven your whole life. But your reason sternly refuses its sanction to that worship, and so long as you consider your individual mind as the only authority by which you can be guided, you must recognize the supremacy of your logical or reasoning faculty over your emotional or feeling faculty.

The Church offers you the restoration of that harmony without which your life is aimless and incomplete. She declares herself to be the supreme reason. She does not ask you to interpret her; she provides her own interpreter in the priest, and suits her doctrine to the individual and the time. You do not renounce the authority of reason, but that only of your individual reason; and this only on a question which it has already proved its incompetency to deal with to the satisfaction of the rest of your nature. So long as you took on yourself the responsibility of deciding what was true, you were morally obliged to abide by the conclusions you arrived at. But in joining the Catholic Church you refer the decision on religious questions to a great association which has been composed, through centuries, of men dedicating their life and thought to the theory and practice of the religious ideal.

Could not the agnostic, if he felt that his nature was not sufficiently developed to live without an emotional religion, could he not renounce his freedom to reason on that one subject, and submit to the authority of the great religious body on the subject of religion; just as he would accept that of the great scientific body on the subject of science, even if in the latter case his own reason should lead him to different conclusions, on any phenomena of nature, to those arrived at by scientific men?

Add to this the beautiful Catholic ritual, and the temptation to commit this intellectual (and perhaps moral) suicide is strong to one whose life without a religious faith is unbearable. [Rome: MS. diary, 14 November 1880.]

From another entry, given out of the order of date, I gather that the Roman Catholic was the only Christian Communion which at that time attracted me.

At their house I read *John Inglesant* – a most originally conceived book – with scenes and passages of great power. Especially interesting to me, as realizing 'sacramental' Christianity, the phase of Christianity for which I have the most sympathy; the author having evidently experienced that striving after inward purity of heart and mind, the continual cleansing and keeping pure of the whole man, as a temple 'built unto God' and suited to this reception in the symbolical form of the supreme and divine sacrifice. Surely there are two ways of viewing the sacrifice of the Mass: one as an atonement to an exacting deity, the other as a grand symbolical expression of the greatest of human characteristics, the power of self-sacrifice in the individual for the good of the community.

If it were only possible for the priesthood to be pure, what an immense power the Roman Catholic Church would become! What a curious psychological fact is that great and mysterious joy in the prostration of soul and body before the symbol of infinite goodness uniting all individuals in one aspiration! [MS. diary, 1882.]

It is impossible for a woman to live in agnosticism. That is a creed which is only the product of one side of our nature, the purely rational, and ought we persistently to refuse authority to that other faculty which George Eliot calls the emotive thought?

And this, when we allow this faculty to govern us in action; when we secretly recognize it as our guide in our highest moments. Again, what is the meaning of our longing for prayer, of our feeling happier and nobler for it? Why should we determine in our minds that the rational faculty should be regarded as the infallible head in our mental constitution? The history of the human mind, shown in the works of the greatest of the race, proves that what has been logically true to one age has been logically untrue to another; whereas we are all able to sympathize and enter into the almost inspired utterances of the emotive thought of philosophers and poets of old. Where is Plato now, in logic? His logic seems almost childish to us from its verbalism; and yet who can read the assertions of his faith without feeling humbled and awed, and willing almost to be his disciple? Is it not possible that *our* logic also is verbal, and that we are foolish to insist on the finality of its conclusions? But perhaps the real difficulty is that the emotional faculty, thought it gives us a yearning, a longing for, perhaps even a distinct consciousness of, something above us, refuses to formulate and to systematize; and even forces us to see moral flaws in all the present religious systems. I suppose with most people it is the sense of what is *morally* untrue which first shakes your faith in Christianity; it is moral disapprobation of some of its dogmas which forces you to question rationally the rest. And this would be still more the case in an attempt to join the Catholic Church. You would be obliged to stifle your sense of what was right as well as that of what was true. [MS. diary, 2 February 1881.]

There is a good deal of interesting argument and demonstration in this chapter [that on 'Necessary Truths' in George Henry Lewes's *History of Philosophy*], but I, alas! see nothing in it to convince me of the soundness of his view of the human being. It is the philosophy which my logical faculty has always dictated to the rest of my nature, and which the emotional part has always resented. Moreover, evolutional and agnostic philosophy seems to me to be more the clearance away of false ideas than the presentation of a system of thought on which we can base our lives. It destroys all our present grounds for believing in immortality, in any being higher than humanity; but how dare we measure the great discoveries of the future, and limit the progress of human thought? There is little doubt that at present this philosophy darkens the life of man; and the greater his egotism the blacker appears to him the impersonality of the universe. Still, this very darkness may force us to keep the light of human sympathy burning clearly in our hearts; may oblige us to study and insist on the conditions for health of body and mind. [MS. diary, 22 September 1881.]

We all joined with Father in that beautiful communion service. [The Sunday after my mother's funeral.]

Now that I have experienced what the death of a dear one is, and have watched it and waited for it, a deep yearning arises for some religion by which to console grief and stimulate action. I have, if anything, less faith in the possibility of another life. As I looked at our mother dying I *felt* it was a final dissolution of body and soul – an end of that personality which we call the spirit. This was an instinctive conviction: on this great question we cannot reason. But, though my disbelief in what we call immortality was strengthened, a new and wondrous faith has arisen within me – a faith in goodness – in God. I must pray, I do pray and I feel better for it; and more able to put aside all compromise with worldliness and to devote myself with singleheartedness to my duty.

Surely the sacrifice of the body and blood of Christ is the greatest symbol of the sacrifice we all ought to strive to make, by which we may gain a noble immortality. In this spirit I took the holy communion, for the first time for six years – years of more or less dreary materialism.

Rationally, I am still an agnostic, but I know not where my religious feeling, once awakened from the dreams of a vague idealism, and acknowledged as helpful in times of trial, sorrow and endeavour – where this religious feeling will lead me: whether I may not be forced to acknowledge its supremacy over my whole nature. [23 April 1882.]

Mother's death opened out a new world to me in thought and action [I write a month later]. It stamped, by a new experience, the conviction which had been slowly growing from the first dawning of conscious thought within me, a conviction that the world was either an infernal chaos, or that all life was a manifestation of goodness; and death, disease and misery horrible only to our imperfect vision.

The death of one dear and near to me did not strike me as sadder than the death of the thousands who vanish unknown around us. Either 'the all' is so inexpressibly sad that there is no room for an increase of sadness through personal affliction; or else there is a mysterious meaning which, if we could divine it and accept it, would hallow all things, and give even to death and misery a holiness which would be akin to happiness. And the result of this ultimatum, presented by the thoughtful to the practical part of my nature, was a partial reversion to religion; I was satisfied that this would be the last word of thought unaided by experience gathered in action. The question remained, how am I to live and for what object? Is the chopped-up happiness of the world worth anything if the first alternative be true. Physical annihilation is impracticable. One's own life and one's own nature are facts with which one must deal; and with me they must be directed by some one consistent principle.

Even if the instinctive faith in a mysterious goodness is a fiction of the mind, would it not on the whole be happier to live by the light of this delusion, and blind oneself wilfully to the awful vision of unmeaning misery? Perhaps it would be difficult to direct a life on this negative basis. In truth one has a faith within one which persists in the absence of direct contradiction. [2 January 1883.]

Thus the long-drawn-out controversy, between the Ego that affirms and the Ego that denies the validity of religious mysticism, ended, not in a reversion to the creed of Christianity, not even in an affirmation by the intellect of the existence of a spiritual power with whom man could enter into communion, but in an intuitive use of prayer as, for one of my temperament, essential to the right conduct of life. A secularist friend once cross-examined me as to what exactly I meant by prayer; he challenged me to define the process of prayer, to describe its happening. I answered that I would gladly do so if I could find the words. The trouble is, as Tagore observed about poetry, that words have meanings, or, as I should prefer to say, *predominantly intellectual meanings*; and that in prayer, even more than in poetry, it is emotion and not reason that seeks transmission. Religion is love; in no case is it logic. That is why, down all the ages of human development, prayer has been intimately associated, whether as a cause or as an effect, with the nobler and more enduring forms of architecture and music; associated, too, with poetry and painting, with the awe-inspiring aspects of nature, with the great emotional mysteries of maternity, mating and death. In another place I may try (and probably fail) to express, by the clumsy mechanism of the written word, the faith I hold; that it is by prayer, by communion with an all-pervading spiritual force, that the soul of man discovers the purpose or goal of human endeavour, as distinguished from the means or process by which human beings may attain their ends. For science is bankrupt in deciding the destiny of man; she lends herself indifferently to the destroyer and to the preserver of life, to the hater and to the lover of mankind. Yet any avoidance of the scientific method in disentangling 'the order of things', any reliance on magic or on mystical intuition in selecting the process by which to reach the chosen end, spells superstition and usually results in disaster.

But this metaphysical resting-place was not reached until middle life. At this point in my narrative it suffices to record the fact that, during the ten years intervening between my mother's death (1882; aet. 24) and my father's death and my own marriage (1892; aet. 34) – crucial years during which I acquired the craft of a social investigator, experienced intense emotional strain, and persisted in continuous intellectual toil under adverse circumstances – it was the habit of prayer which enabled me to survive, and to emerge relatively sound in body and sane in mind.

## CHAPTER 3

*The Choice of a Craft*

1882-5

ONE of the puzzle-questions about human nature in society is the relative significance, in determining the life-work of individual men, of nature and nurture, of innate tendency and social environment. It gratifies self-conceit to imagine 'that every author hath his own Genius, directing him by a secret inspiration to that wherein he may most excel'. But, as the expounder of this seventeenth-century saying reflects, this 'inborn and, as it were, inspired element' was, in those days, assumed to belong to authors possessed of genius as distinguished from talent; authors 'who were indebted to their natural endowments alone', and not to the study and imitation of other writers.[1] So far as I am concerned, the

---

1. *Words and Idioms*, by Logan Pearsall Smith, 1925, p. 98. The distinction drawn in this delightful book (from which I take the quotation from Sir William Alexander's *Anacrisis*, 1634) is between authors who acquire their raw material by direct observation of and original reflection on nature, and authors who study and imitate other writers: a distinction akin to that between original work in art or in science, on the one hand, and book-learning on the other. The distinction made in the present chapter is slightly different: it is between minds that follow their natural bent or native gifts, and succeed or fail to impose themselves and their product on their contemporaries; and minds that, consciously or unconsciously, seek to satisfy an existing demand in the way of intellectual products; guided, to use a coarse expression, by 'the smell of the market'. It appears that I belonged to the latter category of instinctive caterers. The question to my mind was, not whether I liked or did not like the particular task, but whether the job needed doing and whether it was within my capacity. The alternative to doing such a job myself was to add to the function of caterer the function of *entrepreneur*, and to get someone else to accomplish that part of the work which I found unpleasant or difficult. Hence the employment of research secretaries.

conclusion is obvious: in choosing the craft of a social investigator I proved, once for all, that I had no genius. For I had neither aptitude nor liking for much of the technique of sociology; some would say, for the vital parts of it. I had, for instance, no gifts for that rapid reading and judgement of original documents, which is indispensable to the historian; though by sheer persistency and long practice I acquired this faculty. And whilst I could plan out an admirable system of note-taking, the actual execution of the plan was, owing to an inveterate tendency to paraphrase extracts which I intended to copy, not to mention an irredeemably illegible handwriting, a wearisome irritation to me. As for the use of figures, whether mathematical or statistical, I might as well have attempted to turn water into wine! The only outcome of an agonizing effort to master the rudiments of algebra, under the tuition of a local cleric who happened also to be a Cambridge wrangler, was that, for the first and last time in my life, I saw a ghost. It happened this wise. In the autumn after my mother's death (1882) my sister, Mary Playne, was staying with us in our Westmorland home. Out of sisterly affection, she became anxious lest my mania for study should interfere with the prospect of a happy and successful marriage. 'Beatrice's intellect, or rather what she attempts to develop into an intellect,' sister Georgie was reported to have said to sister Mary, 'what's the good of it? It's no use to her or anyone else – it's all done to make a show before old and young philosophers.' (MS. diary, 17 April 1882.) Spurred by some such vision of matrimonial futility (for what sensible woman wants a philosopher for a husband?), my sister Mary broke into my bedroom early one morning to find me sitting by an open window in an untidy dressing-gown, with dishevelled hair, and pale and spotty complexion, straining hand and brain to copy out and solve some elementary algebraical problems. 'What nonsense this is,' she began, half chaff, half compliment, 'trying to be a blue-stocking when you are meant to be a pretty woman.' 'This is *my* room and *my* time – go away,' I snapped at her. Immediately after breakfast, probably in order to assert my independence of domestic criticism, I resumed my mathematical strivings in the hours usually devoted to family talk. Towards the middle of the morning the door opened again, and my sister, silent and reproachful, seemed about to continue her remonstrance. 'Leave the room!' I shouted, at the ragged end of my temper. The door closed. And then it flashed into my consciousness that she was not in her usual tailor-made coat and skirt but in a white flannel wrap with dark blue spots, which I remembered her wearing when we were together in Germany. I shut my book and hurried downstairs. 'Where is Mrs Playne?' I asked the butler. 'She went out with Mr Potter some time ago,' he replied. For the next hour I sat in the hall, miserable with brain-fag, pretending to read the morning paper, but overcome with superstitious fear lest mishap had befallen her. In due course my sister reappeared; quite obviously in the flesh; glad to welcome my relaxed expression and affectionate greeting. Ashamed of my bad temper and unwilling to reopen the dispute, I did not reveal to her until many years afterwards the cause of my penitence.

Three weeks passed in mental contortions consequent on attempting mathematics without possessing mathematical faculty. Algebraical signs or numbers are to me half-believed-in facts which my mind persists in deeming fictions. I naturally refuse to believe that mathematics is the highest faculty of the brain; tho' perhaps a necessary tool in the application of the highest faculties to the most important subjects. [MS. diary, 4 November 1882.]

'What you needed,' observes The Other One, 'was not a tutor but a partner.' 'But how could I select the partner until I had chosen the craft?' I ask.

In the following pages I seek to describe my reaction to the curiously compelling quality in the social environment in which I lived; whether this was manifested in the books that I read, in the persons with whom I associated, or in the domestic, social and political events that formed the framework of my life. Granted intellectual curiosity, and an overpowering impulse towards self-expression, it now seems to me that, whatever had been my inborn gifts and defects, the weight of circumstance would have compelled me to investigate the history and working of social institutions.

To win recognition as an intellectual worker was, even before my mother's death, my secret ambition. I longed to write a book that would be read; but I had no notion about what I wanted to write. From my diary entries I infer that, if I had followed my taste and my temperament (I will not say my talent), I should have become, not a worker in the field of sociology, but a descriptive psychologist; either in the novel, to which I was from time to time tempted; or (if I had been born thirty years later) in a scientific analysis of the mental make-up of individual men and women, and their behaviour under particular conditions. For there begin to appear in my diary, from 1882 onwards, realistic scenes from country and town life, descriptions of manners and morals, analytic portraits of relations and friends – written, not with any view to self-education, as were my abstracts, extracts and reviews, but merely because I enjoyed writing them. It is, however, significant that these sketches from life nearly always concern the relation of the individual to some particular social organization: to big enterprise, or to Parliament, to the profession of law, or of medicine or of the Church. As a sample, I give two entries descriptive of the lower ranges of human nature in the Church of England in mid-Victorian times.

Talk at table d'hôte across the table to three young men, common, commoner, commonest – tho' perhaps more commonplace than common [I note during a tour with my father and little sister to Switzerland in the summer of 1882]. Find the next morning that Father has arranged (while we have been lying lazily in bed) that we two should spend the whole day with Common and Commoner on the other glacier. 'At any rate it will be a study of human nature, Rosebud,' say I. And really on that dreary ice, half the time enveloped in mist and rain, Common and Commoner were not amiss. The latter, a regular wild young Irishman, with harum-scarum intelligence, fell to my lot. Like his two companions, he was a pillar of the Church! I was soon in his confidence. His language was so characteristic of the man, that I scribble it down.

'I was a year and a half in Germany at school – terrible place for work – the master an awful fellare for false doctrine, about eternity and punishment and that sort of thing. . . . But a fellare only wants to have those things explained to him by a clever man. I got it all out of my head when I came to England. Nevare meant to take orders – but was always a terrible one for brain work – it just knocks me down. I'm nevare jolly in a place for more than three months. My only brothare, he spends his life in scenting trouble – wherevare there's war, he's there – got an awful keen scent for it. Last time we heard of him, was one of the mounted constabulary in Australia, just on the track of the natives: that sort of thing is in the family.'

'How did you manage to pass your examination?' I venture to ask.

'Oh, I'm one of those lucky fellares – get through without reading, manage on lectures, can put a little stuff in a deal of pallavar – the examiners they much prefer being told what they've said than what you find in books.'

'And your sermons?'

'Oh, I was well coached in them by Canon Fleming. I'd to preach before him – didn't I shake!'

'I suppose you don't go in for doctrine?'

'Oh yes! a fellare must hang it on to something – I like similes, plenty of similes, they go down; but near Hereford, where I live, is an awful dull place. Vicar, regular driver for work. Really it was awful hard on a young fellare – four days after I got there, he and his family left – I'd the whole work, four-and-twenty young fellares to prepare for Confirmation. And they're a dull lot there, it is hard to drive stuff into their heads. Really, if I hadn't my garden and my fowls, I don't know what I should do. As for the society, it's made up of parsons – I hate them – they get hold of a young fellare, and preach to him, and tell him what to do and what to think, until a young fellare doesn't know where he is. The vicar and his family are awfully kind to me – five daughters – whole family deaf – have to preach into a trough with speaking-trumpets into the vicar's face! He's a wonderful man for politics, get all my politics from him. – Awful old Tory – gives his congregation regular political speeches as sermons. Began the other day, after blowing his nose and clearing his throat, which always takes him a deal of time, "I can congratulate you most heartily, my brethren – that that blaguard

Bradlaugh has been expelled the floor of the House!" Country doctor, awful little cad – wanted me to be always in his house, but really couldn't stand him. Had to make him understand that – but I had some awful shindies about him in the parish.'

'What sort of rows,' ask I, my curiosity aroused, 'are you not on speaking terms with him?'

'Oh yes! when I meet him, I bow and palaver – wouldn't do if I didn't.'

Short pause, as we clamber up a very steep place.

'Do you like your profession?'

'Well, what I should have liked would have been to go to sea, but it was too late, and my brain was too weak for office work, my father was a clergyman and I've five uncles in the Church – I know a lot of young curates, some take to flowers, some to bicycling, some have fowls. Some have told me that they are awfully flabbergasted at a death-bed – don't know what to say – that's the thing that makes a young fellare serious,' said the young Irishman, with a passing expression of sadness. 'It is seeing sickness and death . . .'

Just as I was meditating bed, father came up, with Mrs R., wife of the rector of T. This lady was a comely, clerical-looking dame, with decided aquiline features, pallid face, large cold grey eyes, which, together with the mouth, were slightly turned down at the corners, giving an air of piety; cap and dress of solid respectability, and general look of satisfaction with this world, and firm conviction as to her place in the next.

'It is such a pity we did not make your acquaintance before,' she was kind enough to remark, with a drawling emphasis on particular syllables. 'There are such a *queer* set of people here. Last night I was talking to one of the nicest-looking men here, really quite a presentable man, and what do you think he turned out to be?' 'No! what?' 'A *dissenting* minister! Of course I had to stop my conversation; those dissenters have such queer notions and are so touchy about their social position, and of course as a churchwoman, as the wife of a clergyman of the established church, I could not talk to him, without probably offending him.' 'Of course not,' say I, tho' inwardly wondering why offence need be given. 'Then this morning I sat down on a bench near quite a *ladylike*-looking girl; where do you think she came from?' 'No! where?' 'From *Birmingham*.' 'Dear me,' ejaculate I sympathetically. At this point we seated ourselves and began to reconnoitre as to our acquaintance with the Gloucestershire Vale families. 'I know Mr P.[2] – intimately – *delightful* man – the Miss P.-s, four very accomplished girls – it is a pity they are *still* the Miss P.-s.' Here indeed was a bond of union; who does not enjoy gentle disparagement of their next-door neighbour, especially when that neighbour happens to be a 'leetle' above them in social position? Warmed by this we ascended to the subject of education. 'It is very sad, near us,' continued the rector's wife; 'the whole education of the daughters of the tradespeople, of the solicitors and of *that* class of persons, is in the hands of dissenters – where of course they get no *sound* religious training. My husband is trying to start a Church middle-class school, which will be *entirely* under him – we have secured two *excellent* Church-women as mistresses. A lady, who has great experience of these High Schools, which seem to me *most* objectionable, told me that the girls were so pressed with work, that they had not time for their daily prayers; and that the education was so *high*, that they frequently procured for themselves books on modern thought. And it seems, that in many of these High Schools, all classes are educated together – the teaching is thought *so* good that many parents of good position (tho' of course of limited means) are induced to send their daughters there, and it is quite *impossible* for them to tell next whom their daughters may be sitting!' ... [MS. diary, June 1882.]

The death of my mother revolutionized my life. From being a subordinate, carrying out directions, and having to fit into the framework of family circumstance, studies and travels, friendship and flirtation, I became a principal, a person in authority, determining not only my own but other people's conduct; the head of a large household perpetually on the move; the home, wherever located, serving as the meeting-place of seven married sisters and their growing families; a busy hostess in town and country, entertaining my father's, my own and my sisters' friends. More significant than any of these routine activities was the fact that I was my father's counsellor and my youngest sister's virtual guardian. This position of responsibility and authority was accentuated by my father's temperament; if he had any

2. For obvious reasons, names are frequently omitted in the entries in this and following chapters.

defect as a parent it was an over-indulgent disposition, an over-appreciation of the character and intelligence of those whom he loved and those with whom he lived. And though I was not one of the daughters who attracted his more romantic sentiments, I was certainly one in whose judgement and business shrewdness he had complete confidence; a confidence due partly to my having acted, off and on, as his private secretary and confidential attendant: memorizing for him the various details of the unwritten 'understandings' between men of affairs which form so large a part of the machinery of big business. I note, in passing, that apprehending, recollecting, and afterwards recording complicated series of facts, gathered in conversation, is part of the technique of a social investigator: and I owe the skill I had as an interviewer to this preliminary practice with my father. When I became the head of his household, he left it to me to settle the why, the when and the wherefore of the expenditure of a considerable income; indeed, he had more than once suggested that if I 'did not want to marry' I might become his recognized associate in business. Thus, for two or three years, I experienced that unrestricted and unregulated use of money which the *rentiers* term personal freedom, and the wage-earners, who feel that they produce the commodities and services consumed by men and women of leisure, regard as personal power. Moreover, coincident with this increased freedom of power, perhaps arising out of it, was a bound upward in physical and mental vigour. From being an anaemic girl, always paying for spells of dissipation or study by periods of nervous exhaustion, often of positive illness, I became an exceptionally energetic woman, carrying on, persistently and methodically, several separate, and, in some ways, conflicting, phases of life – undergoing, in fact, much of the strain and stress of a multiple personality.

Driving through the streets of London on my way from Paddington [I recall in a summary of the year's work], I had that curious 'sensation' of power, which I suppose comes to most people who have lived within themselves, who have seldom had their self-estimation righted by competition with others. Every face in the crowded streets seemed ready to tell me its secret history if only I would watch closely enough. Again, that vain hope for a 'bird's-eye view' of mankind floated before my eyes; a grasping after some spectral idea which vanished as I tried to describe its outline. My energy and my power for work were suddenly increased. I remained in a state of exaltation all the summer, possibly to some extent due to the physical effect of the high air at Mürren. (General abundance of blood is a cause of emotional exaltation! H. S.) The state of 'exaltation', whether moral or intellectual, must be the same, in its inherent nature, in the genius and in the ordinary person; but it is vastly different in its result. It is a spiritual isolation of yourself; a questioning of your capability of doing useful work outside the duty incumbent on an ordinary individual of the special class to which you belong.

The penalty attached to a wrong answer is greater if it err on the side of vanity. There is the probability of ridicule, and what is worse infinitely, the certainty of comparative uselessness. Cynicism, too, helps humility to conquer in this crisis. It is so very doubtful whether works (either of thought or of action) of the moderately gifted man have any permanent effect. If he is representative, he is a mere instrument, and many as good ones lie to hand. If he resist the stream, he is powerless to divert the fearful current of human tendency. My little dream was broken by the friendly shake of kindly persons who caught me napping, and neglecting work in which they were interested. Mathematics, too, effectually sobered me. It is a good foot-measure of ability which can be used in private. On the whole, the new year begins with a determination to devote myself first of all to practical life; if there is energy to spare, 'surely I can do what I like with mine own!'

It would be amusing to make studies of human beings, with the same care I bestowed on imitating bits of rock, stick and root. The six months spent on drawing, though wasted as far as accomplishment goes, certainly increased sensitiveness to colour and form. I remember, that winter, what keen delight the curve of a tree branch, the gradation of colour in a carrot or turnip, gave me. The vilest things in Nature had an interest and even a beauty of their own. And, since my life will be much spent in society, an attempt to describe the men and women I meet will add interest to it, and give me a more delicate appreciation of their characteristics.

In most of us there is a desire to express our thoughts, feelings or impressions. Women generally choose music or drawing, but there is really no more pretension in writing, so long as one does not humbug oneself as to the value of the stuff written. And there is this advantage, that language is the ordinary medium for influence in practical life; and that, even if we ignore the great advantage of writing in its development of thought, clearness and plausibility of expression are good allied to the more important qualities of character and mind. Morley says we moderns limit our ideas of redeeming the time to the two pursuits of reading books and making money; and, roughly speaking, the number of books read and digested during this past year is equivalent in one's own estimation to work done!

It is a difficult question whether the present 'intellectualism' is over-estimated in its good effects. Just at present, I fancy, there is a reaction against the idea that intellectual education is the cure for all evils. Certainly, the persons who are universally interested and universally useless make up rather a dreary society. Does culture increase power to act? I am inclined to think it increases the power but decreases the desire? [MS. diary, 3 January 1883.]

The first point to be settled was how to reconcile the rival pulls on time and energy, on the one hand, of family affection, backed up by the Victorian code of feminine domesticity; and, on the other, of a domineering curiosity into the nature of things, reinforced by an awakening desire for creative thought and literary expression. Some claims were beyond doubt. To be my father's companion in business and travel was not merely a continuous delight but also a liberal education. Personal sympathy as well as a sense of duty were roused by my little sister's chronic ill-health. But there were other assumptions with regard to the whole duty of woman that I refused to accept. According to the current code, the entire time and energy of an unmarried daughter – especially if she was the responsible mistress of the home – was assumed to be spent, either in serving the family group, or in entertaining and being entertained by the social circle to which she belonged. There was, it is true, a recognized counter-claim, the right to end this apprenticeship by accomplishing her masterpiece, making a 'good marriage', by which she would graduate into the goodly company of prosperous matrons, thus adding to the corporate influence of the family. A code implies a court to interpret it. In my case, the solid phalanx of seven married sisters; with the seven brothers-in-law in reserve as assessors, proved to be, I gladly admit it, a tolerant and kindly jury of inquiry and presentment. But, like other potential law-breakers, I was determined to evade, or at any rate to limit, the court's jurisdiction. In so far as the health and happiness of father and sister was concerned, or the disposal of the family income, I fully recognized the right of the family jury to intervene. But I silently withdrew all my own aspirations and plans for self-culture and self-expression from family discussion – a reserve which entailed isolation and loneliness.

Alongside of this inward conflict is a recognition that (probably owing to this egotism) I am losing ground in the affections of my sisters. Of course there will be unavoidable criticism, and some of it will be unjustified. It is no use being over-sensitive – but if one wishes to feel philosophically towards it, one must be honestly convinced of the rightness and thoroughness of one's own intentions. [MS. diary, December 1882.]

The rival claims on time and energy were rapidly adjusted by the habit of getting through my intellectual work in my own room between five and eight in the morning, leaving the rest of the day for domestic cares and social duties.

Reading H. S.'s *Psychology* diligently every morning. These quiet three hours of study are the happiest ones in the day. Only one trouble continually arises – the stimulus a congenial study gives to my ambition, which is continually mortified by a gleam of self-knowledge; meeting with the most ordinarily clever person forces me to appreciate my own inferiority. And yet, fool that I am, I can't help feeling that could I only devote myself to one subject I could do something. However, I suppose that the most commonplace person every now and again catches sight of possibilities in his nature which, from lack of other qualities, are doomed to remain undeveloped. And why should we strain every nerve to know, when every fresh atom of knowledge increases the surface exposed to the irritating action of the unknown? What good does it to ourselves or others, even if we increase (which is an impossibility for the ordinary mortal) the sum total of human knowledge? Character is much more in need of development than intelligence, which in these latter days has taken the bit between its teeth and run away with human energy. Perhaps thought, with the philosophy it breeds, *does* influence moral development, by raising our minds above the consideration of personal mortification and personal gratification; by enlarging our sympathies and by opening a safety valve to our mental activity through which it can escape harmlessly. After all, one sees more mischief done by unoccupied but active minds than duties omitted by minds interested in other things besides their own concerns. What distresses me about my own little work is the small amount of material I have to work upon – the trivial subjectiveness of my thought. That is what I am painfully conscious of when I meet really clever men. My work, if it can be dignified by that name, is so amateurish; and yet I don't know that I have a right to pretend to anything better and more business-like. All my duties lie in the practical direction. Why should I, wretched little frog, try and puff myself into a professional? If I could rid myself of that mischievous desire to achieve, I could defend the few hours I devote to study, by the truly satisfactory effect it has on my physical nature. It does keep me in health – whether through its direct influence on my circulation or through the indirect effect of a certain self-satisfaction it induces. Dissipation doesn't suit me, morally or physically; and I don't see why I shouldn't be true to my own nature and resist it. [MS. diary, January 1883.]

The following entries in my diary, during the first year of my newly found position of an independent hostess in London society, reveal the strain and stress of this internal struggle between the desire for self-development and self-expression and the more conventional calls of family duty, reinforced by the promptings of personal vanity and social ambition.

Shall I give myself up to society [I ask the day before we take possession of our London house] and make it my aim to succeed therein; or shall I only do so far as duty calls me, keeping my private life much as it has been for the last nine months? On the whole, the balance is in favour of society. It is going with the stream, and pleasing my people. It is doing a thing thoroughly that I must do partially. It is taking opportunities instead of making them. It is risking less, and walking on a well-beaten track in pleasant company. The destination is not far distant; no unusual amount of power is wanted to arrive there; and lastly, and perhaps this is the reason which weighs most with me, there is less presumption in the choice.

Therefore, I solemnly dedicate my energies for the next five months to the cultivation of the social instincts – trusting that the good demon within me will keep me from all vulgarity of mind, insincerity and falseness. I would like to go amongst men and women with a determination to know them; to humbly observe and consider their characteristics; always remembering how much there is in the most inferior individual which is outside and beyond one's understanding. Every fresh intimacy strengthens the conviction of one's own powerlessness to comprehend fully any other nature, even when one watches it with love. And without sympathy there is an impassable barrier to the real knowledge of the inner workings which guide the outer actions of human beings. Sympathy, or rather *accepted* sympathy, is the only instrument for the dissection of character. All great knowers and describers of human nature must have possessed this instrument. The perfection of the instrument depends no doubt on a purely intellectual quality, analytical imagination – this again, originating in subjective complexity of motive and thought. But unless this latter quality is possessed to an extraordinary degree, insight into other natures is impossible, unless we subordinate our interest in self and its workings to a greater desire to understand others. Therefore the resolution which has been growing in my mind is, that I will fight against my natural love of impressing others, and prepare my mind to receive impressions. And as fast as I receive impressions I will formulate them, thereby avoiding the general haziness of outline which follows a period of receptivity without an attempt at expression. [MS. diary, 22 February 1883.]

A pleasant bedroom in front of the house and looking towards the west [I write when we are settled in Prince's Gate for the London season]. In the afternoon I can sit here and watch the sun slowly setting behind the Museum buildings and gardens ...

undisturbed by the rushing life of the great city; only the brisk trottings and even rollings of the well-fed horses and well-cushioned carriages. Altogether, we are in the land of luxury; we are living in an atmosphere of ease, satiety and boredom, with prospect and retrospect of gratified and mortified vanity. Father has found occupation in inquiring into, and to some extent organizing, a large railway amalgamation scheme: the promoters anxious to get his time, and still more his name. Secretary Price called this afternoon. Cleverly managed to insinuate the 'we' into it. Father really anxious for work. Still suffers silent agony and lonely grief for mother; his sorrow is permanent though intermittent. There is a deep sadness in decaying power, more terrible to me than death itself. And all who have passed the prime of life, who have lived those few golden years for work, must exhibit this decline in the power for *persistent* work. I do not wonder that men should turn from human nature to study, with absorbing interest, life in the lower forms. There is so much that is terrible and awful in mental organization, lit up as it is by one's own self-consciousness, and surrounded by that dark background of annihilation. Constantly, as I walk in one of the crowded streets of London, and watch the faces of the men and women who push past me, lined, furrowed, and sometimes contorted by work, struggle and passion, and think that all this desire and pain, this manifold feeling and thought is but a condition of force and matter, phantomlike forms built up to be destroyed, a hopelessness overtakes me, paralysing all power of wishing and doing. Then I sink into inertia, relieved only by a languid curiosity as to the variations in structure and function of those individuals who will let me observe them and inquire of them. Cold-blooded inquiry takes the place of heartfelt sympathy. But this one should shake off sternly . . . [MS. diary, February 1883.]

Huge party at the Speaker's – one or two of such would last one a lifetime. Find it so difficult to be the universally pleasant. Can't think what to say. Prefer on the whole the crowd in Oxford Street, certainly the feminine part of it. 'Ladies' are so expressionless. Should fancy mental superiority of men greatest in our class. Could it be otherwise with the daily life of women in society? What is there in the life which is so attractive? How can intelligent women wish to marry into the set where this is the social regime? [MS. diary, 1 March 1883.]

Made calls. Lady P., great heiress of common extraction, married baronet: this last a bland individual whose abilities have been swamped in money. Large house in Prince's Gate, magnificently equipped with 'rarities' in china and furniture resulting in general sombre and heavy look. She, a small, pretty, delicate-featured woman, with *maladive* expression and certain seedy stylishness of appearance and manner. Sitting next her a stout plain woman gorgeously got up. Interrupted them in conversation on servants. After first civilities:

Lady P. 'I was telling Mrs B. that the last cook who applied to me asked £250 per year, perquisites and freedom to buy his own materials, and his Sundays to himself. Very kind and condescending, was it not – and he was actually an old servant of ours, who had left us only two years; but really the presumption and dishonesty of servants nowadays is preposterous. I found out only the other day that my cook was disposing of £14 worth of butter per week.'

'Good gracious,' I exclaimed, 'how very disgraceful!'

Lady P. 'But it is quite impossible to check it; one's whole household is in the pay of the tradesmen who supply it. How *can* one check it?'

Mrs B. 'The worst is that whatever you pay, for *that* after all one *does* not mind, you cannot get what you want. Now *do* you think it a right thing for the butler to be out every evening, and not only the butler, but the first footman, and leave only the boy of the establishment to bring up coffee?'

Lady P. 'The day after that happened both of them would go. But then, as you said, there is the difficulty of masters. Only yesterday Lady Wolseley was calling here and was complaining of Sir Garnet – I mean Lord Wolseley. – She had actually rung the bell and told Lord Wolseley exactly what to say to the man about his abominable behaviour; she left the room, and as she went upstairs she heard Lord Wolseley tell the man to put some coals on the fire!'

Mrs B. 'Really!' (Short pause while she is thinking whether she could possibly bring in the Spanish Ambassador who called on her some months ago, which she afterwards succeeded in doing.) 'I see you have got that chest from Christie's last sale; my husband said there was little better than rubbish there, of course *that* excepted. . . .' And so on . . . [MS. diary, 11 March 1883.]

Now my life is divided sharply into the thoughtful part and

the active part [I note a month later], completely unconnected one with the other. They are, in fact, an attempt to realize the different and almost conflicting ideals, necessitating a compromise as to energy and time which has to be perpetually readjusted. My only hope is that the ideal one is hidden from the world, the truth being, that in my heart of hearts I'm ashamed of it and yet it *is* actually the dominant internal power. Fortunately for me, all external forces support the other motive, so perhaps the balance is a pretty just one. But it is a curious experience, moving about among men and women, talking much, as you are obliged to do, and never mentioning those thoughts and problems which are your *real life*, and which absorb, in their pursuit and solution, all the earnestness of your nature. This doubleness of motive, still more this dissemblance towards the world you live in, extending even to your own family, must bring with it a feeling of unreality; worse, a loss of energy in the sudden transitions from the one life to the other. Happily, one thing is clear to me – the state of doubtfulness will not be of long duration; and the work that is done during that state will not be useless to me in whichever vocation my nature and my circumstances eventually force me into. I shall surely some day have the veil withdrawn and be allowed to gaze unblinded on the narrow limits of my own possibilities. [MS. diary, 24 April 1883.]

How comic this is, all this excitement about nothing. After a dinner when I have talked, I am absolutely useless in the way of brain-work. Francis Galton in his *Enquiry into Human Faculty* speaks of the mind 'rumbling over its old stories', but in the society-life one leads in London one's little brain is for the most part engaged in chattering over its newest impressions. Conversation becomes a mania and a most demoralizing one. Even when alone, it is continued in a sort of undertone; and the men and women one has met strut about on the ghostly stage, monopolizing, in their dematerialized form, the little time and energy left. I suppose persons with real capacity can take society as relaxation, without becoming absorbed by it; but then, if it is to be relaxation, one must not have much to do with all that elaborate machinery which moves it. As it is, what between arrangements (which seem endless) and the strangeness of this disconnected companionship with many different minds, all superior in strength and experience to my own, the little mind I ever had is out of joint and useless. When I am not organizing I am either talking with my tongue, or a lively conversation is going on within the 'precinct' of my brain. Reading and meditating are equally impossible. A train of thought is an unknown experience. A series of pictures, in which the human beings represented have the capacity of speech and gesture, succeed one another. The mind seems for the time to lose its personality, to be transformed into a mirror reflecting men and women with their various surroundings; one's own little ego walking in and out amongst them. . . . Certainly 'society' has carried the day – my own pursuits have gone pretty well to the dogs. . . . One gets precious little by talking [I reflect after another dinner party], let it be hoped that one gives amusement. . . . If only one could get some one nature, and examine it thoroughly. Except those of one's own family, observation of different individuals is so hopelessly piecemeal; and is so interfered with by a consciousness of one's own personality; by the continual attempt to make use of the people one meets as self-reflectors. [MS. diary, 5 May 1883.]

Interesting dinner here on the 18th. A Whig Peer on one side of me – Joseph Chamberlain on the other. Whig Peer talked of his own possessions; Chamberlain passionately of getting hold of other people's – *for the masses!* Curious and interesting character, dominated by intellectual passions, with little self-control but with any amount of purpose. Herbert Spencer on Chamberlain: 'A man who may mean well, but who does, and will do, an incalculable amount of mischief.' Chamberlain on Herbert Spencer: 'Happily, for the majority of the world, his writing is unintelligible, otherwise his life would have been spent in doing harm.' No personal animus between them, but a fundamental antipathy of mind. In what does this originate? I understand the working of Herbert Spencer's reason; but I do not understand the reason of Chamberlain's passion. But the motive force which moves the man of action is seldom rational. Philosophers will influence but never rule the world, at any rate not until the human nature of the masses is fundamentally altered; and then I imagine the philosopher will have advanced into a still calmer sphere . . . [MS. diary, June 1883.]

The following entries, six months later, giving my impression of Mr Chamberlain when he was the leader of the Radicals, may interest some readers:

He told me the history of his political career; how his creed grew up on a basis of experience and sympathy; how his desire to benefit the many had become gradually a passion absorbing within itself his whole nature. 'Hitherto, the well-to-do have governed this country for their own interest; and I will do them this credit – they have achieved their object. Now I trust the time is approaching for those who work and have not. My aim in life is to make life pleasanter for this great majority; I do not care if it becomes in the process less pleasant for the well-to-do minority. Take America, for instance. Cultured persons complain that the society there is vulgar; less agreeable to the delicate tastes of delicately trained minds. But it is infinitely preferable to the ordinary worker ...'

The political creed is the whole man – the outcome of his peculiar physical and mental temperament. He is neither a reasoner, nor an observer in the scientific sense. He does not deduce his opinions by the aid of certain well-thought-out principles, from certain carefully ascertained facts. He aims, rather, at being the organ to express the *desires* – or what he considers the desires – of the majority of his countrymen. His power rests on his intuitive knowledge of the wishes of a certain class of his countrymen; on his faculty of formulating the same, and of re-impressing them forcibly on a mass of indifferent-minded men, who, because these desires are co-extensive with their real or apparent interests, have these desires latent in them. Whether these desires are normal, and the gratification of them consistent with the health and well-being of the English body politic, is a question upon which I certainly do not presume to have an opinion. Chamberlain is an organ of great individual force: the extent of his influence will depend on the relative power of the class he is adapted to represent.

By temperament he is an enthusiast and a despot. A deep sympathy with the misery and incompleteness of most men's lives, and an earnest desire to right this, transforms political action into a religious crusade; but running alongside this genuine enthusiasm is a passionate desire to crush opposition to his will, a longing to feel his foot on the necks of others, though he would persuade himself that he represents the right and his adversaries the wrong. [MS. diary, 12 January 1884.]

And here is a description of a political demonstration at Birmingham a few weeks after the date of the foregoing entry:

Below us, packed as close as may be, stand some thousands of men. Strong barriers divide the hall into sections, and, as a new-comer pushed in or a faint-hearted one attempts to retire, the whole section sways to and fro. Cheers rise out of the general hum as a favourite member of the 'nine hundred' seats himself; and friendly voices from the crowd greet the MPs from neigh-bouring constituencies, or delegates from other caucuses, as they take their places on the platform.

The band strikes up, and the three members for Birmingham enter. John Bright is received with affectionate and loyal applause, as he stands for a moment before the children and the children's children of his old friends and contemporaries. Muntz, a feeble-looking elderly gentleman, with rabbit-like countenance and shambling gait, forms an interval between Bright and Chamberlain; and, in his weak mediocrity, looks comically out of place – a materialized vacuum – between these two strong embodiments of humanity. Chamberlain, the master and the darling of his town, is received with deafening shouts. The Birmingham citizen (unless he belongs to the despised minority) adores 'our Joe'; for has he not raised Birmingham to the proud position of one of the great political centres of the universe?

I was disappointed in Bright as an orator. Still, there was some-thing nobly pathetic in the old old story of Tory sinfulness told by the stern-looking old man, who seemed gradually to lose con-sciousness of the crowd beneath him, and see himself confronted with the forces of the past. The people listened with reverence and interest, and as one looked down upon them, and one's eye wandered from face to face, this mass of human beings, now under the influence of one mind, seemed to be animated by one soul. Perhaps the intoxicating effect of the people's sympathy is due to the great fact of the one in the many.

While Philip Muntz meandered through political com-monplaces, and defended himself from charges of lukewarmness and want of loyalty to the Radical programme, the crowd once more became a concourse of disconnected individuals. The subtle bond was broken which had bound man to man and fused all into one substance worked upon by an outside force. Laughter and loud-toned chaff passed from neighbour to neighbour.

Conflicting cries of 'Speak up, Philip', 'Make way for a better man', 'We'll hear you', and hissed-down attempts to clap him into a speedy end, showed the varying tempers of the mixed multitude. As the time advanced, the backward portion became more and more unruly, whilst the eyes of those in front gradually concentrated themselves on the face of the next speaker. He seemed lost in intent thought. You could watch in his expression some form of feeling working itself into the mastery of his mind. Was that feeling spontaneous or intentioned? Was it created by an intense desire to dominate, to impress his own personality and his own aim on that pliable material beneath him; or did it arise from the consciousness of helpful power, from genuine sympathy with the wants and cravings of the great mass who trusted him?

As he rose slowly, and stood silently before his people, his whole face and form seemed transformed. The crowd became wild with enthusiasm. Hats, handkerchiefs, even coats, were waved frantically as an outlet for feeling. The few hundreds of privileged individuals seated in the balcony rose to their feet. There was one loud uproar of applause and, in the intervals between each fresh outburst, one could distinguish the cheers of the crowd outside, sending its tribute of sympathy. Perfectly still stood the people's Tribune, till the people, exhausted and expectant, gradually subsided into fitful and murmuring cries. At the first sound of his voice they became as one man. Into the tones of his voice he threw the warmth of feeling which was lacking in his words; and every thought, every feeling, the slightest intonation of irony or contempt was reflected on the face of the crowd. It might have been a woman listening to the words of her lover! Perfect response, and unquestioning receptivity. Who reasons with his mistress? The wise man asserts his will, urges it with warmth or bitterness, and flavours it with flattery and occasional appeals to moral sentiments. No wonder that the modern politician turns with disgust from the cantankerous debates of an educated 'House' to the undisputing sympathy of an uneducated and like-thinking crowd. Not extraordinary that the man of passionate conviction, or of the will which simulates it and clothes it in finely worded general principles, who ignores all complexity in things, should become the ruling spirit, when the ultimate appeal, the moving force rests with the masses whose desires are prompted by passion and unqualified by thought.

That evening at supper were entertained some twenty of the caucus. The Chief sat silent in a state of suppressed exaltation; acutely sensitive to sympathy or indifference, even from an outsider. His faithful followers talked amongst themselves on local matters – questions of party strategy and discipline – and looked at him from time to time with respectful admiration.

The man's power as a leader and controller of men is proved by his position in his own town. As far as one could judge from watching the large parties of adherents who humbly ate and drank at the great man's table, noon and night, and from listening attentively to their conversation with each other and with him, his authority over the organization he has created is absolute. He recognizes no distinction of class, and in this, as in all other matters, he is supported by the powerful clan to which he belongs. The Kenricks and Chamberlains form the aristocracy and plutocracy of Birmingham. They stand far above the town society in social position, wealth and culture; and yet they spend their lives, as great citizens, taking an active and leading part in the municipal, political and educational life of their town. There is one eternal refrain in a Chamberlain–Kenrick household: Birmingham society is superior in earnestness, sincerity and natural intelligence, to any society in the United Kingdom! Apparently, the conviction remains unshaken by wider social experience, for the Cabinet Minister and his womenkind repeat with warmth the same assertion in the London drawing-room. Certainly, as far as my own experience went of the family and its immediate surroundings, earnestness and simplicity of motive were strikingly present.

The devotion of his electors no doubt springs partly from their consciousness of his genuine loyalty and affection for them. But the submission of the whole town to his autocratic rule arises from his power of dealing with different types of men; of enforcing submission by high-handed arbitrariness, attracting devotion by the mesmeric quality of his passion, and manipulating the remainder through clever presentation of their interests and consideration for their petty weaknesses.

In his treatment of some members of the Association (I noticed this particularly in his attitude towards Schnadhorst) he used the simple power of 'You shall, and you go to the devil if you don't.' The second power – that of attraction – is shown to a certain extent in private intercourse with his intimate friends, but chiefly in his public relationship towards his own constituency; and it is proved by the emotional nature of their enthusiasm. It is to this power that Chamberlain owes all the happiness of his life, and it is the reaction of this power which intensifies his sympathies and also his egotism. Whether it will develop so as to assume a form which will extend beyond the immediate influence of his personality is one of the questions which will decide his future greatness. At present he fails to express it in his written words, except in the bitterness of his hatred and contempt, which is but one side of his passion.

His diplomatic talent is unquestioned, and is shown in his administration of public and local affairs and in his Parliamentary work. [MS. diary, February 1884.]

In this whirl of town society life [I sum up towards the end of the season of 1883] the superficial part of my small intellect and the animal part of my nature are alike stimulated. My aim in life, the motives which have moved me in the best times of the past are blurred and misty. All now is uncertain. I wander hither and thither in search after gratification, gradually exhausting the credit account of 'good motive'; the small experience I pick up being saturated by an ever-increasing perplexity at the queerness of things. Possibly, in our mental life, when we are not forced into a groove of activity, we have periods of effort and periods of receptivity, during which latter state we collect the materials we afterwards form into action; into a governing motive. Anyhow, though, on the whole, life in this phase is pleasurable, there still remains lurking in the depths of one's nature a profound discontent; a doubt as to the usefulness of this careless noting of things, and a contempt for one's own nature in its enjoyment of these petty gratifications, and a somewhat unpleasant surprise at the presence of feelings hitherto ignored or quietly passed over as transient and unimportant. [MS. diary, 3 June 1883.]

This is the last word in my diary about what used to be called, in the reign of Queen Victoria, 'Society', with a big S. The picture stored in my memory of that unpleasing social entity, a state of mind and form of activity, on the part of the upper ten thousand, which, I am told by those who ought to know, was finally killed by the Great War, has been set forth in the first chapter of this book. Here I recall that the special characteristic which most distressed me, during the two years I acted as hostess in my father's London and country homes, was the cynical effrontery with which that particular crowd courted those who possessed, or were assumed to possess, personal power; and the cold swiftness with which the same individuals turned away from former favourites when these men or women had passed out of the limelight. Moreover, it was clear that personal vanity, with its humiliating ups and downs of inflation and depression, and with its still meaner falsification, was an 'occupational disease' of entertaining and being entertained; and, realizing my own constitutional weakness in this direction, flight from temptation seemed the better part of valour. But dissatisfaction with my own and other people's human nature was not the only, not perhaps the main reason for my gradual withdrawal from social functions throughout 1884 and 1885, in order to spend my free time as a rent-collector in the East End of London. What happened was that the time-spirit had, at last, seized me and compelled me to concentrate all my free energy in getting the training and the raw material for applied socio- logy; that is, for research into the constitution and working of social organization, with a view to bettering the life and labour of the people.

Looking back from the standpoint of today (1926), it seems to me that two outstanding tenets, some would say, two idols of the mind, were united in this mid-Victorian trend of thought and feeling. There was the current belief in the scientific method, in that intellectual synthesis of obser- vation and experiment, hypothesis and verification, by means of which alone all mundane problems were to be solved. And added to this belief in science was the consciousness of a new motive; the transference of the emotion of self-sacrificing service from God to man.

*The Cult of Science*

In these latter days of deep disillusionment, now that we have learnt, by the bitter experience of the Great War, to what vile uses the methods and results of science may be put, when these are inspired and directed by brutal instinct and base motive, it is hard to understand the naïve belief of the most original and vigorous minds of the seventies and eighties that it was by science, and by science alone, that all human misery would be ultimately swept away. This almost fanatical faith was perhaps partly due to hero-worship. For who will deny that the men of science were the leading British intellectuals of that period; that it was they who stood out as men of genius with international reputations; that it was they who were the self-confident militants of the period; that it was they who were routing the theologians, confounding the mystics, imposing their theories on philosophers, their inventions on capitalists, and their discoveries on medical men; whilst they were at the same time snubbing the artists, ignoring the poets and even casting doubts on the capacity of the politicians? Nor was the cult of the scientific method confined to intellectuals. 'Halls of Science' were springing up in crowded working-class districts; and Bradlaugh, the fearless exponent of scientific materialism and the 'Fruits of Philosophy', was the most popular demagogue of the hour. Persecuted, proscribed and denounced by those who stood in the high places of Church and State, he nevertheless, by sheer force of character and widespread popular support, imposed himself on the House of Commons, and compelled it finally to abandon its theological test for membership. Indeed, in the seventies and eighties it looked as if whole sections of the British proletariat – and these the élite – would be swept, like the corresponding class on the Continent, into a secularist movement. To illustrate this idolization of science, I give one quotation from a widely read little book published in 1872, which, on account of the broad culture and passionate sincerity with which the author identifies science with the intellect of man, has become a classic, and which foreshadows a universe over which the human intellect will reign as the creator and moulder of all things, whether on earth or in heaven.

His triumph [the triumph of man regarded as pure intellect], indeed, is incomplete; his Kingdom has not yet come. The Prince of Darkness is still triumphant in many regions of the world; epidemics still rage; death is yet victorious. But the God of Light, the Spirit of Knowledge, the Divine Intellect, is gradually spread-

147

ing over the planet, and upwards to the skies. ... Earth, which is now a purgatory, will be made a paradise, not by idle prayers and supplications, but by the efforts of man himself, and by mental achievements analogous to those which have raised him to his present state. Those inventions and discoveries which have made him, by the grace of God, king of animals, lord of the elements, and sovereign of steam and electricity, were all founded on experiment and observation. ... When we have ascertained, by means of Science, the methods of Nature's operation, we shall be able to take her place and to perform them for ourselves. When we understand the laws which regulate the complex phenomena of life, we shall be able to predict the future as we are already able to predict comets and eclipses and the planetary movements. ... Not only will man subdue the forces of evil that are without; he will subdue those that are within. He will repress the base instincts and propensities which he has inherited from the animals below him; he will obey the laws written in his heart; he will worship the divinity that is within him. ... Idleness and stupidity will be regarded with abhorrence. Women will become the companions of men, and the tutors of their children. The whole world will be united by the same sentiment which united the primeval clan, and which made its members think, feel and act as one. ... These bodies which now we wear belong to the lower animals; our minds have already outgrown them; already we look upon them with contempt. A time will come when Science will transform them by means which we cannot conjecture, and which if explained to us we could not now understand, just as the savage cannot understand electricity, magnetism, steam. Disease will be extirpated; the causes of decay will be removed; immortality will be invented. And then the earth being small, mankind will emigrate into space and will cross airless Saharas which separate planet from planet, and sun from sun. The earth will become a Holy Land which will be visited by pilgrims from all the quarters of the universe. Finally, men will master the forces of Nature; they will become themselves architects of systems, manufacturers of worlds. Man will then be perfect; he will be a creator; he will therefore be what the vulgar worship as God.[3]

3. Pages 421, 422 and 425 of The Martyrdom of Man, by Winwood Reade, first published in 1872. A new edition has been recently issued by the Rationalist Press Association, with an introduction by F. Legge, giving a short biography of this remarkable man.

This unhesitating reliance on the particular type of mental activity, which is always associated with modern, or shall I call it Western science, was by far the most potent ferment at work in the mental environment in which I was reared, whether in the books I read or the persons with whom I associated on terms of intimacy. When the brain is young there are written words which serve as master-keys to unlock the mind. Long abstracts of, and extracts from, George Henry Lewes's *History of Philosophy* appear in my diary in the autumn of 1881. The gist of Lewes's argument is a contemptuous dismissal of all metaphysics 'as condemned, by the very nature of its method, to wander forever in one tortuous labyrinth, within whose circumscribed and winding spaces weary seekers are continually finding themselves in the trodden tracks of predecessors who could find no exit.' In contrast with this tragic failure of metaphysical speculation the progress of modern science is eulogized in glowing phrases: 'Onward and ever onward, mightier and forever mightier, rolls this wondrous tide of discovery.' Then follows his definition of the scientific method, a definition which convinced me at the time and still satisfies me. 'Truth is the correspondence between the order of ideas and the order of phenomena, so that the one is the reflection of the other – the movement of thought following the movement of things. This correspondence can never be absolute; it must, from the very structure of the mind, be relative; but this relative accuracy suffices when it enables us to foresee with certainty the changes which will arise in the external order of phenomena under given conditions.' It was this 'odd trick' to be gained by the human intellect – this forecasting leap of the mind – by which alone the game of life could be won, if not for the individual, at any rate for the race, that captivated my imagination.

There is, however, a long way to go between realizing the unique value of an intellectual process, and mastering the technique and obtaining the material essential to its application. The circumstances of my life did not permit me to seek out one of the few University institutions then open to women. It is true that 'the Potter girls' had enjoyed from childhood upwards one of the privileges of University education. We had associated, on terms of conversational equality, with gifted persons; not only with men of affairs in business and politics, but also with men of science and with leaders of thought in philosophy and religion. In particular, owing to our intimacy with Herbert Spencer, we were friendly with the group of distinguished scientific men who met together at the monthly dinner of the famous 'X Club'. And here I should like to recall that, among these scientists, the one who stays in my mind as the ideal man of science is not Huxley or Tyndall, Hooker or Lubbock, still less my friend, philosopher and guide Herbert Spencer, but Francis Galton,[4] whom I used to observe and listen to – I regret to add, without the least reciprocity – with rapt attention. Even today I can conjure up, from memory's misty deep, that tall figure with its attitude of perfect physical and mental poise; the clean-shaven face, the thin, compressed mouth with its enigmatical smile; the long upper lip and firm chin, and, as if presiding over the whole personality of the man, the prominent dark eyebrows from beneath which gleamed, with penetrating humour, contemplative grey eyes. Fascinating to me was Francis Galton's all-embracing but apparently impersonal beneficence. But, to a recent and enthusiastic convert to the scientific method, the most relevant of Galton's many gifts was the unique contribution of three separate and distinct processes of the intellect; a continuous curiosity about, and rapid apprehension of individual facts, whether common or uncommon; the faculty for ingenious trains of

4. Francis Galton and his wife were intimate with my sister Georgie and her husband Daniel Meinertzhagen, at whose house in Rutland Gate I first met them. Afterwards they frequented our house in Prince's Gardens, where my sister Margaret became a special favourite, and undertook to furnish him with a detailed descriptive chart of our family history, which I believe he included in his work on family histories.

Professor Karl Pearson's elaborate *Life of Francis Galton* gives a singularly interesting account of Francis Galton's train of thought and methods of investigation.

reasoning; and, more admirable than either of these, because the talent was wholly beyond my reach, the capacity for correcting and verifying his own hypotheses, by the statistical handling of masses of data, whether collected by himself or supplied by other students of the problem.

However stimulating and enlightening may be social intercourse with men of mark, their casual conversations at London dinner-parties or during country-house visits cannot take the place of disciplined experiment and observation under expert direction in University laboratories or hospital wards. Any such training, even where open to women, was flagrantly out of bounds for a woman who had my extensive and complicated home duties. Hence the pitifully ineffectual attempts, recorded in my diary, to educate myself, first in algebra and geometry, described in the opening of this chapter as ending in nothing more substantial than a ghost; and secondly in the following London season, in the intervals of home-keeping for my father and little sister, and of entertaining and being entertained, in physiology, partly under the direction of a woman science-teacher, and partly by casual attendance on my brother-in-law, William Harrison Cripps,[5] the well-known surgeon, while he was making his microscopic examination into cancer.

The first morning's work with Willie Cripps preparing specimens [here follows an elaborate description of technique of microscopic work]; read through W. H. C.'s *Adenoid Diseases of the Rectum*; had great difficulty in understanding owing to technical phraseology and my ignorance of the subject-matter which he discusses. In my physiological studies must keep clear and distinct two lines of inquiry (1) how a particular organic substance became as it now is, (2) and what is at present its actual structure. Surely a full knowledge of the present structure should

5. William Harrison Cripps, F.R.C.S., the husband of my sister Blanche, became afterwards senior surgeon at St Bartholomew's Hospital, London. His researches into cancer led him to the conclusion that the undiscovered bacillus was localized in particular districts, streets or houses; a conclusion for which there seems some further evidence.

precede the study of 'becoming'; unless one was able to see every stage of the evolution. [MS. diary, 22 April 1883.]

Enjoy sitting in that cool room, with fresh breeze through, and green trees on both sides, in an out-of-the-way corner of London [I write about one of the lessons with the science-teacher]. Before us on the table, diagrams, microscopic sections, and various dissections – these last do not distress me but give me genuine pleasure to pick to pieces. One leaves behind all personalities, and strives hard to ascertain the constitution of things, a constitution which to us is eternal and dependent on no one manifestation of it. To me there is a deep and perplexing pathos in this study of life and death, which to some natures might become almost tragic, while in others it develops that half-sad, half-enjoyable, spectator's interest, pleasant in so far as it removes us far above the petty struggles of mean motive and conflicting interest, and sad in as much as it withdraws from our affections their permanency and from our aspirations their motive. In me, such a study strengthens necessarianism; and as I hurry down Tottenham Court Road, and jostle up against the men and women of the people, with their various expressions of determined struggle, weak self-indulgence, and discontented effort, the conviction that the fate of each individual is governed by conditions born of 'the distant past' is irresistibly forced upon me. [MS. diary, May 1883.]

'Referring to your microscopic work,' writes my guide, philosopher and friend in the following autumn, 'I wish you would take up some line of inquiry, say such an one as the absorbent organs in the leaves, roots and seeds of plants (you will find an indication of them at the end of the *Biology*, but nobody has worked at them to any extent). Great zest is given to work when you have a definite end in view and it becomes both an interest and a discipline. By Xmas I hope you will have something to show me.' (Letter from Herbert Spencer, 8 October 1883.)

But in spite of this injunction, and although I realized the value of physical science as a training in scientific method, the whole subject-matter of natural science bored me. I was not interested in rocks and plants, grubs and animals, not even in man considered merely as a biped, with the organs of a biped.

What roused and absorbed my curiosity were men and women, regarded – if I may use an old-fashioned word – as 'souls', their past and present conditions of life, their thoughts and feelings and their constantly changing behaviour. This field of inquiry was not, as yet, recognized in the laboratories of the universities, or in other disciplined explorations of the varieties of human experience. I may add, by the way, that what turned me away from psychology, even the 'psychology' to be found in books, was what seemed to me the barren futility of the text books then current. Instead of the exact descriptions of the actual facts of individual minds, reacting to particular environments and developing in various directions, I seemed to find nothing but arbitrary definitions of mind in the abstract, which did not correspond with the mental life of any one person, and were, in fact, nothing but hypothetical abstractions from an idealized reflection of the working of the author's own mind – that is, of a superior person of a highly developed race – an idealization which apparently led to an ungrounded belief in the universal prevalence, throughout human society, of that rare synthetic gift, enlightened self-interest! I am afraid that, in my haste, I regarded the manipulation of these psychological abstractions as yielding no more accurate information about the world around me than did the syllogisms of formal logic. For any detailed description of the complexity of human nature, of the variety and mixture in human motive, of the insurgence of instinct in the garb of reason, of the multifarious play of the social environment on the individual ego and of the individual ego on the social environment, I had to turn to novelists and poets, to Fielding and Flaubert, to Balzac and Browning, to Thackeray and Goethe. In all this range of truth-telling fiction the verification of the facts or of the conclusions drawn from the facts was impracticable. If I have any vain regrets for absent opportunities it is exactly this: that I grew up to maturity as a sociological investigator without a spell of observation and experiment in the modern science of psychology.

Thrown back on books, books, and again books, I began to

select these, not in order to satisfy curiosity and extend interest in life but deliberately so as to forge an instrument of discovery about human nature in society. The autumn and winter of 1881–2 finds me using Lewes's *History of Philosophy* as a guide through many English, French and German thinkers and translations of Greek philosophers. The following summer, the summer after my mother's death, I begin a systematic study, lasting for over a year, of the *Synthetic Philosophy*. But in spite of the guidance of its author I remain a 'doubting Thomas' though a miserably feeble one, about the validity of the Spencerian generalizations.

The following entries in my diary are given, not in strict order of date, but so as to illustrate my response to the current faith in the scientific method and my attempts to grapple with some of the problems involved in its application to human nature in society.

Mr Spencer called yesterday, and left the *Athenaeum* with us with a letter of his to Mr Mozley – who had insulted him by stating that he (Mr Mozley) had in boyhood derived similar ideas to Mr Herbert Spencer's from Mr Spencer's father. In Mr Spencer's reply he states his doctrine of evolution so clearly and shortly, that though I confess to but dimly understanding it, yet with a view to the future I shall here transcribe it. [MS. diary, 3 August 1882.] [Here follows transcript.]

Alfred[6] and I had a long discussion over Mr Spencer's résumé of his philosophy [I note ten days later], resulting in my taking it up to bed and spending a couple of hours over it – eventually rushing downstairs, and plunging into *First Principles* – a plunge producing such agreeable sensations that I have since continued the practice every morning before breakfast.

A delicious early morning [I note during our sojourn in our Gloucestershire home] looking towards the hill with sun, shadow and mist uniting in effect, and spreading a mystic joy over trees and slope. Quite clear in my mind that I am on the right way in

6. The husband of my sister Theresa – C. A. Cripps (Lord Parmoor), younger brother of William Harrison Cripps.

reading Herbert Spencer, and in the study of mathematics and geometry; but not so clear as regards literary reading: was tempted, by foolish vanity and desire to accomplish, to read French literature with a view to an article on Balzac, whose extraordinary power of analysis always attracts me. Surely these great analytical students of human nature will be found of use in any future science of the mental life of humanity, when psychology has advanced beyond the study of primitive man, that is, of human characteristics in so far as they distinguish man from other animals. But my instinct tells me that I must work with order; that any attempt to escape from the direct path of historical study will only produce friction of contending purpose. [MS. diary, July 1882.]

There was one riddle in the application of the scientific method to human nature which continuously worried me, and which still leaves me doubtful. Can the objective method, pure and undefiled, be applied to human mentality: can you, for instance, observe, sufficiently correctly to forecast consequences, mental characteristics which you do not yourself possess? Another stumbling-block was the use, by Herbert Spencer and other sociologists, of the analogy between the animal organism and the social organism for the purpose of interpreting the facts of social life.

This objectivity [observation and verification] is possible in all sciences which do not deal with human character and mind [I note in a long review of the philosophy of Schopenhauer]. Even this must be qualified; a certain subjective element creeps in when we discuss the nature of animal intelligence, if once you admit that it differs in degree and not in kind from human intelligence; and without this admission the discussion is baseless and we must restrict ourselves to the purely physical phenomena of animal life. But, when we come to analyse human intelligence, the subjective is prior to the objective element. The elements which build up these complex existences which we call feelings, ideas and acts of will, can only be discovered and examined within our consciousness. By a long and involved series of inferences, the conclusion of which recommends itself to our faith by its congruity with all other experience, and by its confirmation through correct anticipation, we assert that these elements exist in other minds. An appreciation of the exact combination of these elements in the thoughts, feelings and actions of men can result only from a delicate interchange of an objective and subjective experience. In the appreciation of a thought or feeling no thoroughness of observation will make up for the deficiency in personal experience of the thought or feeling [concerned] ... *the possession of a mental quality is necessary to the perception of it.*[7] The subject-matter with which the student starts is rigidly limited by the limits of his own moral and intellectual nature. The full realization of this fact seems to me of immense importance. Something beyond keen intellectual faculty is necessary to the psychologist and sociologist. He must himself have experienced types of those mental forces the action of which he desires to foretell or the origin and nature of which he desires to discover ...

And this enormous advance in complexity seems to me to vitiate the justice of the analogy between the animal and social organism, used as an argument and not simply as an illustration: though it does not in any way diminish the necessity and usefulness of a thorough knowledge of the working of the great laws of evolution on comparatively simple matter, before attempting to study their action on matter which is infinitely more complicated. In order to arrive at true theories regarding the past and future development of society we must study arduously the great social organism itself (a process of incalculable difficulty in the present state of historical knowledge), and not only such among

7. The following quotation from Hazlitt's essay on Shakespeare seems to bear out the suggestion that the psychologist requires to have experienced or to be capable of experiencing the emotions and thought which he desires to portray or analyse: 'The striking peculiarity of Shakespeare's mind was its generic quality, its power of communication with all other minds—so that it contained a universe of thought and feeling within itself, and had no one peculiar bias, or exclusive excellence more than another. He was just like any other man, but that he was like all other men. He was the least of an egotist that it was possible to be. He was nothing in himself; but he was all that others were, or that they could become. He not only had in himself the germs of every faculty and feeling, but he could follow them by anticipation, intuitively, into all their conceivable ramifications, through every change of fortune or conflict of passion, or turn of thought. He had a 'mind reflecting ages past", and present: all the people that ever lived are there' (*Lectures on the English Poets*, by William Hazlitt, p. 71, World's Classics Edition, 1924).

social facts as seem to illustrate a preconceived theory deduced from the elementary workings of nature's laws on the lower planes of life. A conscientious study of animal evolution will teach us the method of investigation to be pursued, will train us in the processes of classification and induction, and will provide us with innumerable illustrations and suggestions; and further, it is absolutely necessary as forming the physical side of the preliminary study into the nature of the social unit man. [MS. diary, October 1884.]

Got back to books again: and stopped as usual by poor health. The whole of my life, from the age of nine, when I wrote a priggish little note on the right books for a child to read, has been one continuous struggle to learn and to think, sacrificing all to this, even physical comfort. When I think of the minuteness of my faculties, which, so far as persistent work goes, are below the average, and of the really Herculean nature of my persistency, my own nature puzzles me. Why should a mortal be born with so much aspiration, so much courage and patience in the pursuit of an ideal, and with such a beggarly allowance of power wherewith to do it? And even now, now that I have fully realized my powerlessness to achieve, have perhaps ceased to value any achievement which I in my dearest dreams thought open to me, even now, my only peaceful and satisfactory life lies in continuous inquiry. Endless questionings of the nature of things, more especially of the queer animal man, and of the laws which force him onward, heaven knows where to? Of the nature of that destination, whether it will answer the wherefore of the long ages of misery and struggle? That old dream of a bird's-eye view of the past, and through it a glimpse into the future – that old dream, now recognized as a dream – fascinates me still. With labour and pain I master some poor fact, I clutch it, look at it over and over again like a miser with a coin of gold. At times, I pour before me my little hoard of facts, a tiny heap it is, some of it base coin too. I pass these facts through and through my brain, like a miser passes the gold through his fingers, trying to imagine that before me lies a world of knowledge wherewith I may unite the knots of human destiny. [MS. diary, 24 October 1884.]

## The Religion of Humanity

So much for the belief in science and the scientific method, which was certainly the most salient, as it was the most original, element of the mid-Victorian Time-Spirit. But the scientific method of reasoning, so it seemed to my practical mind, was not an end in itself; it was the means by which a given end could be pursued. It did not, and as I thought could not, yield the purpose of life. What it did was to show the way, and the only way, in which the chosen purpose could be fulfilled. To what end, for what purpose, and therefore *upon what subject-matter* was the new faculty of the intellect to be exercised? And here I come to the second element of the mid-Victorian Time-Spirit: the emotion, which like the warp before the woof, gives strength and direction to the activities of the intellect. I suggest it was during the middle decades of the nineteenth century that, in England, the impulse of self-subordinating service was transferred, consciously and overtly, from God to man. It would be interesting to trace the first beginnings of this elusive change of feeling. How far was it latent in the dogma that underlay the rise of American Democracy, that all men are born free and equal, with equal rights to life, liberty and the pursuit of happiness? I recall the saying of a well-known leader of the American ethical movement: 'As a free-born citizen, I deny the existence of an autocratic Supreme Being to whom I, and all other men, owe obedience and worship; it offends my American sense of independence and equality!' How far was the passing of the Kingdom of God and the coming of the Kingdom of Man implicit in the 'Liberty, Equality, and Fraternity' of the French Revolution, with its worship of the Goddess of Reason? We certainly find this new version of 'the whole duty of man' in the characteristic political maxim of the British Utilitarians, which prescribed, as the object of human effort, the greatest happiness of the greatest number. With a more romantic content we see it in the life and work of Robert Owen, with his 'worship of the supremely good principle in human nature', which became a 'social bible', promulgated by 'social missionaries' in a 'social cathedral'.

In the particular social and intellectual environment in which I lived, this stream of tendencies culminated in Auguste Comte's union of the 'religion of humanity' with a glorification of science, in opposition to both theology and metaphysics, as the final stage in the development of the human intellect. And once again I note that the reading of books was in my case directed and supplemented by friendly intercourse with the men and women most concerned with the subject-matter of the books. As a student I was familiar with the writings of the most famous of the English disciples and admirers of Auguste Comte. I had learnt my lesson from George Henry Lewes. I delighted in John Stuart Mill's *Autobiography*, and had given to his *System of Logic* and *Principles of Political Economy* an assiduous though somewhat strained attention. Above all, the novels of George Eliot had been eagerly read and discussed in the family circle. But I doubt whether my sister Margaret and I would have ordered from the London Library all the works of Comte himself if it had not been for a continuously friendly intercourse with the Frederic Harrisons,[8] at reciprocal dinner-parties in London, picnics in the Cliveden Woods and weekend parties in our respective country homes. In after years the Frederic Harrisons stand out from a host of former London acquaintances as loyal friends, encouraging me in my first attempt at authorship, and in due course welcoming as another friend The Other One. But in those early days they appeared to me as 'society folk'. For, in spite of heterodox opinions and courageous association with men and women deemed to be undesirable and even pernicious, this accomplished couple, possibly because they were at once well-to-do and personally

8. Frederic Harrison (1831–1923), M.A., D.C.L. (Oxford), Hon. Litt. D.(Camb.), Hon. LL.D. (Aberdeen); president of the English Positivist Committee, 1880–1905; member of Royal Commission on Trade Unions, 1867–9; author of more than a score of books published from 1862 to 1919, and of innumerable articles, addresses, introductions, prefaces, etc.; Professor of Jurisprudence and International Law to the Council of Legal Education, London, 1877–89; Alderman, London County Council, 1889–93.

attractive, were full-fledged members of political society, as distinguished from the narrower Court circle and the more fashionable sporting set. At the social functions of the Gladstonian Administration of 1880–86 they were much in evidence; more especially were they on terms of intimate comradeship with the rising group of Radical statesmen and journalists. Unlike the ruck of clever authors, successful barristers, and minor politicians on the make, they selected their acquaintances according to their own scale of values; and, once chosen, they stood through good and evil repute by those whom they deemed to be friends. A brilliant publicist, an insistent lecturer, a most versatile and sympathetic conversationalist, Frederic Harrison had also the greater distinction of being an original thinker and public-spirited citizen, always eager to appreciate new ideas and encourage unrecognized intellectuals. It was he who first explained to me the economic validity of trade unionism and factory legislation; who taught me to resist the current depreciation of the medieval social organization; and who, in spite of his extreme 'positivism', emphasized the real achievements in their own time of the Catholic Church and the craft guilds. The wife, with her luminous dark eyes and consummate coils of hair, her statuesque figure and graceful garments, was a befitting mate to the most eloquent preacher of the religion of humanity. Always a 'St Clothilde' to her Auguste, she listened with reverence to his words from the lectern of Newton Hall, and added cultured comments to his table-talk; whilst in his absence she regaled her friends with the pleasantest form of gossip – the gossip about political and literary personages – phrased with motherly beneficence, but spiced with just enough denigrating wit to make the mixture thoroughly delectable.

To return to the pile of books from the London Library. The result is memorized in a scene on the Westmorland moors in the autumn of 1879, two or three years before my mother's death.

Two girls, aged twenty-five and twenty-one respectively, stride across the Rusland bog towards the Old Man of Coniston, in a driving mist, with packets of sandwiches and cases of cigarettes bulging out of short and shabby waterproofs. They are discussing vigorously their readings from Auguste Comte. In these discussions the elder one, Margaret, always takes the leading part, as she reads six hours to the younger girl's two. The three stages in the development of the human intellect are accepted without demur; 'Though how does this fit in with Buckle's climatic and increased productivity theory?' reflects Beatrice, conscious of having just completed a painstaking review of Buckle's *History of Civilization* in her private MS. book – secret writing which not even her one pal among her sisters is invited to read. Presently they come to rest on a dripping stone wall. After vainly attempting to light a cigarette, Margaret, with genial smile, glittering black eyes and long wisps of lank brown hair flying in the winds, sums up her criticism.

'Dreadful old pedant; horrid French; what a dark chasm in style between him and Voltaire. Some of his ideas detestable; others absurd. That spiritual power, I hate it. Having kicked religion out of the front door of the human intellect, why should it sneak in through the servants' hall? For after all, Beatrice,' with rising acerbity, 'all Comte's humans are servile. The man worships the woman. Who wants to worship anyone, leave alone a woman? And the woman turns out, in the end, to be no better than a domestic servant with no life of her own. Thank heavens, he puts the working man in his right place; Great Hearts, may be; we've all got to think of them in order to do them good. But they've just got to obey; no more strikes; jolly good thing too!'

Short pause while Beatrice, having lit her cigarette by manipulating the match-box (a trick taught her sitting out with a ballroom partner in a country-house garden in the early hours of a July morning), hands the stump to Margaret, who lights up and continues in a more complacent tone.

'Rather like that notion of a committee of bankers to rule the world. The Barclays, Buxtons, and Hoares strike me as a solid lot; dull but solid; just the sort father likes us to marry, and one likes one's sisters to marry.'

'But why a committee of *bankers*?' interposes the younger one. 'Why not chairmen of railway companies, shipowners – for that matter, timber merchants? Machinery, raw material, trade routes, what do bankers know about them? And whether you like it or not, there's the working class who've got votes and mean to have more.'

Margaret, with a note of good-tempered contempt – 'My dear child, working men just don't count; it's money that counts, and the bankers have got it. Not brains, but money.' And with a rising crescendo of conviction – 'Credit; credit, Beatrice; it is *credit* that rules the world. Men and women have just got to follow the bankers' loans, or clear out. Over and again I have watched it. Remember how Baring and Glyn beat father about that new railway in Canada, which after all didn't pay. Father had the brains but they had the money; and it was *he* who had to resign, not they.'

Long pause: Beatrice doubts the sister's synonymous use of the terms 'money' and 'credit'. 'Father said,' she muses, 'that the amount of credit depended on the state of mind of the capitalist: a state of mind which does not always correspond with the state of affairs; hence trade booms and depressions. Money was a commodity like any other commodity, except that it had a specialized use and a legalized status. "My little Bee," he added, with his dear beaming smile, "might think out for herself whether cheques are money or credit and let me know." And I never did so,' she ruefully recollects.

Margaret, having swung round and jumped off the wall on the other side – 'Come along, Beatrice, we've got to get up there before we eat our lunch; I'm getting hungry. . . . The plain truth is that all this fantastic stuff about the future is nonsense. No one knows or can know what is going to happen to the world. The root question raised by Comte – the only one that concerns you and me, is whether we are all of us, here and now, to tumble over each other and get in each other's way by trying to better the world, or whether we are each one of us to pursue his or her own interest according to common sense. I'm for each one of us looking after our own affairs. Of course I include family affairs. One has to look after father and mother, husband and children, brothers and sisters. But there it stops. Perhaps,' slowly and doubtfully, 'if there is time and money to spare, sisters' children.' Briskly dogmatic – 'Certainly not uncles or aunts; still less, cousins; they're not as good as business associates, and only a shade better than London acquaintances. As for the service of man, the religion of humanity; heavens, Beatrice, what *does* it mean? It is just underbred theology, with no bishops to bless it.'

So spake the Ego that denies. Some forty years afterwards, roused by a mother's sorrow for one son dead on the battlefield, another in a prison cell on grounds of conscience, the Ego that affirms impels her to stand fast by the brotherhood of man, whether friend or enemy; and in particular to sacrifice fast-failing strength to prison reform, where she builded better than the world knows.[9]

How far, as a young girl, I agreed with my sister's acid testing of the worship of man I do not recollect. Notwithstanding our friendship with the Frederic Harrisons and other leading Comtists, it certainly never occurred to me to join the Church of Humanity. Yet five years afterwards I find, as the prefacing text to a new MS. book, copied out in large letters for my own edification, the following quotation from Auguste Comte:

Our harmony as moral beings is impossible on any other foun-

9. In the autumn of 1880 Margaret married Henry Hobhouse of Hadspen, Somersetshire. She had seven children – her youngest son being killed in the war. She died in 1920, her husband and five children surviving her. In the last years of her life, owing to the imprisonment during the war of her eldest child Stephen (who had joined the Society of Friends, and had refused to be burdened with property or the prospect of property) as an 'absolutist' conscientious objector, she published *An Appeal to Caesar*, and became interested in prison reform, initiating the inquiry which eventuated in the remarkable report by Stephen Hobhouse and Fenner Brockway, entitled *English Prisons To-day*, 1922. Many of the proposals of this report have been embodied in the recent transformation of prison administration in England, effected, not by Act of Parliament, but as a result of the silent conversion of the Home Office bureaucracy.

dation but altruism. Nay more, altruism alone can enable us to live in the highest and truest sense. To live for others is the only means of developing the whole existence of man.

Towards humanity, who is the only true great Being, we, the conscious elements of whom She is the compound, shall henceforth direct every aspect of our life, individual and collective. Our thoughts will be devoted to the knowledge of Humanity, our affections to the love, our actions to her service. [MS. diary, 1884.]

Dined last night with the Frederic Harrisons and went with them to the Positivist Hall in the City. 'Live for others' was the text of Harrison's address. He spoke bitterly of the gibes and sneers with which Comte's doctrine had been received. He pointed out that positivism was the only sincere religious form of the present day; that all religions and sects were making the service of humanity the keynote of religion; but refused to recognize that they did so. His address seemed to me forced – a valiant effort to make a religion out of nothing; a pitiful attempt by poor humanity to turn its head round and worship its tail. Practically we are all positivists; we all make the service of man the leading doctrine of our lives. But in order to serve humanity we need inspiration from a superhuman force towards which we are perpetually striving. [MS. diary, 15 March 1889.]

Social questions [I write in the MS. diary of 1884] are the vital questions of today: they take the place of religion. I do not pretend to solve them. Their solution seems largely a matter of temperament. Still, the most insignificant mind has a certain bias, has an intellectual as well as a moral conscience. If we wilfully defy the laws of our special mental constitution we must suffer the penalty of a diseased and twisted nature, and must leave life conscious of faithlessness to the faith that is in us. ... A higher standard of motive is asked for in social action than in any other. ... The social reformer professes to be an uncompromising idealist; he solemnly declares that he is working for the public weal. His whole authority, derived from public opinion, arises from the faith of the people in his honesty of purpose and strength of understanding. If he uses his mind to manipulate facts, and twist them so that they shall serve his own personal interests, if the craving for power is greater than the desire for truth, he is a traitor to the society towards which he professes loyal service. [MS. diary, 22 April 1884.]

Now, without pretending to sum up the influence of the Time-Spirit on the social activities of the last quarter of the nineteenth century, what is clear is that upon me – in 1883, a woman of twenty-five – it led to a definite conclusion. From the flight of emotion away from the service of God to the service of man, and from the current faith in the scientific method, I drew the inference that the most hopeful form of social service was the craft of a social investigator. And some such conclusion seems to have been reached by many of my contemporaries. For detailed descriptions of the life and labour of the people in all its various aspects, sensational or scientific, derived from personal observation or statistical calculation, became a characteristic feature of the publications of this period, whether newspapers or magazines, plays or novels, the reports of philanthropic organizations or the proceedings of learned societies. It may be said that this novel concentration of attention on the social condition of the people was due neither to intellectual curiosity nor to the spirit of philanthropy, but rather to a panic fear of the newly enfranchised democracy. But this is looking at the same fact from another standpoint. For even the most fanatical Socialist asserted that his hopes for the future depended on a deliberately scientific organization of society, combined with the growth among the whole body of the people of the desire and capacity for disinterested social service.

It was in the autumn of 1883 that I took the first step as a social investigator, though I am afraid the adventure was more a sentimental journey than a scientific exploration. What had been borne into me during my book studies was my utter ignorance of the manual-working class, that is, of four-fifths of my fellow-countrymen. During the preceding London season I had joined a Charity Organization Committee and acted as one of its visitors in the slums of Soho; but it was clear to me that these cases of extreme destitution, often distorted by drink and vice, could no more be regarded as a fair sample of the wage-earning class than the 'sporting set' of London society could be considered representative, either in conduct or in intelligence, of the landed aristocracy and business and professional class, out of which its individual members had usually sprung. How was I to get an opportunity of watching, day by day, in their homes and in their workshops, a sufficient number of normal manual-working families to enable me to visualize the class as a whole; to understand what was meant by chronic poverty and insecurity of livelihood; to ascertain whether such conditions actually existed in any but a small fraction of the great body of the people? Were the manual workers what I was accustomed to call civilized? What were their aspirations, what was their degree of education, what their capacity for self-government? How had this class, without administrative training or literary culture, managed to initiate and maintain the network of Nonconformist chapels, the far-flung friendly societies, the much-abused trade unions, and that queer type of shop, the Co-operative store?

## A Sentimental Journey

The romantic note in this adventure arose from finding, among my own kith and kin, my first chance of personal intimacy, on terms of social equality, with a wage-earning family. For out of the homesteads of the 'domestic manufacturers' of Lancashire and Yorkshire had sprung the Heyworths, my mother's family. During the last quarter of the eighteenth century some few of these master craftsmen had risen to be mill-owners and merchants, the greater number being merged in the new class of factory hands. My grandfather, Lawrence Heyworth, belonged to the master-class; but he married a pretty cousin, who had been born and bred in the home of a power-loom weaver. This unknown grandmother – she died of tuberculosis when my mother was yet a child – was, however, not the nearest tie with the humble folk of Bacup. There was the beloved old nurse and household saint, Martha Mills, nicknamed Dada [see pp. 41–6], who had been selected by my grandfather at the age of eighteen to accompany my mother and her brother on their continental journey, meeting at Rome my father and his sister; she watched the coming of the marriage, and she had remained my mother's inseparable companion until death parted them. With this explanation I fall back on entries in my diary and letters to my father during my visits to Bacup.

I have listened many a time to mother's old stories of Bacup life as we paced up and down the walks of the Standish gardens or along the Rusland lanes.

The last time, I think, was on a March morning at Standish [a few weeks before her sudden death]. I remember well the sensation of the soft west wind and of the sweet sighs and sounds of the coming spring, as I listened dreamily to those well-known tales mother loved to tell – of her grandfather who would put on his old clothes to go to the Manchester market if times were good, and call on his wife to bring him his new hat and best coat if he felt his credit shaky; of the old grandmother sitting bolt upright in her wooden stays in her straight-backed chair, giving sage advice to her four sons; or kneeling by her bed in the midnight hours praying to her God, watched in the dim light of the moon or coming dawn by the awe-struck little Laurencina.

And the sweet old tale of mother's first visit to Bacup.

Father and daughter arriving late after a long coach journey. 'I want my supper,' cried little Miss Heyworth as her father tried to carry her to bed. 'I want my supper; I won't go to bed without my supper.' The idea of bed supperless associated in the little woman's mind with disgrace and punishment. 'Let be, Lawrence,' called out the tall quaint nightcapped figure over the banister; 'let the child have its supper if it will. Here, Sarah, take the child and give it some milksop, the fire will soon be blown up a bit.' So dignified little Miss Heyworth was led into the kitchen by sleepy Sarah and placed in a chair by the table, and the fire blown up a bit. But having saved her dignity, poor little Laurencina, dazed by the light and strangeness of the place, burst out into sobs, between which the willing Sarah distinguished as 'I want to go to bed, I want to go to Papa'.

Eighteen months had passed away since that March morning. Rosebud [my youngest sister], Dada, and I were sitting by the firelight in the cosy little sitting-room at The Argoed [our Monmouthshire home]. I was listening again to old stories of Bacup life. Not the same old stories, but descriptions of chapel and Sunday school, and long walks along dirty lanes to prayer meetings in weavers' cottages.

'Surely, Da,' said I, turning my eyes for a moment from the fascinating scenes in a coal fire, 'some of the Akeds must be our kin.' 'Well, let's see,' says our old nurse, putting her hands on her knees and meditating; 'there's John Aked, he's a reed-maker, now out o' work, nephew of Mrs Heyworth. Then he's got two brothers, James, manager of the waterworks, and William, who is, I fancy, rather queer; I don't think he does much. Then there's Mrs Ashworth, Miss Aked as was. I was apprenticed to her in the dressmaking line before I went to Miss Heyworth. She married James Ashworth, a mill-owner, a rich man; she's a widow now, and what you call rather close with her money. I don't think there's any other of your grandmother's relations left besides them as I have mentioned; at least I am not aware of it.'

'Da,' said I, as I watched a narrow bridge of black coal give way, tumble into the red-hot mass below and burst into flame; 'I should dearly love to go to Bacup next time you go.' 'Well, you know I can always go; there's no occasion to wait for that,' answered the dear old woman, 'but my friends up there would be astonished to see a Miss Potter coming along with me; they are not accustomed to such grand folk. I think they would be what they call "flayed" by you.' 'Oh!' cried I, jumping up with the delightful consciousness of an original idea, 'I wouldn't be Miss Potter, I would be Miss Jones, farmer's daughter, near Monmouth.'

Somewhat to my surprise the God-fearing Martha Mills eagerly agreed to carry out the 'pious fraud'.

It was a wet November evening 1883, when Mrs Mills and Miss Jones picked their way along the irregularly paved and badly lighted back-streets of Bacup. The place seemed deserted. There was that curious stillness in the air which overtakes a purely manufacturing town when the mills with their noise and their lights are closed – the mill-hands with their free loud voices are 'cleaning up' or enjoying 'Biffin' by their own fireside. 'There, m'am, there's Irwell Terrace Chapel,' said Mrs Mills as they stood for a moment on a little stone bridge, under which the small river Irwell splashed as merrily as it could, considering its free mountain descent, over bits of broken crockery, old boots and pieces of worn-out machinery; 'and there's the chapel-house adjoining it,' continued she, 'where John Ashworth the chapel-keeper lives, him as we're going to stay with.' 'Da,' said Miss Jones in an emphatic tone, 'you really must not call me m'am; now wait a bit and summon up your courage to tell that little lie, and remember the words of the Apostle Paul, "Whatever ye do, do heartily".'

Here follow letters to my father dated November 1883:

[*First Letter.*] – We arrived at Bacup about 6.30 and found our way along very ill-lighted back-streets to this old-fashioned house at the back of the chapel. We were received by a regular old Puritan and his daughter (a mill-hand) in the most hearty fashion; prayers being offered up for our safety and spiritual well-being while under their roof. After we had enjoyed some delicious tea and home-made bread and butter, various of the elders dropped in to welcome Mrs Mills, to whom they are evidently devoted, and who is quite a great lady amongst them. She introduced me with the most bare-faced effrontery as 'Miss Jones, farmer's daughter, who had come here to see town life and manufactures', and they all showed themselves anxious to 'lighten my ignorance' on things material and spiritual. I have been quite received into the charmed circle of artisan and small bourgeois life, and have made special friends with John Aked, a meek, gentle-hearted man, who suffers from the constitutional melancholy of the Aked family. I hear that a brother and sister of Grandmamma Heyworth committed suicide, and two or three of the family have been threatened with suicidal mania. Perhaps it is from that quarter that we get our 'Weltschmerz'. This morning he escorted us through Bacup, and I saw Rose Cottage and Willow Cottage, where our grandmama lived and died. Also Bankside and Fern Hill, the houses of the great Heyworth and Ormerod families. We dined with John Wooded, his wife and only son (cousins of Da's) and I have been listening to one continuous kind-hearted gossip interspersed with pious ejaculations and shrewd remarks on the most likely method of getting the good things of this world. Certainly the way to see industrial life is to live amongst the workers, and I am surprised at the complete way they have adopted me as one of their own class. I find it less amusing and much more interesting than I expected; and I am heartily glad that I made the venture.

[*Second Letter.*] – I am going on most satisfactorily. I find a diary out of the question; one has neither the time nor the place for writing. These folk live all day in 'coompany'; there are always some mill-hands [cotton-weavers] out of work who spend their days chatting in each other's houses. This house, too, is the centre of chapel-goers, and is used by the relieving officer to distribute the poor-rate.

Bacup is quite a small manufacturing town. The 'old gentry', 'them as really was gentry', have disappeared, and the present manufacturers are self-made men, 'who are much more greedy like than the old lot'. The Whitakers still own the land, but they come only to drain the land of money, to the evident indignation of the inhabitants. The Ormerods and Heyworths were looked upon 'as real gentry'. John Aked told me yesterday (in a six-miles' walk with him across the country; he is out of work) that 'Lawrence Heyworth was one of those men who married his servant, and she was my aunt; but I've heard tell by those who've seen her, she was a bonny one to look at.' I asked him what had become of the family, and he said, 'I've not heard mich of them, save Mrs Potter, and folk say she was an able, stirring body; you've a look of that, Miss Jones, far more like a male than a female to talk wi''.'

They have not as yet the slightest suspicion: the old hands look at me with admiration, 'as a right useful sort of body as would be a comfort to my father', and the young men with a certain amount of amazement and fear. One shrewd old man smelt a rat and asked me whether my father was not a Lord, and when I told him he was an honest farmer, he strained all my knowledge of farming by cross-questions as to stock, etc.; but at last he was disarmed, and remarked that if he came south he would 'coom un 'ave a chat wi' ye father', and he would like to see these Welsh lasses 'if they'd all got sich white teeth and glistening 'air' as I; but he thought we had it 'middling snod (smooth) wi' ye, e'en warty' (even on weekdays). The same shrewd old man told me a lot about the failure of the company mills owned by working men; how the managers were invariably tipped to take worse goods for the same money, and how the committees of working men 'got talkin' like'.

Many of these are shut up; in fact, trade here is worse now than it has ever been; but there is comparatively little poverty, and those who remain out of work move on to the big towns where there are more 'odd jobs'. The wife of the old man with whom we were 'ta in' was a jolly fat woman who talked such broad Lancashire that I could scarce understand her; but in the course of the evening she bashfully admitted that she 'summat took a bit of backy', whereupon I produced my cigarette-case and offered the company some 'Welsh cigars'. You would have laughed, father, to see me sitting amongst four or five mill-hands smoking quietly, having been voted 'good company', 'interesting like' to talk wi'. Under the benign influence of tobacco the elder ones came out with the history of their lives, gave me a list of their various successive occupations, and some of them of their series of wives. I was surprised at their fair-mindedness, and at the kindliness of their view of men and things; now they all recognize that men got on from having certain qualities and that 'na makin' of laws can alter that'. This class of respectable working man takes little or no interest in politics (they have no votes); their thoughts are set on getting on in this world and the next; their conversation consists chiefly of personalities and religion. The old man and his daughter with whom we were staying are a veritable study in Puritan life on its more kindly side; worth a dozen history books on the subject. We always have prayers in the evening, and I have been constituted the reader as I pronounce 'so distinct like'. It is curious how completely at home I feel with these people, and how they open their hearts to me and say that I'm 'the sort of woman "they" can talk straight away with'. I can't help thinking that it would be as well if politicians would live amongst the various classes they legislate for, and find out what are their wishes and ideas. It seems to me we stand the chance, in our so-called representative government, of representing and working out the wishes of the idler sort of people, who, because they have no quiet occupation absorbing their time and energy, have time and energy to make a row, and wish to alter things because they don't fit themselves. Of course it would be absurd to generalize from such a narrow basis; but much that one sees and hears whilst living with the working men and women as one of them, sets one thinking that a little more patient observation might be advisable before carrying out great organic changes, which may or may not be right. Mere philanthropists are apt to overlook the existence of an independent working class, and when they talk sentimentally of the 'people' they mean really the 'ne'er-do-wells'. It is almost a pity that the whole attention of this politician should be directed towards the latter class.

[*Third Letter.*] – I have just received your letter. I will certainly meet you at Manchester Monday, but don't on any account come here; Da says they would never forgive her if they found it out!

The dear people have accepted me so heartily and entertained me so hospitably as one of themselves that it would be cruel to undeceive them.

We dined this morning in a most comfortable cottage, owned by a mill-hand with three sons, mill-hands. (The) afternoon I spent in going over two or three mills, introduced by my friends to their managers, and finished up by going through the Co-op. stores with the manager. I told him I had been sent by my father to inquire into the management of Co-ops. as you wanted to start one; and he took me into his counting-house, showed me his books and explained the whole thing. It is entirely owned and managed by working men. Membership entails spending a certain amount there; and the dividend is paid according to the amount spent per quarter, though it is not paid out until the share is paid up through accumulation. In this way there is a double check on the management; the shareholder requiring his dividend, and the consumer requiring cheap and good articles, and as the manager remarked, 'Females look pretty sharp arter that.' It has been established twenty years or more and has never paid less than $12\frac{1}{2}$ per cent; the working expenses only come to 5 per cent on capital turned over. No member can have more than £100 in stock, and any one can become a member on the payment of three shillings and sixpence entrance fee, and on the original terms. The manager gave me a graphic account of his trouble with the committee of working men; and interested me by explaining the reasons of the failure of most of the Co-op. mills, all of which I will tell you over our cigarettes.

We went to tea in another cottage, and have just been listening to a somewhat dreary 'spiritual oration' from our religiously minded host. A miner by profession, he finished up by saying that 'God Almighty did all things right; that 'e'd *bouried* the coal sa deep 'cause if it 'ud been o' the top the women would 'ave ta'en all the cobs and left all the small.' You would be amused at my piety, dear father; yesterday, in one of the Sunday schools, I came to the rescue of a meek elderly teacher who was being pertly questioned by a forward young woman as to Adam's responsibility for our sin. I asked her whether 'she did not "favour" her parents' and made her draw the rather far-fetched inference.

The meek elderly man shook me warmly by the hand as we left, and inquired if 'he could do ought for me while I was in Bacup'. But the only way to understand these people is, for the time, to adopt their faith, and look at things in their light; then one gets a clear picture (undisturbed by any critically antagonistic spirit) of their life, both material and mental. And to me, there is a certain charm and restfulness in their simple piety and absolute ignorance of the world.

As regard the 'material life' I am sometimes rather hard up for meat, and my diet is principally oatcake and cheese, with the butter which we brought with us. Every evening I have my cigarette in a rocking-chair by the kitchen fire, having persuaded my friends that all Welshwomen smoke. My host accepted a cigarette the first night, saying, 'I main 'ave a bit but a bitter 'ull go a long wa' '; so after puffing once or twice he snuffs it out and puts it carefully on the corner of the mantelpiece for the next night: 'On musna' tak too mich o' a gude thing, fur mooney is a slattering thing' (easily spent). Their income is only £1 a week, so that without the hospitality of our neighbours we should not have much to live on. We go to Mrs Ashworth's tomorrow. She is universally disliked, being very rich and very closefisted; and nobody receiving ought from her now or knowing where it will go to at her death. In order to avoid paying the tax on her carriage, she has taken it off the wheels, and has some arrangement by which it is mounted when wanted: (so say her cousins). I expect a good deal of condescension from her, as when we met her the other day in the butcher's shop, where we were paying a friendly visit, she gave me the slightest nod and did not shake hands ...

Two memories arise out of the above-mentioned visit to Mrs Ashworth. In order to impress the Welsh farmer's daughter, my purse-proud cousin brought out the photographs of her much-honoured relatives, my grandfather Heyworth and his brothers, and his sons and their children; luckily for me, she had no photographs of the Potter family! And her death in 1892, without a will, led to a rare example of unworldliness and moral fastidiousness on the part of these Bacup cotton operatives. No less than eighty thousand pounds was divided, according to the law of intestacy, in equal portions among her next-of-kin, who happened to be two groups of surviving first cousins; consisting, on the one hand, of eleven wage-earners, one earning less than twenty shillings a week, and, on the other, of the relatively wealthy sons of Grandmother Heyworth – the only daughter, my mother, being dead. The eleven wage-earners met together, and, after prayer, decided that it was against Christian brotherhood and natural equity for them to monopolize this unexpected heritage, to the exclusion of the children of the deceased first cousins; and they proceeded to divide their share in equal amounts, among themselves and some thirty of the younger generation, whose parents, being also first cousins of Mrs Ashworth, were dead. Thus the eleven legal heirs found themselves possessed, not of thousands, but of hundreds of pounds each. They naïvely notified their action to the Heyworth brothers in order that these also might share out their portion with the children of their dead sister. Needless to say, these 'men of property' refused to follow suit, on the common-sense ground that 'law was law, and property was property'; and that there was no more reason for them to share their own windfall with well-to-do nephews and nieces than that they should give it away in charity, which no one would expect of them.

[*Third Letter continued.*] – I have spent the day in the chapels and schools. After dinner, a dissenting minister dropped in and I had a long talk with him; he is coming for a cigarette this evening after chapel. He told me that in all the chapels there was a growing desire among the congregation to have political and social subjects treated in the pulpit, and that it was very difficult for a minister, now, to please. He also remarked that, in districts where cooperation amongst the workmen (in industrial enterprise) existed, they were a much more independent and free-thinking set.

There is an immense amount of cooperation in the whole of this district; the stores seem to succeed well, both as regards supplying the people with cheap articles and as savings banks paying good interest. Of course, I am just in the centre of the dissenting organization; and as our host is the chapel keeper and entertains all the ministers who come here, I hear all about the internal management. Each chapel, even of the same denomination, manages its own affairs; and there are monthly meetings of all the members (male and female) to discuss questions of expenditure, etc. In fact each chapel is a self-governing community, regulating not only chapel matters but overlooking the private life of its members.

One cannot help feeling what an excellent thing these dissenting organizations have been for educating this class for self-government. I can't help thinking, too, that one of the best preventatives against the socialistic tendency of the coming democracy would lie in local government; which would force the respectable working man to consider political questions as they come up in local administration. Parliament is such a far-off thing, that the more practical and industrious lot say that it is 'gormless meddling with it' (useless), and they leave it to the 'gabblers'. But they are keen enough on any local question which comes within their own experiences, and would bring plenty of shrewd sound sense to bear on the actual management of things.

Certainly the earnest successful working man is essentially conservative as regards the rights of property and the non-interference of the central government; and though religious feeling still has an immense hold on this class, and forms a real basis for many lives, the most religious of them agree that the younger generation are looking elsewhere for subjects of thought and feeling.

It seems to me of great importance that the political thought should take a practical instead of a theoretical line; that each section of the community should try experiments on a small scale, and that the promoters should see and reap the difficulties and disadvantages of each experiment as it is executed. There is an immense amount of spare energy in this class, now that it is educated, which is by no means used up in their mechanical occupation. When the religious channel is closed up it must go somewhere. It can be employed either in the *practical* solution of social and economic questions, or in the purely intellectual exercise of political theorizing and political discussion about problems considered in the abstract.

Forgive all these crudely expressed ideas. I have jotted them down just as they have crossed my mind. I am immensely interested in what I hear and see. But it is a daring thing in a young woman to drop 'caste'; and that is why I am anxious it should not be talked about. I have sufficient knowledge of men to

make them be to me as I choose; but not every one would understand that one had that power, and without it, it would not be a
profitful or wise adventure. I have seen two more Aked brothers.
They are all delicate-featured, melancholy men, with beautiful
*hands*. There is a universal interest in our family. I think they
would be somewhat horrified if they knew that this 'stirring lass
who is up in everything' was one of 'the fashionable Miss Potters
who live in grand houses and beautiful gardens and marry enor-
mously wealthy men'. But they evidently feel that there is something very strange about me. Their generalizations about 'Welsh
women' will be rather quaint by the time I go!

In living amongst mill-hands of East Lancashire [I reflect a
few months later] I was impressed with the depth and realism of
their religious faith. It seemed to absorb the entire nature, to
claim as its own all the energy unused in the actual struggle for
existence. Once the simple animal instincts were satisfied, the
surplus power, whether physical, intellectual or moral, was devoted to religion. Even the social intercourse was based on religious sympathy and common religious effort. It was just this
one-idea'd-ness and transparentness of life which attracted my
interest and admiration. For a time it contrasted favourably with
the extraordinarily complex mental activity arising in the cos-
mopolitan life of London – an activity which in some natures
tends to paralyse action and dissipate thought.

The same quality of one-idea'd-ness is present in the Birmingham Radical set, earnestness and simplicity of motive
being strikingly present. Political conviction takes the place here
of religious faith; and intolerance of scepticism of the main
articles of the creed is as bitter in the one case as in the other.
Possibly the Bible, from its inherent self-contradiction, is a more
promising ground for the individualism than the Radical programme, and the less likely to favour the supremacy of one interpreter. Heine said some fifty years ago, 'Talk to an
Englishman on religion and he is a fanatic; talk to him on politics and he is a man of the world.' It would seem to me, from my
slight experience of Bacup and Birmingham, that that part of the
Englishman's nature which has found gratification in religion is
now drifting into political life. When I suggested this to Mr
Chamberlain he answered, 'I quite agree with you, and I rejoice
in it. I have always had a grudge against religion for absorbing
the passion in man's nature.' It is only natural then that, this
being his view, he should find in the uncompromising belief of

his own set a more sympathetic atmosphere wherein to recruit his forces to battle with the powers of evil, than in the somewhat cynical, or at any rate indefinitely varied and qualified, political opinions of London society. [MS. diary, 16 March 1884.]

To complete the tale, I give the entries and letters relating to other visits in 1886 and 1889, after I had become an investigator in the East End of London.

Three years passed away – and Miss Jones again came to Bacup. She had lost her bloom of body and mind; some of her old friends hardly recognized her. The now familiar scene of working-class life had lost its freshness – adventure had lost its charm, and conscience had become more uneasy, even of white lies! So she lived among the people, keenly observant of the larger features of their life – but haunted with a spiritless melancholy. The grand old puritan with his vigorous, homely, religious feeling had passed away; the amiable and gentle John Aked had gone to the rest vouchsafed by heaven even to melancholy Akeds; young children had grown up to years of discretion. Old Bacup remained unaltered along the bleak high hills. The mills, now working busily overtime, nestled in the valley, long unpaved streets of two-storied cottages straggled irregularly up the hills. The old coaching inn, with its air of refined age, still stood behind the new buildings representing municipal life; a 'Co-op.' shop asserted its existence with almost vulgar prominence. The twenty chapels of all denominations, the parish church, and the 'gentry-built' new church, stood on the same ground and are as yet unemptied. Bacup life is still religious – the book of science, insinuating itself into the mill-hand's cottage, has not yet ousted the 'book of life'. The young man goes to chapel, but he will not teach in the Bible class or the Sunday school. The books from the free 'Co-op.' library interest him more; his talk about God is no longer inspired by the spirit of self-devoting faith. But Bacup, in spite of municipal life and cooperative industry, is spiritually still part of the 'old world'. It knows nothing of the complexities of modern life, and in the monotony of its daily existence likens the hand-loom village of a century ago. The restless ambition, the complicated motive and the far-stretching imagination of cosmopolitanism find no place in the gentle minds of Bacup folk. They are content with the doings of their little town – and say that even in Manchester they feel oppressed – and not 'homely like'.

I was interested in the mill-hand's life. So long as the hours do not include overtime, the work is as healthful to body and mind as it well could be. Sitting by the hands at work, watching the invigorating quickness of the machinery, the pleasant fellowship of men, women and children, the absence of care and the presence of common interest – the general well-being of well-earned and well-paid work – one was tempted to think that here, indeed, was happiness – unknown to the strained brain-worker, the idle and overfed rich, or the hardly pressed very poor. Young men and women mix freely; they know each other as fellow-workers, members of the same or kindred chapels; they watch each other from childhood upwards, live always in each other's company. They pair naturally, according to well-tested affinity, physical and spiritual. Public opinion – which means religiously guided opinion – presses heavily on the misdoer or the non-worker – the outcasting process, the reverse of the attracting force of East End life, is seen clearly in this small community, ridding it of the ne'er-do-weel and the habitual out-o'-work. There are no attractions for those who have not sources of love and interest within them; no work for those who cannot or will not work constantly. On the other hand, ill-success and unmerited failure are dealt with gently – for these people are, in the main, thinking of another world, and judge people not according to the position they have scrambled into in this, but according to their place in a future Heaven – won by godliness and self-renunciation.

Overtime brings needless waste of strength, taking more from the worker and giving less to the employer. It means an existence of physical drudgery, wearing out the body and rusting out the mind. It leaves men with no appetite for food and a strong desire for drink – brutalizes them by unfitting them for social intercourse or common interest.

This class eats too little, and above all, sleeps too little – growing boys getting only six or seven hours' bed; and the unfortunate mother who calls them lying awake half the night so as to be in time, and sitting up for the latest and oldest to get to bed. But overtime is forbidden for women and children – and it is here that one sees the benefit of the Factory Acts, and consequent inspection. *Laissez-faire* breaks down, when one watches these things from the inside. The individual worker cannot refuse to work overtime – if he does he loses his employment. Neither does he always wish to refuse, for many are ignorant of the meaning of constant strain on future life. It is idle to say that this bad effect of overwork is not restricted to manual labour; but is more felt by brain-workers. True, but in one case the remedy is easy to administer, in another impossible. Factories are easily stopped – briefs, consultations and literary study cannot be checked. Perhaps it would be far happier if they could be. [MS. diary, October 1886.]

LETTERS TO MY FATHER, OCTOBER 1886

[*First Letter.*] – I should have written to you before but I have had a wretched cold in my head, which has made me feel stupid. I nearly always have a cold once a year and generally about this time, but it is unfortunate that it should come in this visit. Still, it has not been bad enough to prevent me from going out among the people. Mrs Aked, with whom I am staying, is a jolly little Yorkshire widow, delighted with an excuse for going again into 'coompany', so we spend most of our time in and out of the neighbours' cottages, and very old friends insist on entertaining me. I can assure you 'Miss Jones' is a very popular person; and her London experiences draw quite an audience in the cottages in which she takes her 'tiffen'. . . . I am more and more charmed with the life of these people; with their warm-hearted integrity and power to act together. I suppose they are more or less a picked people from among the working class; if not, this section of the working class are more refined in their motives and feelings than the majority of the money-getting or money-inheriting class. There is a total absence of vulgarity; no attempt to seem what they are not, or to struggle and strive to be better off than their neighbours. Then, it is the only society I have ever lived in, in which religious faith really guides thought and action, and forms the basis to the whole life of the individual and the community.

The religious socialism of the dissenting communities is very remarkable, each circle forming a 'law unto itself' to which the individual must submit or be an outcast. And as all the denominations work heartily together (except the Church, which has here, on account of an ill-conducted parson, a contemptible position), the censorship on private morality is very severe, and a man or a woman cannot well escape it without leaving Bacup. One sees here the other side of the process through which bad workmen and bad characters are attracted to the large town. In East End life one notices this attraction, here one can watch the outcasting force. In the first place, there are no odd jobs in a small community which depends on productive industries. Unless a man can work regularly he cannot work at all. Then a bad character is socially an outcast, the whole social life depending on the chapel and the 'Co-op.'.

The 'Co-op.' furnishes amusement and interest, free of expense to all members, and through the system of deposit account, a mutual insurance company. Trade unionism is not strong here; class spirit hardly exists because there is no capitalist class; those mills which are not companies being owned by quite small men of working-class origin and connected with working people. Then, as a great many working people have shares in the co-operative mills, there is a recognized desire to keep down wages, which reacts on the public opinion, and makes even the non-owning men take a fairer view of the employer's position.

Three or four mill-hands were smoking here yesterday (my cigarettes!) and they were saying that the workers were getting the best of the bargain just at present. There is no bitter, uneasy feeling among the inhabitants of Bacup, for there is practically social equality; perhaps this accounts for the total absence of vulgarity. But one wonders what will happen when the religious feeling of the people is undermined by advancing scientific culture; for though the 'Co-op.' and the chapel at present work together, the secularism of the 'Co-op.' is half unconsciously recognized by earnest chapel-goers as a rival attraction to the prayer-meeting and the Bible class. One wonders where all the *feeling* will go, and all the capacity for *moral* self-government.

I think the safeguard will be in a strong local government, with considerable power to check individual action; and of a sufficiently small area to allow of the working people taking a real everyday part, and not only at election times. For the active regulation of their own and their neighbours' lives will be far less dangerous than theorizing and talking about things of which they have no knowledge. They have been trained to *act* but not to *think* – and in talking over 'imperial politics' they do not show much intelligence – for their one leading idea seems to be to cut down salaries!

Labouchere seems the principal favourite – a man they would not tolerate as a 'Co-op.' or 'chapel' leader.

I am glad to say the better class stick to Mr Chamberlain [my father was an ardent 'Unionist']. The G.O.M. has sadly gone down since I was last here – some good Liberals saying openly that he is in his dotage.

Tomorrow, if my cold is well enough, I am going to Manchester with the draper's daughter to buy goods from the Manchester warehouseman. Ask Mary to let me know how you got over your journey; my address is Miss Jones, 5 Angel Street, Tony Lane, Bacup.

[*Second Letter.*] – This is my last day here, as I am not going on to Oldham; the weather is so raw and disagreeable and I cannot get rid of my cold. I must tell you something about our daily life.

It begins at 5.30 with Mrs Aked's pleasant voice: 'Willie, Willie, be sharp, first bell's rung.' Willie is the youngest son, a pretty blue-eyed youth, who 'favours' Grandmamma Heyworth. He is tenter to a sheet weaver; is fifteen years old and earns five shillings. The last week his wages have been pulled down to four shillings and ninepence and he threatens to strike off work, but his mother tells him if he does he shall be 'without money'. Titus (the oldest) is off to work the same time (to the Keld' (*sic*) manufacture) and his mother gives them both a 'cup of tea' before they leave. Then the good little woman sits down to her Bible and struggles through her chapter (she is no scholar) until it is time for Walter to get off to his work (eight o'clock) at the 'Coop.' shop. He is a dull, heavy boy, whose chief interest is in his smart ties. We breakfast at 8.30. Titus and a fellow-worker joining us – bread and butter and tea-cake and good strong tea. Titus is a good, sensible lad, very fond of music and still fonder of 'his woman' – reads a good many 'Co-op.' books on science, and wins prizes at the night schools. The fellow-worker is an unmarried woman of thirty-seven, who says in a cheery way that 'she's had her chance a' lost it, and canna look for another' (in which sentiment I sympathize!).

Yesterday, I put a shawl over my head and went off with her to the mill – stayed an hour or so chatting with the hands while they worked. They are a happy lot of people – quiet workers and very sociable – men and women mixing together in a free-and-easy manner – but without any coarseness that I can see; the masculine sentiment about marriage being 'that a man's got no friend until he's a woman of his own'. Parties of young men and women go off together for a week to Blackpool, sometimes on cheaps trips to London – and as the women earn as much or nearly as much as the men (except the skilled work) there is no assumption of masculine superiority. Certainly this regular mechanical work, with all the invigorating brightness of machines, and plenty of fellow-workers of both sexes, seems about the happiest lot for a human being – so long as the hours are not too long. The factory inspectors keep a sharp look-out on 'overtime' for women and children; and this week two masters were fined forty pounds and costs. There is a strong feeling among the hands that overtime ought to be stopped for the men; and I think it would be better if it were. Latterly Titus has worked on till eight o'clock, and looks thoroughly worn out. It seems to waste their strength compared to the amount of work they do extra, and changes an existence of wholesome exertion into wearisome drudgery. Yesterday I went to middle-day meal with my old friend Alice Ashworth – an ugly, rough, warm-hearted single woman of forty, daughter to the delightful old puritan (now dead) we stayed with last time. Poor Alice lives alone in a two-roomed cottage, works at the mill, and has nothing but the memory of her father (who was a leader in all good things) and her strong religious feeling to warm the desolate loneliness of her life. 'Set ye down in the vacant chair, Miss Jones (after a hearty embrace); it does me good to see anyone who loved my father'; and her ugly rough features were lit up with strong feeling. She talks the broadest 'Lankey', sometimes I cannot understand her – and her language is Biblical – all her simplest ideas illustrated with Bible texts. She is devoted to me, looks upon me with quite a wondering admiration, and yet with a strong fellow-feeling of another 'lonesome' working woman. It was a high day for Alice, for she had asked the chapel minister and other friends of former days to meet me at tea. The minister, one of the 'new college men', with measured phrases and long words; a poor exchange for the old-fashioned minister 'called of God from among the people', no more educated than his fellows but rising to leadership by force of character. This man is more of a politician than a preacher – a politician of the shallowest and most unreal type, using endless words and not touching facts. He has a certain influence over the people, through his gift of the gab; but even they half unconsciously feel that the 'real thing' is passing away, and grieve that there [are] 'na more plain men as *feel* the word of Christ'. He is a snob into the bargain, and talks of Stephen Gladstone as if he were his most intimate friend – but then he is not of 'Lankey' breed – he is a Welshman. His wife and sister-in-law are of the shabby-genteel – aping the ways of the leisured class. Watching him among a large company of simple-minded, clear-headed mill-hands, mal-using his long words and affectedly twisting his hands, one felt the presence of the 'inferior animal', and dreaded the making of others of the like pattern by the shallow intellectualism of 'higher education'.

But I have got off the 'order of the day!'

We generally dine at home off mutton and potatoes, and have gone out 'a tayin'' every day. That means going about three o'clock and staying until nine, sometimes the whole party adjourning to another cottage.

The people are wonderfully friendly – the cottages comfortable and well furnished, and the teas excellent. Of course the living is trying to anyone unaccustomed to a farinaceous diet, and after a certain time the conversation would become wearisome to our restless, excited minds, always searching after new things. Still, living actually with these people has given me an insight, that is difficult to express in words, into higher working-class life – with all its charm of direct thinking, honest work and warm feeling; and above all, taught me the real part played by religion in making the English people, and of dissent teaching them the art of self-government, or rather serving as a means to develop their capacity for it. It saddens one to think that the religious faith that has united them together with a strong bond of spiritual effort and sustained them individually, throwing its warmth of light into the more lonely and unloved lives, is destined to pass away. For with their lives of mechanical work – with the many chances of breakdown and failure meaning absence of physical comfort, they need more than intellectualisms – more than any form of 'high thinking', which, even if it were worth anything to those who have it, is beyond the reach of these people from their lack of physical energy.

Intellectual culture is a relaxation to the more active-minded and successful, but it cannot be a resting-place to the worn-out or failed lives. 'Life in Christ' and hope in another world brings ease and refinement into a mere struggle for existence, calming the restless craving after the good things of this world by an 'other worldliness', and making failure a 'means of grace' instead of despicable want of success.

Poor Mary! who has had to read this letter to you!

On the last evening of my second visit I told my gentle

cousins who I was. I feared they would be offended: on the contrary, they were delighted, and glad I had not told them before they had got to know me.

The Akeds, mother and son, have been staying with me [I write a year afterwards]. They are simple, true-hearted people, strong Christians; I love these Lancashire folk. I showed them all over London; the one thing they delighted in was the endless galleries of books in the British Museum [the iron galleries where the books are stored]. Olive Schreiner [author of the *South African Farm*] was staying here; she is a wonderfully attractive little woman brimming over with sympathy. Titus Aked lost his heart to her; her charm of manner and conversation bowled over the simple-hearted Lancashire laddie, with his straight and narrow understanding. He gazed at the wee little woman with reverence and tenderness, and listened intently to every word she said. [MS. diary, 4 October 1887.]

Among my dear old friends [I write when visiting Bacup in 1889], with their kindly simplicity. Cousin Titus is now married to a young girl of sweet and modest expression and gentle ways, a fellow-worker at the mill. Most days she works with him; but often takes a day off and engages a 'knitter' [? word illegible] to do her work. Titus reads newspapers and periodicals, and takes music lessons, and attends the mechanics institute. The young wife spends her spare time in visiting and needlework, and does not attempt 'higher interests'. But she is full of kindness and affection for her mother-in-law, and fairly worships her Titus. ... [MS. diary, Bacup, April 1889.]

... When I was at Bacup [I meditate after my first visit] I felt as if I were living through a page of puritan history; felt that I saw the actual thing, human beings governed by one idea; devotion to Christ, with no struggle or thought about the world; in every action of their daily life living unto God. And I realized the strength of the motive which enlightened persons believe is passing away. I realized the permeating influence, and wondered what would fill the void it would leave, what inspiring motive would take its place? [MS. diary, February 1884.]

The Bacup adventure gave a decisive turn to my self-development.

Every day actual observation of men and things takes the place of accumulation of facts from books and boudoir trains of thought. Undoubtedly the Bacup trip is the right direction. To profit by that kind of observation I must gain more knowledge of legal and commercial matters, understand the theory of government before I can appreciate deficiencies in practice. The time is come now for a defined object towards which all my energies must be bent. [MS. diary, 24 January 1884.]

The die was cast, the craft was chosen. Through the pressure of circumstances and the inspiration of the Time-Spirit, I had decided to become an investigator of social institutions.

CHAPTER 4

*The Field of Controversy*

THE decisive influence of social environment on the activities of the individual was in my case even more immediate and obvious in the selection of a subject for investigation than in the choice of a craft.

Why did I select the chronic destitution of whole sections of the people, whether illustrated by overcrowded homes, by the demoralized casual labour at the docks, or by the low wages, long hours and insanitary conditions of the sweated industries, as the first subject for inquiry? Unlike my sister Kate, who had toiled for six years as a volunteer rent-collector, I was not led into the homes of the poor by the spirit of charity. I had never been moved by the 'hard cases' which, as I thought, 'make bad law'. What impelled me to concentrate on the condition of the people as the immediate question for investigation was the state of mind in the most vital centres of business enterprise, of political agitation and of academic reasoning.

There were, in fact, in the eighties and nineties two controversies raging in periodicals and books, and giving rise to perpetual argument within my own circle of relations and acquaintances: on the one hand, the meaning of the poverty of masses of men; and, on the other, the practicability and desirability of political and industrial democracy as a set-off to, perhaps as a means of redressing, the grievances of the majority of the people. Was the poverty of the many a necessary condition of the wealth of the nation and of its progress in civilization? And if the bulk of the people were to remain poor and uneducated, was it desirable, was it even safe, to entrust them with the weapon of trade unionism, and, through the ballot-box, with making and controlling the government of Great Britain with its enormous wealth and its far-flung dominions?

In the first chapter of this book I described how, in my childhood and youth, the outlook of the family circle, though unusually extended and diversified, did not include the 'world of labour'. I described how 'the very term "labour" stood for an abstraction – for an arithmetically calculable mass of human beings, each individual being merely a repetition of the others'. . . . 'Water plentiful and labour docile was a typical sentence in a company-promoter's report.'

Owing to a shifting in business and family relationships, reinforced by the transformation in British public opinion presently to be described, this closed eye came to be opened, and opened widely. In 1879 my father resigned the presidency of the Grand Trunk Railway of Canada, which he had held for ten years, and became once more actively engaged in British business enterprises. To an alien railway administrator, speeding over the vast spaces of a continent that was steadily filling up with immigrants of all races, white and yellow, brown and black, the conception of the manual workers as so many 'Robots' was natural, perhaps inevitable. To the manufacturer or merchant of Great Britain, as to the financiers standing behind them, faced as they were in 1879–85 by lock-outs and strikes conducted by trade unions of undeniable power; having to meet in official relations the workmen leaders, not only as negotiators on equal terms, but also as members of the House of Commons, even, in 1885, as part of the Administration – the term 'Labour' had come to mean no abstraction at all, but a multitude of restless, self-assertive, and loss-creating fellow-citizens, who could no longer be ignored and therefore had to be studied. Hence there began to appear, on my mother's boudoir table, pamphlets and treatises for and against the Wage-Fund Theory; whilst my father, with a puzzled expression, sought enlightenment from Carlyle's *Past and Present*, and began to take an interest in the experiences (as a volunteer rent-collector in the East End of London) of his daughter Kate, and in the conversation of such co-workers, thus introduced into the family circle, as Octavia Hill and Samuel and Henrietta Barnett. Moreover, it happened to be during these years that three political-minded brothers-in-law joined the family group. There was Henry Hobhouse (afterwards one of the members for Somerset and the Chairman of its County Council and Quarter-Sessions), who married my sister Margaret in 1880, and brought with him the cultivated refinement and sense of social obligation characteristic of such country gentlemen and public-service families as the Hobhouses, Farrers, Aclands and Stracheys. There was Charles Alfred Cripps, who married my sister Theresa in 1881; a brilliantly successful young barrister, an accomplished dialectician, with a tolerant and benevolent outlook on life; in after years destined to become a Conservative M.P., and eventually, as Lord Parmoor, owing to his hatred of war and distrust of 'capitalist imperialism', to swing into sympathy with the Labour and Socialist Movement, and to enter the short-lived Labour Cabinet of 1924. I delighted in arguments with him. And, last to join us, but eldest and most influential of the trio, Leonard Courtney, then Financial Secretary to the Treasury in Gladstone's Administration, won my sister Kate from her philanthropic work in 1883, and brought to bear on our discussions a massive intelligence and an amazing memory, combined with the intellectual integrity and personal disinterestedness of a superman. He and my sister, with a wide circle of political and literary friends, made a new centre of light and leading to the whole family. Of more immediate significance to myself was my deepened friendship with my cousin Mary Booth and with her husband Charles Booth, whose outstanding inquiry into the life and labour of the people of London I describe in the following chapter. All these stimulating personalities were so many 'live wires' connecting me with the larger worlds of politics, philanthropy and statistical investigation in these very years subjected to the working of a new ferment of thought and feeling.

## The World of Politics

'What is outside Parliament', wrote Mr Gladstone to Lord Rosebery in the first year of the triumphant Gladstonian Government of 1880–85, 'seems to me to be fast mounting – nay, to have already mounted – to an importance much exceeding what is inside.'[1]

The new ferment was, in fact, barely discernible in the proceedings of the House of Commons directed by the Gladstonian Cabinet of 1880–85. For half a century British politics had been based on a continuous rivalry between Whig and Tory; between landlordism on the one hand, rooted in privilege and protection, and on the other, capitalism claiming unrestricted freedom of enterprise in pursuit of pecuniary profit. To these must be added the distinct but parallel conflict between Nonconformity and the Established Church. From time to time there had arisen a demand for a further extension of the suffrage, and hot had been the disputes between the two great parties as to the exact amount of property or degree of social position necessary to fit a man for the exercise of the suffrage, and as to the devices that might be invented for curbing the power of majorities.

Now it was these old forces that were, in the main, represented by the House of Commons elected in 1880. For it must be remembered that the general election of that year had turned almost entirely on an emotional, even a religious view, of foreign affairs, to the exclusion of domestic issues, save for a repugnance to any increase in public expenditure and a desire for an actual reduction of taxation. Partly owing to this lack of lead, and partly to sheer bad luck, this Parliament failed altogether to control its own destinies, and floundered in the bogs of Bradlaughism, Ireland, the Transvaal, and Egypt – all of them issues remote from the needs and thoughts of the British electorate. Yet, as Gladstone had realized, there were already portents of politics of a new type.

1. Mr Gladstone to Lord Rosebery, 16 September 1880. Quoted in *The Life of William Ewart Gladstone*, by John Morley, vol. iii. p. 4.

Lord Randolph Churchill, with his queerly assorted three fellow-benchers, Arthur Balfour, Drummond Wolff and John Gorst, was feverishly stimulating the organization of the Tory working men into a ubiquitous electoral network which would enable him, from time to time, to shake his fist at Lord Salisbury. And there was Joseph Chamberlain, already controlling a powerful Radical caucus, who had administered Birmingham on the bold principle of 'high rates and a healthy city', and who was now talking of taxation as a ransom due from those 'who toil not neither do they spin', and who was demanding, in his new role of Cabinet Minister, adult manhood suffrage, free secular education, and three acres and a cow for those who preferred individual production on the land to work at wages in the mine or factory. 'There is a process of slow modification and development, mainly in directions which I view with misgiving,' wrote the veteran statesman to Lord Acton in February 1885. ' "Tory Democracy", the favourite idea on that side, is no more like the Conservative Party in which I was bred than it is like Liberalism. In fact less. It is demagogism; only a demagogism not ennobled by love and appreciation of liberty, but applied in the worst way, to put down the pacific, law-respecting, economic elements which ennobled the old Conservatism; living on the fomentation of angry passions, and still, in secret, as obstinately attached as ever to the evil principle of class interests. The Liberalism of today is better in what I have described as ennobling the old Conservatism: nay much better, yet far from being good. Its pet idea is what they call construction, that is to say, taking into the hands of the State the business of the individual man. Both the one and the other have much to estrange me, and have had for many, many years.'[2] It was this demoniacal constructiveness

2. Mr Gladstone to Lord Acton, 11 February 1885. *The Life of William Ewart Gladstone*, by John Morley, 1903, vol. iii. pp. 172–3. As early as 1877 Goschen, in the House of Commons, speaking as a Cabinet Minister, declared: 'It might be an unpopular thing to say it, but Political Economy had been dethroned in that House and Philanthropy had been allowed to take its place' [*Life of Lord Goschen*, by A. D. Elliot (1911), vol. i. p. 163].

that a few years later the aged and weary leader anathematized as 'whole vistas of social quackery'.

Why this demand for State intervention from a generation reared amidst rapidly rising riches and disciplined in the school of philosophic radicalism and orthodox political economy? For it was not the sweated workers, massed in overcrowded city tenements or scattered, as agricultural labourers and home workers, in village hovels; it was not the so-called aristocracy of labour – the cotton operatives, engineers and miners who were, during this period, enrolling themselves in friendly societies, organizing trade unions, and managing their own co-operative stores – it was, in truth, no section of the manual workers that was secreting what Mr Asquith lived to denounce in the 1924 election as 'the poison of socialism'. The working-class revolt against the misery and humiliation brought about by the Industrial Revolution – a revolt, in spasmodic violence, aping revolution – had had its fling in the twenties and thirties and its apotheosis in the Chartist Movement of the forties. During the relative prosperity of the fifties and sixties the revolutionary tradition of the first decades of the nineteenth century faded away; and by 1880 it had become little more than a romantic memory among old men in their anecdotage. Born and bred in chronic destitution and enfeebling disease, the denizens of the slums had sunk into a brutalized apathy, whilst the more fortunate members of skilled occupations, entrenched in craft unionism, had been converted to the 'administrative nihilism' of Cobden, Bright and Bradlaugh.

The origin of the ferment is to be discovered in a new consciousness of sin among men of intellect and men of property; a consciousness at first philanthropic and practical – Oastler, Shaftesbury and Chadwick; then literary and artistic – Dickens, Carlyle, Ruskin and William Morris; and finally, analytic, historical and explanatory – in his latter days John Stuart Mill;[3] Karl Marx and his English in-

3. In his *Autobiography* (The World's Classics Edition, pp. 195–6) John Stuart Mill thus describes his conversion to socialism. 'In those days I had seen little further than the old school of political economists

terpreters; Alfred Russel Wallace and Henry George; Arnold Toynbee and the Fabians. I might perhaps add a theological category – Charles Kingsley, F. D. Maurice, General Booth and Cardinal Manning. 'The sense of sin has been the starting-point of progress' was, during these years, the oft-repeated saying of Samuel Barnett, rector of St Jude's, Whitechapel, and founder of Toynbee Hall.

When I say the consciousness of sin, I do not mean the consciousness of personal sin: the agricultural labourers on

---

into the possibilities of fundamental improvement in social arrange-ments. Private property, as now understood, and inheritance, appeared to me, as to them, the *dernier mot* of legislation: and I looked no further than to mitigating the inequalities consequent on these institutions, by getting rid of primogeniture and entails. The notion that it was possible to go further than this in removing the injustice – for injustice it is, whether admitting of a complete remedy or not – involved in the fact that some are born to riches and the vast majority to poverty, I then reckoned chimerical, and only hoped that by universal education, leading to voluntary restraint on population, the portion of the poor might be made more tolerable. In short, I was a democrat, but not the least of a Socialist. We [Mills and his wife] were now much less democrats than I had been, because so long as educa-tion continues to be so wretchedly imperfect, we dreaded the ignorance and especially the selfishness and brutality of the mass: but our ideal of ultimate improvement went far beyond Democracy, and would class us decidedly under the general designation of Socialists. While we repudiated with the greatest energy that tyranny of society over the individual which most Socialist systems are supposed to involve, we yet looked forward to a time when society will no longer be divided into the idle and the industrious; when the rule that they who do not work shall not eat will be applied not to paupers only, but impartially to all; when the division of the produce of labour, instead of depending, as in so great a degree it now does, on the accident of birth, will be made by concert on an acknowledged principle of justice; and when it will no longer either be, or be thought to be, impossible for human beings to exert themselves strenuously in procuring benefits which are not to be exclusively their own, but to be shared with the society they belong to.' The sentence that follows I put in italics as it contains John Stuart Mill's pregnant definition of socialism. '*The social problem of the future we consider to be, how to unite the greatest individual liberty of action, with a common owner-ship in the raw material of the globe, and an equal participation of all in the benefits of combined labour.*'

Lord Shaftesbury's estate were no better off than others in Dorset; Ruskin and William Morris were surrounded in their homes with things which were costly as well as beautiful; John Stuart Mill did not alter his modest but comfortable way of life when he became a Socialist; and H. M. Hyndman gloried in the garments habitual to the members of exclusive West End clubs. The consciousness of sin was a collective or class consciousness; a growing uneasiness, amounting to conviction, that the industrial organization, which had yielded rent, interest and profits on a stupendous scale, had failed to provide a decent livelihood and tolerable conditions for a majority of the inhabitants of Great Britain. 'England', said Carlyle in the forties, 'is full of wealth, of multifarious produce, supply for human want in every kind; yet England is dying of inanition.'[4] 'This association of poverty with progress', argued the American advocate of taxation of land values, some forty years later, 'is the great enigma of our times. It is the central fact from which spring industrial, social and political difficulties that perplex the world, and with which statesmanship and philanthropy and education grapple in vain. ... So long as all the increased wealth which modern progress brings goes but to build up great fortunes, to increase luxury and make sharper the contrast between the House of Have and the House of Want, progress is not real and cannot be permanent. The reaction must come.'[5] 'At this very time', wrote William Morris and H. M. Hyndman in 1884, 'official returns prove conclusively that vast masses of our countrymen are living on the very verge of starvation; that much of the factory population is undergoing steady physical deterioration; that the agricultural labourers rarely get enough food to keep them clear of diseases arising from insufficient nourishment; while such is the housing of the wage-earners in our great cities and in our country districts, that even the leading partisans of our pol-

4. *Past and Present*, by Thomas Carlyle, p. 1.
5. *Progress and Poverty, An Inquiry into the Cause of Industrial Depressions, and of Increase of Want with Increase of Wealth – The Remedy*, by Henry George, 1883, pp. 6, 7.

itical factions at length have awakened to the fact that civilization for the poor has been impossible for nearly two generations under these conditions, and that some steps ought really to be taken to remedy so monstrous an evil. Drink, debauchery, vice, crime inevitably arise under such conditions. For indigestion arising from bad food, cold arising from insufficient firing, depression arising from unhealthy air and lack of amusement, necessarily drive the poor to the public-house; while even the sober have had, too often, no education which should fit them for the full enjoyment of life. And drunken and sober, virtuous and vicious – if they can be called vicious who are steeped in immorality from their very babyhood – are all subject to never-ceasing uncertainty of earning a livelihood, due to the constant introduction of fresh machines over which they have no control, or the great commercial crises which come more frequently and last for a longer time at each recurrence. There is therefore complete anarchy of life and anarchy of production around us. Order exists, morality exists, comfort, happiness, education, as a whole, exist only for the class which has the means of production, at the expense of the class which supplies the labour-force that produces wealth.'[6] 'The state of the houses,' declared Cardinal Manning two years later, 'families living in single rooms, sometimes many families in one room, a corner apiece – these things cannot go on. The accumulation of wealth in the land, the piling up of wealth like mountains in the possession of classes or of individuals, cannot go on if these moral conditions of our people are not healed. No commonwealth can rest on such foundations.'[7]

This class-consciousness of sin was usually accompanied by devoted personal service, sometimes by open confession and a deliberate dedication of means and strength to the re-

6. *A Summary of the Principles of Socialism*, by H. M. Hyndman and William Morris, published 1884.

7. *The Rights of Labour*, by Cardinal Manning, republished and revised in 1887, quoted in *Life of Cardinal Manning*, by Edmund Sheridan Purcell, vol. ii. p. 647.

organization of society on a more equalitarian basis. One of the noblest and most original of these latter-day confessors, Arnold Toynbee, expressed, on the eve of his premature death – in words charged, it may be overcharged, with emotion – at once his penitence and his hope for a nobler life for the mass of his fellow-countrymen.

We – the middle classes, I mean, not merely the very rich – we have neglected you; instead of justice we have offered you charity, and instead of sympathy we have offered you hard and unreal advice; but I think we are changing. If you would only believe it and trust us, I think that many of us would spend our lives in your service. You have – I say it clearly and advisedly – you have to forgive us, for we have wronged you; we have sinned against you grievously – not knowingly always, but still we have sinned, and let us confess it; but if you will forgive us – nay, whether you will forgive us or not – we will serve you, we will devote our lives to your service, and we cannot do more. It is not that we care about public life, for what is public life but the miserable, arid waste of barren controversies and personal jealousies, and grievous loss of time? Who would live in public life if he could help it? But we students, we would help you if we could. We are willing to give up something much dearer than fame and social position. We are willing to give up the life we care for, the life with books and with those we love. We will do this, and only ask you to remember one thing in return. We will ask you to remember this – that we work for you in the hope and trust that if you get material civilization, if you get a better life, if you have opened up to you the possibility of a better life, you will really lead a better life. If, that is, you get material civilization, remember that it is not an end in itself. Remember that man, like trees and plants, has his roots in the earth; but like the trees and plants, he must grow upwards towards the heavens. If you will only keep to the love of your fellow-men and to great ideals, then we shall find our happiness in helping you; but if you do not, then our reparation will be in vain.[8]

Now what infuriated the philosophic individualist, what

8. Arnold Toynbee, M.A., on ' "Progress and Poverty": a Criticism of Mr Henry George', being a lecture entitled 'Mr George in England', delivered 18 January 1883, in St Andrew's Hall, Newman Street, London.

upset the equanimity of Tory squire, Whig capitalist and Conservative professional man, was not the vicarious conscience of a pious peer or philanthropic employer, it was not the abstract or historical analysis of the industrial revolution by heterodox thinkers and rhetorical authors, still less the seemingly hysterical outpourings of university dons and sentimental divines; it was the grim fact that each successive administration, whether Whig or Tory, indeed every new session of Parliament, led to further state regulation of private enterprise, to fresh developments of central and municipal administration, and, worst of all, to the steadily increasing taxation of the rich for the benefit of the poor. The reaction against the theory and practice of empirical Socialism came to a head under Mr Gladstone's administration of 1880–85, an administration which may be fitly termed the 'no man's land' between the old Radicalism and the new Socialism. For this ministry of all the talents wandered in and out of the trenches of the old individualists and the scouting parties of the new Socialists with an 'absence of mind' concerning social and economic questions that became, in the following decades, the characteristic feature of Liberal statesmanship. Hence it was neither in Parliament nor in the Cabinet that the battle of the empirical Socialists with the philosophic Radicals was fought and won. Though the slow but continuous retreat of the individualist forces was signalized by annual increments of Socialistic legislation and administration, the controversy was carried out in periodicals, pamphlets, books, and in the evidence and reports of Royal Commissions and government committees of inquiry.

Foremost at that time among the literary defenders of the existing order – shall I say the passing order! – was my old friend Herbert Spencer, in the early eighties at the zenith of his world fame as England's greatest philosopher. Under challenging titles – *The Sins of Legislators*, *The New Toryism*, *The Coming Slavery*, and *The Great Political Superstition* – he contributed a series of articles in the *Contemporary Review* of 1884, published a few months later in *Man versus The State*, in which he ingeniously combined a destructive analysis of current legislation and a deductive demonstration of the validity of individualist economics and ethics, with a slashing attack on the Liberal party for having forsworn its faith in personal freedom. The gist of his indictment can best be given in his own words:

Dictatorial measures, rapidly multiplied, have tended continually to narrow the liberties of individuals; and have done this in a double way. Regulations have been made in yearly growing numbers, restraining the citizen in directions where his actions were previously unchecked, and compelling actions which previously he might perform or not as he liked; and at the same time heavier public burdens, chiefly local, have further restricted his freedom, by lessening that portion of his earnings which he can spend as he pleases, and augmenting the portion taken from him to be spent as public agents please. ... Thus, either directly or indirectly, and in most cases both at once, the citizen is at each further stage in the growth of this compulsory legislation, deprived of some liberty which he previously had.[9] ... How is it [asks the indignant philosopher] that Liberalism, getting more and more into power, has grown more and more coercive in its legislation? How is it that, either directly through its own majorities or indirectly through aid given in such cases to the majorities of its opponents, Liberalism has to an increasing extent adopted the policy of dictating the actions of citizens, and, by consequence diminishing the range throughout which their actions remain free? How are we to explain this spreading confusion of thought which has led it, in pursuit of what appears to be public good, to invert the method by which in earlier days it achieved public good?

Then he defines the distinctive policies of Whig and Tory parties throughout the eighteenth and early nineteenth centuries: 'If we compare these descriptions, we see that in the one party there was a desire to resist and decrease the coercive power of the ruler over the subject, and in the other

9. I quote from the revised edition included in the volume entitled *Social Statics, Abridged and Revised; together with The Man versus The State*, by Herbert Spencer, 1892, pp. 271 and 290. In the introduction to this reprint Spencer notes that as far back as 1860 he had foreseen the trend towards Socialism inherent in political democracy. [*Westminster Review*, April 1860.]

party to maintain or increase his coercive power. This distinction in their aims – a distinction which transcends in meaning and importance all other political distinctions – was displayed in their early doings.' And this degeneration of Liberalism the philosopher attributes to a mistaken belief in the validity of democratic institutions. 'The great political superstition of the past was the divine right of kings. The great political superstition of the present is the divine right of parliaments. The oil of anointing seems unawares to have dripped from the head of the one on to the heads of the many, and given sacredness to them also and to their decrees.' ... 'The function of Liberalism in the past was that of putting a limit to the powers of kings. The function of true Liberalism in the future will be that of putting a limit to the powers of parliaments.'[10]

Alas! poor Liberals! The outraged survivors of philosophic Radicalism were far more eager to drive the Gladstonians back into the rear-trenches of what was assumed to be orthodox political economy than to stop the advancing scouts of the tiny sect of Socialists. Indeed, these rival fanatics became the pets of Conservative drawing-rooms and the sought-for opponents on individualist platforms. 'Anyway, I declare that I positively look forward with pleasure to the day when Lewin's Socialists will increase in numbers and power,' says the cynical mugwump M.P. in Auberon Herbert's brilliant symposium, *A Politician in Trouble about his Soul*. 'It will be refreshing to escape, even by their help, from this atmosphere of perfumed lying. The real Socialists – I don't mean any of the half-breeds, the Tory democrats, or the Gladstonites, or the Christian *sans-culottes*, or whatever they call themselves – have convictions, even if they are of the "blood and iron" kind. I should feel it a true pleasure to be shot by a genuine Socialist – or to shoot him, as the matter might turn out – if only in return we might be quit of the modern politician, who smirks and bows like the draper's assistant, while he cheats us out of an inch in every yard. Only, may it please the Lord to shorten the time and deliver us from this univer-

10. *Man versus The State*, pp. 277, 279, 369, 403.

sal sloppiness! If "justice as our guide", generosity, and "gracious messages" may be consigned once for all to the rhetorical dust-hole, I shall breathe freely again, and feel grateful to the men who say in a straightforward dialect, "You are the few, we are the many; we have the force, and we intend to have the enjoyment. Do you keep, if you can; and we will take, if we can." '[11]

And here I venture on an interlude – an entry in my diary (an irrelevance, corrects The Other One) descriptive of Auberon Herbert[12] at home in the New Forest.

Across the forest and the moor we rode on that February day; the man and the elder girl and I to the home in the wilds. ... From the forest glade the ground slopes gently to a boggy boundary separating the meadow from a vast expanse of moor. Round about reigns solitude. The rough forest pony, the picturesque Channel Isle cattle, and the wild deer, roam with equal freedom on the common land; but the wooden fence bars them from the sacred precincts of a forest freehold. On the highest part of this ground stands a little colony of queer red-painted buildings; two large cottages and various small outhouses, huddled together indistinct from one another and free from any architectural plan. No attempt at a drive or even a path, not even a gate. To enter the enclosure the visitor must needs dip under a wooden paling. But once inside the larger cottage, there is comfort, even taste. The floors are bare and clean scoured; here and there warm-coloured rugs thrown across, while the monotony of the wooden wall is broken by draped Eastern hangings. In the dining-room the old forest hearth, bringing with it commoners' rights, stands intact: the only part of the 'Old House', still the name of the colony, left unchanged; it forms a half circle, the chimney arising straight from the stone hearth whereon a mass of peat and wood burns brightly. Another

11. A Politician in Trouble about his Soul, by Auberon Herbert, pp. 183–4 (1884).

12. Auberon Herbert, 1838–1906: third son of third Earl of Carnarvon. Conservative candidate for Isle of Wight, 1865; Liberal candidate for Berkshire, 1868; elected for Nottingham, 1870; retired, 1874. One of Herbert Spencer's three trustees. Besides A Politician in Trouble about his Soul, his principal publications were: The Sacrifice of Education to Examination, 1889; A Plea for Liberty, 1891; The Right and Wrong of Compulsion by the State, 1885; A Voluntaryist Creed, 1908.

sitting-room, a guest-chamber, the kitchen and pantry on either side of the entrance, complete the rooms on the ground floor. Above, three bedrooms and the family sitting-room – this latter gable shape, with a ladder leading on to the roof. There is comfort, even elegance, though a lack of finish, and a certain roughness which has its own charm. Refined eccentricity, not poverty, lives here. The outhouses clustering round the larger cottages are still unfinished. Five ponies of all sorts and conditions, safely termed 'screws', stand in the stalls, and a shaggy Shetland wanders in the meadow. I think there are cows, but these are out in the forest during the day. Happily, no cocks and hens to break the silence. A mangey dog, a time-worn retriever, and three or four lively, well-fed cats compose the rest of the livestock. In the smaller cottage live three maidservants; two men, formerly 'Shakers', serve in all capacities, for ponies, cows, drawing of water, hewing of wood, and as messengers to the civilized world.

Auberon Herbert, head of this little home, is a tall stooping man; he is already grey though only fifty years of age; and the look of failing physical strength is stamped on face and figure. His bearing, manner, voice – all tell the courtesy and sensitiveness of good breeding; his expression is that of an intellectual dreamer, tempered by the love of his fellow-creatures, whether human or otherwise; and in the truthful sympathy of his grey eyes and in the lines of his face you read past suffering and present resignation. The younger son of a great English peer, he was brought up to the amusements and occupations of his own class: public school, university, army, sport and racing, and, lastly, politics, followed in quick succession, with the always-present background of big country houses and sparkling London drawing-rooms. But his choice was not there. He married a woman of his own caste and, strangely enough, sharing his own tastes, and these two refused to move in the grooves of aristocratic custom. They settled down in a country farm and carved life out according to their own conscience. Strange stories floated up to London Society of their doings: Shaker settlements, gipsy vans, spirit-rapping and medium-hunting; and, worst of all, eating with their own servants! Now and again the literary world was charmed by brilliant articles in the *Fortnightly* or letters in *The Times*, and the political set was flustered and amused by the outspoken and well-worded dialogue, *A Politician in Trouble about his Soul*; which actually seemed written for the purpose of

disproving the usefulness of the politician! But generally Auberon Herbert was looked upon as an enthusiast, a Don Quixote of
the nineteenth century, who had left the real battle of life to fight
a strange ogre of his own imagination – an *always immoral State
interference*: a creature, the uncouthness of whose name was a
sufficient guarantee for its non-existence.

Now the loved companion is dead. Two little girls, one thirteen
and the other seven, a boy away at a grammar school, are the
beloved of the solitary man. Both the girls are dressed in grey
smocks, worsted stockings, and thick clump boots. The elder is
largely and loosely made, with a warm complexion, dark eyes,
and constantly changing expression; sometimes awkward plain-
ness, at other times bright beauty; at all times a simplicity and
directness and ready sympathy attracting love. The younger is a
quick, grey-eyed, phlegmatic-tempered child, with compressed
mouth and decided little ways; a toss of the head and a sparkle of
the eye speaking decision and purpose of character. A young
Oxford man, pleasant, fairly intelligent, but in no way out-of-
the-common, lives in the house as tutor. Here in the midst of
great natural beauty, far away from all human intercourse, these
three lives slip slowly onward; the man towards old age and
death, the girls towards the joys and the troubles, the risks and
burdens of mature womanhood ...

After our long ride, fourteen miles round about from the
station, we were tired. Lunch over, we sank into comfortable
chairs round the blaze of peat and wood fire, sipped coffee, and
smoked cigarettes. Religiously minded individualism disputing
with scientific fact-finding; discordant tendencies, it is true, but
mutually tolerant. 'A woman without a soul,' said Auberon
Herbert playfully, 'looking upon struggling society as a young
surgeon looks on a case as another subject for diagnosis. Cannot
you see it is moral law that should guide our action; and that the
only moral axiom in social life is free action for every man's
faculties? [MS. diary, 8 February 1888.]

Another two days with Auberon Herbert in the New Forest [I
write nine months later]. Long talks with him riding through the
tangled forest groves or by the peat fire in his small attic sanc-
tum, these latter lasting far into the night. The same gentle-
natured well-bred man, but new lights on his character bringing
out weaker qualities. 'All through my life I have formed sudden
fancies, I have been wrapped up in a man or woman and then

discovered some imperfection and turned from them. I am perpetually seeking the ideal and as perpetually being disappointed.
Like all idealists I am a little inhuman.'

There is a touch of egotism in his eccentric life; unwillingness
to bear the burdens of everyday existence. And his career proves
the impossibility of influencing men without constant contact;
even to me (a woman!) his proposals seem manifestly absurd in
inadequacy of means to ends. All the same, he has an attractive
and highly original personality, touching heights of moral
beauty but showing sometimes a ground-work of self-deceiving
egotism. There is a want of masculine qualities, of healthy
sturdiness. It is only the transparent honesty of his nature and
the absence of 'earthiness' that prevents this weakness leading to
morbid and untrue feeling.

I enjoyed the rides and scenery, and the constant companionship with a refined and highly intellectual man, and his
idealism is refreshing – I wish to believe it is true. [MS. diary, 14
December 1888.]

So far as I was concerned, the net effect of this dialectical
duel between the philosophic Radical and the Socialist or
socialistically-minded politician is best described in a letter
which I drafted to a London acquaintance – a letter which
apparently I lacked the courage to send, as it remains
unfinished, undated and unsigned in the MS. diary of July
1884. Today, forty years afterwards, this presumptuous and, I
fear, priggish pronouncement has incidentally the merit of
demonstrating the anti-democratic and anti-collectivist bias
with which I started out to investigate the working of social
institutions.

I send you *Man versus The State*. I feel very penitent for talking to you on social subjects, which I do not, and never hope to,
understand. Nevertheless, it is very distressing to be reduced to a
state of absolute agnosticism on all questions, divine and human:
and that state appears to me nowadays the fate of the ordinary
mortal born with an intellectual tendency.

Social questions would seem to me to require for their solution
greater intellectual power and more freedom from bias than the
problems of other sciences – and I do not quite understand the
democratic theory that by multiplying ignorant opinions
indefinitely you produce wisdom! I know the democrat would

answer: 'The political instincts of the masses are truer than the political theories of the wise men.' But if we approach this great idol 'the majority' and examine the minds of those individuals of it who are within our reach, we find them roughly divided into three classes: those who are indifferent – whose nervous energy is absorbed in the struggle for existence and well-being; those who accept political opinions as a party faith without really understanding the words they use; and lastly, that more promising material, politically considered, that large section of the working classes who are passionately discontented with things as they are and desirous to obtain what they would consider a *fairer* share of the good things of this world. But we all agree that there are laws governing distribution, though we may differ as to their nature.

Are these discontented men anxious for immediate relief, *likely* to arrive at the truth about these laws? Would desperate anxiety to relieve pain teach the patient or his friend the medicine likely to affect it – if they had no knowledge of medicine?

Certainly, if one judges the political intelligence of the masses by the speeches addressed to it by party speakers, especially the speeches of those most successful in pleasing it – one cannot estimate it very highly.

What body of scientific men, or even of ordinary shrewd business men, spoken to on the subject that interested them most, whether intellectually or materially, would *tolerate* that extraordinary mixture of personalities, dogmatic assertions as to fact and principle, metaphysical theories, grand and vague moral sentiments, appeals to personal devotion on the one hand, and self-interest on the other, this extraordinary medley of sentiment, passion, and expediency which makes up the argument of the politician?

And then if one turns from the practical man to the theorist I do not know that one finds much rest there. Herbert Spencer seems to me to be guilty of what Comte defines as materialism: he applies the laws of a lower to the subject-matter of a higher science – his social theories are biological laws illustrated by social facts.

He bases sociological laws on the analogy of the organism; and this analogy, in so far as it deals with the identity of the functions of the 'being' called society with the function of the 'being' called the individual, seems to me unproved hypothesis.

One might as well attempt to describe the nature of organic life by the laws which govern inorganic existence.

Then this analogy of the organism cuts both ways. Herbert Spencer maintains that because society is a natural growth it should not be interfered with. But it is quite possible to argue that the government is a 'naturally differentiated organ' (as he would express it) developed by the organism to gratify its own sensations. This might lead straight to a state socialism – logically it leads to pure necessarianism, since whatever happens is natural, even the death of the organism!

So I think, if I were a man, and had an intellect, I would leave political action and political theorizing to those with faith, and examine and try to describe correctly and proportionately what actually happened in the different strata of society; more especially the spontaneous growth of organization – to try and discover the laws governing its birth, life and death.

I do not believe we can deduce social laws from the laws of another science; nor do I believe that there is an intuitive perception of them in the majority of men's minds – I believe they will only be discovered by great minds working on carefully prepared data, and for the most part I think these data have yet to be collected and classified.

In the meantime, as a citizen looking to the material and spiritual welfare of my descendants, I object to these gigantic experiments, state-education and state-intervention in other matters, which are now being inaugurated and which flavour of inadequately thought-out theories – the most dangerous of all social poisons. Neither do they seem to me to be the result of the spontaneously expressed desires of the people; but rather the crude prescriptions of social quacks seeking to relieve vague feelings of pain and discomfort experienced by the masses. [MS. diary, July 1884.]

Less self-conscious and elaborately composed is an entry in my diary three months later, after a discussion with my brother-in-law, C. A. Cripps. I add it here because it reveals the deep-lying controversy, between the Ego that affirms and the Ego that denies, upon the issue, which was continuously present in my mind: Can we have a science of society, and if so, will its conclusions be accepted as a guiding light in public policy?

Stayed with the Alfred Cripps: Theresa fascinating as ever, slightly depressed with poor health, but sweetly happy in her marriage. Alfred keeps up his success at the Bar. Bought the family place and taken to farming in these bad times, as a recreation! Evidently will not go into politics, except as 'a scholar and a gentleman'. He is not a leader of men; his opinions do not represent the desires of the masses; they are the result of an attempt to deduce laws of government from certain first principles of morality. His theory as to the present state of political life is that the tendency is to ignore principle and follow instinct; that this is based on the fallacious belief that what the people wish is right. He believes in principle, and in the possibility of reducing politics to a science. Many cultivated men think, with him, that political action should be governed by principle. But there is no body of doctrine upon which they can agree. Hence they cannot organize themselves into a party for working purposes. A reaction has set in against the doctrine of the philosophical Radicals; [a doctrine] insisted upon with so much dogmatism. . . . [This doctrine] seems to me to be a queer mixture of metaphysical principles, such as the equal rights of men, etc., and of laws such as those of political economy; laws true, no doubt, of the facts from which they were deduced, but recklessly applied to cover facts with which they have no proper relationship or connection . . .

When one comes to ponder on this situation one feels how hopelessly incapable one really is of forming political opinions. The most one can do is to attempt to see truly what is actually happening, without attempting to foretell what will, from that, result. And even this more modest effort is immensely difficult for the observer of moderate power and with moderate opportunities. Possibly within that great organism, society, there may be changes now taking place, unregistered by any outward action in political life; growth or decomposition outside the activity of the political organ. And these changes, whether for good or for evil, can only be discovered by the most patient observation, by men of highly sensitive feeling and well-trained intellect, and furnished with a comprehensive knowledge of social facts, past and present. Great genius will be required in social science. [MS. diary, 6 November 1884.]

## The World of Philanthropy

The world of politics in the seventies and eighties was intimately associated with the world of philanthropy.[13] The social reformers in Parliament, whether Conservatives or Liberals, belonged, almost invariably, to the groups of public-spirited and benevolent men and women within the metropolis or in the provincial towns who were initiating and directing the perpetual flow of charitable gifts from the nation of the rich to the nation of the poor. Now, it was exactly in these decades that there arose, among the more enlightened philanthropists, a reactionary movement – a movement more potent in deterrence than the arguments of ratiocinating philosophers or the protests of cross-bench politicians, because it was based on the study of facts, and took the form of an alternative scheme for grappling, then and there, with the problem of poverty. And here I bring on the stage my friend the enemy – the Charity Organization Society – one of the most typical of mid-Victorian social offsprings. In after years, when the latter-day leaders of

13. Among the social changes in my lifetime, in the London that I have known, none is more striking than the passing 'out of the picture' of personal almsgiving. I do not pretend to estimate to what extent the aggregate gifts of moneyed persons to individuals in distress (including gifts to such organizations as Lord Mayor's Funds, soup kitchens, shelters, etc.) may have fallen off; whilst the total of benefactions to hospitals, colleges and other institutions has plainly increased. But in the seventies and eighties individual almsgiving not only filled a large part of the attention of the philanthropically-minded, but also overflowed into Parliament, where, irrespective of political parties, these philanthropists exercised an important influence on governments. One of the effects of the Charity Organization Society was, first to discredit individual almsgiving; and secondly, whilst replacing the habit of unthinking charity by a doctrine repellent in its apparent hardness, unwittingly to make it impossible for politicians to become associated with it. The divorce between Parliament and the once-influential doctrines of 'enlightened charity' promulgated by the C.O.S. was completed by the rise, in the twentieth century, of the Labour Party, with its insistence on social reconstruction, based not on charity but on equity, and on a scientifically ascertained advantage to the community as a whole.

charity organization and I had become respectively propagandists of rival political and economic theories, we fought each other's views to the death. But in these years of my apprenticeship (1883-7) the C.O.S. appeared to me as an honest though short-circuited attempt to apply the scientific method of observation and experiment, reasoning and verification, to the task of delivering the poor from their miseries by the personal service and pecuniary assistance tendered by their leisured and wealthy fellow-citizens.

The leading spirits of the Charity Organization Society, when I first came across it in the spring of 1883, had been, in 1869, its principal founders – Octavia Hill,[14] Samuel Barnett, W. H. Fremantle,[15] and a younger man who had recently become its secretary and was to become its chief protagonist – C. S. Loch.[16] These initiators of charity organization were

14. Octavia Hill (1838–1912) – not related to Matthew Davenport Hill and his equally well-known daughters, who were also active workers in social reform and philanthropy – see *Life of Octavia Hill*, by her brother-in-law, C. E. Maurice (1913); also 'Miss Octavia Hill', by Sir C. S. Loch, *Charity Organization Review* for September and October 1912. Octavia Hill gave evidence before the Royal Commission on the Housing of the Working Classes in 1884, and before the Royal Commission on the Aged Poor in 1893, and was a member of the Royal Commission on the Poor Laws and Relief of Distress, 1905–9.

15. W. H. Fremantle, at that time rector of the parish church of St Marylebone, afterwards Dean of Ripon.

16. Charles Stewart Loch (1849–1923), son of an Indian judge; created a knight, 1915, on his resignation, owing to ill-health, of the secretaryship that he had held for nearly forty years. 'That he was educated at Glenalmond and Balliol means comparatively little [writes the editor of the *Oxford Magazine* in 1905, when C. S. Loch was given the honorary degree of D.C.L.]; his life begins with his appointment as Secretary to the Charity Organization Society, and even more, the life of the Society dates from his appointment. He has formulated a principle, and created a type. The Society, when he joined it, represented a praiseworthy, if somewhat Utopian, effort to bring about co-operation in the charitable world, and unity among its workers. It has since become the repository of wise counsels in all matters concerning the relief of the poor. It is widely disliked and universally trusted. Its friends are few, and they are *voces in deserto*, but they win a hearing. That independence is among the most valuable of the goods and chattels that a man possesses; that to wound independence is to do

all of them distinguished for moral fervour and intellectual integrity. The immediate purpose of the Society was to organize all forms of charitable assistance so as to prevent overlapping and competition between the innumerable and heterogeneous agencies. And from the standpoint of the mid-Victorian Time-Spirit there was no gainsaying the worth of the three principles upon which this much-praised and much-abused organization was avowedly based: patient and persistent personal service on the part of the well-to-do; an acceptance of personal responsibility for the ulterior consequences, alike to the individual recipient and to others who might be indirectly affected, of charitable assistance; and finally, as the only way of carrying out this service and fulfilling this responsibility, the application of the scientific method to each separate case of a damaged body or a lost soul; so that the assistance given should be based on a correct forecast of what would actually happen, as a result of the gift, to the character and circumstances of the individual recipient and to the destitute class to which he belonged. In the life of her husband Mrs Barnett gives a graphic description of the state of mind of Octavia Hill and Samuel Barnett in the early days of charity organization. 'Counting that the only method of improving social conditions was by raising individuals, she [Octavia Hill] held that it was impertinent to the poor and injurious to their characters to offer them doles. They should be lifted out of pauperism by being expected to be self-dependent, and, in evidence of respect, be offered work instead of doles, even if work has to be created artificially.'[17] 'One old gentleman I remember who sat at the end

---

grievous harm; to foster independence is true charity; that character is nine-tenths of life; that the State shares with indiscriminate charity the distinction of being a mighty engine for evil – these and kindred precepts are summed up under the name.' He served on many Royal Commissions and committees of inquiry, and published many papers and articles. His principal book was *Charity and Social Life*, 1910. For sympathetic appreciations of his work, see *Charity Organization Review* for April 1923.

17. *Canon Barnett, His Life, Work, and Friends*, by his wife, vol. i. p. 35.

of the table, and therefore next to the applicants,' reports to Mrs Barnett a member of one of the first C.O.S. committees, 'slipped a sixpence under the corner of it into a poor woman's hand, as Miss Hill was pointing out to her the reasons why we could not give her money, and offering her the soundest advice. The old gentleman was afterwards called to account by your husband and melted into tears for his own delinquency!'[18]

Now this trivial incident illustrates better than any general explanation the subversive character of the movement, alike in thought and feeling, initiated by the founders of the Charity Organization Society. To the unsophisticated Christian, even of the nineteenth century, almsgiving was essentially a religious exercise, a manifestation of his love of God, of his obedience to the commands of his Lord and Saviour. 'Give unto every one that asketh thee', 'Sell all that thou hast and give unto the poor', were perhaps counsels of perfection impracticable for the householder with family responsibilities, and fit only for the saint whose entire life was dedicated to the service of God. Yet this universal and unquestioning yielding up of personal possessions for common consumption was thought to be the ideal conduct; the precious fruit of divine compassion. The spirit of unquestioning, of unrestricted – in short of infinite – charity was, to the orthodox Christian, not a process by which a given end could be attained, but an end in itself – a state of mind – one of the main channels through which the individual entered into communion with the supreme spirit of love at work in the universe.[19]

18. ibid., p. 29.

19. This conception of almsgiving as an end in itself, a desirable state of the soul comparable to prayer and fasting, seems still to be the predominant attitude of orthodox Roman Catholics, derived as it undoubtedly is from the teaching of the Fathers of the Church. According to Origen, we are told by the historian of *Christian Charity in the Ancient Church*, the first forgiveness of sins is obtained by baptism, the second by martyrdom, the third is that which is procured by almsgiving. Prayer and alms from the beginning always accompanied each other, as the Scriptures had always combined them. They form

How opposite was the state of mind and consequent conduct of the enlightened philanthropists of mid-Victorian times! To the pioneer of the new philanthropy, 'to give unto every one who asketh thee' was a mean and cruel form of self-indulgence. 'These petty and oft-repeated, while heedless, liberalities, by which many a sentimentalist scatters poison on every side', had been the contemptuous dismissal of almsgiving from the category of virtues by the great Scot – Robert Chalmers – the pioneer of charity reform in the first half of the nineteenth century. 'What educationalists have to do', thunders an early exponent of the new doctrine,

is to instruct (if they can be taught) the large dole-giving community, and to get them punished, as did our ancestors some centuries ago; but, above all, to purge the nation of the hypocrisy which sends the mendicant to prison, while for the great parent central vice of dole-giving it has only mild reproofs, or even gentle commendation. If you will bring about the due punishment of this low vice; if you will somehow contrive to handcuff the indiscriminate almsgiver, I will promise you, for reasons which I could assign, these inevitable consequences: no destitution, little poverty, lessened poor-rates, prisons emptier, fewer gin-shops, less crowded madhouses, sure signs of under-population, and an England worth living in.[20]

Or take a saner statement by Samuel Barnett in 1774:

Indiscriminate charity is among the curses of London. To put the result of our observation in the strongest form, I would say that 'the poor starve because of the alms they receive'. The people of this parish live in rooms the state of which is a disgrace

---

together the outward expression of the inward sacrifice of the heart. Clement of Alexandria warns the faithful not to judge who is deserving and who is undeserving. 'For by being fastidious and setting thyself to try who are fit for thy benevolence, and who are not, it is possible that thou mayest neglect some who are the friends of God.' (See *Christian Charity in the Ancient Church*, by G. Uhlhorn, pp. 121–50.)

20. Dr Guy, in Walker's *Original*, p. 239 (quoted in *Social Works in London, 1869–1912*, by Helen Bosanquet, pp. 6 and 7).

to us as a nation. Living such a life, they are constantly brought into contact with soft-hearted people. Alms are given them – a shilling by one, a sixpence by another, a dinner here and some clothing there; the gift is not sufficient if they are really struggling, the care is not sufficient if they are thriftless or wicked. The effect of this charity is that a state of things to make one's heart bleed is perpetuated. The people never learn to work or to save; out-relief from 'the House', or the dole of the charitable, has stood in the way of providence, which God their Father would have taught them.[21]

The belief – it may almost be called an obsession – that the mass-misery of great cities arose mainly, if not entirely, from spasmodic, indiscriminate and unconditional doles, whether in the form of alms or in that of Poor Law relief, was, in the sixties and seventies, the common opinion of such enlightened members of the governing class as were interested in the problem of poverty. Their hypothesis seemed to be borne out alike by personal observation, the teaching of history and the deductions of the Political Economists. There was the patent fact, crystal clear to intelligent workers among the poor, that casually and arbitrarily administered doles undermined, in the average sensual man, the desire to work; cultivated, in recipients and would-be recipients, deceitfulness, servility and greed; and, worst of all, attracted to the dole-giving district the unemployed, under-employed and unemployable from the adjacent country. Thus were formed, in the slums of great cities, stagnant pools of deteriorated men and women, incapable of steady work, demoralizing their children and all new-comers, and perpetually dragging down each other into ever lower depths of mendicancy, sickness and vice. Nor was historical proof lacking. How often were we told of the success of the reform of the Poor Law in 1834, when the summary stoppage of Outdoor Relief to the able-bodied and their families resulted in a quick transformation of an idle and rebellious people into the industrious and docile population of the countryside, ready to accept the ministrations of the clergy and the steady

21. *Canon Barnett, His Life, Work, and Friends*, by his wife, vol. i. p. 83.

employment at low wages tendered by the farmer and the squire! To the abstract economist of the period, the giving of alms or Poor Law relief seemed, indeed, to have the double evil of not merely discouraging the poor from working, but also of actually injuring the more industrious by lessening the amount of the wage-fund distributed among them in return for their labour. When we realize that behind all this array of inductive and deductive proof of the disastrous effect on the wage-earning class of any kind of subvention, there lay the subconscious bias of 'the haves' against taxing themselves for 'the have nots', it is not surprising that the demonstration carried all before it; and the tenets of the originators of the idea of charity organization found ready acceptance among the enlightened members of the propertied class.

The argument pointed, indeed, not to any organization of philanthropy, but to its abandonment as a harmful futility. And yet these devoted men and women, unlike the mass of property owners, were yearning to spend their lives in the service of the poor. What was clear to them was that the first requisite was the thorough investigation of each case, in order to save themselves from being taken in by the plausible tales of those who hastened to prey upon their credulity. But when the circumstances had been investigated, and genuine need had been established, what line was the enlightened 'friend of the poor' to pursue? The first idea was to eliminate those whose evil state could be plausibly ascribed to their own culpable negligence or misconduct. All enlightened philanthropy was to be concentrated on 'the deserving', the others being left to a penal Poor Law. Any such line of demarcation was, however, soon found impracticable. It was only in a small proportion of extreme cases, on one side or the other, that any confident judgement could be pronounced as to whether the past life of an unfortunate family had or had not been marked, not only by freedom from patent vice or crime, but by such a degree of consistent sobriety, industry, integrity and thrift as warranted its classification among the deserving. Moreover, any such classification by merit was found to have no relation to the necessary classification according to needs. The most deserving cases often proved to be those whom it was plainly impossible to help effectively either by money or by the philanthropic jobbery that got its favourites into situations. Most numerous were the cases of chronic sickness, or those needing prolonged and expensive medical treatment. Others, again, were hopeless without a complete change of environment. There were innumerable other varieties ruled out, in practice, because any adequate dealing with them involved an expense altogether beyond the means available. Eventually the Charity Organization Society was driven to drop the criterion of desert; 'the test is not whether the applicant be deserving but whether he is helpable', we were told.[22] No relief was to be given that was not 'adequate', that is to say, such as could be hoped, in due time, to render the person or family self-supporting. No relief was to be given where the person was either so bad in point of character, or so chronic in need, as to be incapable of permanent restoration to the ranks of the self-supporting. All 'hopeless' cases – that is, persons whom there was no helpful prospect of rendering permanently self-supporting (perhaps 'because no suitable charity exists') – were, however blameless and morally deserving had been their lives, to be handed over to the semi-penal Poor Law. We may admit that some such principles as these were, in practice, almost forced upon any systematic private philanthropists. But it is difficult to see how they could be made consistent with the duty, persistently inculcated, of personal friendship with the poor. The intruder in the poor man's hovel, mixing rigorous questioning as to the conduct and income of every member of the family with expressions of friendly sympathy, was supposed finally to decide in innumerable instances that the case, though thoroughly deserving, was so desperately necessitous as to be incapable of adequate help, and so hopeless of permanent restoration that no aid whatsoever could possibly be given. The one door opened by these 'friends of the poor' to all

22. Principles of Decision, C.O.S. Papers, No. 5, revised edition, July 1905.

those they were unable to help privately, deserving as well as undeserving, was that of the workhouse with its penal discipline 'according to the principles of 1834'. Thus, well-to-do men and women of goodwill who had gone out to offer personal service and friendship to the dwellers in the slums found themselves transformed into a body of amateur detectives, in some cases initiating prosecutions of persons they thought to be impostors, and arousing more suspicion and hatred than the recognized officers of the law. The pioneers of organized charity had made unwittingly an ominous discovery. By rudely tearing off the wrappings of medieval almsgiving disguising the skeleton at the feast of capitalist civilization, they had let loose the tragic truth that, wherever society is divided into a minority of 'haves' and a multitude of 'have nots', charity is twice cursed, it curseth him that gives and him that takes. Under such circumstances, to quote the phrase of Louise Michel, 'philanthropy is a lie'. For human relationships, whether between individuals, groups or races, do not thrive in an emotional vacuum; if you tune out fellow-feeling and the common consciousness of a social equity, you tune in insolence, envy and 'the wrath that is to come'.

The theory and practice of the Charity Organization Society, in spite of its vogue among those who counted themselves enlightened, found small acceptance among the Christian Churches, any more than among the impulsive givers of alms. Thus the C.O.S. found itself baulked in its purpose of organizing the multifarious charities of the metropolis; neither the Churches nor the hospitals, neither the orphanages nor the agencies for providing the destitute with food, clothing or shelter, would have anything to do with a society which sought to impose methods that appeared the very negation of Christian charity. Instead of serving as a co-ordinating body to all the other charities, in order to prevent their harmful overlapping and wasteful competition, the C.O.S. became itself the most exclusive of sects, making a merit of disapproving and denouncing much of the practice of other charitable agencies (for instance, the social activities of the Salvation Army); and at the same time failing to obtain anything like the army of personal 'friends of the poor', or anything approaching the great amount of money, that would have enabled it to cope, on its own principles, with the vast ocean of poverty that had somehow to be dealt with. The C.O.S. went yet one step further. It had become apparent, even in early Victorian times, that the greater part of the work of preventing destitution, as distinguished from relieving it after it had occurred, necessarily transcended individual capacity, and must be undertaken, if at all, by a public authority, with compulsory powers of dealing with private property, and at the expense of public funds. The great Scottish forerunner of charity organization, Thomas Chalmers, whilst strongly objecting both to almsgiving and to the outdoor relief of the Poor Law authorities, had equally strenuously supported the public provision, even, if need be, gratuitously, of universal schooling for the children and of universal medical and surgical treatment, both institutional and domiciliary, for the sick and infirm of all kinds; and most remarkable of all, a universal provision, preferably by private philanthropy, of honourable pensions and almshouses for all the aged who found themselves in need of such aid. In London, Edwin Chadwick, who had so large a share in the great Poor Law Report of 1834, was in these years still able to describe how he had been at first convinced that it was the indiscriminate, inadequate and unconditional outdoor relief of the old Poor Law that was the cause of the great mass of destitution. A very few years of actual administration of the Act of 1834 had, however, taught him that the mere arrest of demoralizing dole-giving, admirable as it was, left untouched the fundamental causes of destitution, especially among the most deserving. Within a decade Edwin Chadwick had become as infatuated an advocate of positive municipal action in the provision of drainage, paving, water supply, open spaces, improved dwellings, hospitals and what not, as he had ever been of the stoppage of outdoor relief and charitable doles. But the C.O.S. had apparently forgotten the experience of these forerunners. Its leading members added to their sectarian creed as to the necessary restrictions of the impulse of charity, an equally determined resistance to any extension of State or municipal action, whether in the way of physical care of children at school, housing accommodation, medical attendance, or old-age pensions, however plausibly it might be argued, in the spirit of Chalmers and Chadwick, that only by such collective action could there be any effective prevention of the perennial recruiting of the army of destitutes. Hence Octavia Hill, C. S. Loch and their immediate followers concentrated their activities on schooling the poor in industry, honesty, thrift and filial piety; whilst advocating, in occasional asides, or by parenthetical phrases, the moralization of the existing governing class, and its spontaneous conversion to a benevolent use of its necessarily dominant wealth and power.

The common basis underlying the principle of restricting private charity to exceptional cases, and the analogous but not necessarily related principle of governmental *laissez-faire*, is easily discovered. However well aware these estimable leaders of the C.O.S. may have been of personal shortcomings, they, unlike many of their contemporaries, had not the faintest glimmer of what I have called 'the consciousness of collective sin'.[23] In their opinion, modern

23. One of the jarring notes of the C.O.S. was their calm assumption of social and mental superiority over the poor whom they visited. In these more democratic days, how odd sounds the following description of Octavia Hill's 'At Home' to her old tenants, related by Mrs Barnett with perhaps a touch of irony. 'I recall the guests coming in shyly by the back entrance, and the rather exaggerated cordiality of Miss Octavia's greeting in the effort to make them feel welcome; and Miss Miranda's bright tender way of speaking to everyone exactly alike, were they rich or poor; and old Mrs Hill's curious voice with its rather rasping purr of pride and pleasure and large-heartedness, as she surveyed her motley groups of friends; and the two Miss Harrisons [who presumably had entered the house by the front door], those beautiful and generous artistic souls, the one so fat and short and the other so tall and thin, and their duet, purposely wrongly rendered to provoke the communion of laughter, ending with the invitation to everyone to say 'Quack, quack', as loudly as each was able, if only to prove they were all 'ducks'. Miss F. Davenport Hill was there, and Mr C. E. Maurice and Miss Emma Cons and Miss Emily Hill and

capitalism was the best of all possible ways of organizing industries and services; and if only meddlesome persons would refrain from interfering with its operations, the maximum social welfare as well as the maximum national wealth would be secured for the whole community. Barring accident to life and health, which happens to both rich and poor, any family could, they assumed, maintain its 'independence' from the cradle to the grave, if only its members were reasonably industrious, thrifty, honest, sober and dutiful. Thus any attempt by private or public expenditure to alter 'artificially' the economic environment of the manual-working class so as to lessen the severity of the 'natural' struggle for existence must, they imagined, inevitably undermine these essential elements of personal character, and would, in the vast majority of cases, make the state of affairs worse than before, if not for the individual, at any rate for the class and the race. Thus, in the world of philanthropy as in the world of politics, as I knew it in the eighties, there seemed to be one predominant question: Were we or were we not to assume the continuance of the capitalist system as it then existed and if not, could we, by taking thought, mend or end it?

The break-away of Samuel and Henrietta Barnett in 1886 from the narrow and continuously hardening dogma of the Charity Organization Society sent a thrill through the philanthropic world of London. The denunciation of indiscriminate charity in 1874 (quoted above) was not recanted. But during the intervening twelve years' residence in the very midst of the worst misery of the East End of London, the Barnetts had followed in the footsteps of Robert Chalmers and Edwin Chadwick. They had discovered for themselves that there was a deeper and more continuous evil than unrestricted and unregulated charity, namely, unrestricted and unregulated capitalism and landlordism. They had become aware of the employment of labour at starvation rates; of the rack-renting of insanitary tenements; of the ab-

Mr Barnett. . . .' (*Canon Barnett, His Life, Work, and Friends*, by his wife, vol. i. p. 34).

sence of opportunities for education, for refined leisure and for the enjoyment of nature, literature and art among the denizens of the mean streets; they had come to realize that the principles of personal service and personal responsibility for ulterior consequences, together with the application of the scientific method, ought to be extended, from the comparatively trivial activity of almsgiving to the behaviour of the employer, the landlord and the consumer of wealth without work. Their eyes had been opened, in fact, to all the sins of commission and omission, whether voluntary or involuntary, committed by the relatively small minority of the nation who, by means of their status or possessions, exercised economic power over the masses of their fellow-countrymen. Thus without becoming Socialists, in either the academic or the revolutionary meaning of the term, they initiated or furthered a long series of socialistic measures, all involving increased public expenditure and public administration, of which Samuel Barnett's advocacy in 1883 of universal state-provided old-age pensions may be taken as a type – an advocacy which, be it added, eventually converted Charles Booth, and led to his remarkable demonstration of the expediency and practicability of pensions to the aged poor. But what appealed most insistently to the rector of St Jude's was not the provision of the necessaries of life, but the provision of the pleasures of life. 'I do not want many alterations in the law,' modestly explained Samuel Barnett to an interviewer in 1892,

but I should like the best things made free. We want many more baths and wash-houses, especially swimming baths; and they should be free and open in every district. Books and pictures should be freely shown, so that every man may have a public library or a picture gallery as his drawing-room, where he can enjoy what is good with his boys and girls. We want more open spaces, so that every man, woman and child might sit in the open air and see the sky and the sunset. . . . We want free provision of the best forms of pleasure. Denmark provides travelling scholarships, and our school authorities are taking steps in that direction. . . . Poverty cannot pay for the pleasure which satisfies, and yet, without that pleasure, the people perish.[24]

24. ibid., vol. ii. p. 12.

How can I make my readers see, as they are engraved in memory, the figures of Samuel and Henrietta Barnett, and the impression they made on the philanthropic workers and social investigators of the London of the eighties?

First Rector of St Jude's and founder of Toynbee Hall, a diminutive body clothed in shabby and badly assorted garments, big knobby and prematurely bald head, small black eyes set close together, sallow complexion and a thin and patchy pretence of a beard, Barnett, at first sight, was not pleasing to contemplate! Yet, with growing intimacy, you found yourself continuously looking at him, watching the swift changes in expression, detached but keen observation of the persons present, followed by a warmly appreciative smile at something said; the far-away, wondering look of a questioning mind, passing suddenly and unexpectedly into emotional enthusiasm or moral indignation, and then melting back again into the calmness of an argumentative intelligence. And as an always present background for these rapid transformations, an utter absence of personal vanity, an almost exaggerated Christian humility, arising perhaps from what the modern psychologist calls a permanent 'inferiority complex' – an attitude especially marked towards his adored and gifted wife!

What charmed his comrades at work in the East End, and I speak from personal experience, was Barnett's fathomless sympathy; his 'quickness at the uptake' of your moral and intellectual perplexities; his inspiring encouragement for your strivings after the nobler self. But this nineteenth-century saint had his limitations, alike as an ecclesiastic and a citizen. He had no special intellectual or artistic gifts; he was neither a scholar nor a skilled researcher; he was not a reasoner nor a scientific observer; he had no personal magnetism as a preacher, no fluency as a lecturer; he had no special talent in the choice and use of words. Meticulous lawyers found him muddle-headed when explaining schemes of reform; fanatics discovered indispensable links absent in the consistent working out of a creed; and hard-sensed and literal-minded men and women felt that he was Jesuitical in the way he jumped from standpoint to standpoint in search of common ground upon which might be based united action in the direction he desired.[25] He was, in fact, far too intent on what he conceived to be the purpose of human life – a noble state of mind in each individual and in the community as a whole – to concentrate on the processes by which this end could be reached. These shortcomings were the defects of one outstanding characteristic. Samuel Barnett journeyed through life 'as if' he was in continuous communion with an external spirit of love; and 'as if' man's purpose on earth was to make this spirit of love supreme in society. Men and women, however vicious or stupid they might be, were approached 'as if' each one of them had an immortal soul. 'Do you believe in personal immortality?' his wife asked him. 'I can imagine life on no other basis,' he replied.[26] More expressive of Barnett's mentality than any words of mine is an entry in his diary when a very young man, which his wife tells us was always kept in his private drawer as his ideal of life. 'When I calmly think what is best in life I see it is goodness; that which I feel to be good, which means restraint from spite, impurity, or greed, and which manifests itself in love. Goodness is more desirable than power. I set myself to gain goodness. I check all emotions towards its opposite and I reach out to contemplate itself. I try to find what that is of which I feel my impressions of goodness to be but a shadow. There is somewhere perfect goodness. I commune with ideas of goodness which is equivalent to praying to God. Across my vision passes a figure of perfect Man. I am seized, borne

25. Mrs Barnett, with characteristic candour, quotes C. S. Loch's somewhat ungenerous characterization of her husband – be it added, in the heat of controversy! 'With Mr Barnett progress is a series of reactions. He must be in harmony with the current philanthropic opinion of the moment or perhaps just a few seconds ahead of it. Then having laid great stress on a new point, he would "turn his back on himself" and lay equal stress on the point that he had before insisted on. Thus, he was at one time in favour of suppressing outdoor relief and promoting thrift, now he favours outdoor relief in a new guise' (this is Mr Loch's phrase for old-age pensions) and depreciates thrift' (ibid., p. 267).

26. ibid., p. 379.

on by Jesus Christ. In communing with Him I find the greatest help to reaching goodness. I pray to Jesus Christ and through Him come to the Father.'[27] Hence his never-failing optimism about the future; tempered, be it added, by recurring waves of depression with regard to the actual working of human nature as he surveyed it, in his day-by-day experience of men and affairs, from the heights of his own scale of values.

Thus Samuel Barnett was not wholly representative of the mid-Victorian Time-Spirit: he carried over some of the mysticism of what we are apt to call 'primitive christianity'; an overwhelming faith in the validity of the dominant impulse of the Christ and the Buddha; beneficence towards all human beings irrespective of their characteristics.

Is it an impertinence to write about one who is still with us? My excuse is that the Barnetts were an early example of a new type of human personality, in after years not uncommon; a double-star-personality, the light of the one being indistinguishable from that of the other.

At nineteen years of age, pretty, witty, and well-to-do, Henrietta Rowland married the plain and insignificant curate who was her fellow-worker in the parish of St Marylebone; not solely, so I gather from her own account, because he had won her admiration and affection, but also as a way of dedicating her life to the service of the poor. In many of her characteristics she was the direct antithesis of her husband, and, exactly on this account, she served as complement to him, as he did to her. Assuredly she was not hampered by the 'inferiority complex!' A breezy self-confidence, a naïve self-assertion – sometimes to the border-line of bad manners – was her note towards the world at large. Lavishly admiring, loving and loyal towards friends and comrades, her attitude towards those whose conduct she condemned – for instance, towards the heartless rich, the sweating employer, or the rack-renting landlord – was that they required 'spanking', and that she was prepared to carry out this chastisement, always assuming that she thought it would lead to their

27. ibid., p. 97.

reformation! She may have been influenced by her husband's mysticism, but her native bent was a rationalist interpretation of the facts of life. The emotion that was the warp of her weft was not the merging of self in a force that makes for righteousness, but the service of man, or rather of the men and women in her near neighbourhood. To this vocation she brought a keener and more practical intellect than her husband; a directness of intention and of speech which excited sometimes admiration, sometimes consternation, in her associates; and, be it added, a sense of humour which was 'masculine' in its broadness, offensive to the fastidious and invigorating to those who enjoyed laughter at the absurdities of their own and other people's human nature. For all the business side of philanthropy, for initiation, advertisement, negotiation and execution, her gifts rose at times to veritable genius.

To this sketch I add an entry in the MS. diary illustrating the influence of the Barnetts over their fellow-workers.

Visit of three days from the Barnetts, which has confirmed my friendship with them. Mr Barnett distinguished for unselfconsciousness, humility and faith. Intellectually he is suggestive; with a sort of moral insight almost like that of a woman. And in another respect he is like a strong woman. He is much more anxious that human nature should *feel rightly* than that they should *think truly*, and *being* is more important with him than doing. He told me that Comte, F. D. Maurice and history had influenced him most. But evidently the influence had been more on his character than on his intellect; for intellectually he has no system of thought, no consistent bias – his thought is only the tool whereby his feeling expresses itself.

He was very sympathetic about my work and anxious to be helpful. But he foresaw in it dangers to my character; and it was curious to watch the minister's anxiety about the *morale* of his friend creep out in all kinds of hints. He held up as a moral scarecrow the 'Osford Don' – the man or woman without human ties – with no care for the details of life. He told his wife that I reminded him of Octavia Hill; and as he described Miss Hill's life as one of isolation from superiors and from inferiors, it is clear what rocks he saw ahead. I tried to explain to him my doctrine of nervous energy: that you are only gifted with a certain quantity, and that if it were spent in detail it could not be reserved for large undertakings. But as he suggested very truly, if all the thought and time spent on egotistical castle-building or brooding were spent on others, your neighbourly and household duties would be well fulfilled without encroaching on the fund reserved for your work.

Mrs Barnett is an active-minded, true and warm-hearted woman. She is conceited; she would be objectionably conceited if it were not for her genuine belief in her husband's superiority – not only to the rest of the world (which would be only another form of conceit) – but to herself. Her constant flow of spirits, her invigorating energy, is incalculably helpful to her husband. Her nature is saturated with courage and with truthfulness; her sympathies are keen, and her power of admiration for others strong. Her personal aim in life is to raise womanhood to its rightful position; as equal [to] though unlike manhood. The crusade she has undertaken is the fight against impurity as the main factor in debasing women from a status of independence to one of physical dependence. The common opinion that a woman is a nonentity unless joined to a man, she resents as a 'blasphemy'. Like all crusaders, she is bigoted, and does not recognize all the facts that tell against her faith. I told her that the only way in which we can convince the world of our power is to show it. And for that it will be needful for women with strong natures to remain celibate; so that the special force of womanhood – motherly feeling – may be forced into public work.

In religious faith Mr Barnett is an idealistic Christian without dogma, and Mrs Barnett an agnostic with idealism; in social faith, the man a Christian Socialist, the woman an individualist. The woman is really the more masculine-minded of the two. Mr Barnett's personal aim is to raise the desires of men and women – to cultivate their higher tastes: to give the poor the luxuries and not the necessaries of life. The danger which I foresee of mental strain, and thence melancholy, he looks upon as imaginary. And I think myself, that in my fear of melancholy for the race, I am governed by the bias of my own rather morbid constitution. It was not an overstrained mind which made our Aked relations suicidal: they were innocent of intellectual effort. And I have inherited the suicidal constitution, and, naturally enough, I connect it with other qualities of my nature, whereas it may be only co-existent with these qualities.

The Barnetts' visit braced me up to further effort and stronger resignation. But in my work of observation, I must endeavour to get in front of my own shadow – else I shall end by disbelieving in sunshine! [MS. diary, 29 August 1887.]

The result upon my mind of the controversy between the rigid voluntaryism of the Charity Organization Society, on the one hand, and on the other, the empirical socialism of Samuel and Henrietta Barnett, was a deepening conviction that the facts collected by philanthropists – by small groups of heroic men and women struggling, day in and day out, under depressing circumstances, with crowds of destitute persons clamouring for alms – were too doubtful and restricted to lead to any proven conclusion as to the meaning of poverty in the midst of riches. What was the actual extent and intensity of this destitution? Could it be explained by the shortcomings of the destitute persons or families themselves, whether by delinquency, drunkenness, unwillingness to work, or a lack of practicable thrift, all forms of bad behaviour which were likely to be aggravated by the thoughtless alms-giving of the rich? And in the case of admittedly deserving persons, was the destitution existing in East London confined to particular areas, or to groups of families exceptionally affected by epidemics or by temporary dislocations of trade? Or were we confronted, as the Socialists were perpetually re-iterating, with a mass of fellow-citizens, constituting a large proportion of the inhabitants of Great Britain, and made up of men and women of all degrees of sobriety, honesty and capacity, who were habitually in a state of chronic poverty, and who throughout their lives were shut out from all that makes civilization worth having? My state of mind at that date can, I think, be best expressed in the words of Charles Darwin, when he was puzzling over the problem of the emergence of man.

I have often experienced [he writes to Sir Joseph Hooker] what you call the humiliating feeling of getting more and more in-volved in doubt, the more one thinks of the facts and reasoning on doubtful points. But I always comfort myself with thinking of the future, and in the full belief that the problems which we are just entering on, will some day be solved; and if we just break the ground we shall have done some service, even if we reap no harvest.[28]

Now it is exactly this process of 'breaking the ground' over a sufficiently large area, without too anxiously reckoning the harvest, that I shall describe in the following chapter.

28. Letter from C. Darwin to J. D. Hooker, 20 January 1859, *Life and Letters of Charles Darwin*, by Francis Darwin, vol. ii. p. 144 (1887).

## CHAPTER 5

※·c··ɔ·※

## A Grand Inquest into the Condition
## of the People of London

So far, I have described as my intellectual environment the then closely interrelated worlds of politics and metropolitan philanthropy. I now come to a great enterprise which aroused my whole-hearted sympathy and admiration; an enterprise in which I played the minor part of an industrious apprentice. Here the impulse came neither from politics nor from philanthropy, but from scientific curiosity; from the desire to apply the method of observation, reasoning and verification to the problem of poverty in the midst of riches.

Now, every man is apt to overrate the significance of an event with which he has been intimately associated. But the grand inquest into the conditions of life and labour of the four million inhabitants of the richest city in the world – an investigation carried on by Charles Booth (entirely at his own expense) over a period of seventeen years and published in as many volumes – seems to me to stand out as a landmark alike in social politics and in economic science. Prior to this inquiry, neither the individualist nor the Socialist could state with any approach to accuracy what exactly was the condition of the people of Great Britain. Hence the unreality of their controversy. And if, as I am inclined to believe, a subtle combination of quantitative and qualitative analysis is a necessary factor in social studies, it may well be that Charles Booth's elaborate plan of wide statistical verification of data obtained by detailed observation of individual families and social institutions will be recognized as an indispensable basis of sociological science. In comparison with the preceding generations of social researchers, I suggest that his method of analysis constitutes, if not the starting-point, certainly the first sign-post directing the student on one of the main ways to discovery. Unfortunately Charles Booth, partly owing to his modesty and partly owing to his voluminous output, failed, like so many other successful organizers, to describe his own plan of campaign; and for this reason I do not hesitate to attempt to sketch into my picture this eminent Victorian and his work.

In the short and modest memoir by his wife[1] we are given in bare outline the circumstance of his birth and breeding. We are introduced into the family circle of the Booths, Fletchers, Cromptons and Holts, for the most part Liverpool merchants and shipowners, Liberals or Radicals in political opinion, and Unitarian by religious conviction. We are told that he lived at home with his brothers and sisters, getting his education at the first-grade secondary day school of the Royal Institution of Liverpool; and passing, whilst yet in his teens, into a business career through the office of Messrs Lamport & Holt; spending his leisure either in study or in disputatious talk within the large family circle of brothers, sisters, and cousins; or engaging in enthusiastic propaganda as a member of the newly formed Birmingham Education League, with its programme of universal secular education; or, through his friendship with working men, taking thought about the affairs of the Liverpool Trades Council. One has a vision of a group of families living simple and strenuous lives, with a high standard of work, and small requirements in the way of games, sport and less desirable forms of pleasure. Nor was the higher thought neglected; for, owing to his intimacy with his two cousins Harry and Albert Crompton, leading members of the 'Church of Humanity', Charles Booth came under the influence of Auguste

1. *Charles Booth – A Memoir* (Macmillan, 1918) [by Mrs Charles Booth]. Shipowner and merchant by profession, Charles Booth became in later life a Privy Councillor, F.R.S., and Honorary Doctor of Oxford, Cambridge and Liverpool. He married Mary, daughter of Charles Zachary Macaulay (brother of the historian), and granddaughter of my own grandfather, Richard Potter, M.P. for Wigan.

Comte. Perpetually discussing the philosophy of Positivism and the social theories arising out of it with such leading Positivists as Dr Bridges and Professor Beesly, the Frederic Harrisons and the Lushingtons, Charles Booth – to quote the words of the *Memoir* – 'was fairly captivated, and his formal adhesion to the ranks of Positivism was held to be only a matter of time' – an expectation which was not fulfilled; for 'his nature, though enthusiastic, had many needs, many aspirations difficult to satisfy, and not easily combined within the limits of any formal body of doctrine'. In 1871 he married the attractive and accomplished daughter of Charles Macaulay, who happened to be my cousin, and who had met him for the first time at the house of my eldest sister, the wife of R. D. Holt.[2] Meanwhile, his multifarious activities, carried on from early morning to late at night, whether in the ship-owning venture which he started with his brother, or in political propaganda or continuous reading, caused a severe breakdown in health, which necessitated some years abroad, and a long period of inability to work or even read.

It was during the period of his convalescence, I think in the late seventies, that my cousin brought her husband for the first time to stay with us. I recall with some amusement the impression made on a girl's mind by this interesting new relative. Nearing forty years of age, tall, abnormally thin, garments hanging as if on pegs, the complexion of a consumptive girl, and the slight stoop of the sedentary worker, a prominent aquiline nose, with moustache and pointed beard

2. Robert Durning Holt, who married my eldest sister Laurencina in 1867, was the youngest of five brothers of a remarkable family, Unitarians and Liberals, which for a whole generation dominated the management of two great and successful shipping companies of Liverpool, took a prominent part in the municipal life, and were munificent benefactors of the local University. My brother-in-law was a member of the Royal Commission on London Government, 1893–4. He was probably the only man who found himself actually gazetted as a baronet against his will, his humorous letter of refusal having been taken by Lord Rosebery as an acceptance. Reinforced by the indignant protests of his wife (who vehemently objected, as a good Radical, to all social inequalities) he insisted on the honour being cancelled.

barely hiding a noticeable Adam's apple, the whole countenance dominated by a finely-moulded brow and large, observant grey eyes, Charles Booth was an attractive but
distinctly queer figure of a man. One quaint sight stays in
my mind: Cousin Charlie sitting through the family meals,
'like patience on a monument smiling at' – other people
eating, whilst, as a concession to good manners, he occasionally picked at a potato with his fork or nibbled a dry biscuit.
Fascinating was his unselfconscious manner and eager curiosity to know what you thought and why you thought it;
what you knew and how you had learnt it. And there was the
additional interest of trying to place this strange individual
in the general scheme of things. No longer young, he had
neither failed nor succeeded in life, and one was left in doubt
whether the striking unconventionality betokened an initiating brain or a futile eccentricity. Observed by a stranger,
he might have passed for a self-educated idealistic compositor or engineering draughtsman; or as the wayward
member of an aristocratic family of the Auberon Herbert
type; or as a university professor; or, clean shaven and with
the appropriate collar, as an ascetic priest, Roman or Anglican; with another change of attire, he would have 'made
up' as an artist in the Latin Quarter. The one vocation which
seemed ruled out, alike by his appearance and by his idealistic temperament, was that of a great captain of industry
pushing his way, by sheer will-power and methodical industry, hardened and sharpened by an independent attitude
towards other people's intentions and views – except as circumstances which had to be wisely handled – into new countries, new processes and new business connections. And yet
this kind of adventurous and, as it turned out, successful
profit-making enterprise proved to be his destiny, bringing
in its train the personal power and free initiative due to a
large income generously spent.

Though I gather from the *Memoir* that business organization was the career of his choice,[3] Charles Booth had also

3. The attitude of Charles Booth towards profit-making enterprise is
described in the *Memoir*: 'Those who imagined that a business life

the scientific impulse, in his case directed towards the structure and working of society. Without the specific genius of Charles Darwin and Francis Galton for imaginative hypothesis and for verification by observation, experiment and reasoning, he likened these two great scientists in possessing, in a high degree, the scientific temperament: an overpowering curiosity about the nature of things; originality in designing ways and means of research; and above all, a splendid courage and persistency in the pursuit of knowledge. Further, Charles Booth was singularly appreciative of any suggestions, however irrelevant or far-fetched these might seem, from fellow-workers and subordinates. In the prime of life he delighted in upsetting generally accepted views, whether the free-trade orthodoxy of Manchester capitalism, at that time in the ascendant, or the cut and dried creed of the Marxian socialist. Indeed, if he had a bias as an investigator, it was in favour of the unlikely and unpopular explanation of a given series of facts. And combined with intellectual curiosity was the positivist conception of the service of man. In short, Charles Booth was, within my circle of friends, perhaps the most perfect embodiment of what I have described in a former chapter as the mid-Victorian timespirit – the union of faith in the scientific method with the transference of the emotion of self-sacrificing service from God to man.

I will end this slight sketch of Charles Booth's personality

---

must be dull, wanting in the interest and charm attending political, literary, or scientific pursuits, filled him with amazement. To him the living forces that stir the great pendulum of trade; the hazards to be incurred in new portions of the work of a great concern; the sharp reminders of failure given by the actual loss of money when any undertaking had been begun too rashly, or conducted with insufficient insight; above all, the contact with a set of men working towards one end, and in hourly touch with the realities of existence: all this delighted and absorbed him' (p. 93).

A significant and well-documented analysis of his outlook on public affairs after twenty years of successful business and sociological investigation is given in the chapter on Business, pp. 93–103, and in that on Industrial Policy, pp. 155–71, in the *Memoir* by his wife.

by an entry from my diary giving a glimpse of these favourite cousins as I knew them in the first years of intimacy.

The last six weeks spent in London, with friends and sisters. The Booths' house dark and airless, but the inmates exceedingly charming and lovable. Mary, really a remarkable woman, with an unusual power of expression, and a well-trained and cultivated mind. She makes one feel, in spite of her appreciative and almost flattering attitude, 'a very ignoramus'. To me there is a slight narrowness in her literary judgements; they are too correct, too resting on authority? hardly the result of original thought? Perhaps it is this very orderliness of mind and deference to authority which makes her so attractive as a woman; for, added to this culture and polish of the intellect, there is a deep vein of emotion, of almost passionate feeling.

Charlie Booth has a stronger and clearer reason, with a singular absence of bias and prejudice. It is difficult to discover the presence of any vice or even weakness in him. Conscience, reason and dutiful affection, are his great qualities; other characteristics are not observable by the ordinary friend. He interests me as a man who has his nature completely under control; who has passed through a period of terrible illness and weakness, and who has risen out of it, uncynical, vigorous and energetic in mind, and without egotism. Many delightful conversations I had with these two charming cousins, generally acting as a listening third to their discussions. [MS. diary, 9 February 1882.]

## Poverty in the Midst of Riches

It pleases me to find in the *Memoir* by his wife, confirmed by his own words, that Charles Booth, in selecting the subject for investigation, was influenced by exactly the currents of thought and feeling, notably the controversies in the worlds of politics and philanthropy, which I have described in the foregoing pages as determining my own choice of a field for research.

Settled in London, where he had opened a branch of his shipowning and merchant business, he became aware of the new ferment.

People's minds were very full of the various problems connected with the position of the poor, and opinions the most diverse were expressed, remedies of the most contradictory nature were proposed [we are told by the author of the *Memoir*]. The works of Ruskin, the labours of Miss Octavia Hill, the principles and practice of the C.O.S., all contributed to the upheaval of thought and feeling. The simple, warm-hearted and thoughtless benevolence of former ages was held up to reprobation. . . . In the opinion of some, the great evils to be met were improvidence and self-indulgence. To relieve from the consequences of these was to aggravate the mischief. Yet another view was held, that the selfishness and vice of low lives was the result of the selfishness and vice of high lives; that the first duty of the rich was to produce among their poorer neighbours the physical condition which alone could render decent existence possible. Good air, more room, better clothes, better food and similar advantages would exorcize the demon which ran rife. 'Stimulate private charity,' said one school. 'Relieve the rates. It is the State-paid pauper who is the source of all harm.' 'Down with charity,' said another set; 'the very word has become a degradation. Let the State see to it that the toiling millions are fed and housed as they should be.' 'Toiling millions!' would be replied. 'The people who are in want never really toil at all. They are wastrels, lazy and ill-tempered. No one in England who will work need want.' . . . These various views, and many others, were listened to by Charles Booth, and ever more earnestly did he seek an answer to the question. Who are the people of England? How do they really live? What do they really want? Do they want what is good, and if so, how is it to be given to them?[4]

It is the sense of helplessness that tries everyone [explains Charles Booth in the paper read before the Royal Statistical Society on the Condition and Occupations of the people of the Tower Hamlets in May 1887]. The wage-earners are helpless to regulate or obtain the value of their work; the manufacturer or dealer can only work within the limits of competition; the rich are helpless to relieve want without stimulating its sources; the legislature is helpless because the limits of successful interference by change of law are closely circumscribed. From the helpless feelings spring socialistic theories, passionate suggestions of ignorance, setting at naught the nature of man and neglecting all the fundamental facts of human existence.

4. *Charles Booth – A Memoir* (Macmillan, 1918), by Mrs Charles Booth, pp. 13–15.

To relieve this sense of helplessness, the problems of human life must be better stated. The *à priori* reasoning of political economy, orthodox and unorthodox alike, fails from want of reality. At its base are a series of assumptions very imperfectly connected with the observed facts of life. We need to begin with a true picture of the modern industrial organism, the interchange of service, the exercise of faculty, the demands and satisfaction of desire. It is the possibility of such a picture as this that I wish to suggest, and it is as a contribution to it that I have written this paper.[5]

## The Scope of the Inquiry

The East End of London, an area made up of the Tower Hamlets and the Hackney School Board divisions, and comprising one million inhabitants, was first surveyed. He chose this particular district of the metropolis, one quarter of the whole, because, to cite his own words, 'it is supposed to contain the most destitute population in England, and to be, as it were, the focus of the problem of poverty in the midst of wealth, which is troubling the minds and hearts of so many people'.[6] Of this vast aggregate in its completeness, he sought 'to produce an instantaneous picture, fixing the facts on my negative as they appear at a given moment, and the imagination of my readers must add the movement, the constant changes, the whirl and turmoil of life' [Poverty, i. p. 26].[7] He made no attempt at history or even at describing

5. *Condition and Occupations of the People of the Tower Hamlets, 1886–87*, by Charles Booth, 1887, p. 7.

6. ibid., p. 4; a paper read before the Royal Statistical Society, May 1887.

7. This huge inquiry, begun in 1886, resulted in a series of volumes the publication of which extended over many years. The first volume, dealing with the East End of London, appeared in 1889; and those relating to Central and South London in 1891. These were included, in 1902–3, with the remaining results of the inquiry, in a new and definitive edition entitled *Life and Labour of the People in London*, in which the subject-matter was rearranged, revised by the 1891 census, and extended to seventeen volumes. These volumes comprised four on 'Poverty' (which I shall cite as Poverty i. to iv.); five on 'Industry' (Industry i. to v.); seven on 'Religious Influences' (with which I do

233

contemporary development, but set himself to obtain, so to speak, an exact cross-section at a given moment, full from end to end of precise details, equally complete and equally microscopic over the whole field. Out of this multitudinous and infinitely diversified subject-matter he concentrated on two series of facts; first, the relative destitution, poverty or comfort of the home, and secondly, the character of the work from which the various bread-winners in the family derived their livelihood. Thus there were two separate and distinct inquiries carried on concurrently, each involving its own group of investigators and its own methods of investigation.

The general plan of the inquiry, as applying to the whole of London, is to divide the entire population by districts and by groups of trades, each answering to a similar division in the census; and then to deal with each district by a local inquiry, and with each group of trades by a trade inquiry. The principal object of the district inquiry would be to show the conditions under which the people live, but it would also give their employments; the principal object of the trade inquiry would be to show the conditions under which the people work, but it would indirectly deal with their manner of life. The double method would provide a check upon the results of each, and much light be thrown upon the one inquiry by the other.[8]

*Methods of Investigation*

How did Charles Booth obtain the mass and range of data required to complete this scientific exploration into the life and labour of the people of London?

The statistical framework outlining the whole, and defining the parts of the gigantic undertaking, was afforded by the census figures of 1881, afterwards corrected and

not deal except incidentally to the poverty and industry inquiry); and a 'Final Volume' entitled 'Notes on Social Influences and Conclusion' (to be cited as Final); together with a case of coloured maps, mounted and divided into convenient sections.

8. *Condition and Occupations of the People of the Tower Hamlets, 1886-7*, p. 2.

amplified by the more detailed census of 1891. With the scope and limitations of these statistical documents Charles Booth was already familiar; for prior to 1886 he had made a painstaking analysis of the figures giving the occupations of the people of the United Kingdom in the series of censuses from 1841 to 1881.[9] This inquiry was undertaken in order to ascertain how many persons depended at any one time for their subsistence on any particular trade; and how the distribution of the population among different industries and services had shifted from decade to decade. Owing to the divergent classification of persons and industries adopted by successive Registrars-General, the scientific result of this analysis and re-classification was disappointing. But it had given its author facility in the handling of such figures and an influential introduction to the census authorities. Thus, at the very outset of his inquiry he was able to obtain, not only all the published documents giving the numerical totals and rough classifications of the latest census, that of 1881, but he was also given access, by special favour of the Registrar-General, to the information, correct and incorrect, recorded in the Householders' Schedules. The census of 1891 proved to be of even greater value owing to the addition, in the Householders' Schedule, of two new questions, vital to the completion of the inquiry.[10] Each head of family or occupier

9. *Journal of Royal Statistical Society*, vol. 49, pp. 314-444, 1886.

10. It was stated by an official of the Board of Trade at the meeting of the Statistical Society, December 1893, that Charles Booth was a member of the official committee appointed to draw up the Householders' Schedules and make other arrangements for the 1891 census. He himself tells us that 'to meet the difficulty of novelty, and to make sure that the enumerators' work was carefully and intelligently performed, at any rate in London, I obtained the Registrar-General's permission to place myself in communication with the Registrars in each sub-district of the Metropolis, and through them with the enumerators themselves. I personally saw all the Registrars more than once, and discussed the subject with them, pointing out the object to be attained, and the important uses that could be made of the material to be collected; and my appeal was very heartily responded to both by them and by the enumerators. Amongst so many men (there were over three thousand enumerators in all) there could not be uniform

living in fewer than five rooms was asked to state the number of rooms occupied; and, in London at least, this information was in most instances obtained by the enumerators. Further, householders employing domestic servants were called upon to state the number they employed. Thus, Charles Booth was able to verify and revise, by the practically contemporary and complete enumeration of the Registrar-General, his classification of the entire population, from top to bottom, testing poverty by the degree of crowding in the dwelling, and affluence by the number of servants employed.

But it was clear to a scientific investigator that an inquiry dependent on the filling up of a form by each household had to restrict itself to the barest numerical data, and that such details as were given could not always be depended upon as accurate. Even so elementary a 'qualitative' fact as occupation had proved to be stated so vaguely as to be almost useless – employers, manual working wage-earners and salaried managers, together with the superannuated and those who had merely left the trade, being, for instance, all included under 'builders'. Hence individual inquiry and personal observation were indispensable. Many such investigations had been made, by all sorts of people and the most diverse agencies. But these had always been carried out over small fields, specially selected for one or other reason; and there were no means of deciding whether, and to what extent, they were representative of the whole people even of a single street. Charles Booth's invention was the combination of the census with the personal inquiry into each family, for the double purpose of making his survey co-extensive with the entire field, without selection, and of uniting the qualitative with the quantitative information thus obtained. By this cross-verification of wholesale statistics, by personal observation of individual cases, and the verification of the sum of individual cases obtained by personal obser-

---

excellence, and no doubt some may have performed the work in a perfunctory manner, but, on the whole, I was assured, and feel quite satisfied, that the work was well and conscientiously done.' [Industry, i. p. 12.]

vation by the statistics of the census, Charles Booth was not only able to produce a complete series of qualitative as well as quantitative descriptions of the households and their environment, but also to present this triumph of personal observation in a statistical framework covering the whole four millions of people.

Such a colossal investigation, dealing with nearly a million households, could obviously not be carried out, even in a decade, by one investigator or by any ordinary group of investigators. Some other instrument had to be found. This Charles Booth discovered in what I shall term the *Method of Wholesale Interviewing*. 'The root idea with which I began the work,' he tells us, 'was that every fact I needed was known to someone, and that the information had simply to be collected and put together.' [Final, p. 32.] In giving evidence before the Royal Commission on the Housing of the Poor, Joseph Chamberlain had incidentally mentioned that the Birmingham Town Council, in preparing its schemes for the clearance of slum areas, had found useful the very complete knowledge of each family possessed by the school attendance officers. Following this suggestion, Charles Booth obtained permission to arrange, with each of the sixty-six school attendance officers at work in the East End, to give a series of evenings, with his notebooks, as a witness submitting to patient examination by Charles Booth or one of his secretaries as to the facts of each household.

In the Tower Hamlets division, which was completed first, we gave on the average 19¾ hours' work to each School Board visitor; in the Hackney division this was increased to 23½ hours. St George's-in-the-East, when first done in 1886, cost 60 hours' work with the visitors; when revised it occupied 83 hours ... the task was so tremendous, the prospect of its completion so remote; and every detail cost time. ... [But] without this nothing could have been done. The merit of the information so obtained, looked at statistically, lies mainly in the breadth of view obtained. It is in effect the whole population that comes under review. Other agencies usually seek out some particular class or deal with some particular condition of people. The knowledge so obtained may be more exact, but it is circumscribed and very apt to produce a distortion of judgement. For this reason, the information to be had from the School Board visitors, with all its inequalities and imperfections, is excellent as a framework for a picture of the Life and Labour of the People. [Poverty, i. pp. 25–6.]

When Charles Booth extended the same methods of investigation to the whole of the county of London, thus including a total of four million inhabitants, he shortened his procedure of interviewing the school attendance officers.

In passing from the special study of East London to a review of the whole Metropolis the method of inquiry into the condition of the people was slightly changed. In dealing with East London (and afterwards with Central London and Battersea) the unit taken was the family. In extending over the larger area the street has been substituted as a working basis. Instead of noting the number of children going to school from each household with the employment and social position of its head, we have contented ourselves with stating the number of children street by street, dividing them as to class according to what is known of the parents, but giving only general particulars of the occupations. The result is, that the division of the population according to the conditions under which they live has been maintained, but that according to employment has been dropped. [Poverty, ii. p. 1.]

The information thus obtained, when fitted into the framework of the census figures and used to verify and amplify the inevitable inaccuracy of the Householders' Schedules, formed, as he told us, the solid groundwork of the inquiry.

They [school attendance officers] are in daily contact with the people and have a very considerable knowledge of the parents of the school children, especially of the poorest among them, and of the conditions under which they live. No one can go, as I have done, over the description of the inhabitants of street after street in this huge district [East London], taken house by house and family by family – full as it is of picturesque details noted down from the lips of the visitor to whose mind they have been recalled by the open pages of his own schedules – and doubt the genuine character of the information and its truth. Of the wealth of my material I have no doubt. I am indeed embarrassed by its mass, and by my resolution to make use of no fact to which I cannot give a quantitative value. The materials for sensational stories lie plentifully in every book of our notes; but, even if I had the skill to use my material in this way – that gift of the imagination which is called 'realistic' – I should not wish to use it here. There is struggling poverty, there is destitution, there is hunger, drunkenness, brutality, and crime; no one doubts that it is so. My object has been to attempt to show the numerical relation which poverty, misery, and depravity bear to regular earnings and comparative comfort, and to describe the general conditions under which each class lives. [Poverty, i. pp. 5—6.]

And here is a characteristic warning, from one who was primarily a statistician, to the eager observer of individual persons and families.

To judge rightly we need to bear both in mind, never to forget the numbers when thinking of the percentages, nor the percentages when thinking of the numbers. This last is difficult to those whose daily experience or whose imagination brings vividly before them the trials and sorrows of individual lives. They refuse to set off and balance the happy hours of the same class, or even of the same people, against these miseries; much less can they consent to bring the lot of other classes into the account, add up the opposing figures, and contentedly carry forward a credit balance. In the arithmetic of woe they can only add or multiply, they cannot subtract or divide. In intensity of feeling such as this, and not in statistics, lies the power to move the world. But by statistics must this power be guided if it would move the world aright. [Poverty, i. p. 179.]

On the few occasions when I attended these interviews it was enlightening to watch how Charles Booth, or one or other of his secretaries, would extract from the school attendance officer, bit by bit, the extensive and intimate information with regard to each family, the memory of these willing witnesses amplifying and illustrating the precisely recorded facts in their notebooks. What was of greater significance to 'the industrious apprentice' than any of the facts revealed was the way in which this method of wholesale interviewing and automatic recording blocked the working of personal bias. Each of the two or three hundred school attendance officers had doubtless his own predilections; one would be an optimist, another a pessimist; some were 'proletarian' in their sympathies, others were inclined to think an unemployed person was unemployable. But with so large a group of witnesses these different types of prejudice cancelled out. The same differences in temperament or experience may have been at work with the interviewers. But short of deliberate and malicious falsification it was impracticable for anyone taking part in extracting and swiftly recording specific facts about every individual in every house in every street throughout the metropolis, to produce a result which seriously, and a total which materially, falsified the aggregate of particulars. In a wholly beneficent sense, the inquirers, during the actual process of investigation, were not able to 'see the wood for the trees'; and were therefore incapable of prejudging, according to their several expectations, the size, the shape or the value of the wood as a whole. To change the metaphor, it was impracticable for the investigators so to minimize or maximize each separate item so as to produce a picture of the life and labour of the whole people according to the predilections of any or all of them. Hence it is not surprising that the completed results of the investigation frequently contradicted (as we are told by the chief organizer) the expectations of one or other investigator, and even of all of them.[11]

The information obtained through the census papers and the school attendance officers was extended and verified by innumerable other witnesses, such as the teachers[12] in the

11. 'I undoubtedly expected that this investigation would expose exaggerations, and it did so; but the actual poverty disclosed was so great, both in mass and in degree, and so absolutely certain, that I have gradually become equally anxious not to overstate.' [Poverty, i. p. 5.]

12. 'In describing the streets and various portions of London we have drawn upon many sources of information, but it must be borne in mind that the classification of the people rests in effect upon what

schools, the superintendents of artisans' dwellings and rent-collectors, sanitary inspectors and relieving officers, ministers of religion, district visitors, the C.O.S. and other philanthropic agencies. In the later stages of the inquiry the results obtained by this process of interviewing were supplemented and verified by the personal observation of the organizer of the inquiry and his staff of investigators.

At the outset we shut our eyes, fearing lest any prejudice of our own should colour the information we received. It was not till the books were finished that I or my secretaries ourselves visited the streets amongst which we had been living in imagination. But later we gained confidence, and made it a rule to see each street ourselves at the time we received the visitor's account of it. [Poverty, i. p. 25.]

Finally, Charles Booth completed his survey by the kind of personal experience of working-class life which I had enjoyed in 1883 among the Lancashire cotton operatives, and which I have described in the preceding chapter.

For three separate periods I have taken up quarters, each time for several weeks, where I was not known; and as a lodger have shared the lives of people who would figure in my schedules as belonging to Classes C, D and E. Being more or less boarded, as well as lodged, I became intimately acquainted with some of those I met, and the lives and habits of many others came naturally under observation. [Poverty, i. p. 158.]

---

the School Board attendance officers have told us of the homes and parents of the children in elementary schools. It has therefore seemed desirable to check the results thus obtained by looking at the same facts from the point of view of the teachers in the schools, who, though lacking some means of information open to the attendance officers as to the parents and homes, have a much more intimate knowledge of the children themselves. Moreover, from the regularity or irregularity of attendance, the condition in which the children come to school, the demands for remission of fees, and in many other ways, the teachers can, and usually do, acquire a very considerable knowledge of the parents, and a fair idea of the character of the home.' [Poverty, iii. p. 195.]

## The Eightfold Classification of the People

As I have already explained, the main purpose of Charles Booth's inquiry was to obtain an accurate statement of the number and proportion of families living in a state of misery, poverty, decent comfort and luxury respectively. But these vague words, which no two persons will interpret alike, were plainly insufficient for any purpose. He therefore formed for himself, after careful consideration, an eightfold classification according to the actual facts of each case, leaving it to the reader to affix to each class what descriptive adjective he pleased. The table of the eight classes under which all the four millions of people are marshalled, together with the explanatory note, I give below.

A. The lowest class of occasional labourers, loafers and semi-criminals.
B. Casual earnings – 'very poor'.
C. Intermittent earnings. ⎫
D. Small regular earnings. ⎬ together the 'poor'.
E. Regular standard earnings – above the line of poverty.
F. Higher class labour.
G. Lower middle class.
H. Upper middle class.

The divisions indicated here by 'poor' and 'very poor' are necessarily arbitrary. By the word 'poor' I mean to describe those who have a sufficiently regular though bare income, such as 18s. to 21s. per week for a moderate family, and by 'very poor' those who from any cause fall much below this standard. The 'poor' are those whose means may be sufficient, but are barely sufficient, for decent independent life; the 'very poor' those whose means are insufficient for this according to the usual standard of life in this country. My 'poor' may be described as living under a struggle to obtain the necessaries of life and make both ends meet; while the 'very poor' live in a state of chronic want. [Poverty, i. p. 33.]

And now we are in sight of the principal goal of Charles Booth's scientific exploration into the life and labour of the people of London. Sorting out the million families into his eight classes, he was able to give a definitive estimate of the economic and social condition of the whole of the inhabitants of the county of London. This descriptive analysis was, it is needless to say, far more accurate and complete in respect of the 80 per cent of the community coming under the jurisdiction of the school attendance officers than it was of the 20 per cent consisting of the upper and lower middle classes, about whom no information was obtained except the number of domestic servants employed. But this restriction of the data was of slight significance, seeing that the purpose of the investigation was to ascertain, in relation to the total, the number of persons living in a state of chronic destitution, the number of persons who might be accounted as poor – that is, living on the line of bare subsistence – and the number of persons belonging to the wage-earning class who were in a state of comparative comfort. The information obtained enabled him to construct a table showing the relative percentages of the whole contributed by these three classes of the population, together with another table classifying all this 80 per cent according to the degree of overcrowding. In the two compact tables given below the reader will find concentrated and condensed the quantitive results of Charles Booth's stupendous analysis of a million 'Householders' Schedule', tested and amplified by the method of wholesale interviewing of the school attendance officers and also by the testimony of all sorts and conditions of men, and reinforced by his own and his staff's personal observations.

## TABLE I
### Classification by Family Income

In volume ii of the Poverty Series the whole population (overestimated at the time at 4,309,000) is divided and described as follows:

| | | |
|---|---|---|
| Classes A and B (the very poor) | 354,444 or | 8·4% |
| Classes C and D (the poor) | 938,293 or | 22·3% |
| Classes E and F (comfortable working class, including all servants) | 2,166,503 or | 51·5% |
| Classes G and H ('lower middle', 'middle' and 'upper classes') | 749,930 or | 17·8% |
| | 4,209,170 | |
| Inmates of institutions | 99,830 | |
| | 4,309,000 (Estimated population, 1889.) | |

## TABLE 2
### *Classification by Number of Rooms Occupied*

| | | | | |
|---|---|---|---|---|
| Poor | (1) and (2) 3 or more persons per room | 492,370 or | 12·0% | |
| | (3) 2 and under 3 persons per room | 781,615 or | 19·0% | 19·5% |
| | Common lodging houses, etc. | 20,087 or | 0·5% | |
| Central | (4) 1 and under 2 persons per room | 962,780 or | 23·4% | |
| | (5) Less than 1 person per room | 153,471 or | 3·7% | |
| | (6) Occupying more than 4 rooms | 981,553 or | 23·9% | 56·4% |
| | Servants | 205,858 or | 5·0% | |
| | Persons living in large shops, etc. | 15,321 or | 0·4% | |
| Upper | (a) 4 or more persons to 1 servant | 227,832 or | 5·5% | |
| | (b) to (h) 3 or less persons to 1 servant | 248,493 or | 6·0% | 12·1% |
| | Inmates of hotels and boarding houses where servants are kept | 25,726 or | 0·6% | |
| | | 4,115,106 | | |
| | Inmates of institutions | 96,637 | | |
| | | 4,211,743 | | |

[Final, p. 9. It may be explained that the 'servants' in Table 2 are those employed by the 'Upper' section (Classes G and H of Table 1); and they are included in the 'Central' section as being of much the same social grade as this 56.4 per cent of the whole.]

## *The Physical and Social Environment of the Poor*

These tables, however, whilst revealing the standard of life measured in income and house-room, afford no information with regard to the physical and social environment in which the different classes of the community had perforce to live.

In the modern industrial city it is the poverty of the poor that, in a quite literal sense, is their destruction. In the sunlit and wind-swept spaces of a sparsely inhabited country, insufficient food and scanty clothing do not necessarily spell either disease or demoralization. But huddled in the poor quarters of a great city, a million poverty-stricken men, women and children, working, sleeping, eating, mating and being born under the perpetual shadow of buildings belching out smoke, sweating vermin, and excreting filth, make for themselves (though not, in the main, through their individual misdoing) a physical and social environment in which all but the strongest bodies and minds suffer continuous deterioration. These evil circumstances do not admit of quantitative measurement and statistical expression; even if we could weigh up and record the smoke, the vermin and the foul gases, it would tell us little or nothing about the physical misery and spiritual defilement of the victims. Realizing the importance of social environment, Charles Booth added to his investigations into income and house-room a detailed survey of the physical and social environment, an early but elaborate essay in what I may call social topography, from which I take one or two samples.

In the inner ring nearly all available space is used for building, and almost every house is filled up with families. It is easy to trace the process. One can see what were the original buildings; in many cases they are still standing, and between them, on the large gardens of a past state of things, has been built the small cottage property of today. Houses of three rooms, houses of two rooms, houses of one room – houses set back against a wall or back to back, fronting it may be on a narrow footway, with posts at each end and a gutter down the middle. Small courts contrived to utilize some space in the rear, and approached by an archway under the building which fronts the street. Of such sort are the poorest class of houses. Besides the evidence of configuration, these little places are often called 'gardens', telling their story with unintended irony. But in other cases all sentiment is dropped, and another tale about their origin finds expression in the name of 'So-and-so's rents' – not houses, nor dwellings, nor cottages, nor buildings, nor even a court or a yard, suggesting human needs, but just 'rents'. [Poverty, i. p. 30.]

The property is all very old, and it has been patched up and altered until it is difficult to distinguish one house from another. Small back yards have been utilized for building additional tenements. The property throughout is in a very bad condition, unsanitary and over-crowded; and it is stated (as a suggestive reason why so little has been done in the way of remedy) that until very recently the rent collector of the property was a brother of the sanitary inspector! A number of rooms are occupied by prostitutes of the most pronounced order. [Poverty, i. pp. 10, 11.]

Here the streets are blocked with those coming to buy, or sell, pigeons, canaries, rabbits, fowls, parrots, or guinea-pigs, and with them or separately all the appurtenances of bird or pet keeping. Through this crowd the seller of shell-fish pushes his barrow; on the outskirts of it are movable shooting galleries and patent

Aunt Sallies, while some man standing up in a dog-cart will dispose of racing tips in sealed envelopes to the East End sportsman. [Poverty, i. p. 67.]

Shelton Street was just wide enough for a vehicle to pass either way, with room between curb-stone and houses for one foot-passenger to walk; but vehicles would pass seldom, and foot-passengers would prefer the roadway to the risk of tearing their clothes against projecting nails. The houses, about forty in number, contained cellars, parlours, and first, second, and third floors, mostly two rooms on a floor, and few of the 200 families who lived here occupied more than one room. In little rooms no more than 8 ft square would be found living father, mother and several children. Some of the rooms, from the peculiar build of the houses (shallow houses with double frontage) would be fairly large and have a recess 6 ft wide for the bed, which in rare instances would be curtained off. If there was no curtain, anyone lying on the bed would perhaps be covered up and hidden, head and all, when a visitor was admitted, or perhaps no shyness would be felt. ... Drunkenness and dirt and bad language prevailed, and violence was common, reaching at times even to murder. Fifteen rooms out of twenty were filthy to the last degree, and the furniture in none of these would be worth 20s., in some cases not 5s. Not a room would be free from vermin, and in many life at night was unbearable. Several occupants have said that in hot weather they don't go to bed, but sit in their clothes in the least infested part of the room. What good is it, they said, to go to bed when you can't get a wink of sleep for bugs and fleas? A visitor in these rooms was fortunate indeed if he carried nothing of the kind away with him. ... The passage from the street to the back-door would be scarcely ever swept, to say nothing of being scrubbed. Most of the doors stood open all night as well as all day, and the passage and stairs gave shelter to many who were altogether homeless. Here the mother could stand with her baby, or sit with it on the stairs, or companions would huddle together in cold weather. The little yard at the back was only sufficient for dust-bin and closet and water-tap, serving for six or seven families. The water would be drawn from cisterns which were receptacles for refuse, and perhaps occasionally a dead cat. At one time the street was fever-stricken; the mortality was high, and the authorities interfered with good effect so that the sanitary condition of the street just before it was destroyed was better than it had been formerly. The houses looked ready to fall, many of them being out of the perpendicular. Gambling was the amusement of the street. Sentries would be posted, and if the police made a rush the offenders would slip into the open houses and hide until danger was past. Sunday afternoon and evening was the heyday time for this street. Every doorstep would be crowded by those who sat or stood with pipe and jug of beer, while lads lounged about, and the gutters would find amusement for not a few children with bare feet, their faces and hands besmeared, while the mud oozed through between their toes. Add to this a group of fifteen or twenty young men gambling in the middle of the street and you complete the general picture. [Poverty, ii. pp. 46–8.]

But all the inhabitants of these mean streets were not addicted to gambling and drink; a fair number were respectable citizens; though experience of their own environment sometimes led to seditious views, if not with regard to the government of their country, at any rate with regard to the government of the universe.

So, too, on the second floor there were till lately a father and son, billposters, of good character. The man is a notorious Atheist, one who holds forth on behalf of his creed under railway arches, saying that if there be a God he must be a monster to permit such misery as exists. This man suffers from heart disease, and the doctor tells him that some day in his excitement he will drop down dead. His room is full of Free-thought publications. On the third floor, and in the other rooms below, there lived people of orderly habits, the landlord being particular about his tenants. [Poverty, ii. p. 65.]

## The Map of Poverty

And here I come to what was perhaps the most impressive achievement, and certainly the most picturesque outcome of the whole inquiry. The economic and social circumstances of all the families of London were graphically displayed in a series of maps, carefully coloured, street by street, according to the actual data obtained for each street. Charles Booth had ascertained with precision the class in which the residents in each street stood with regard to the number of rooms occupied by each family. For the 80 per cent who were wage-earners he had approximate figures of the level of family incomes and of the degree of overcrowding in the homes. For the remainder he had the number of domestic servants employed in proportion to the numbers in the families. The streets could, in fact, be put into eightfold classification with as much accuracy as the individual families. Thus, it was possible, with the labour and time that Charles Booth never stinted, to display graphically on these wonderful maps, by an eightfold coloration, the extent, the local distribution and even the exact location of the misery, the poverty, the comfort and the luxury of the whole Metropolis.

There is a map of the whole Metropolitan area divided into compound blocks of about 30,000 inhabitants each, and shaded according to the percentage of poverty found in each. And there is a map on a larger scale (divided into four sections), on which is indicated the character of every street so far as it extends, but this map is squared off in some way within the Metropolitan boundaries. The marking of the streets in different shades and colours according to their prevailing social character was done, in the first instance, from the particulars given in the notebooks, of which some specimen pages have been given. It was then revised by my secretaries, who for this purpose walked over the whole ground, and also by the School Board visitors. After this it was referred to the parish relieving officers for each Union, and to the agents of the Charity Organization Society throughout London. The police were also referred to with regard to the streets marked black. Finally, I have consulted the clergy and their district visitors as to most of the poorer parts, obtaining from them, by the way, interesting details of typical streets. At each stage of revision amendments have been introduced where needed, and the map may now, I think, be accepted as practically correct. [Poverty, i. pp. 16, 17.]

*Classification According to Occupation*

Meanwhile the second part of Charles Booth's plan of campaign was proceeding: that relating to the occupations of the people, 'How they work' as distinguished from 'How they live.' There was first a trial trip, in which I cooperated, concerning the conditions of employment and industries peculiarly associated with the East End of London, such as labour in the London docks and wharves, and the various branches of what was then called the 'sweating system' in the manufacture of slop clothing and the cheaper lines of boots, furniture and cigarettes, and in women's work generally. These monographs were completed and published in 1889 before the figures of the 1891 census were available; and in the definitive edition of 1902–3 they find their place, not in the 'Industry' series but in vol. iv of the 'Poverty' series. In the elaborate and systematic investigation into the occupations of the whole people, embodied in the five volumes of the 'Industry' series, I took no part; and I am no more competent to describe it than any other student of the published results. But in order to complete this survey of Charles Booth's methods of investigation I will endeavour to give some indication of the lines on which he proceeded.

We find again the plan of combining the personal observation and testimony afforded by a large number of witnesses, with the statistical framework given by the census of the whole population. Unfortunately, the Registrar-General's classification of the occupations to which the million families had ascribed themselves ran to no fewer than three hundred and fifty 'trades' or vocations of one sort or another, and these, moreover, were lessened in value by the fact that the terms used by those who filled up the 'Householders' Schedules' were in many instances ambiguous. Charles Booth undertook the herculean task of re-classifying, on this point of occupation, the whole million schedules, according to a scheme of his own, arranging the aggregate into sixteen main 'industries', subdivided into about ninety subclasses. . . . For each of the sixteen 'industries' he was able to give an exact classification of those engaged in it from top to bottom, according to their social condition; and to show this graphically by tables exhibiting the number and percentage existing at eight separate grades, according to the number of persons per occupied room, and of the domestic servants kept by each family – these particular indices of social condition having been conclusively proved by the 'Poverty' inquiry to correspond closely with grades of family income. These graphic diagrams of social condition 'by industry' are in some cases illuminating, though opinions differ as to whether the particular grouping of occupations in an 'industry' corresponds with any 'organic' character of the group, or with any particular problem to be solved. In some cases (as for instance that of 'the building industry'), in spite of the inclusion of the relatively tiny numbers of the great contractors and the architects with the manual working operatives, the diagram has obvious significance. At the other extreme of the Public Services and Professional Classes, which include in a single 'industry' the Civil Service, the doctors, lawyers, teachers, artists and ministers of religion, with sweepers and dustmen and the water-works employees, the diagram of the social condition of the whole aggregate of families can have but little value. Charles Booth's idea seems to have been to class those occupations together in an 'industry' which cooperated in producing a particular commodity or a particular service, with a view to discovering what grade of social conditions was being afforded to those engaged in the production of each of them – a classification which, in the opinion of some competent critics, is not feasible on account of the interlocking of finance, commerce and manufacture; and if it were feasible would not be of scientific value, owing to the inclusion of persons of unrelated vocations and widely separated standards of expenditure in each of the so-called 'industries'.

More plainly significant were the results yielded by the classification into the eight separate grades of social condition of each of the ninety relatively homogeneous subclasses,[13] such as woodworkers, municipal employees, etc.; to

13. Even in this re-grouping of the census figures, many of the subclasses seem to me too heterogeneous to be of much value; for instance, the tables and diagrams relating to the persons occupied in medical pursuits include physicians and surgeons, nurses and mid-

which was added a graphic diagram, the product of immense industry, showing how the age distribution of those engaged in the occupation compared with the age distribution of the whole of the 'occupied persons' of London. These tabular statements and graphic diagrams were supplemented by detailed statements as to whether the individuals concerned were born in or out of London; where and how the occupation was carried on; the rates of wages and methods of remuneration of the wage-earners; the amount of 'slack time'; the hours of labour and sanitary conditions of the trade; the organizations existing in it; and innumerable other details gathered from employers, foremen, trade union officials and the personal observation of the investigators.

The method adopted has been varied according to the character of the employment, but everywhere we have tried to obtain information from all sides. Employers, trades union officials and individual workmen have all been applied to. . . . As regards employers in each trade, the plan adopted has been to approach as many as possible by circular, asking from each an exact account of those employed, whether men, women or boys, and the wages paid to each in an average, or, better still, in a maximum and minimum week. This appeal brought in every case a fair proportion of replies, and the tabulated results may be accepted as showing the earnings ordinarily made in the best class of firms. . . . For each section of industry I have endeavoured to ascertain the extent to which the workpeople are organized for trade purposes. Particulars of every trade union or society of importance have been obtained. It is, however, possible that some small society has, here and there, been omitted, owing either to the difficulty of tracing it, or to information being refused. The evidence of individual workers, I fear, falls short of what might be desired. It is not always easy to obtain; but when available adds much to the life of the picture. [Industry, i. pp. 27, 28.]

I have been very kindly allowed to use the wages returns from many London trades collected by the Statistical Department of the Board of Trade in 1886–7, but not published, because it con-

wives, chemists and druggists, mineral tooth-makers and bone-setters – vocations too widely divergent from each other in income, social status, degree of skill and character of training, to yield any common measure of social condition.

cerned trades which were not of sufficient general importance. I have set my figures and those of the Board of Trade side by side for comparison. . . . The queries of the Board of Trade asked for the maximum and minimum numbers employed in any weeks in 1885, with the total amound paid for the same week, and also the numbers employed in the first week of October 1886, with full particulars of character of employment, standard of hours worked, and wages for an ordinary full week's work. We could not venture to ask so much, and contented ourselves with the actual wages earned in an ordinary week (or in a busy and slack week, of which we ourselves took the average). Our figures are therefore actual, and include overtime or short time, whereas the figures of the Board of Trade are for a full week's work, taking no account of time lost or extra time made. [Industry, i. p. 28.]

## Charles Booth as a Pioneer in Social Science

In the foregoing pages I have attempted to give in bare outline Charles Booth's plan of campaign. I have now to estimate, I fear even more imperfectly, the value of the product.

From the standpoint of science it seems to me that Charles Booth's principal contribution was not the discovery of particular facts, though, as I shall presently show, this revelation of the life and labour of the people in London reverberated in the world of politics, and philanthropy, but his elaboration of an adequate technique in obtaining a vision of the condition of the whole population, within a given area, at a given time. For it is only by this static account of a given population that we can discover the relative proportions of particular attributes – that we can make sure that the particular instances of good or evil that have been observed are not merely sensational exceptions. We may admit that the static method has well-defined limits to its power of discovery. When not repeated at intervals, according to strictly analogous schemes of classification, it seldom discovers what has happened in the past, or what is likely to happen in the future.[14] And even when repeated, these

14. Charles Booth realized this limitation of the static method: 'My principal aim is still confined to the description of things as they are.

statements of contemporaneous facts, however analogous to one another and photographic they may be, do not reveal the actual processes of birth, growth, decay and death of the social institutions existing at the time of each successive investigation. The experienced investigator knows that, in order to discover the processes underlying the structure and function, or the conditions of health and disease for any given piece of social organization, the historical method[15] is imperative; with its use of the documents and contemporaneous literature belonging to each successive stage of the organization concerned, with its own ways of interviewing, and its more continuous personal observation of particular organizations, to which may occasionally be added freedom to experiment in constitution-making and day-by-day administration. Only by watching *the processes* of growth and decay during a period of time, can we understand even the contemporary facts at whatever may be their stage of development; and only by such a comprehension of the past and present processes can we get an insight into the means of change. But every method, like every instrument, has its limitations, and we do not abuse a knife because it turns out not to be a fork!

Further, Charles Booth showed us for the first time how best to combine the qualitative with the quantitative exam-

I have not undertaken to investigate how they came to be so, nor, except incidentally, to indicate whither they are tending; and only to a very limited extent, or very occasionally, has any comparison been made with the past. These points of view are deeply interesting and not to be ignored, but are beyond the scope of my own work. ... In a similar way an attempt is made to show in what manner the action of Local Authorities and County Council, Poor Law Guardians and Local Government Board, affects the condition of the people, but there is no pretence of going deeply into the principles of government involved.' [Religious Influences, i. p. 5.]

15. I use the term 'historical' rather than any of the alternative terms – evolutionary, genetic, kinetic and comparative method – because it seems to me least open to misunderstanding by the general reader. The 'industrious apprentice' can be referred to the concise textbook, *Essentials of Scientific Method* (by A. Wolf, Professor of Logic and Scientific Method in the University of London, 1925).

ination of social structure. By a masterly use of the method of wholesale interviewing (*i.e.* the use of a set of intermediaries who, in manageable numbers, were themselves acquainted with the whole aggregate of individuals to be investigated), amplified and verified by all sorts of independent testimony and personal observation of various parts of the immense field, he succeeded in making a qualitative examination of a magnitude never before attempted. By combining this with the merely mechanical enumeration of all the individuals in successive censuses, and by drawing out the eightfold indices of social condition that he had discovered, he was able to give to his qualitative categories a numerical measurement of an accuracy and over a field far greater than had ever before been attempted. In short, Charles Booth was much more than a statistician. He was the boldest pioneer, in my judgement, and the achiever of the greatest results, in the methodology of the social sciences of the nineteenth century.

## The Political Effect of the Grand Inquest

What was the effect on public opinion, what were the reactions in politics and philanthropy, of the revelation of the life and labour of the common people made by this 'Grand Inquest'? I was so intimately associated as an 'industrious apprentice' with the first stage of these investigations, and my mind was, at the time, so sensitive to impressions, implications and inferences, that I may easily overstate the political and administrative results of Charles Booth's labours. All I can do is to give my own conclusions; and it is for the reader to discount them as he thinks fit.

The authoritative demonstration – a fact which could not be gainsaid after the publication of Charles Booth's tables – that as many as 30 per cent of the inhabitants of the richest as well as the largest city in the world lived actually at or beneath the level of bare subsistence – came as a shock to the governing class.[16] It is true that the assertions of the Marx-

16. Subsequent inquiries into the condition of the people in other

ian Socialists, that the manual workers as a whole were in a state of chronic destitution, and that the poor were steadily becoming poorer whilst the rich were becoming richer, were not borne out. Indeed, the high proportion of manual workers – as many as 50 per cent of the whole population – who were described as existing in relative comfort and security, was the consoling feature of Charles Booth's table. But the philanthropist and the politician were confronted with a million men, women and children in London alone, who were existing, at the best, on a family income of under 20s. a week, and, at worst, in a state of chronic want; whilst this whole class of 'poor' and 'very poor' were subject to physical and social surroundings which were proved by innumerable tests – from the death-rate at all ages, the prevalence of endemic disease, and the raging of epidemics to the number of vermin-infested and dinnerless children,[17] from prosecutions for drunkenness to convictions for 'indecent occupation' of tenements – to be disastrously deteriorating to the race, alike

---

urban centres of population, on the Booth plan (varied by such statistical devices as 'sampling', the population and extended by a more intensive study of family obligations), have borne out, with startling exactitude, the London statistics of poverty of 1881–91, i.e. 30 per cent on or under the line of bare subsistence. See *Poverty, A Study of Town Life* (York, 1902), by Seebohm Rowntree, and *Livelihood and Poverty* (Northampton and Warrington), 1915, by A. L. Bowley and A. R. Burnett Hurst. In view of the alarm arising out of the present condition of the people owing to persistent unemployment, it would be of outstanding value if there could be started new inquiries on analogous lines in all these places, including the Metropolitan area.

17. The condition of the child was perhaps the saddest feature in Charles Booth's picture: 'Further than this, an official return, made in 1889, gives over 40,000 children in the London Board Schools, or nearly 10 per cent of the number on the roll, as habitually attending in want of food, to which number returns from Voluntary schools add about 11,000 in the same condition. ... Puny, pale-faced, scantily clad and badly shod, these small and feeble folk may be found sitting limp and chill on the school benches in all the poorer parts of London. They swell the bills of mortality as want and sickness thin them off, or survive to be the needy and enfeebled adults whose burden of helplessness the next generation will have to bear.' [Poverty, iii. p. 207.]

in body and mind. How had this morass of destitution and chronic poverty arisen during a period of unprecedented national prosperity?

Now the static method of investigation may not be able to discover causes – that is, the processes by which things happen – but it frequently yields invaluable clues, for other investigators to follow up by one or other of the methods of research. What this practically simultaneous examination of four millions of English urban society revealed was a series of affiliations or concomitants with the various degrees of destitution and poverty; not merely overcrowding but also the analogous condition of the state of repair of the houses; the sanitation; the lighting, paving and cleansing of the streets, and, generally speaking, the degree of dirt, squalor, noise and disorderly conduct characteristic of the various neighbourhoods: all these conditions rising and falling with the amount and the security of the livelihood of the family. An even more significant fact was the rise and fall of the death-rate and birth-rate according to the degree of destitution or poverty of the families concerned. That the death-rate, and especially the infantile death-rate, should be found to rise with a shortage of food, warmth and breathing space, and above all, in the presence of ubiquitous dirt and conse-quent flies, was of course expected; though the actual doub-ling of the infantile death-rate among the denizens of mean streets relatively to that of the inhabitants of West End squares was sensational. But to one who had been brought up in the political economy of Malthus, and taught to believe that every increment of income and security would inevitably be accompanied by additional children in working-class families, it was disconcerting to discover that the greater the poverty and overcrowding, and especially the greater the insecurity of the livelihood, the more reckless became the breeding of children; whilst every increment in income, and especially every rise in the regularity and the security of the income in working-class families, was found to be accom-panied, according to the statistics, by a more successful control of the birth-rate. And among other circumstances or conditions found to be closely related to destitution and poverty were the character of the occupations followed by the bread-winners, the unsatisfactory methods of remuneration, the irregularity of the hours of labour, the low degree of responsibility of landlord and employer for the sanitation and the cubic space of the workplace. On these points I shall have more to say in the following chapter. On the other hand, popular illusions about certain malign forces at work in the poorer districts were dispelled by these investigations. The careful inquiry made by H. Llewellyn Smith (afterwards Sir Hubert Llewellyn Smith, G.C.B., of the Board of Trade) disproved the common complaint that underpaid agricultural labourers swarmed into London and dragged down the rate of wages. It was proved beyond dispute that the country labour almost always came in at the top, and not at the bottom, of the wage levels. And the more sensational indictment of what was assumed to be a constant stream of aliens flooding the East End was finally disposed of by a precise enumeration of the aliens already living in the East End, and an accurate estimate of the relatively small annual increment afforded by the residuum between the total entering the Port of London and the numbers recorded as merely passing through London on their way to the United States of America.

## The Irrelevance of Charity

In the rough and tumble of day-by-day public administration and private enterprise we cannot stand and wait for an authoritative social science: politicians, philanthropists and the plain citizen alike have, here and now, to act or refrain from acting according to any clues that may be available. Now I venture to suggest that perhaps the most noteworthy clue afforded by Charles Booth's investigation was the irrelevance of charitable assistance, whether regarded as a good or evil influence, in determining the social environment of the common people. Some forms of indiscriminate and unconditional almsgiving – for instance, when competing religious communities recklessly scattered gifts, in money and in kind, in order to bring into their several folds persons who were indifferent and even contemptuous of the religion that they were bribed to confess – proved to be as diabolically black as they had been painted by the C.O.S.; but it was a mere fraction of the population that was thus debased. On the other hand, the administration of the Poor Law 'according to the principles of 1834', supplemented by charitable assistance according to the tenets of the C.O.S., though it reduced the Poor Rate and possibly diminished the amount spent in charity by enlightened persons, had next to no effect either on the poverty or on the misery of the poor. In the second volume of the 'Religious Influences Series', Charles Booth sums up his general impression of the effect of the rich man's charity, even when tempered by a strictly administered Poor Law and the active intervention of the Charity Organization Society. In the light of this conclusion – surely the most weighty judgement ever passed on a social experiment, all the more weighty because it is expressed with moderation and kindliness – the whole controversy between rival schools of poor relief and private charity is seen to be obsolete in so far as the prevention of destitution is concerned.

It is very difficult to give any adequate idea of the extent of the religious and philanthropic effort that has been, and is, made in this district [Whitechapel, etc.]. No statistical device would be of much avail to measure the work done, and description fails to realize it. Great as the effort is in many other parts of London, it is greatest here. Nowhere else are the leading churches so completely organized to cover the whole field of their work; and nowhere else are the auxiliary missions on so huge a scale. Money has been supplied without stint; the total expended is enormous; and behind and beneath it all, much of the work is sustained by the self-devotion of very many and the exalted enthusiasm of not a few. It can hardly be but that the sense of present help and kindly sympathy brought home to the people must do good, and that the world would be a blacker world without it. But these results are difficult to gauge. Much that is done seems rather to do harm than good, and on the whole all this effort results in disappointment and causes men to turn to other methods.

Whitechapel, St George's, and Stepney have been the scene of a very great experiment in the reform of the Poor Law on the anti-out-relief side. These three Unions, covering a very considerable area and including a population that is in the aggregate equal to that of a large provincial town, constitute in effect the district with which we are now dealing. The experiment has been an almost unique attempt. When it began the people were not only very poor, but terribly pauperized, and the object was to instil independence and so to raise the standard of life. A generation has elapsed, and we can take stock of the results. ... The district, owing to the unusually small proportion of cases which from any point of view are suitable for out-relief, is well adapted for such an attempt, and, moreover, since it is part of their theory that private charity is much less injurious to the spirit of independence than parish aid, it has had the advantage (if it really be one) of being carried out contemporaneously with an unexampled flood of private benevolence. In this effort they have had the advantage also of close cooperation with the Charity Organization Society, for whose methods no greater opportunity could ever be offered.

Complete success has been achieved in reducing outdoor relief without any corresponding increase in indoor pauperism. But to those who have advocated the principles which have produced these great results it is the more disheartening to find that they meet with no general acceptance. The example is not followed elsewhere, and even here the principle is not beyond the risk of abandonment. The continued presence and influence of the men I have named have been needed to prevent relapse, and at Stepney with the change of personnel there is already to some extent a change of policy.

Tested by the condition of the people, it is not possible to claim any great improvement. The people are no less poor, nor much, if at all, more independent. There are fewer paupers, but not any fewer who rely on charity in some form. Private charity defies control, and the work of the Charity Organization Society has, in spite of itself, become largely that of providing, under careful management, one more source of assistance for those who would otherwise be obliged to apply to the Guardians. [Religious Influences, ii. pp. 50 – 53.]

## Charles Booth as Social Reformer

So much for the negative influence on opinion of Charles Booth's work. Was there no remedy for this condition of a million people, over 30 per cent, of the richest city in the world? It is surely significant that this wealthy captain of industry, by this time Conservative in politics and strongly anti-Socialist in temper and economic views, should have come out of his prolonged study with proposals the very reverse of individualist. The one force at work of which he is wholeheartedly admiring, and in which he finds most hope, is the essentially collectivist organization of compulsory education by the London Education Authority at the public expense – an organization that was, in these very years, being hotly denounced as a form of Socialism.[18] 'The disease from which society suffers is unrestricted competition in industry of the needy and the helpless.' [Poverty, i. p. 162.] His par-

18. 'Among the public buildings of the Metropolis the London Board Schools occupy a conspicuous place. In every quarter the eye is arrested by their distinctive architecture, as they stand, closest where the need is greatest, each one 'like a tall sentinel at his post', keeping watch and ward over the interests of the generation that is to replace our own. The School Board buildings, as befits their purpose, are uniformly handsome, commodious, and for the most part substantial and well arranged. The health and convenience of both children and teachers have been carefully considered, and, in the later ones especially, have been increasingly secured. They accommodate a little over 443,000 children, and have been erected at a cost of about four and a half million sterling. Taken as a whole, they may be said fairly to represent the high-water mark of the public conscience in this country in its relation to the education of the children of the people.' [Poverty, iii. p. 204.] '. . . Of these general influences the greatest of all is elementary education, which, however, presents here no special features, and embodies no special effort. . . . Habits of cleanliness and of order have been formed; a higher standard of dress and of decency have been attained, and this reacts upon the homes; and when children who have themselves been to school become parents, they accept and are ready to uphold the system, and support the authority of the teachers, instead of being prone to espouse with hand and tongue the cause of the refractory child. Schoolmasters need no longer fear the tongue of the mother or the horsewhip of an indignant father.' [Religious Influences, ii. pp. 53, 54.]

ticular remedy for the conditions that he had revealed was for 'the State' compulsorily to take entire charge of the lives of the whole of 'Class B' – 'the entire removal of this very poor class out of the daily struggle for existence I believe to be the only solution of the problem' (Poverty, i. p. 154) '. . . for the State to nurse the helpless and incompetent as we in our own families nurse the old, the young, and the sick, and provide for those who are not competent to provide for themselves' (Poverty, i. p. 165). When we remember that, in London alone, Class B numbered over three hundred thousand people, apart from those actually in institutions; and that for the whole kingdom they would number over three million people, the magnitude and the daring of this piece of 'Collectivism' was startling.

Nothing less than this [summed up Charles Booth] will enable self-respecting labour to obtain its full remuneration, and the nation its raised standard of life [Poverty, i. p. 165]. . . . My idea is to make the dual system, Socialism in the arms of Individualism, under which we already live, more efficient by extending somewhat the sphere of the former and making the division of function more distinct. Our Individualism fails because our Socialism is incomplete. In taking charge of the lives of the incapable, State Socialism finds its proper work, and by doing it completely, would relieve us of a serious danger. The Individualist system breaks down as things are, and is invaded on every side by Socialistic innovations, but its hardy doctrines would have a far better chance in a society purged of those who cannot stand alone. Thorough interference on the part of the State with the lives of a small fraction of the population would tend to make it possible, ultimately, to dispense with any Socialistic interference in the lives of all the rest. [Poverty, i. p. 167.]

This proposal, it is needless to say, found supporters neither among the individualists, who objected to state intervention as such, nor among the Socialists, who preferred the 'state tutelage' of the rack-renting landlord and rate-cutting employer to that of the very poor who were their victims. But a more popular and practicable proposal – one already advocated by Samuel Barnett and the Fabian Society – was given an immense prestige by Charles Booth's concurrent investigation into the conditions of the aged poor throughout England and Wales;[19] and by his advocacy of the grant by the State of non-contributary, universal old-age pensions, given as of right, irrespective of affluence, to every person attaining a given age. It was certainly due to his statistical investigations and incessant propaganda, more than to any other factor, that the Old Age Pensions Act was passed in 1908, to be greatly enlarged and extended in 1911, 1919 and 1924. And is it a mere coincidence that the two most distinguished members of his staff of investigators were, within a very few years of the publication of the completed edition in 1902–3, influentially associated with perhaps the two biggest experiments in public administration and public control in the interest of the manual workers that the century has yet seen? The brilliant young statistician, who was Charles Booth's chief intellectual adviser in the first stage of the great inquiry, found himself, as Sir Hubert Llewellyn Smith, G.C.B., in 1906–10 initiating and organizing the national network of State Labour Exchanges, and in 1911–14 of the elaborate provisions for the able-bodied outside the Poor Law by compulsory unemployment insurance, involving, as amended in 1918–24, an annual issue which has run up, in the worst times, to over forty million pounds a year. The other, who, Mrs Charles Booth tells us, was 'in many respects the ablest of all'[20] – the late Ernest Aves – played a leading part in the initiation and administration of the Boards established under the Trade Boards Act of 1909 (extended in 1913–18), by which, in a wide series of so-called sweated trades, employers were compelled by law to pay to all their employees not less than a prescribed legal minimum wage. Thus we have as the outcome of Charles Booth's poverty statistics, not indeed State provision for Class B as such, but State provision for the children of school age, State provision for those over seventy (and State provision for the blind over fifty), State

19. *The Aged Poor in England and Wales*, 1894, by Charles Booth; also *Charles Booth – A Memoir* op. cit., pp. 141–54.
20. ibid., p. 130.

provision (under health insurance) for the sick and disabled, and State provision for all those without employment (under unemployment insurance). Meanwhile, in the sphere of collective regulation, we have seen the repeated extensions of the Factory and Workshops, Mines and Merchant Shipping, Railways and Shop Hours Acts; and the far-reaching ramifications of minimum wage and maximum hours legislation. Indeed – perhaps being 'wise after the event' – if I had to sum up, in a sentence, the net effect of Charles Booth's work, I should say that it was to give an entirely fresh impetus to the general adoption, by the British people, of what Fourier, three quarters of a century before, had foreseen as the precursor of his organized communism, and had styled 'guaranteeism'; or, as we now call it, the policy of securing to every individual, as the very basis of his life and work, a prescribed national minimum of the requisites for efficient parenthood and citizenship. This policy may, or may not be Socialism, but it is assuredly a decisive denial of the economic individualism of the eighties.

It was under the continuous pressure of this peculiarly stimulating social environment – political, philanthropic and scientific – that I sought and found a field of inquiry, and began the series of observations and experiments described in the following chapter.

CHAPTER 6

❦

*Observation and Experiment*
1884–90

THE four years between my visit to Bacup in 1883 and the publication in 1887 of my first contribution to Charles Booth's *The Life and Labour of the People in London* were the crucial years of my life; the period of greatest risk to health and happiness, a veritable testing-time of character and intelligence. From being a lively and, at times, good-looking society girl, assumed to be ready to follow her elder sisters' example in making a happy and otherwise satisfactory marriage, I was transformed into, I will not say a professional, but a professed brain-worker, overtly out for a career of my own. What had altered my looks, if not my outlook, was my frantic attempt, in the first two of these years, to combine three or four lives in one: housekeeping and entertaining for my father and sister in our London and country homes, with C.O.S. visiting in Soho, and a short spell of rent-collecting in a block of low-class dwellings at the East End of London; perpetual controversies with politicians and philanthropists with an assiduous study of blue books, social histories and economic treatises. 'A rather hard and learned woman, with a clear and analytic mind', so records a brilliant journalist in his reminiscences of these days. Some of the opinions attributed to me by this friendly and too flattering critic I do not recognize; but his observation about my general attitude strikes me as singularly apt. 'I'm afraid there is something a little hard about it all. Unhappily, man has bowels of compassion, and the individual case appeals so much more to compassion than an undefined and unimaginable "class".'[1]

1. *Changes and Chances*, by H. W. Nevinson, pp. 86–7.'

To me 'a million sick' have always seemed actually more worthy of self-sacrificing devotion than the 'child sick in a fever', preferred by Mrs Browning's *Aurora Leigh*. And why not? The medical officer of health, who, made aware by statistical investigation of the presence of malaria in his district, spends toilsome days and troubled nights in devising schemes for draining stagnant pools and providing for the wholesale distribution of quinine, has a compassion for human misery as deep-rooted as, and certainly more effective than that of the devoted nurse who soothes the fever-stricken patient in the last hours of life. This type of broad-based beneficence has been exquisitely expressed in two poems by Sir Ronald Ross, the discoverer of the cause of malaria:

[Before his discovery, 1890–93.]
> The painful faces ask, can we not cure?
> We answer, No, not yet; we seek the laws.
> O God, reveal thro' all this thing obscure
> The unseen, small, but million-murdering cause.

[After his discovery, 1897.]
> This day relenting God
> Has placed within my hand
> A wondrous thing; and God
> Be praised. At His command,
> Seeking His secret deeds
> With tears and toiling breath,
> I find thy cunning seeds,
> O million-murdering Death.
> I know this little thing
> A myriad men will save.
> O Death, where is thy sting?
> Thy victory, O Grave?[2]

Not that I wish to imply that research, still less my own investigation, into the cause and cure of poverty has yielded, as yet, results in any way commensurate with Sir Ronald Ross's researches into the origin and prevention of malaria.

2. *Philosophies*, by Sir Ronald Ross, pp. 21 and 53.

Still in its infancy, the science of society has barely reached the years of fruitful discovery. All I suggest is that the impulse of pity for the needless misery of men, as distinguished from the suffering of those individuals whom you happen to know, can be as operative in the study of human nature in society as it is in that of the pestilential poisons besetting the human body.

## Management of Working-class Dwellings

Casting about for some way of observing the life and labour of the people, I seized the opportunity of my sister Kate's marriage[3] to assist Miss Ella Pycroft[4] in taking over one of my sister's commitments in the management of working-class dwellings in the East End of London. About the harmlessness of this intrusion of the relatively well-to-do into the homes of the very poor I had no misgiving; rents had to be collected, and it seemed to me, on balance, advantageous to the tenants of low-class property to have to pay their money to persons of intelligence and goodwill who were able to bring hardships and grievances to the notice of those who had power to mitigate or remedy them. And this occupation was certainly well fitted to form part of my apprenticeship as

3. About my sister's work and marriage Canon Barnett writes: 'This year we lose Miss Potter. She has been a rent-collector since 1878, and has found here so many friends that, desiring on her wedding day to be among her "own people", she could only be among her friends at St Jude's. 15 March, 1883, will be long remembered by the many who, on that day, followed their friend with kindly thoughts into her new life, and shared the first meal which she took with her husband. We shall not forget her, and she, I know, will not forget us.' (*Canon Barnett, His Life, Work, and Friends*, by his Wife, vol. i. pp. 106–7.)

4. Miss Ella Pycroft, who became a lifelong friend, retained the management of Katherine Buildings, together with another block of dwellings under the East End Dwellings Co., until May 1890. At that time turning to educational work, after a year at the Cambridge Training College for Teachers, and after adding to the qualifications she had already held, she became, in 1893, Chief Organizer of Domestic Economy Subjects under the Technical Education Board of the London County Council, from which post she retired in 1904.

a social investigator. Unlike philanthropic visiting under the parochial clergy, or detective visiting under a C.O.S. committee, one was not watching instances of failure in the way of adaptation to this world or the next. What was under observation was the whole of a given section of the population: a group of families spontaneously associated in accordance with the social and economic circumstances of the particular district. From the outset the tenants regarded us, not as visitors of superior social status still less as investigators, but as part of the normal machinery of their lives, like the school attendance officer or the pawnbroker; indeed, there was familiarity in their attitude, for they would refer to one or other of us as 'my woman collector', a friendly neighbour being given the superior social status of 'the lady next door'. And as the management of this block of buildings was handed over to us from the day of its opening in January 1885, my colleague and I had to learn, by actual experiment, how to choose, from a crowd of applicants, the tenants for 281 separate rooms; how to judge at sight relative sobriety and trustworthiness; how to test by the spoken and the written word the worth of references. Incidentally, it was an advantage that Katherine Buildings, situated close to St Katherine's Docks, was itself an experiment. A group of philanthropists, inspired by Octavia Hill, had undertaken the difficult task of rehousing without financial loss, in a manner both sanitary and cheap, the poorest of the poor: in particular, the dock labourers who had been ousted from their homes by the Metropolitan Board of Works in its demolition of insanitary slum property. The policy adopted by these experimenters in working-class housing was outlined by Octavia Hill in her evidence before the Select Committee of the House of Commons on Artisans' and Labourers' Dwellings Improvement, 1882, and before the Royal Commission on the Housing of the Working Classes, 1885.

It seems to me that one great difficulty that has been before the people who have been interested in the Artisans' Dwellings Act is that they want to take too many steps at once: they want to move the very lowest class of poor out of, we will say, damp underground cellars, where a large number of them have been living in one room, at once into an ideal working-man's home. Now I grant that the problem is very difficult, but supposing they take the two steps separately, and be satisfied, for the moment, to build clean, light, dry rooms above ground; and instead of building them in suites, build them, as it is very easy to do, opening from a little lobby from which four rooms enter, instead of making any of them passage rooms; and they can let either one, two, three or four rooms, as the people require; and whenever the standard of working people is raised higher they can take more rooms.' [Question 3002, Select Committee on Artisans' and Labourers' Dwellings Improvement, H.C. 235 of 1882.]

I think a very great deal more simplicity is needed in the construction of the houses. It seems to me that where you remove the very lowest class of dwelling, and wish to reaccommodate the same people, you must adopt the very simplest manner of building, and that I am afraid has not been done. [Question 8833.] . . . They should build what really is wanted, and what is essential to health. . . . Primarily, I should not carry the water and the drains all over the place; I think that is ridiculous. If you have water on every floor, that is quite sufficient for working people. It is no hardship to have to carry a pail of water along a flat surface. You would not dream of altering the water supply in a tiny little house now, and yet people carry their water up three or four floors there. You would not dream of legislating to prevent that. Surely, if you bring the water on each floor that is quite sufficient. In most of the blocks of workmen's dwellings the water is laid on into every tenement. That is not only a large cost to begin with, but it means an enormous cost in keeping the thing up, and a larger cost still in proportion as the tenants are destructive and careless. Of course, the same thing applies to the drains, and it is not in the least necessary that they should be laid on everywhere. [Question 8852, Royal Commission on the Housing of the Working Classes, C. 4402 of 1885.]

You ought to be able to give people things that they do not break. I should make everything as strong as I could, and above all as simple as I could. These people are not at all accustomed to the use of appliances, and everything of that sort is a difficulty to them; and I am quite certain that we ought not to give them elaborate appliances for a long time yet. [Question 9003-4, ibid.]

So far as Katherine Buildings was concerned, the outcome of this policy was a long double-faced building in five tiers; on one side overlooking a street; on the other, looking on to a narrow yard hemmed in by a high blank brick wall forming the back of the premises of the Royal Mint. Right along the whole length of the building confronting the blank wall ran four open galleries, out of which led narrow passages, each passage to five rooms, identical in size and shape, except that the one at the end of the passage was much smaller than the others. All the rooms were 'decorated' in the same dull, dead-red distemper, unpleasantly reminiscent of a butcher's shop. Within these uniform, cell-like apartments there were no labour-saving appliances, not even a sink and water-tap! Three narrow stone staircases led from the yard to the topmost gallery; on the landings between the galleries and the stairs were sinks and taps (three sinks and six taps to about sixty rooms); behind a tall wooden screen were placed sets of six closets on the trough system, sluiced every three hours; and these were allotted to the inhabitants of the rooms on either side of them; in the yard below were the dustbins. From a sanitary standpoint there was perhaps little to be said against this super-economical structure. But the sanitary arrangements, taken as a whole, had the drawback that the sets of six closets, used in common by a miscellaneous crowd of men, women and children, became the obtrusively dominant feature of the several staircases, up and down which trooped, morning, noon and night, the 600 or more inhabitants of the buildings. In short, all amenity, some would say all decency, was sacrificed to the two requirements of relatively low rents and physically sanitary buildings. 'Benevolence has had much to do with the erection of dwellings in the neighbourhood,' caustically observed Samuel Barnett, a few years after the opening of Katherine Buildings, 'and in the name of benevolence, so as to encourage benevolence, some argue that decoration must be given up, so that such dwellings may be made to pay. Probably this is a mistake in economy: it is certainly a mistake in benevolence. To treat one's neighbour as oneself is not to decorate one's own house with the art of the world, and to leave one's neighbour's house with nothing but the drain-pipes to relieve the bareness of its walls.'[5]

With this slight introduction I fall back on entries in the MS. diary – mere jottings of facts and impressions, the distracted and diversified life I was leading forbidding lengthy explanation or detailed description.

Another day at Whitechapel. Met Mr Bond[6] there and looked over fittings. Stove suggested by architect a failure; the management fails to go straight to the best authority and find out whether what is proposed is likely to succeed. Afterwards talked with Mr Barnett. He anxious that I should spend this unoccupied time in getting more general information, and find out particulars about medical officer, sanitary officer, relieving officer, School Board visitor, and voluntary sanitary committee, their powers and duties. [There follows an analysis of a manual of local government law, and a summary of Sanitary Acts and Metropolitan Local Management Act, etc., with details as to the Local Government officials in Whitechapel.] Miss Pycroft spent three days with me; daughter of a country physician. Free-thinking, had somewhat similar life to ours, isolated from other country neighbours by opinions. Decided business capacity, strong will and placid temper. Devoted to her father, with whom she has the same intimate companionable relationship as we have. Very anxious for work, and indifferent to life! We shall get on, and we are anxious to have no other workers on the block. [MS. diary, January 1885.]

5. *Canon Barnett, His Life, Work, and Friends*, vol. i. p. 139.
6. Edward Bond (1844–1920). An Oxford 'Double First' and Fellow of Queen's College, and endowed with sufficient private means to lead the life of unpaid public service, he became one of the leaders of the Charity Organization movement, and among other things, one of the original directors of the East End Dwellings Co. He remained throughout his life an uncompromising individualist; served for a few years as a 'Moderate' on the London County Council, and as the Conservative M.P. for East Nottingham from 1895 to 1906. A fine figure of a man with handsome features, large soulful grey eyes, attractively set in dark pencilled brows and long silken lashes, he alternated cultured comments with thrilling silences; and was the beloved of the philanthropic set. Indeed, it was said that George Eliot had him in mind in the characterization of the most romantic of her heroes – Daniel Deronda – though, unlike Deronda, he never married.

I spend my time now in alternate days of work and rest. The physical part of my work absorbs so much energy that I have little left for thought and feeling. Work is the best narcotic, providing the patient is strong enough to take it. All is chaos at present. Long trudges through Whitechapel after applicants and references, and tenants tumbling in anyhow. A drift population of all classes and races; a constantly decomposing mass of human beings; few arising out of it, but many dropping down dead, pressed out of existence by the struggle. A certain weird romance with neither beginning nor end; visiting amongst these people in their dingy homes. They seem light-hearted enough, in spite of misery and disease. More often feel envy than pity. Shall in the future, when other workers are found, and when once I am fairly started in the practical work, undertake less of the management, and use the work more as an opportunity for observation. Mean some day to master, as far as my power goes, what is theoretically thought out in social questions. Earnestly hope I shall never get conceited again, or look upon my work as more than the means for remaining contented and free from pain. Relief to be alone. . . . Society constantly increasing; have none of that terrible nightmare feeling about it of last year. But work brings Society into its proper place as a rest and relaxation, instead of an effort and an excitement. Trust I shall never make social capital out of my work. That with me is a danger, as I enjoy retailing my experiences, independently of any effect I may produce, and the 'vanity motive' comes in to strengthen desire. Perhaps the past year of suffering will decrease my egotism, and instead of cold observation and analysis, all done with the egotistical purpose of increasing knowledge, there will be the interest which comes from feeling, and from the desire humbly to serve those around me. [MS. diary, 8 March 1885.]

Feel rather depressed by the bigness of my work. When I look at those long balconies, and think of all the queer characters, tenants and would-be tenants, and realize that the character of the community will depend on our personal influence, and that, again, not only on character but on persistent health, I feel rather dizzy. Home life adds to strain. Have cleared away all instructive books and taken to poetry and beautiful prose. Find restfulness in beauty now that I have hard practical work and constant friction. Emerson's essays delight me. [Review of Emerson follows.] [MS. diary, 15 March 1885.]

Here for two or three days' rest. My work takes a great deal out of me, and sometimes wonder how much of it I shall eventually do. Feel so utterly done when I come back from Whitechapel, too tired to think or feel. [MS. diary, The Argoed, our Monmouthshire home, 12 April 1885.]

Working hard. Buildings are satisfactory; caretaker hopelessly inadequate. Tenants rough lot – the aborigines of the East End. Pressure to exclude these and take in only the respectable – follow Peabody's example. Interview with superintendent of Peabody's. 'We had a rough lot to begin with; had to weed them of the old inhabitants; now only take in men with regular employment.'

The practical problem of management: are the tenants to be picked, and all doubtful or inconvenient persons excluded? Or are the former inhabitants to be housed so long as they are not manifestly disreputable? May have some rough work to do, and I am gaining experience. When overtired, the tenants haunt me with their wretched, disorderly lives. Wish I had started with more experience, and had been able to give my whole time to it. Half-hearted work is always bad. [MS. diary, 4 June 1885.]

Visited Miss Cons[7] at Surrey Buildings (South London Building Company, cost £20,887, pays four per cent; no depreciation fund). According to evidence before Royal Commission, only

7. Emma Cons (1838–1912), one of the most saintly as well as the most far-sighted of Victorian women philanthropists, deserves to be more widely known. Trained under Octavia Hill as a rent-collector, she revolted against the self-complacent harshness of doctrine of the C.O.S. of the eighties and became an independent manager of working-class dwellings on the Surrey side. Realizing that what was needed, even more than sanitary but dismal homes, was the organization of the pleasures of the poor in great cities, she, in 1880, took over the management of the Victoria music hall, at that time a disreputable centre for all that was bad – Charles Kingsley's 'licensed pit of darkness' – and ran it as a place of popular musical entertainment, free from vice, and unsubsidized by the sale of alcoholic drink. Supported by Samuel Morley, Miss Martineau and Lord Mount Temple, Miss Cons kept this enterprise going until her death in 1912, when she was succeeded by her niece, Miss Lilian Baylis, who had been assisting her; and whose genius has since transformed 'the Vic', with its excellent operas, and its admirable productions of nearly all Shakespeare's plays, appreciated by a wide circle of enthusiastic wage-earning patrons, into something approaching the British National Theatre.

three quarters let. Working-class tenements, together with shops and cottages; outside staircase, balconies round pleasure ground; water-closets together, one to each tenement with keys. No sinks. Wash-houses and drying grounds on roof. Trained by Octavia Hill. Not a lady by birth, with the face and manner of a distinguished woman, almost a ruler of men. Absolute absorption in work; strong religious feeling, very little culture or interest in things outside the sphere of her own action. Certainly, she is not a lover of fact or theory: she was not clear as to the total number of rooms, unlets or arrears. No description of tenants kept. Did not attempt to theorize about her work. Kept all particulars as to families in her head. To her people she spoke with that peculiar combination of sympathy and authority which characterizes the modern type of governing woman. I felt ashamed of the way I cross-questioned her. As far as I could make out from her books, her arrears amounted to within £1 of her weekly rent – that is to say, on her working-class tenants. She lives on the premises; collects other blocks, but devotes much time to other work in connection with amusement and instruction of the people. A calm enthusiasm in her face, giving her all to others. 'Why withhold any of your time and strength?' seems to be her spirit. All her energy devoted to the practical side of the work. No desire to solve the general questions of the hour. These governing and guiding women may become important factors if they increase as they have done lately; women who give up their lives to the management of men; their whole energy, body and mind, absorbed in it. Unlike the learned woman, the emotional part of their nature is fully developed; their sympathy almost painfully active, expressed in eyes clear of self-consciousness, and bright with love and the pity from which it springs. They have the dignity of habitual authority; often they have the narrow-mindedness and social gaucherie due to complete absorption, physical and mental, in one set of feelings and ideas. The pure organizer belongs to a different type; she is represented by the active secretary of a growing society, or the matron of a big hospital; and she is to a certain extent unsexed by the justice, push and severity required. Not that I despise these qualities, they are indispensable to any work. But with the organizer, *justice is a technical and not a moral characteristic*. Push and severity are not prominent qualities in such guiding women as Miss Cons. For the guiding of men they use personal influence based on feeling more than on reasoning.

Desirable that I should thoroughly master details of South London Building Company management. [MS. diary, 12 August 1885.]

Took over the whole work from Miss Pycroft. Aim during her absence – collecting and accounting, thoroughly and methodically. Arrears diminished; rooms let; first-rate broker engaged; caretaker's work observed; amount of repairs done by him estimated. Morality enforced on buildings. Advantages of clear account of my own tenants written, and general knowledge of Miss Pycroft's. Boys' club started; notes on reading room taken. To do this must live a great deal on the buildings, but not take rents on all days. Bullying people all the week round system a waste of time. [MS. diary, 13 August 1885.]

Delightful two days with Booths. . . . Discussed possibilities of social diagnosis. Charlie working away with [a] clerk, on the Mansion House inquiry into unemployment, and other work of statistical sort. Plenty of workers engaged in examination of facts collected by others; *personal investigation* required. *Pall Mall [Gazette]* has started this but in worst possible way; shallow and sensational. As to ideal of work: collecting well done; accounts not yet done; arrears diminished and a few rooms let. Many of the most respectable persons will not come in, owing to prejudice against buildings, and to ours in particular. The coarseness of the arrangements, want of attractiveness, and uniformity of the rooms a great disadvantage. Broker found; or rather a broker, typical Jew, found me! Was I done? Paid 5s. for three warning visits. If he gets two disreputable women out without further charge, I have made a good bargain. Accounts of tenants got on with. If I get the facts during the next four weeks, can write up the stories of East End lives later on. [MS. diary, 22 August 1885.]

Struggling through the end of my work with painful effort: the old physical longing for the night that knows no morning. Given up books to Miss Pycroft. As to ideal of work, this much realized. Collecting and accounts on the whole well and thoroughly done; arrears diminished; twenty new tenants. On the other hand nine gone of their own accord, six left under notice – balance of five. A very indifferently written account of my own tenants. Boys' club started by Maurice Paul.[8] Reading

8. Maurice Eden Paul (younger son of Kegan Paul, the accomplished

Room carried on by him. Spent three evenings there, and started the idea, in my own mind, of introducing a committee of men gradually into management of buildings. Roadnight's work [a porter] not estimated; not satisfied with him; wants more supervision than he gets. Suspect him of drinking; not sufficiently to be a scandal, but too much to keep respect of tenants. Failed in respect of Roadnight. Disagreeable row with one of Miss Pycroft's tenants, and had to use summary measures. Badly managed. Softness would have paid better than hardness. Difficult ideal of conduct to be realized. Firmness in enforcing obligation and respect for law, together with patient gentleness in the manner. Succeeded in case of Haggarty, and failed in case of Schmidts, because of this difference in my manner. Interesting conversation with Ansing family; man Prussian Catholic, settled in Whitechapel twenty-five years ago; woman English. Sweaters, that is, middlemen between [retail] shop and hands, for the making of men's clothes. Man with a rigid disapproval of Whitechapel population – not pity. Woman more heart (on her tongue); should think she was fairly kind, though naturally enough treating the hands for her own advantage, not for theirs. Give melancholy account of their habits in regard to work. She told me, and one of her hands corroborated, that she frequently spent the whole day hunting them up in public-houses, to persuade them to finish work for which she had contracted. The account she and her husband gave of the class we have to do with is much the same as I should give with my small experience; except that they omit certain lovable qualities, which apparently a lady arouses into activity and appreciates. We all designate them as on the whole a *leisure* class; picking up their livelihood by casual work, poor in quality; by borrowing from their more industrious friends, and by petty theft. Drunken, thieving and loose in their morality. I should add, generous-hearted and affectionate, capable of self-control when once you have gained their affection. As a class, not beggars; do not expect you to give.

---

publisher of the eighties and nineties), at that time studying for the medical profession. Today he is, in conjunction with his wife, a well-known translator of erudite foreign works, among many others the seven volumes of Treitschke's *History of Germany in the Nineteenth Century*. He has also been prominent as a member of the Left of the International Socialist Movement, and has contributed pamphlets and books on communism and invented the term 'Proletcult' as the title of a book (Parsons) on 'proletarian' culture.

Unlike the country poor in this matter. Also warm in their feeling for family and friends. As a class, in a purely business relationship in which no other moral principle enters than that of fulfilling contracts – hopelessly unsatisfactory. ... To return to sweaters themselves. Seemed from their own account to work hard enough: their whole energy of body and mind going into their work. Apparently no recreations – always excepting their Sunday spent at Chapel. Live well. Women mentioned incidentally that their butcher's bill for a party of eight came to eighteen shillings per week. Bad debts, that is, stolen work, came to a considerable item in their accounts. Intend to see more of them. [MS. diary, 15 September 1885.]

A pleasant holiday among the hills [our Westmorland home]. Read Taine's *Ancien Régime* with real enjoyment after ten days of artisans' dwellings Blue Books. These philosophic histories are delightful to ignoramuses. ... [Then follows a review of Taine.] I do not know how little or how much my energy will be equal to. But while I hope to devote the greater part to my own subject, yet I feel my knowledge of history is wholly inadequate even for my special purpose. At the same time, a thorough detailed knowledge of what actually is, will give me a much stronger imagination, will furnish me with the raw material, the knowledge of men and women under different conditions, by the aid of which, added to a knowledge of past circumstances, the history of former men and women may be instructive. A rigmarole way of expressing myself! ... As to scientific theories as to the evolution of society, a main principle upon which to graft knowledge of special fact, I have none except perhaps Comte's great generalization of the processes of human thought. I read with a sort of fervid enthusiasm Herbert Spencer's *First Principles*, and accepted his perfect formula of the course of life in all being. But his deductions from general theory, used as first principles of social science, are to my mind suggestive hypotheses, not proven laws. He irritates me by trying to palm off illustrations as data; by transcribing biological laws into the terms of social facts, and then reasoning from them as social laws. A deeper knowledge of his work, based on a wider experience of life, may make me in the end his true disciple. At present I am *not*. I am biased by his individualism, not converted to it. I should like to understand clearly what his theory is; and apart from mere deduction from *First Principles* and general analogies, which seem to me only to require skilful handling to cut into facts anyway, how he has worked it out. I should like also to have mastered the general outline of the reasoning of the scientific socialist. But I will keep my own mind from theorizing about society . . .

One needs more knowledge of antecedent facts. . . . For instance, a general knowledge of English history, with a due proportion of 'setting' from other contemporary history; a special knowledge of the state of the working man in the different periods of our history, and of the laws regulating commerce and industry: the growth of industrial organization and of its rival organization; influence of religion in determining political and social action; rise and fall of various religious sects with the peculiar activities belonging to them; the difference of race in the working-class communities; the growth of towns and the occupations necessitated by these, and the reaction of these occupations on the minds and bodies of the people; the formation and dissolution of classes, with their peculiar habits of body and mind. There is a study for a lifetime! That is to be my general aim. My special aim is to understand the condition of the working class in the way of housing, by digesting the evidence of other people; testing and supplementing it by my own observation and experiment. [MS. diary, October 1885.]

Tomorrow to London to begin a new year of work. The report I sent to my Directors had an effect, and has made them reconsider their plan for the new building. When Mr Bond's letter asking my attendance came I had forgotten all about my letter to him. Must look up details to support my case. [This letter was a detailed criticism of the sanitary arrangements at Katherine Buildings, more especially concerning the water-closets – their dominating position at the head of each flight of stairs; their common use; and their periodical sluicing; and a plea for self-contained tenements in the new block, on the ground that, the more brutalized the class of tenants, the more imperative it became to provide tolerably refined arrangements.]

Wish to get a complete account of the tenants of Katherine Buildings; must think out facts I want to ascertain about each family, and go straight at it. Will be obliged to go more deeply into practical work in order to get opportunities of observation. It is no use fighting against an irresistible tendency, however humble one may be as to the worth of it. And why should not I have the enjoyment, now that I am young, of a thoroughly congenial pursuit? Through the management of men, one will always get the opportunity of studying them. Do not intend to become nauseated with my subject – intend to go through a course of reading in history and social science. Shall digest Herbert Spencer's *Sociology* and read Maine's *Popular Government*. Shall begin the study of the English People in periods – so as to learn their characteristics and compare them with their present ones, and understand the growth of local and political organization, and the transfer of power from class to class; the material necessities and the ideas which lead to this transfer. [MS. diary, 23 October 1885.]

I meant this morning to have worked at my Katherine Buildings book, but unfortunately, or fortunately, my rent books were away. I think I will keep Sunday for rest and writing a short account of my work for the past week. ... Met Directors, but I think failed to convince them, as I had no alternative to offer which was based on experience. Two long conversations with Mr Barnett: I making my suggestion of associating all agencies for housing in one body. Had not thought this out, and was rather astounded at the way he took it up and wanted me to elaborate a plan and become the moving spirit. Shall I always disappoint myself and others when my strength comes to be tested; or will my strength increase and enable me to carry out what I intend? ... As for work, I have done only my bare duty at Katherine Buildings. I have begun a careful account of tenants. Oh, for more energy! Went with two fellow-workers to the Vic[toria Theatre]; managed by that grand woman, Miss Cons. To me a dreary performance, sinking to the level of the audience, while omitting the dash of coarseness, irreverence and low humour which give the spice and the reality to such entertainments. To my mind the devil is preferable, and in every way more wholesome, than a shapeless mediocrity.

Let me see what I mean by the association of the agencies for the housing of the poor. About 150,000 persons live under the superintendence of these agencies. I should like the experience of each class of agency to be tabulated, giving a complete account of their population, with occupation, family, income, where they came from, whether employed in the neighbourhood, and other details. Also method of superintendence (cause of ejectment, etc.); relative expense of management and repairs, etc. I should like an annual meeting and a reading of reports, and for these reports to be made as complete as possible and published as proceedings. Also, that this association should serve as a central office to provide caretakers, superintendents and lady collectors. This is the outline of what I wish to discover about the inhabitants of Katherine Buildings: number of family, dead and alive; occupation of all members; actual income from work, charity or private property; race; whether born in London; if so, belonging to London stock? If not, reason for immigration, and from what part of the country; religion. As much of previous history as obtainable. [MS. diary, 8 November 1885.]

A long day, from 9.30 to 5 o'clock, with Alfred [Cripps] and Colonel Martindale at Albert and Victoria Docks, some way out of London on the Essex Marshes. Labourers a much finer class [than those of St Katherine Docks], English, practically permanently employed; live in small two-storey houses. [Then follows a description of the methods of employment.] But I should like to master the whole thing. The courteous old gentleman seemed somewhat taken aback by my questions and demand for statistics. But I shall get them if I have patience. [Then follows a list of questions about methods of remuneration and the way of engaging labour, which I intend to get answered.] [MS. diary, 12 November 1885.]

Worked well: Monday, Katherine Buildings, one to nine o'clock; afterwards saw over Whittingham Club. Tuesday, Katherine Buildings, four hours; Wednesday, Albert and Victoria Docks from 10 p.m. to 6 a.m.; Thursday, idle morning, afternoon, Katherine Buildings; Friday, seven hours' work on Katherine Buildings book; Saturday, Katherine Buildings twelve to seven o'clock. Altogether forty hours, including railway journeys. [MS. diary, 15 November 1885.]

And here is an extract from a letter dated November 1885 to my father, who was staying in our Westmorland home, whilst I had returned to York House, Kensington:

In the afternoon I had four men who stayed from three to seven o'clock. First a young S—, a meek and mild pretty-looking young man, whom I had always put down as a dancing idiot, but, remembering Mrs Barnett's admonition, I plunged into philanthropy and found out that he was a hard-working 'cooperator'; and he gave us a most interesting account of the progress of the cooperative movement in London.

He has half promised to help me with the boys' club. It is extraordinary how much earnestness there is in the air, and how shy everyone is of owning to it. Then entered the great Major W. who is now quartered at (I can't remember the name, I am so stupid today), who was most good-natured and tried valiantly to enter into our conversation . . .[9]

Professor Newton[10] and Mr Bond (who had come to talk business) completed our party, and we had a lengthy discussion on State education, etc. Mr Bond stayed afterwards. He said he regretted he had shown my letter to the Board, as it had created a commotion, and delayed the final issue of the plans. They are not going to decide until Monday next, when they meet again. They have given way to us about some minor points on our own buildings.

Anyway, one will have done one's duty and given them a fair warning. I am working hard now at a book of all the tenants, past and present, with description of occupation, family, etc., and a statement of income and previous history and cause of leaving or ejectment. I have undertaken to do the whole of it; and Miss Pycroft [is] to give me particulars about her tenants. She and I are cut out to work with each other, as she has the practical ability and power to carry things through with steady work, and I have more initiative and power of expression. What I lack is method and strength; both fail me in critical times. I have a much greater *show* of ability than reality, arising from my audacity of mind and plausible way of putting things. My dear old Father, I am a sort of weak edition of you! There is no doubt about it. I enjoy planting, but don't care for the tending!

9. This gallant officer had commanded the Black Watch when it was quartered at the barracks, Church Street, Kensington (the next building to York House; an attractive Queen Anne mansion, standing in an extensive garden, which my father had recently bought, now (1926) demolished), and he had sent his 'Bagpipes' in their kilts to march round and round our garden, whilst I was entertaining a party of East End school children. Insisting on being initiated into rent-collecting, he had scandalized my tenants by offering to pay up the arrears of the most impecunious!

10. Professor Newton, afterwards Sir Charles Newton (1816–94), Keeper of Greek and Roman Antiquities at British Museum and holder of Yates Chair of Classical Archaeology at University College, London, was the most personally attractive, as Dr Richard Garnett, the Keeper of the Books, was the most lovable member, of the B.M. officials with whom I was then intimate.

On Monday I went to bed directly I came from Whitechapel.
... Yesterday I again went to Whitechapel, and dropped into the
Barnetts' to lunch. Mr Barnett is very full of the idea of a conference which would result in an association of the agencies for
Housing of the Poor. About 160,000 persons live under the
superintendence of these bodies; it seems a pity there should not
be some intercommunication and exchange of valuable experience and a sifting of it for public purposes. But the whole thing
wants thinking out. Miss Hill was dining there that night to
discuss it. Mr Barnett thought she would be adverse to it. But it
seems that the lady collectors are deteriorating as a body, and
that some stimulus is wanted to attract stronger and finer women
into the profession; and Mr Barnett evidently grasps at any plan
likely to furnish this. *I* believe in the attraction of belonging to a
*body* who have a definite mission and a definite expression, and
where the stronger and more ambitious natures rise and lead. I
admire and reverence women most who are content to be among
the 'unknown saints'. But it is no use shutting one's eyes to the
fact that there is an increasing number of women to whom a
matrimonial career is shut, and who seek a masculine reward for
masculine qualities. There is in these women something exceedingly pathetic, and I would do anything to open careers to them
in which their somewhat abnormal but useful qualities would get
their own reward. They are a product of civilization, and civilization should use them for what they fit, and be thankful. At
the best, their lives are sad and without joy or light-heartedness;
they are now beginning to be deeply interested and warmed with
enthusiasm. I think these strong women have a great future
before them in the solution of social questions. They are not just
inferior men; they may have masculine faculty, but they have
the woman's temperament, and the stronger they are the more
distinctively feminine they are in this.

I only hope that, instead of trying to ape men and take up
men's pursuits, they will carve out their own careers, and not be
satisfied until they have found the careers in which their particular form of power will achieve most ...

The next entry in the diary, early in December 1885, is a
gloomy description of my father's sudden breakdown in
health, the beginning of a long and lingering illness lasting
for six years. But in order to complete the episode of rent-
collecting I give a final entry, when, a year afterwards, as a

relaxation from daily attendance on my father, I take over Miss Pycroft's work and her room in Wentworth Dwellings, near to Katherine Buildings, during her month's holiday.

It would not do for me to live alone. I should become morbid. . . . But this East End life, with its dirt, drunkenness and immorality, absence of cooperation or common interests, saddens me and weighs down my spirit. I could not live down here; I should lose heart and become worthless as a worker. And practical work does not satisfy me; it seems like walking on shifting sand, with the forlorn hope that the impress of one's steps will be lasting, and guide others across the desert.

Where is the wish for better things in these myriads of beings hurrying along the streets night and day? Even their careless, sensual laugh, coarse jokes, and unloving words depress one as one presses through the crowd, and almost shudders to touch them. It is not so much the actual vice, it is the low level of monotonous and yet excited life; the regular recurrence to street sensations, quarrels and fights; the greedy street-bargaining, and the petty theft and gambling. The better natures keep apart from their degraded fellow-citizens and fellow-workers, live lonely and perforce selfish lives, not desiring to lead their more ignorant and unself-controlled neighbours. Social intercourse brings out, and springs from, the worst qualities in East London; as a society it is an ever-increasing and ever-decomposing mass; the huge mass smothering the small centres containing within them the seeds of social life and growth. Even the faculty for manual labour becomes demoralized, and its capability is reduced.

These buildings, too, are to my mind an utter failure. In spite of Ella Pycroft's heroic efforts, they are not an influence for good. The free intercourse has here, as elsewhere in this dismal mass, a demoralizing effect. The bad and indifferent, the drunken, mean and lowering elements overwhelm the effect of higher motive and noble example. The respectable tenants keep rigidly to themselves. To isolate yourself from your surroundings seems to be here the acme of social morality: in truth, it is the only creed one dare preach. 'Do not meddle with your neighbours' is perforce the burden of one's advice to the newcomer. The meeting-places, there is something grotesquely coarse in this, are the water-closets! Boys and girls crowd on these landings – they are the only lighted places in the buildings – to gamble and flirt. The lady collectors are an altogether superficial thing. Undoubtedly their gentleness and kindness brings light into many homes: but what are they in face of this collective brutality, heaped up together in infectious contact; adding to each other's dirt, physical and moral?

And how can one raise these beings to better things without the hope of a better world, the faith in the usefulness of effort? Why resist the drink demon? A short life and a merry one, why not? A woman diseased with drink came up to me screaming, in her hand the quart pot, her face directed to the Public [House]. What could I say? Why dissuade her? She is half-way to death – let her go – if death ends all. But with her go others; and these others may be only on the first step downwards. Alas! *there* is the pitifulness in this long chain of iniquity, children linked on to parents, friends to friends, and lovers to lovers, bearing down to that bottomless pit of decaying life.

The bright side of the East End life is the sociability and generous sharing of small means. This, of course, brings in its train quarrels and backbiting; for it is easier to give than to bear ingratitude, or to be grateful. And as the 'Public' is the only meeting-place, the more social and generous nature is led away even by its good qualities; while the crabbed mind and sickly constitution isolates itself, and possibly thrives in isolation. The drink demon destroys the fittest and spares the meaner nature: undermines the constitution of one family, and then passes on to stronger stuff. There are times when one loses faith in *laissez-faire* and would suppress this poison at all hazards, for it eats the life of the nation. For hardworking men are tied to drunken wives, and hardworking women to drunken husbands; so that the good are weighted down, and their striving after a better life made meaningless.

And yet there are glimpses into happy homes; sights of love between men and women, and towards little children, and, rarely enough, devotion to the aged and the sick. And, possibly, it is this occasional rest from dirt and disorder that makes the work more depressing; for one must hear unheeded the sickening cry of the sinking man or woman dragging the little ones down into poverty from which there is no rising.

In spite of the numberless out-of-work it is difficult to find really good workmen; for they become quickly demoralized and lose their workfulness. This again is depressing, for how can one help these people if they are not worthy of life from an economic point of view? [MS. diary, 8 November 1886.]

During the spell of rent-collecting I had only one interview with Octavia Hill, about which I find the following entry in my diary:

I met Miss Octavia Hill the other night at the Barnetts'. She is a small woman, with large head finely set on her shoulders. The form of her head and features, and the expression of the eyes and mouth, have the attractiveness of mental power. A peculiar charm in her smile. We talked on artisans' dwellings. I asked her whether she thought it necessary to keep accurate descriptions of the tenants. No, she did not see the use of it. 'Surely it was wise to write down observations so as to be able to give true information,' I suggested. She objected that there was already too much 'windy talk': what you wanted was action; for men and women to go and work day by day among the less fortunate. And so there was a slight clash between us, and I felt penitent for my presumption. But not convinced. [MS. diary, July 1886.]

## The Dead Point

The sympathetic reader may have noted a black thread of personal unhappiness woven into the texture of my observations on East End life. From the entries in my diary I gather that I saw myself as one suffering from a divided personality; the normal woman seeking personal happiness in love given and taken within the framework of a successful marriage; whilst the other self claimed, in season and out of season, the right to the free activity of 'a clear and analytic mind'. But did the extent of my brain power – I was always asking myself – warrant sacrificing happiness, and even risking a peaceful acceptance of life, through the insurgent spirit of a defiant intellect? For in those days of customary subordination of the woman to the man – a condition accentuated in my case by special circumstances – it would not have been practicable to unite the life of love and the life of reason. The following entries in the diary – the first written on the eve of taking over the management of Katherine Buildings, and the others when my father's breakdown in health had led to my withdrawal from active work – reveal me in the grip of self-pity, 'the commonest of all human failings', as Mr Arthur Ponsonby observes in his fascinating introduction to *English Diaries*.[11]

I don't suppose I shall ever again take that interest in myself to make me care to tell my thoughts and feelings to the impersonal confidant – my diary. At any rate there is a long lapse in my habit of writing down what I see, think and feel. And yet I am loath to say good-bye to an old friend, one who has been with me since I first had experiences, and wished to tell them to someone,

11. *English Diaries from the XVIth to the XXth Century*, by Arthur Ponsonby, 1924, p. 9. The following is Mr Ponsonby's criticism of the value of introspective diaries: 'Although the honesty and sincerity of the introspective writers may be beyond question, they do not necessarily by their method give a faithful picture of themselves. . . . We think we know ourselves better than others know us. But the truth is we only know the inside half, and it is doubtful whether any human being in varying moods can describe even that accurately. Moreover, the little shop window we dress and expose to view is by no means all that others see of us. We may be very self-conscious about things which others hardly notice, and throughout our lives we may be entirely unaware of some glaring peculiarity which continually strikes our neighbours. A pelican is not the least self-conscious about the size of his beak. A peacock may be self-conscious about his tail; but he thinks, too, that he has a beautiful voice. On the other hand, outsiders may believe that some person is quite oblivious of certain failings till it is discovered by his diary that he had been struggling with them all along.

'We have said that the honesty and sincerity of indiscreet and un-reticent writers are beyond question. This perhaps requires some qualification. Self-deception is very prevalent. There is a good deal of truth in Byron's remark in his diary, "I fear one lies more to one's self than to anyone else"; or as Gladstone puts it, "I do not enter on interior matters. It is so easy to write, but to write honestly nearly impossible".' (pp. 10–11).

I find that I had my own view of the use of introspective diaries: 'Now that observation is my work I find it is necessary to keep two books, as I did when reading was my source of information. Otherwise the autobiography is eaten up by statistics of wages, hours of work, interviews with employers and workpeople – no space for the history of a woman's life. And without egotistical brooding, it is still necessary to keep a record of individual growth; not merely as a stepping-stone to higher life, but as a help in the future. How often have I found strength in turning over back pages, in watching the inevitable work its way in spite of my desperate clutches at happiness, which were seemingly foredoomed to failure.' [MS. diary, 1 November 1887.]

tho' it were only to a phantom of myself. It would be curious to discover *who it is* to whom one writes in a diary? Possibly to some mysterious personification of one's own identity, to the Unknown, which lies below the constant change in matter and ideas, constituting the individual at any given moment. This unknown one was once my only friend; the being to whom I went for advice and consolation in all the small troubles of a child's life. Well do I remember, as a small thing, sitting under the damp bushes, and brooding over the want of love around one (possibly I could not discern it), and turning in upon myself, and saying, 'Thou and I will live alone and if life be unbearable we will die.' Poor little meagre-hearted thing! And then I said, 'I will teach thee what I feel, think and see, and we will grow wise together; then shall we be happy.' So I went my own little way, and noted diligently what I saw, and began on that to reason. Soon I found that there were other minds seeing and reasoning, who would in their strength carry me on my way. I clutched at this help and they for pity's sake gave it me. But still I loved only the Unknown one, and my feeling was constantly looking inward, though my reason was straining its utmost to grasp what was outside. Then came friendship in the guise of intellectual sympathy; in later years, discovering its true nature in affection, gently putting reason, with its eternal analysis, on one side. And last of all came passion, with its burning heat; and emotion, which had for long smouldered unseen, burst into flame, and burnt down intellectual interests, personal ambition, and all other self-developing motives.

And now the Unknown one is a mere phantom, seldom conjured up, and then not grasped. Reason and emotion alike have turned towards the outer world. Today, I say humbly, 'we have learnt, poor thing, that we can neither see, think nor feel alone, much less live, without the help of others. Therefore we must live *for* others, and take what happiness comes to us by the way.'

And all the time I was travelling in Bavaria this was the eternal refrain running in my mind. I saw things; wrote about them; I lived with an intimate friend. But day and night I cried secretly over my past, and regretted the form which my past life had given me. For who can undo the moulding work of years? We must live with the self we have made. [MS. diary, 15 October 1884.]

On 26 November, the day that London polled in the general election of 1885, my father, who had gone out to vote, was struck down by paralysis; and complete withdrawal, not only from business but also from all social intercourse, became imperative. For me there ensued months of anxiety and gloom, deepened and darkened by my own personal unhappiness. My youngest sister, always in delicate health, had to be persuaded to winter abroad with friends. My father's business engagements and commitments had to be straightened out. As for my own career, it looked as if it had come to a sudden and disastrous end. The new occupation of rent-collecting had to be given up; the comradeship with fellow-workers had to be severed; the attempts at social investigation had to be abandoned. Spending the winter months with my father at Bournemouth, I was deprived of the narcotic of work, and, for the first few weeks, this abstinence was tormenting.

Life seems to my consciousness a horrible fact [I write in my diary, 12 February 1886]. Sometimes I wonder how long I shall support it. . . . I am never at peace with myself now; the whole of my past life looks like an irretrievable blunder. I have mistaken the facts of human life as far as my own existence is concerned. I am not strong enough to live without happiness. . . . I struggle through each new day, waking with suicidal thoughts early in the morning; I try by determined effort to force my thoughts on to the old lines of continuous inquiry, and to beat back feeling into the narrow rut of duty. . . . I look out tonight on that hateful grey sea, the breaking and the vanishing of the surf on the shore; the waves break and vanish like my spasms of feeling; but they return again and again, and behind them is the bottomless ocean of despair. Eight-and-twenty, and living without hope! Now and again deceived by a movement of physical energy, and then falling back on the monotony of despair. No future but a vain repetition of the breaking waves of feeling. [MS. diary, 12 February 1886.]

But when intellectual curiosity is coupled with the habit of work there is always the chance of recovery, and the needful stimulus to renewed hope came quickly. Two days after that wail of egotistical misery there came a letter! Not a love letter, dear reader, but a prosaic communication from the editor of the *Pall Mall Gazette*. There had been a controversy in the newspapers about relief works in the neighbourhood of London for the East End unemployed. Concerned for the work and wages of the tenants of Katherine Buildings, I wrote to protest against the attraction of still more labour to its most over-stocked market by any widely advertised public employment, this letter being my first bid for publicity. 'May we place your signature at the head of your article?' was the gracious reply by return of post. This slight recognition of my capacity as a writer on social questions undoubtedly helped me over the 'dead point'. But other influences were at work.

It is curious that old associations with this place [Bournemouth] and perhaps other causes, have brought me again under the influence of religion [I write in my diary a month later]. ... Is it vanity, this intense desire to devote my life to clearing up social questions? The desire to do it is so strong with me that if I had faith in my own power I could accept an existence of daily toil, devoid of excitement, or what most persons call pleasure, and wanting in the holier happiness of wife and mother. If I believed I had, in my intellect and character, a fit instrument for scientific inquiry, and that I should strike truth, I could pass years of uneventful learning, living to work, and sleeping to rest from work in order to work again. But I dread self-deception. The most pathetic of all lives are men and women cursed with a false estimate of their own ability, and waking up late in life to the waste blankness of unfulfilled instinct, missing even what is open to all men.

And then the isolation in the last days of existence. Surely one would always have friends whatever happened? And I love my friends, have never yet lost one. Even if I did not succeed in my main aim, my life need not be quite cast away! I could still be a practical help to those around me; an odd hand when help was needed. [MS. diary, 15 March, 1886.]

It is strange that the spirit of religion [I write more than a year afterwards] always dwells on an unmarried life, devoted to work, rather than on the restful usefulness of wifehood and motherhood. Sometimes I wonder whether it is inflation; but the consciousness of a special mission to society at large, rather than to individuals, is certainly present in my better moments, ceasing only when I am a prey to passion, selfconsciousness and egotism. In those dark days of worldliness and sensual feeling it died away; it rose again with the resigned fulfilment of my daily duties. Faith in my own capacity to do this work burns in communion with my faith in the Great Spirit, before whom all things are equally small: it brightens or darkens with this higher faith. And yet, when I examine myself with sober judgement, I can see no reason for this faith in myself; any more than, when I examine the outside world, do I find a reason for my faith in God, and in all that God means. Neither can I see the connection between these two faiths – why one should be dependent on the other? . . .

And it is partly this consciousness of a special mission, and this faith in my own capacity, that brings a strained feeling into many of my relationships even to my nearest and dearest friends. To them, whenever I hint at it, the whole idea seems ludicrously out of proportion to what they know of my abilities. But for the most part I hide this faith away, and my best friends know not the spirit that moves me, slowly but inevitably, either to specialized usefulness or to life-failure. [MS. diary, July 1888.]

At this point in my narrative I am tempted to make a trite reflection because it is peculiarly applicable to this dead point in my career. How little we mortals know what is good for us! When I look back on that slough of despond into which I had been slowly sinking from 1884 onward, the deepest and darkest pit being my father's catastrophic illness in the winter of 1885-6, I seem to see a guardian angel busily at work hardening my own purpose and perhaps another person's heart! . . . ('Saved for me,' interjects The Other One.) However that may be, so far as progress in my craft was concerned, this compulsory withdrawal from the distracted and diversified life I had been leading was, on the whole, a gain. Having sampled the method of observation and experiment, and discovered my field of inquiry, what I most needed was historical background; some knowledge of constitutional law and industrial development, and some acquaintance with past and present political and economic theory. With my small reserve of energy, the carrying out of the elaborate scheme of study mapped out in the autumn, concurrently with rent-collecting at Katherine Buildings, and housekeeping and entertaining at York House, was beyond my powers. But what troubles the short-time brain-worker (had I not observed it in the tragic case of Herbert Spencer?) is how to pass the time, after you have exhausted your small store of mental energy, without indulging in ego-tistical brooding over imaginary grievances. This problem was happily solved in the life I had to lead as companion to an invalid. Owing to my habit of early rising, I was able to get through a good three hours' sustained study and con-centrated thought before breakfast; and this was about as much intellectual effort as I was equal to. For the rest of the morning there was plenty of occupation without strain: deal-ing with my father's correspondence; reading aloud the morning papers; walking by the side of his bath-chair, or driving out with him. After the mid-day meal there was the ride, or the walk across country, meditating on the morning's work, followed by another spell of reading aloud, sometimes the favourite novels of Miss Austen or Sir Walter Scott, or some newly published political biography. This peaceful existence was varied by frequent visits of married sisters, and by dashes up to London to meet a friend, or to look up a pamphlet or a Blue Book in the British Museum reading-room.

In one respect I was exceptionally fortunate. Throughout his long lingering illness my father retained his charm of character and temperament.

He has indeed the reward of a loving and self-devoted nature [I write in my diary three months after his first stroke of para-lysis]. His life is without friction and without regret; his only sadness that deeply religious sorrow for mother's death. And even in that there is more tenderness than bitterness; for he loves to dwell on it, and lives over and over again in his imagination those years of married life of which nothing but the good is remembered. These two months have been especially happy; en-joying his physical healthiness, and not regretting his absence of strength, probably because he is unconscious of it. Living in the lives of his children who have been constantly round him — perhaps thinking that these lives of nine women are more important to the world than they are – still, that is pardonable in an aged parent tottering to the grave. [MS. diary, 4 April 1885.]

## Essays in Social Theory

During the following six months the current MS. books multiply rapidly, packed with abstracts and criticisms of historical works – I will spare the reader the catalogue.

There are two uses of historical study in its largest sense [I write in the first weeks of these studies], indispensable knowledge of fact as it enlightens social structure, and the equally indispensable cultivation of imagination to enable you to realize the multiform conditions and temperaments which make up human society. The difficulty lies in keeping off by-ways: mastering the leading facts thoroughly, and not attempting to study all the excrescences, often the most fascinating part of the whole. [MS. diary, 17 April 1886.]

Reading books and writing about them had, however, ceased to be the main instrument of self-education; I was beginning to have ideas of my own, and I was intent on expressing them. In particular, I was puzzling over the methodology of social science – What, for instance, was the right relation of personal observation to statistical inquiry? – a problem which was, in these very months, being raised by the first phases of Charles Booth's inquiry into the life and labour of the people in London. The following entries describe my attempt to solve this problem:

Charles Booth's first meeting of his board of Statistical Research at City Office. Present: Charles Booth, Maurice Paul, Benjamin Jones,[12] secretary of the Working Men's Co-operative Society, London; Radley, secretary to a Trade Society, and myself. Object of this committee to get a fair picture of the whole of London society: that is of the four miles, by district and employment, the two methods to be based on census returns. We passed Charles Booth's elaborate and detailed plan for the work,

12. Benjamin Jones, for many years General Manager of the London Branch of the Co-operative Wholesale Society, became one of my most intimate associates in my inquiry into the Co-operative Movement; author of *Co-operation Production* [2 vols., 1894], and jointly with [Right Honourable] Arthur Dyke Acland, of *Working Men Co-operators* [1884].

and a short abstract of it for general purposes. At present Charles
Booth is the sole worker in this gigantic undertaking. If I were
more advanced in knowledge of previous conditions it is just the
sort of work I should like to undertake, if I were free. . . . [MS.
diary, 17 April 1886.]

Lunched with Mr Barnett: he threw cold water on C. B.'s
scheme; said it was impossible to get the information required,
and was evidently sceptical of the value of such facts. [This
remark, probably a reaction from my super-enthusiasm for fact-
finding, cannot have represented Canon Barnett's eventual
opinion of the value of Charles Booth's Grand Inquest, for he
proved to be a most helpful associate in the inquiry.]

I suggested that 'practical men', those who have actually to do
with the management of society, will not listen to general principles, but will only believe in special application of these principles demonstrated by fact. He replied that, if he had read
history right, it taught that ideas had more influence than facts,
that ideas influence character, and that character was the secret
of all life – all reforms should be judged by their effect on
character. (I believe in ideas, but in ideas following facts. . . .)
I agreed to this, adding that this truth or fact was one that required to be carefully demonstrated: that no amount of *a priori*
reason would be of much value in persuading people; that the
scientific spirit had produced scepticism as to general principles,
and yet was not sufficiently far advanced to give faith in the
scientific method [MS. diary, 18 April 1886.]

Met at C. B.'s office Mr Loch, secretary of C.O.S. Enthusiastic
for accurate knowledge of the conditions of the poor. Evidently,
from his account, there are many who would like to devote themselves to investigation. Borrowed from C. B. volumes of Statistical Society. . . . Statistics defined as the science which treats of
the structure of human society, *i.e.* of society in all its constituents, however minute; and in all its relations, however complex; embracing alike the highest phenomena of education,
commerce, crime, and the so-called 'statistics' of pin-making and
the London dustbin. . . . I am thinking that I might do well to
explain what I mean by social diagnosis, and publish it as an
article in the autumn. If it were well written it would help
Charles Booth's organization. [MS. diary, 4 May 1886.]

I have quite made up my mind to try an article on social diagnosis. It would take the form of showing, first how much we were

influenced in thought and action by descriptions of social facts; that social sentiment was formed by these descriptions, giving rise to a cry for political action or venting itself in voluntary effort; that political action, when taken, was based on these descriptions of social facts (see Commission on Artisans' Dwellings); therefore, the question is not whether we ought to be governed by the sentiment and thought arising from a complete or incomplete knowledge of social facts; whether it would not be wiser to guide our action by the decalogue, or the principles of Herbert Spencer. That is not the question of the practical politics of the social science of the present day. General principles are discredited with the public at large, and with the type of man who they elect to govern us.

Disagreement of the sociologists.

Very careful description of the rise of medical science – comparison between politicians and doctors in their debates. [MS. diary, 6 May 1886.]

Do not get on much with the accumulation of knowledge for my article. It is absolutely necessary that I should get a proof from history that we *do* act from the thought and sentiment formed by the description of social facts. To a large extent, as Charles Booth remarked the other day, legislation is based on class feeling, or on religious or anti-religious feeling, and merely uses facts to prove its points, giving facts as data when they are really illustrations. There are four points I must make: two only have I in any way thought out.

(1) The method of statistical inquiry; illustrations of it in Giffen's *Progress of the Working Classes*. The data used. (2) Fallacy of the equal or identical nature of the units; and the illustrations of this fallacy from Giffen's article, and in the various estimates made of the income of the working class. Here I would insert description of demoralized labour in big towns. (3) Fallacy of the law that labour, like water, goes to where it is best paid. Statement of the other attractions of town life. (4) Fallacy underlying the doctrine of averages as applying to wages.

Personal observation, and its liability to gross error unless checked by the statistical method. Bias in the selection of facts. The superior attraction of certain facts to certain temperaments; instance women's work. Tendency of personal observation to take its own experience of a class as a sample of the whole. This tendency marked in philanthropists, and in politicians who draw their inspiration from philanthropists. Paternal government possibly based to some extent on this mistaken notion of the working class? . . . Great difficulty lying in the way of the observation of social organization is the absence of certain qualities in the observers' minds present in the subject observed. For instance, religion, Bohemianism. Numerous inquiries check each other. [MS. diary, 24 May 1886.]

The essay on Social Diagnosis, designed for immediate publication, failed to get written. During the summer months of 1886, which were spent with my father and sister at The Argoed, our Monmouthshire home, I turned aside to develop a train of thought arising out of the study of the writings of the political economists, from Adam Smith to Karl Marx, from Karl Marx to Alfred Marshall, a notion with regard to the relation of economics to sociology, with a consequent theory of value. But among my manuscripts dated eighteen months later I find one entitled 'Personal Observation and Statistical Enquiry'. The reader who is today what I was then, an industrious apprentice, may find it useful; not merely because it explains, with the zest of an amateur, an essential part of the technique of investigation, but also because it reveals my ignorance of other methods of research. There is, for instance, no sign that I had realized the need for the historical method, with its use of documents and contemporaneous literature, and its special task of discovering the sequence of events leading to changes in the constitution and activities of particular organizations.

The 'little thing of my own', with which I became infatuated during the summer and autumn of 1886, took form in two long essays, one on 'The History of English Economics' and the other on 'The Economic Theory of Karl Marx' – neither the one nor the other being ever presented for publication. I do not suggest that there is any intrinsic originality in these essays; it may well be that all the fallacies are to be found in the writings of other cranks, whilst the grain of truth is in the books of the recognized political economists. All I wish to imply is that the ideas embodied in these essays did in fact originate in my own mind.

The diary brings back to memory both the pains and the purpose of the discipline to which I was subjecting myself.

Oh! my head aches and my ambitious idea looms unreachably large and distant. Political economy is hateful – most hateful drudgery. Still, it is evident to me I must master it. What is more, I must master the grounds of it; for each fresh development [of theory] corresponds with some unconscious observation of the leading features of the contemporary industrial life. At present the form *I* want is not imaginable in this mass of deductions and illustrative facts. I need to understand what are in fact the data upon which political economy is based – what are its necessary assumptions. [MS. diary, 2 July 1886.]

I have broken the back of the economic science as far as I want it – there is perhaps another fortnight's study to fit me to write that one paragraph correctly. Principles of political economy have never been fixed – they have not only grown in number as fresh matter was brought under observation, but the principles themselves have developed with the greater care in the observation of each section of the subject-matter already subjected to generalization. [MS. diary, 18 July 1886.]

Finished my essay on 'The Rise and Growth of English Economics'. I think I have expressed my central idea so that it can be understood, and gives a fairly correct sketch of the historical development. I wonder whether, if it is published, it will be thought very conceited? It isn't so. I can't help my ideas taking a positive form; and if I try to express them in a hesitating way I am only affected. It is either 'I don't know, for I am not capable of judging', or 'I believe with my whole heart and soul that black is black, and nothing will persuade me to say it is white'. It is this hopeless independence of thought that makes my mind so distasteful to many people; and rightly so, for a woman should be more or less dependent and receptive. However, I must go through the world with my mind as it is, and be true to myself. [MS. diary, 14 September 1886.]

The essay on 'The Economic Theory of Karl Marx' was not finished until the following spring.

Three weeks absorbed in my review of Karl Marx, now nearly ended. It has cleared my own ideas; but whether it is written in a form that will be accepted and 'take' I don't know. Sometimes I feel elated, and think that I have got the right end of the stick; at other times, when I am depressed by fatigue, I see in my writing only disjointed half-truths. Anyhow, intellectual production makes life for a time enjoyable; lends to it a personal meaning. And now that I must face many years of this loneliness, and absence of practical interests, constant intellectual endeavour is the only safeguard against morbid feeling. [MS. diary, 25 February 1887.]

Here again I will not burden my narrative by recalling generalizations which I ultimately left on one side, partly because I recognized that I had been carried out of my depth as a reasoner, and partly because I doubted the desirability of a water-tight science of political economy. This intolerable toil of thought was an essential part of the apprenticeship I am trying to describe. Indeed, I can conscientiously recommend the 'industrious apprentice' to go and do likewise! For however futile may have been these imaginings as a contribution to sociology, they served me as illuminating hypotheses – suggesting what proved fruitful lines of investigation – in subsequent inquiries into East End labour and into the Co-operative Movement.

My definition of the sphere of economics, involving, as it did, studies in social pathology, brought me upstanding against the dogmatic conclusions of my revered teacher, Herbert Spencer, whose objections to my speculations I give hereunder.

'So far as I understand them,' he wrote in answer to an abstract of my argument which I had sent him, 'the objections which you are making to the doctrines of the elder political economists, are a good deal of the kind that have of late years been made, and as I think, not rightly made. The explanation of my dissent I must put into a few sentences; using to explain my meaning the analogy which you rightly draw between social life and individual life.

'(1) Physiology formulates the laws of the bodily functions in a state of health, and absolutely ignores pathology – cannot take any account whatever of functions that are not normal. Meanwhile, a rational pathology can come into existence only by virtue of the previously established physiology which has ignored it: until there is an understanding of the functions in health, there is no understanding of them in disease.

'(2) Further, when rational pathology has been thus established, the course of treatment indicated by it is the course which aims as far as possible to re-establish the normal functions – *does not aim to readjust physiology in such a way as to adapt it to pathological states.*

'(3) Just so is it with that account of the normal relations of industrial actions constituting political economy properly so-called. No account can be taken by it of disorder among these actions, or impediments to them. It cannot recognize pathological states at all; and further, the understanding of these pathological social states wholly depends upon previous establishment of that part of social physiology which constitutes political economy.

'(4) And moreover, if these pathological states are due to the traversing of free competition and free contract which political economy assumes, the course of treatment is not the readjustment of the principles of political economy, but the establishment as far as possible of free competition and free contract.

'If, as I understand you, you would so modify politico-economical principles as to take practical cognizance of pathological states, then you would simply organize pathological states, and things would go from bad to worse.' [Extract from letter from Herbert Spencer, 2 October 1886.]

The old philosopher's letter is interesting [I write in my diary a few days later].

His first proposition is very characteristic. ... Certainly, as a fact, physiology has grown out of the study of human and animal life in all its manifestations, birth, growth, disease and death. Physiological truths have actually been discovered by the study of pathology; and it is questionable whether the science of disease did not precede the science of health. But Herbert Spencer has no historical sense.

Second proposition [I had numbered the paragraphs in his letter] shows how thoroughly he misunderstands my position. I have no intention of prescribing a course of treatment; and his reference to it proves that his observation and reasoning on social subjects is subordinated to a *parti pris* on the art of government.

As Bella Fisher [13] misunderstands me in the same way, somehow or other I must have expressed myself wrongly.

Third proposition assumes that political economy is an account of the *normal* relations within industry. The first step surely is to find out what are these relations; then possibly we may, through understanding the various economic diseases, discover what is normal, or shall we say, what is healthy?

But, as I understand Ricardo's economics, he does not attempt to discover, he merely assumes. It is possible that his assumptions may turn out to be an account of normal action, but he does not prove that his assumptions represent fact. But then he does not seem to think that proof is necessary.

Fourth proposition. Again the question of treatment. 'You would so modify politico-economical principles as to take practical cognizance of all pathological states.' How strange! Evidently he regards economic science as a branch of the art of government, not as a branch of sociology: that is, the science of one part of human nature. The object of science is to discover what is; not to tell us according to some social ideal what ought to be. [MS. diary, 4 October 1886.]

13. *Née* Arabella Buckley (sister to Lord Wrenbury), formerly secretary to Sir Charles Lyell and author of *A Short History of Natural Science* and other books, was in those days one of my best friends, encouraging me in my lonely studies and criticizing any essay sent her.

The following entries in the diary show that I submitted the article on Karl Marx to other intellectual advisers – to my cousins the Booths and to my brother-in-law Alfred Cripps, with the following result.

The Booths are delighted with my article; Charlie enthusiastic. They sent it to Professor Beesly. Here is his answer. He overlooks the whole point of the article, which is to distinguish between the labour that is useful and the labour that is useless. That distinction rests on the presence of another element – desire. However, if my idea is true it is unlikely that it will be accepted all at once, especially by men who are pledged by past utterances to contrary opinions. But his criticism shows that I have not made my point clear, and his practical suggestions as to writing and proper references are useful. Evidently he does not think much of the article, or rather, he does not like it. [MS. diary, 12 February 1887.]

Alfred Cripps has read my article, and when I came to hear his opinion he greeted me with: 'Well, Beatrice, I have never read a stiffer article; I am not sure I understand it.' We sat down to read it over word by word. . . . I see now that it must be rewritten in a more concise and perfect form. [MS. diary, 20 March 1887.]

A fortnight later there is another entry about my old friend, on a different note; an entry which incidentally reveals the unpleasant effect on mind and body of the 'hateful drudgery of political economy'.

To Brighton to see the old philosopher. A great mind run dry. But I love the poor old man, and my warm feeling gladdens his life. His existence one continual touching of his pulse to see how it fares with himself – a torturing self-analysis of all his physical feelings. Ah! me; there come times when one would recommend universal suicide. For the whole business of living seems too horribly tiresome to all concerned. And I feel seedy today – sick and headachy and discouraged; but my spirit will return. I need a change; and think the world is going to the Devil because *I* am ailing in body and mind. Courage, my friend, courage. [MS. diary, 18 October 1886.]

## Studies in East End Life

Towards the end of the first year of my father's illness a partial return to active life became practicable. During the summer of 1886, with the help of our 'beloved physician' Sir Andrew Clark, my father's friend as well as his medical adviser, I persuaded my father to give my brother-in-law, Daniel Meinertzhagen,[14] a general power of attorney. To the unfailing kindness and courtesy of this near relative and able financier I owe my release from harassing business, for which I was ill-equipped, and which, owing to the speculative character of some of my father's investments, had caused me continuous anxiety. And when it became evident that my father's illness had passed out of the critical into the stationary phase, my married sisters insisted that they should take

14. Daniel Meinertzhagen, who married my sister Georgina in 1873, was the son of the senior partner, and himself eventually the senior partner, in the old-established firm of foreign bankers and merchants, Frederic Huth & Co., one of the leading 'acceptance houses'. See *A Bremen Family*, by Georgina Meinertzhagen, including interesting diaries of the Daniel Meinertzhagen of the period, when touring in Great Britain, France and Switzerland in 1756, 1798 and 1799. My sister wrote also an account of our grandfather, Richard Potter, entitled *From Ploughshare to Parliament*.

turn and turn about for at least four months of the year, so that, as they kindly put it, I might feel free to amuse myself in society, travel or work. The form that this recreation would take was promptly decided.

Two days in London with the Booths [I write at the end of the year]. Charlie is absorbed in his inquiry, working all his evenings with three paid secretaries. I have promised to undertake 'Docks' in my March holiday. Dear sweet little Mary with her loving ways and charming motherhood. ... Leonard [Courtney] says little, and he has no special regard for what I say, but his personality – perfect integrity and courage – stands out like a rock. [MS. diary, 5 December 1886.]

After spending the winter with my father at Bournemouth I betook myself to the headquarters of the 'Friends', the Devonshire House Hotel, Bishopsgate (which for several years became my London home), and started work.

Thoroughly enjoyed the last month [I write towards the middle of my holiday]. Have got statistical outline of dock labour for Tower Hamlets.

Certainly, inquiring into social facts is interesting work: but it needs the devotion of a life to do it thoroughly. I feel that the little bit of work I do will be very superficial, and that, until I can take to inquiry as a life-work, and not only as a holiday task, I shall do very little good with it. But I need much preparation. A general but thorough knowledge of English history and literature: a skeleton, the flesh and blood of which I could at any moment gain by specialized study. A theoretical grasp of the growth of industry, and of the present state of industrial organization. Then the thinking out of principles – of the limits to the subject-matter and the question of method. This, and a good deal more, I need before I am fully prepared for direct observation. A study of this kind is compatible with my home life, with its uniform duty of tender devotedness. Perhaps I shall be free before I am fit for freedom! Even now my freedom is considerable; more considerable than I have enjoyed since mother's death. Four months of the year I shall be able to devote to actual observations, and if I take my rest in the country, that will not leave much more than six months to be spent in literary preparation [of the material collected]. But as the observation will necessarily be disjointed and incomplete, it will serve more to clear my own ideas than to form definite pictures of life. My education is yet to come.

In the meantime I am enjoying my life. I see more reason for believing that the sacrifices I have made to a special intellectual desire were warranted by a certain amount of faculty. As yet I have had no proof of this; my capacity has not been stamped as current coin; the metal is still soft and I know not whether it will bear the right impression. Still, I feel power, I feel capacity, even when I discover clearly my own limitations, for I think I discern the way to overcome them. Alfred Cripps's criticism of my article made me aware how very far off it was from good work; but it was better than the last, and, unlike the last, I see how I can alter and make it good.

And the old faith in individual work is returning – in the sanctity of moral and intellectual conviction. [MS. diary, 30 March 1887.]

I feel rather low about the proposed paper on Dock Labour. Besides bare statistics I want local colouring; a clear description of the various methods of employing men, of types of character of men employed, and where they live. Must realize the 'waiting at the gates', and find out for myself the exact hours at which the different classes are taken on. [MS. diary, May 1887.]

There follow pages and pages of notes of interviews with dock officials and the various grades of dock labourers and their wives. Morning after morning I am up early, watching the struggle for work at the dock gates; and observing the leisurely unloading of sailing vessels compared to the swift discharge of steamers.

This morning [I record early in May] I walked along Billingsgate to the London Docks. Crowded with loungers smoking villainous tobacco; coarse talk with the clash of the halfpenny on the pavement every now and again. Bestial content or hopeless discontent on their faces. The lowest form of leisure – the senseless curiosity about street rows, idle gazing at the street sellers, low jokes – this is 'the chance' the docks offer! I met Dartford, respectable tenant K[atherine] B[uildings], and he greeted me cordially. He is always in work, and complains that he never gets a holiday – says that many of the unemployed do not want to work, and get sacked for not turning up. 'I make a point of not mixing up with anyone. Women get thick together, and then there is always a row. The curse is the daily payment; it is always a mistake not to give the woman the money once a week instead of at odd times.' Said [that] the worse a man is, the more work he will get at the docks. [MS. diary, May 1887.]

Go to docks early in the morning [records another entry]. Permanent men respectable, sober, clean. Casuals low-looking, bestial, content with their own condition. Watch brutal fight and struggle: then sudden dissolution of the crowd with coarse jokes and loud laugh. Look of utter indifference on their faces: among them the one or two who have fallen from better things – their abject misery. The mass of the rejected lounge down to another dock to spread themselves over the entrance to the various wharves. About 100 of the lowest will congregate in the 'cage' in Nightingale Lane waiting for the chance of a foreman needing them as odd men. If a man weary of ennui and of an empty stomach drops off to sleep, his companions will promptly search his pocket for the haphazard penny. [MS. diary, May 1887.]

In the evening went to club in St George's Yard and talked to 'preferables' at London and St Katherine's docks. Robinson, socialist dock labourer; originally tobacconist. Emigrated, and returned to England because he became homesick. A rolling stone, superior and interesting-looking. Bitter and hopelessly illogical. The right to live and to marry and to have children, the basis of his argument. Gives deplorable account of lack of employment at Victoria Dock; an average of two or three days for each man. Contract system spreading fast; eight men under contract system will do the work of thirty employed directly by the Company. Says he himself, when he is working for the Company, tries to do as little as he can. Says that socialism makes little progress among dock labourers; they are incapable of organization. Sees no remedy but a complete reconstruction of society. The State might supply '*pleasant* labour' for everyone. Considers it a grievance that labourers are not allowed to take the tobacco that is being destroyed [by Custom House officials]; if it is found on their persons they are imprisoned for seven days. Says he makes a point of secreting tobacco on his person in order to defy the rule. Complains that the women of the working class are no companions to their husbands. 'When I was courting my wife I could not get a word out of her; it was just walking by her side and giving her an occasional kiss. If a working man gets a good mother, and a woman that does not drink, as his wife, that is as much as he can expect. And my wife was not the first woman I courted. They are all alike in not talking of anything but details.' Kennedy said much the same thing when he told Ella Pycroft that she did not know what it was to talk to a woman without brains. Robinson admitted that capitalists are in a poor way. He hates competition, machinery, employers and the Executives of Trade Unions. [MS. diary, 13 May 1887.]

Among those I interview are the School Board Visitors for the district; and here is an account of two interviews with Kerrigan, School Board Visitor for the Stepney Division.

Describes his casuals, about 900, as hereditary casuals, London-born. The worst scoundrel is the cockney-born Irishman. The woman is the Chinaman of the place: drudges as the women of savage races: she slaves all day and night. Describes the communism of this class. They do not migrate out of the district, but they are constantly changing their lodgings: 'They are like the circle of the suicides in Dante's Inferno; they go round and round within a certain area.' They work for each other: hence low ideal of work. They never see excellence in work. They never leave the neighbourhood. From the dock-gate they lounge back to the street: 'treating' and being 'treated', according to as they have earned a few pence. Live chiefly on 'tobacco' which is a compound of sugar, vinegar, brown paper and German nicotine. The teapot is constantly going – bread and a supply of dried haddock which goes through a domestic preparation: dried in the chimney and acquiring a delicate flavour by lying between the mattresses of the beds. They never read. Except the Catholics, they never go to church. On the Bank Holiday the whole family goes to Victoria Park. 'Permanent' men live outside the neighbourhood – Forest Gate, Hackney, Upton, some even at Walthamstow. Kerrigan does not think that corruption and bribery goes on in the West India Dock, as it does at the London and St Katherine's. 'Permanent' men might be classed just above the artisan and skilled mechanics. They read Herbert Spencer and Huxley, and are speculative of intelligent working men. [MS. diary, May 1887.]

Most amusing day with Kerrigan, School Board Visitor living in Victoria Park [I record a few days later]. Victoria Park lies in the extreme east of London; it is surrounded by streets of small two-storey houses of the genteel type – a porch and one bow-window, Venetian blinds and lace curtain. These houses are inhabited by the lower middle class; now and again there is a row of more modest little dwellings, without the bow-window or the porch, or with a bow of less publicity and consideration – houses inhabited by the tip-top East End working class, mechanics, or 'permanent' labourers.

Sunday afternoon is a great time in Victoria Park, not confined to local people, but the meeting-place of the enthusiasts and the odd-minded of the whole East End district. The first group we came to were congregating around a small organ; they were old men, women with children, and one or two stray youths; and they called themselves 'The Elder Branch of Primitive Methodists' (?). Verily they looked 'primitives'! Another group, larger and more combative, was made up of the Young Men's Christian Association; City clerks, spotty, seedy and smelly, but one or two among them inspired by living enthusiasm. They were singing loudly of the Blood of Jesus; of the eternal happiness, which is to wipe away the feeling of grievance among the failures of this life, and to compensate for an existence of dreary, half-starved drudgery. Some ten yards farther, a small knot of working men crowded round two disputants, an English mechanic and a Russian emigrant. Foreign emigration was the question disputed; apparently both were agreed that the arrival of low-class labour ought to be stopped; but the Englishman insisted that it was the foreigners' fault for coming, while the Russian declared that it was the English Parliament who ought to prevent it by a heavy poll-tax on the invader.

'What is the good of your Government?' jeered the foreigner in a broken accent. 'You call it representative, and say that you working men make it. But you tell them to do a thing, and instead of doing it they go on talking for twenty years, and then the time is past.' 'Yes,' said the wit in the crowd, 'the English Parliament is like the Christian who is always saying, "I will arise and go to my Father", and yet he never gets up and goes.'

The main crowds were gathered on a gravel space under trees. Here was a nauseous nigger mouthing primitive methodism; a mongrel between the unctuous sacramentalist and the Christy Minstrel. Back to back with him, facing another crowd, there was a messenger from the 'Hall of Science'. He was explaining to an attentive audience of working men that man was an animal, and nothing but an animal. His face was lined by sensuality, and moved by shallow quickness and assertiveness of thought. He used scientific phrases, quoted freely from Huxley, Darwin and German physiologists, and assumed a certain impartiality in his treatment of rival religious theories of man's development. The burden of his message from the sphere of science was the animalism of man, the gross unreason of believing in any higher nature. But the thickest crowd surrounded the banner of the social democrat.[15] From a platform a hoarse-voiced man de-

15. My first introduction to the Social Democratic Federation, and the socialism based on 'scientific materialism' which they preached, was an interview with the accomplished daughter of Karl Marx in the spring of 1883. And here is the entry in my diary:

Went in afternoon to British Museum and met Miss Marx in refreshment-room. Daughter of Karl Marx, socialist writer and refugee. Gains her livelihood by teaching literature, etc., and corresponding for socialist newspapers; now editing *Progress* in the enforced absence of Mr. Foote. Very wrath about imprisonment of latter [for blasphemy].

'I couldn't see much joke in those particular extracts but there was nothing wrong in them. Ridicule is quite a legitimate weapon. It is the weapon Voltaire used, and did more good with it than with any amount of serious argument. We think the Christian religion an immoral illusion, and we wish to use any argument to persuade the people that it is false. Ridicule appeals to the people we have to deal with, with much greater force than any amount of serious logical argument. The striking difference of this century and the last is, that free-thought was the privilege of the upper classes then, and it is becoming the privilege of the working classes now. We want to make them disregard the mythical next world and live for this world, and insist on having what will make it pleasant to them.'

It was useless to argue with her—she refused to recognize the beauty of the Christian religion. She read the gospels as the gospel of damnation. Thought that Christ, if he had existed, was a weak-headed individual, with a good deal of sweetness of character, but quite lacking in heroism. 'Did he not in the last moment pray that the cup might pass from him?' When I asked her what the 'socialist programme' was, she very sensibly remarked that I might as well ask her to give me in a short formula the whole theory of mechanics. Socialist programme was a deduction from social science, which was the most complicated of all sciences. I replied that from the very little I knew about political economy (the only social science we English understood) the social philosophers seemed to limit themselves to *describing forces*; they were more or less necessarians. She did not contradict this. I do not know whether it is true or not.

In person she is comely, dressed in a slovenly picturesque way, with curly black hair flying about in all directions. Fine eyes full of life and sympathy, otherwise ugly features and expression, and complexion showing the signs of an unhealthy excited life, kept up with

nounced the iniquities of the social system; in one hand he held Malthus, in the other, *Fruits of Philosophy*. The subject was a delicate one – the rival methods of checking population, late marriage versus preventive checks. He, however, joined issue with both methods, for he asserted that neither was needed. There was bread enough for all if it was equally distributed. Men starving while warehouses were stocked to overflowing; it was the commercial system that was at fault, not the laws of nature. The crowd was not enthusiastic, only interested and eager to listen to new suggestions. For the most part they were men in full employment, and their speculative interest in social reform was not whetted by positive hunger. Now and again, when he denounced employers, there was a grunt of approval; when he pointed out the cul-de-sac of competition there was even slight applause. But when he turned from what is, to what would be if the socialist dogma reigned supreme, there was simply scepticism – readiness to listen but not willingness to perform . . .

We wended our way back between these crowds to Mr Kerrigan's lodging. The back room of a small working-class dwelling served as dining, sitting, sleeping, working room of this humble individual, with the most ingenious arrangements for all his functions. Kerrigan is an amusing Irishman; a seaman by profession, taken to School Board visiting as a livelihood. Intensely interested in his fellow-men, with extensive but uncultivated knowledge of science and literature. He is a lover of books. His language is picturesque and descriptive; he has a knack of ready generalization, and his personal experience among the East End poor falls readily into definite pictures of different classes. In theory he is neither destructive nor constructive, and seems without prejudices. I should think too much entertained and interested to have many vices. There was something pathetic in his intense pleasure in our visit and our conversation. He gave us an excellent tea, and afterwards first-rate cigarettes. What would the conventional West End acquaintance say to two young women smoking and talking in the bed, sitting, smoking, working and bath room of an East End School Board Visitor? [MS. diary, Sunday, May 1887.]

stimulants and tempered by narcotics. Lives alone, is much connected with Bradlaugh set. . . . [MS. diary, 24 May 1883.] For an account of this remarkable woman and her tragic end, see *My Years of Exile*, by Edouard Bernstein, pp. 158–65.

Found it quite impossible to write in London; and wasted a week in attempting to do so. Interesting dinner with B. Jones and Mr Hoffmann – Hoffmann is a Christian Socialist, and hopes that the spirit of true Christianity will make it impossible for a man to need the means of subsistence. Argues that all men have a right to live and to live well. Does not recognize the fact that many men do not fit their conditions and cannot be made to do so. He believes that socialism should be the result of public opinion; and that a socialist should preach at the corners of the streets, the doctrines they believe in. Would not meet the question of increased numbers, assuming that every family were allowed to increase as they chose and provided with the means of so doing. [MS. diary, May 1887.]

As a contrast to my East End experiences, I give a stray note about a West End dinner-party.

Dined with Courtneys: John Morley, Arthur Balfour, Secretary for Ireland, E. Russell, Editor of *Liverpool Post* and rising politician, Mrs Fawcett and Mrs Dugdale. Arthur Balfour a charming person. Tall, good-looking and intellectual. Says cynical and clever things, which are meant to be cleverer than they turn out to be. Easy and well-bred – of the old type of gentleman-politician, a type fast fading out of existence. Is connected with the world of science through his gifted brother, who died sometime since. The party most harmonious; John Morley, evidently in sympathy with Arthur Balfour, in spite of their public opposition. John Morley amused us by describing the Front Opposition Bench, and repeating Gladstone's remarks on the speeches made. The conversation was easy and pleasant, but it was all froth. No one said what they thought, and everyone said what they thought to be clever. [MS. diary, May 1887.]

In after years I learnt to appreciate the subtle intellect and literary gifts of the author of the *Defence of Philosophic Doubt* and the *Foundations of Belief*. Other entries of the MS. diary, of which the following is a sample, reveal a bias against politicians in general, and the gentleman politicians in particular; and my preference for the official peer, as compared with the hereditary legislator.

He [Lord Granville[16]] is an inconsiderable man, pleasant

16. This was the second Earl Granville (1815–91), who, after ten

enough. But mental insignificance, joined to great political position, is irritating to a democratic mind. Like most 'society men' he does not care for the likes of me; and until last night he had not spoken to me. But I having appeared in a pretty black gown, he came up to me while I was discussing vehemently labour questions with Mr Cross, with whom I had struck up friendship. Lord Granville listened with a puzzled air; and when I tried, out of politeness, to bring him in, explaining to him the actual point we were thrashing out, he looked still more utterly at sea, as if I had asked him to join in a discussion on Chinese metaphysics. What could a woman, who really by nightlight looked quite pretty, want with such questions; still less, how could she expect a polished man of the world to know what she was talking about? So the noble Earl stood silently gazing in mild surprise – I remember Chamberlain on Lord Granville 'One does not expect to sit next an old nurse in Cabinet Council' – and turned away to tell a little story to some more congenial party. At breakfast he came and sat next me, and I started him off on Lady Ponsonby, and he seemed perfectly happy. After he had finished with her he meandered on about others of like position, till I was lost in the pursuit of dukes and duchesses, their personal characteristics and pedigrees, and could not give the requisite sympathetic appreciation. So we relapsed into silence.

With Lord Hobhouse[17] I had a great deal of conversation, and very sympathetic conversation it was. Liked him better than I have ever done before and I think he returned the compliment.

---

years in the House of Commons (1836–46), was for a whole generation the leading representative of the Whig and Liberal parties in the House of Lords, and an influential member of every Government from that side of the House. In 1857 he was made a Knight of the Garter. In 1859 the Queen offered him the Prime Ministership, but he was unable to form a Government. When I met him he had been alternately Secretary of State for the Colonies and for Foreign Affairs in Gladstone's three Governments of 1868, 1880 and 1886. He was a Fellow of the Royal Society; and Chancellor of the University of London, 1856–91.

17. Hobhouse, Arthur, first Baron Hobhouse of Hadspen (1819–1904); chancery barrister, 1845; Q.C., 1862; member of Council of Governor-General of India, 1872–7; K.C.S.I., 1877; member of judicial committee of Privy Council (without salary), 1881–1901; raised to the peerage, 1885; see *Lord Hobhouse, a Memoir*, by L. T. Hobhouse and J. L. Hammond, 1905.

There is a genuine ring about him; he lacks play of mind and is deficient in humour, but he is thoughtful and conscientious to an almost painful degree. Kindness and a chivalrous moral tone is his peculiar charm – a sort of fine essence of integrity in all things. He interests me as Henry's [my brother-in-law] uncle. [MS. diary, 21 October, 1888.]

And here are two other entries about John Morley, one before and one after that given above.

Met John Morley yesterday at Kate's, and spent an evening with him and the Courtneys alone. A lovable man I should think to his friends. Quick sympathy and appreciation of the ideas of others. But surely not a man of statesmanlike grasp or of practical sagacity? An 'intellectual', delighting in 'the order of thought', not in 'the order of things'. Spoke enthusiastically of Gladstone's power of work, of his charm, and of his absorption in the idea then present to his mind; he [Gladstone] obviously regarding men as shadows, liking those best who gave him the ease of flattery and perfect agreement. This, joined to what Huxley said at Bournemouth – that Gladstone never sought truth for itself but always regarded principles and opinions in so far as they were held and expressed by a more or less number of people – throws some light on the character of the G.O.M. [MS. diary, April 1886.]

I had a long talk with John Morley. He is anxious about the socialists at Newcastle. Up till now he has treated them with indifference, not to say contempt; but they mustered two thousand votes at the last School Board election, and Morley began to take them seriously. He was preparing for an interview at Newcastle, and was full of the eight hours' movement and other social questions. In his speeches he asserts that the social question is the one thing to live for; he ignores imperial politics and wants to cut off England from all foreign relations. And yet he has evidently never thought about social questions; he does not know even the A B C of labour problems. Oh! ye politicians! [MS. diary, 11 February 1889.]

It is strange, living in close correspondence with all sorts and conditions of men [I wrote as, back in the country, I pondered over the records of my London experiences] how one observes the same fact about classes as about individuals. Each class seems to have a certain range of ideas, and to be incapable of growing out of these ideas, unless it ceases to be a class. And so it is with individuals. Few individuals are capable of continual growth. It is the gift of perpetual youth; and most of us sink, early or late in our lives, into a state of intellectual self-complacency or indolent doubtfulness. We settle down to one point of view, and naturally enough our intellectual horizon remains eternally the same, as we gaze constantly on one side of each object, forgetting that there are at least four other – maybe an indefinite number – of sides. [MS. diary, August 1887.]

And here are my reflections, on the day of publication in the *Nineteenth Century*, of my first essay as a recognized social investigator.

Yesterday we gave up York House; and my article on Dock Life appears in the *Nineteenth Century*:[18] exit hateful association, enter promising beginning ... it is the work I have always longed to do, the realization of my youthful ambition. ... This summer I dawdled, and wrote my paper with no enthusiasm and little effort. It was accepted by the leading review, and is now printed two months after acceptance.[19] Two years ago I should have trembled with delight. Now I look upon it as only the natural result of my labour. ... I know I have no talent, that I am almost lacking in literary faculty. But I have originality of aim and method, and I have faith that I am on the right track, and I have a sort of persistency which comes from despair of my own happiness. My success will depend on my physical strength, and on whether I have sufficient moral back-bone to banish self with its dark shadow, so that I may see things in their true proportion without morbid exaggeration of what is painful. [MS. diary, 30 September 1887.]

One of the results of my notoriety as a female expert on dock labour appears in the following entry:

Meeting at the Tabernacle, Barking Road, Canning Town. I was advertised to appear at this meeting of dock labourers. The hall was crowded, the men fine, determined, though quiet-

18. *Nineteenth Century*, October 1877.

19. This article was afterwards included in the first instalment of Charles Booth's inquiry published in the spring of 1889. In the final edition (1902) it appears as the first chapter of vol. iv., Poverty Series.

looking set, far superior to the run of dock labourers at the dock gates. I was the only woman present, and as I made my way up to the platform enjoyed my first experience of being 'cheered' as a public character. In the little room behind the platform were assembled the speakers of the evening, at which the renowned X. Y. was advertised to appear. The chairman, Alderman Phillips, was a pleasant, good, little fellow, with the small commonplace head and kindly features denoting hard-working philanthropy. Two or three councillors; among others a self-important little man who bustled into the room exclaiming 'Well, what's it all about? what's one to say?' and then, without waiting for an answer, 'I suppose the usual thing, elevation of the working class: grandeur of unity, etc. etc.' There was a considerable confusion in the minds of the other speakers as to what they *were* to say; for, with the exception of the secretary of the newly formed association, they none of them knew anything about labour or dock trade. I was pressed to second the resolution, but absolutely refused to speak. Secretary Tillett opened the proceedings. A light-haired little man with the face of a religious enthusiast; might have been a revivalist. Honest undoubtedly, but ignorant and unwise. He ranted against white slavery, sub-contract and irregular hours. I do not think the meeting was impressed, though they applauded his denunciation of sub-contract. He went on indefinitely until the chairman checked him, and whispered that he had better keep to the point and propose the resolution. There followed the series of councillors, whose words hardly justified their title. A small man with a loud voice, a professional speaker, accustomed to fill up gaps at public meetings, pranced up the platform and shouted loudly, 'When I see on the one side of me the starved dock labourers with faces marked by the intolerable lines of overwork, surrounded by a wretched family, a wife worn by strain, worry and labour, and on the other side of me the bloated official of the dock company with his brougham, his well-built house and his servants, I feel and I say that, etc. etc.' Happily at this moment the bulky form of X.Y. was seen wending its way to the platform. No one knew him except the secretary. He took the seat nearest to me, and asked the chairman to give him the resolution to look at. Then in a stage whisper to the secretary, 'I will give you £20, but don't let my name appear. I don't want it to be known. Of course you will support me about foreign immigration.' When on his legs I examined him. He is a big man, with a red and somewhat bloated face, and an equally corpulent body; black eyes with a suspicious tendency to fiery bloodshot, and a heavy black moustache and somewhat unctuous voice, and an intolerable gift of the gab. I was surprised, after his stage whisper, that the leading feature of his speech was the announcement of his gift of £20. He dwelt on the iniquity of pauper immigration; but to this audience of dock labourers his denunciation fell flat, seeing that foreigners do not patronize the dock gates. He spoke fluently with the customary three adjectives at every turn. No sooner had he sat himself down than he offered to take me back in his brougham, which I promptly accepted. He was considerably 'cheered' as we left the platform: and I followed meekly in the train of the hero who had given £20. The man who opened the door of his brougham refused to take the tip offered, which X. Y. characterized as 'noble'. The interest of the conversation in our long drive homeward was slightly spoilt by the strong smell of spirit which the philanthropist transferred to the atmosphere of the closed brougham. I suggested that the night air was pleasant; and to my extreme relief he forthwith opened the window. His talk was the usual sympathy with the trouble and poverty of the lower classes, interspersed with 'When I saw Gladstone the other day', 'Only this day week I was staying with Tennyson', 'The day I had worked at the docks I went to lunch with Lord Rothschild'. We touched on the population question, and he said somewhat alarmingly, 'I need a noble woman to help me', at which I started back, as just previously he had asked me to supper with him, which I refused. Whether it was the effect of the public meeting or of the spirit, X. Y. became rather too confidential. I was disgusted with his reference to family life as a curse to a man: a delicate wife, it seems, expected him to live with her for seven months out of the twelve. 'Of course if your family sympathizes with your work it is all very well,' was his response to my assertion that family life was the only thing worth living for. [MS. diary, 1 December 1887.]

The essay on 'Dock Life in East London' was, even in my own estimation, an inferior piece of work; the investigations had been scamped for lack of time, and my conclusions with regard to the disease of under-employment and its possible prevention, though sound as far as they went, were neither exhaustive nor sufficiently elaborated to be helpful.[20] But its

20. The conclusions I reached are thus summed up: 'In the indivi-

immediate acceptance for publication by the editor of the *Nineteenth Century* encouraged me to undertake another task in connection with the Booth inquiry.

Settled with Charlie on the autumn's work; The Sweating System is to be the subject of my next paper. I have it in mind to make it more of a picture than the article on Dock Labour, to dramatize it. I cannot get this picture without living among the actual workers. This I think I can do. [MS. diary, 12 August 1887.]

The note of self-pity characteristic of the MS. diary of 1884–7 is now superseded by a strain of self-complacency – 'the second commonest of all human failings', Mr Arthur Ponsonby will doubtless observe in his next volume on English diaries!

Lunched with Knowles [the editor of the *Nineteenth Century*]. He was very polite, and not only offered to take the article on the Sweating System, but proposed one on Co-operation – the very subject I had thought of writing on in the summer. I expect I shall do the Sweating System for C. Booth, and that 'The Present State of Co-operation in England' will be my next paper in the

dualism run wild, in the uncontrolled competition of metropolitan industry, unchecked by public opinion or by any legislative regulation of employment, such as the Factory Acts, it seems impossible for any set of individuals, whether masters or men, to combine together to check the thoughtless and useless caprices of that spoilt child of the nineteenth century – the consumer. A possible remedy is a kind of municipal socialism, which many of us would hesitate to adopt, and which in the case of the docks and waterside would take the form of amalgamation under a Public Trust – a Trust on which the trader, consumer and labourer would be duly represented. This would facilitate a better organization of trade and admit the dovetailing of business. And supposing the Public Board did not undertake to provide the labour, they could at least throw open the gates to a limited number of labour contractors working under legislative regulations, who would be enabled by the extent of their business to maintain permanent staffs of workmen. I believe that the idea of a Public Trust is not regarded as without the sphere of practical politics by dock and waterside authorities.' [Charles Booth's Final Edition (1902), Poverty Series, vol. iv., chapter on 'The Docks', by Beatrice Potter, pp. 33–4.]

*Nineteenth Century*. Altogether, I am hopeful. I have made a steady rise in literary capacity, as my diary shows. There is no reason why I should not rise further. [MS. diary, November 1887.]

The inquiry into the sweating system, eventually narrowed down to sweating in the manufacture of cheap clothing, resulted in five separate essays, four appearing as articles in the *Nineteenth Century* and (including two of the former) three as additional chapters of Charles Booth's first volume, published in the spring of 1889.[21] Moreover, my determination to present 'a picture' as well as a monograph led me into an experiment in the craft of a social investigator which brought in its train some temporary notoriety; and consequences, pleasant and unpleasant.

Whilst yet in the country, I started to plan out my campaign, so that the autumn and spring holiday months should be used to the greatest advantage. All the volumes, blue books, pamphlets and periodicals bearing on the subject of sweating that I could buy or borrow were read and extracted; the Charles Booth secretariat was asked to supply particulars of the workshops within the area selected for exploration, classified according to the numbers employed in each; friends and relatives were pestered for introductions to public authorities, philanthropic agencies and all such business enterprises (not only wholesale and retail clothiers, but also

21. The four essays appearing in the *Nineteenth Century* were 'Dock Life in the East End of London', October 1887; 'The Tailoring Trade of East London', September 1888; 'Pages from a Workgirl's Diary', October 1888; and 'The Lords Committee on the Sweating System', June 1890. Of these, 'Dock Life', 'The Tailoring Trade', together with a separate essay on 'The Jewish Community of East London', were included in Charles Booth's first volume, published in 1889; and in his Final Edition of 1902 are to be found in Poverty Series, vols. iii. and iv. Over and above these essays there was a paper read at the Co-operative Congress, 1892, 'How to do away with the Sweating System'. Three of these essays, 'The Diary of an Investigator', 'The Jews of East London' and 'How to do away with the Sweating System', are re-published in our *Problems of Modern Industry*, by S. and B. Webb, 1898.

shippers, sewing-machine companies and others) as were likely to have contact with East End workers, whether sub-contractors or wage-earners. Once settled at the Devonshire House Hotel, my time was mainly occupied in interviewing employers and employed, School Board Visitors, Factory and Sanitary Inspectors and members of the Jewish Board of Guardians; in visiting home-workers and small masters whom I happened to know and in accompanying rent-collectors, or the collectors of payments due for the hire of sewing-machines, on their rounds of visits. In the intervals of these interviews and observations I trained as a trouser-hand, successively in the workrooms of the Co-operative Wholesale Society and in the 'domestic workshop' of a former tenant of Katherine Buildings, by way of preparation for 'finding work' during the busy season of the spring months.

Here are sample entries from the MS. diary of the autumn and winter of 1887–8:

Read through all the back numbers of the *Briton* [I write early in September while still at The Argoed], a paper devoted to crus-ade against sweating and foreign immigration; sensational outcry and unproven facts; principal contributor a certain Jew, A. B., author of pamphlet on Sweating System. Thinking he was an enthusiast, I asked for interview and enclosed 5s.

We met at C. Booth's office. Small man with low retreating forehead and retreating chin; failed to explain anything, and utterly ignorant of the facts even about the workers. Said he did not believe in usual methods of trade unionism and disapproved of cooperative production (disapproval afterwards explained by Mr Barnett). A 'Member' friend of his was going to introduce a Bill to abolish sweating; he [A. B.] intended 'giving the House of Commons a chance of remedying the grievances of the workers'; if it failed to do so, *he* knew what he should advise the workers to do – though he would not tell us the nature of his advice. The society to which he was secretary numbered two hundred; and yet it was going to transform the condition of the London tailors!

Mr Barnett, with whom I afterwards dined, told me he was a regular scamp, and embezzled the funds of a cooperative society; lived on his wits. I felt rather ashamed of my gift of 5s., and anxious to retreat from my new acquaintanceship. So long as Socialism has as exponents this sort of man there is little danger that it will enlist the sympathies of the better sort of workman. [MS. diary, September 1887.]

Arkell [one of Charles Booth's secretaries] dined here yesterday. Have asked him to colour map, so as to see exactly where the trades are localized. [MS. diary, September 1887.]

My first experience of the tailoring shops was in the easy form of a friendly visit, under my own name, to a 'sweater' to whom I was introduced as an inquirer by one of the tenants of Katherine Buildings. This was, in fact, an 'interview' under informal conditions, and it finds record as such in my diary.

First morning learning how to sweat; Mrs Moses, Oxford Street, Stepney. Four rooms and a kitchen, 12s., one room let, 3s. Street deserted during daytime, with public-houses at each corner. A small backyard. Three rooms on ground floor, two used as workshop; two machinists, Polish Jews; the master acts as presser. In back room mistress and first hand, a Scottish woman, and two girls learning the trade. Coats turned out at 1s. 2d. each, trimmings and thread supplied by the sweater. Buttonholes 4½d. a dozen by woman outside. Mistress said the woman by working very hard could earn 10s. a week, with 2s. deducted for silk. Evidently these people work tremendously hard; woman working from eight to ten without looking round, and master working up to two o'clock, and often beginning at five the next morning. The mistress was too busy to give me much information; and I did nothing but sew on buttons and fell sleeves. They all seemed very pleasant together. Went next morning, but they were too busy to let me in; they had to 'drive' to get [work delivered in time] into shop. The master was grumpy and suspicious; go there on Monday. [MS. diary, October 1887.]

Monday morning the work is slack for plain hands; Moses preparing coats for machines, and Mrs Irons, the Scottish woman, helping him. The other young woman had taken her departure; she was not satisfied with 2s. 6d. a week and her training. ... Mrs Moses was communicative and told me about her business. She and her husband worked for Hollington's; but foreman was brutal and pay wretched; now she worked for

Rylands, export firm. For coats she was paid 1s. 6d. each, she finding the thread. She paid 4½d. a dozen for buttonholes; and the widow who undertook this work might earn 10s. a week, with deductions of 2s. for silk. First machinist paid 6s. a day; second, 3s.; the Scottish woman, 1s. 6d. Mr Moses worked early and late during the coat season. The slack season was the bad time for them; they 'rid' themselves of the little furniture they had. Certainly, if the workshop was indicative of the rest of the house, there was not much capital to fall back on: one or two deal tables whereon to set the work; a broken-down settee and a few chairs; a ragged bit of blue paper tacked on to the mantelpiece, and a broken vase and one or two old lamps were the only visible signs of subsistence for out-of-work days. Mrs Moses's dress was of the dirtiest and most dishevelled. Mrs Moses's history was briefly this. She was born in London, and had never been in the country; three years ago she had been up at the West End to the 'Healtheries' [the Exhibition at South Kensington], treated by a brother-in-law. She went about once a year to the theatre, never to the synagogue. She had children by her first husband, and her second husband had a son. Presently she went out to buy a bit of dinner, returning with a fresh haddock. . . . Later on, I had a chat with Mrs Irons, while Mrs Moses was washing the haddock in the backyard. She also had her history of troubles. Was brought up a tailoress in Glasgow, married a professional street-singer, who had for some time kept a public-house. But her husband turned out badly and now she was back at the tailoring with eyesight failing. Today she had brought a basin of stew for her lunch. She worked as long as Moses wanted her – sometimes till ten o'clock – and spoke in a friendly way of her master and 'Missus', and was kindly with the girl. She had been thirteen weeks out of work before she had found this place. Given to cant, but a sober and respectable woman. Told me that drunkenness had decreased, but not immorality; 'no young girl thought any worse of herself for getting into trouble', and none of them were satisfied with going to service.

The third morning another young woman came in to learn the trade; work wretched, but both Mrs Moses and Mrs Irons were good to her. Told me that she was come to learn the trade, and that she should stay if her work suited them; thought to myself, it will be a long time before your work will be worth the trouble of your training. . . . I worked four days with Moses family, and we parted excellent friends. The work must have been bad, for my sewing, they said, was too good for the trade! [MS. interviews, October 1887.]

Interviewed H. and G. firms [Wholesale Clothiers]. Long conversation with principal partners in each case. J. G. was a haw-hawy young man in 'masher' clothes, with silver-tipped cane and camellia in his buttonhole. Said there had been a revolution in the tailoring trade; small tailors were being wiped out. It was 'now a trade in which capitalists invested money, and worked on wholesale scale'. Profits regulated according to fixed scale based on cost of production. For instance, if two contracts were taken for same cloth and same pattern, at a higher and a lower price, the manager gave out the work at corresponding figures, and if one middleman did not choose to take the lower-priced garment, another did. As to provincial production for stock and export, it was undercutting London. ... For work at a certain figure undoubtedly the factory system was most to be relied on, but of course you could not get style, or even much fit, if all the coats were cut out by machinery. Admitted that starvation wages were given by some middlemen. ... H., wholesale clothier (was a true little grinder), had a fussy self-important air, nervous manner, and shrewd money-making expression. Scrupulously attired, with orchid in his buttonhole. 'Work paid better than it ever was; middlemen confoundedly independent; if one man refuses a job, no one else will take it.' Said that, for strength and honesty of work, undoubtedly provincial factory system was to be preferred, and if he [H.] could afford to wait he sent down to the provinces. He did very little bespoke work; firm entirely wholesale, dealing principally in contracts. Was disgusted with sensationalism and Burnett's Report.[22] [MS. Interviews, Wholesale Clothing Trade, October 1887.]

22. This summarily condemned Parliamentary Paper was the Report to the Board of Trade on the Sweating System at the East End of London, by the Labour Correspondent of the Board of Trade, September 1887, H.C. 331 of 1889.

John Burnett, who became one of my best friends in the world of labour, was born at Alnwick, Northumberland, in 1842, became, after the Nine Hours' Strike, a lecturer for the National Education League, and joined the staff of the *Newcastle Chronicle*. In 1875, on Allan's death, he was elected to the general secretaryship of the Amalgamated Society of Engineers. He was a member of the Parliamentary Committee of the Trades Union Congress from 1876 to 1885. In 1886 he was appointed to the newly created post of Labour Correspondent of the Board of Trade, in which capacity he prepared and issued a series

Amusing interview with L., factory inspector [at] Home Office. Square-built man, with general impression of checked suit: I will not swear that his three garments were all check; but the general effect was a mottled and crossed appearance. Red face, tiny greeny-grey eyes, and fat hands; whiskers and hair of the same tint as his eyes; hair rapidly receding from his forehead. He welcomed me with a funny self-important air; he was 'delighted to see me in connection with a subject that had occupied so much of his thought'. He knew that my object was to do good, etc. etc. That had been *his* object, and he had laboured night and day to accomplish it. And then he opened out in a burst of indignation against the Board of Trade and Burnett's Report. He thought it disgraceful, stealing men's brains; that is what Burnett had done. He had come to him, and cross-examined him and put all he said, without acknowledgement, into this report (Burnett had told me that L. had refused to give him any information). What did the Board of Trade know about sweating? What could it know? 'I, on the other hand,' continued Mr L., 'have ferreted all the evil out, have spent sixteen hours out of the twenty-four in the service of the Government, on this particular question. I know all the iniquity that goes on in the East End; and mind what I say, Miss Potter, it will not stop until the factory inspector has more power.' Charlie [Booth] became very impatient with this tirade and cut it short by asking for special and definite information. L. then gave us the usual hackneyed account of 'Sweating', a great deal of which we recognized as inexact and absurdly sensational. Then Charlie, rather unwisely, asked him bolt out: would he give him list of names and addresses of sweaters? 'No,' said L., somewhat testily, 'I can't do that.' And then as Charlie explained his object, Mr L. smiled at him with conscious superiority, as much as to say, 'You all of you are amateurs, and think you know a great deal; but your ideas are impracticable.' All this was simply the result of the lack of sympathy C. had shown to the man's wounded vanity. Altogether, I

of reports on Trade Unions and strikes. On the establishment of the Labour Department in 1893 he became Chief Labour Correspondent under the Commissioner for Labour and was selected to visit the United States to prepare a report on the effects of Jewish immigration. He retired in 1907 and died in 1914. [See *The History of Trade Unionism 1666–1920*, by S. and B. Webb, 1920 Edition, pp. 314–15, describing the Nine Hours' Strike.]

was sorry I had not been alone with him; I should have managed him better, with softer and less direct treatment. As it was, we got nothing out of him, except the picture of a man smarting under the consciousness of another man reaping the fruits of what he considered he had sown. A good moral. The personal element in work is contemptible. [MS. Interviews, Wholesale Clothing Trade, 5 November 1887.]

At this point my autumn holiday ended, and I returned to attendance on my father.

I have a good amount of loosely gathered material [I write after spending three months with my father at Bournemouth]. C. B. has a certain amount of statistical information. Remains to be done: a complete statistical basis giving proportionate statement of various classes of trades; and description of different types of tailoring, so that I may give picturesque account of technique. The leading ideas to be embodied in the paper: (1) correspondence of low form of faculty with low form of desire; absence of responsible employer; effect of foreign immigration on trade, with proportion of foreigners engaged in trade. [MS. diary, 5 February 1888.]

Last days at Bournemouth. Hardly expect to return here. If father lives, we shall move to Wimbledon next winter.[23] Very happy during these peaceful months, reading English history and literature. Long rides and short walks, and listening to the band. Not felt it waste of time, as I needed more study; though of course I should have preferred to work straight onward with the investigation. But I am so accustomed to take things as they come, and be thankful, that it is little trouble to me to break in upon my plan. And now I enjoy my life. I have fair health, faith in my own capacity to do the work I believe in, and I have regained my old religious feeling, without which life is not worth living to one of my nature. Intend to spend ten days of my holiday in the West End, before I settle in to work. And then a hard pull and a long pull to get the material wherewith to make a

23. After my youngest sister's marriage to Arthur Dyson Williams in the autumn of 1888, and after wintering once again at Bournemouth, I moved my father to a small house (which became my permanent home until my father's death in January 1892) belonging to my sister Mary Playne, and close to her husband's place in Gloucestershire.

really graphic picture of the London tailoring trade. Thirty years is a good deal of sand in the hour-glass; and I must justify all this long period of silent intellectual seed-time by fruit.

One good thing done; Herbert Spencer cured, at least for the present. Living with us gave him courage to rise out of his state of lethargy, and take to active life again. Now I hear he is running about London, and thoroughly enjoying society. Poor old man! It is a comfort to think one has been a help to him, and a small return for his constant intellectual guidance and sympathy.

The leading idea of my paper will be the correspondence of low faculty with low desire: proof of this – picture of life in a sweater's den, picture of life of a man who wears the coat.

Shall turn my back on Society, except in so far as it is likely to be useful to my work . . . [MS. diary, 12 February 1888.]

This question of 'Society' had been troubling me for some time.

I do not wish to forgo the society of my own class – and yet to enjoy means wasted energy [I wrote a few months before the last entry]. Late hours, excitement, stimulants and unwholesome food, all diminish my small stock of strength available for actual work. And society has another drawback; it attracts one's attention away from the facts one is studying, so that the impression is not so keen and deep. To take a clear impression, the intellect must be in a peculiar state – strong, and yet for the moment blank. That is why I find so much difficulty in working at two subjects at the same time – the facts of the one efface the facts of the other. And when striking personalities intervene with the complicated problems of their lives, it is so hard to drive them out of one's thoughts. For the men and women of society are, naturally enough, more interesting, as psychological studies, than the men and women with whose circumstances you are not familiar, whose phraseology you do not quickly understand. Gradually, if you give way, the ogre, society, sucks you in, and you are lost to the bigger world of common-life.

I see before me clearly the ideal life for work – [I continue] I see it attainable in my present circumstances. Love and cheerfulness in my home-life; faithful friendship with a few – to those tied to me by past association, to those bracing me by moral genius, to those who will aid me to judge truthfully – and, lastly, charity and sympathy towards women of my own class who need it, whether they be struggling young girls, hard-pressed married women or disappointed spinsters. Every woman has a mission to other women – more especially to the women of her own class and circumstances. It is difficult to be much help to men (except as an example in the way of persistent effort, and endurance in spite of womanly weakness). For, do what one will, sentiment creeps in, in return for sympathy. Perhaps as one loses one's attractiveness this will wear off – *certainly* it will! At present it is only with working men one feels free to sympathize without fear of unpleasant consequences . . . [MS. diary, December 1887.]

Early in March I am once again at the Devonshire House Hotel: 'trying to grasp my subject – the trade and labour questions of East End Tailoring', I write in my diary; and wishing 'that I had more strength and pluck'.

So the first six weeks of my inquiry ends [I write four weeks later]. Think I have broken the crust, and am now grubbing at the roots of the subject. But much definite work I have not done. Most of my time spent in training as a 'plain hand', and it remains to be seen whether my training will be of real use. Anyway, it has given me an insight into the organization, or, in this case into the want of organization, of a workshop, and into the actual handicraft of tailoring.[24] Otherwise my life has been extremely interesting, and I am more than ever assured that *I have capacity*. . . . And now there are no conflicting desires and few conflicting duties. 'Society', even now that it is unusually gracious and flattering, has no charm for me. The other night, as I returned from a distinguished party to which I had been enticed, I felt that I should not regret the loss of attraction (as I shall inevitably lose it), for I did not care for the result. Only for my work should I fear the loss of the woman's charm; un-

24. The Report of John Burnett, the Labour Correspondent of the Board of Trade, on the Sweating System in Leeds, 1888, recalls to my memory a visit to Leeds at Whitsuntide 1888 (unrecorded in the MS. diary), in order to compare provincial with metropolitan conditions. 'Miss Beatrice Potter was in Leeds collecting facts on the state of trade there, and by her kindness I was allowed to attend meetings which she had arranged between herself and the workmen, and herself and the masters. With her I also saw Mr Abraham, a Jewish Rabbi stationed at Leeds, who is remarkably well informed on most phases of the question then interesting the Jewish community.' [Report to the Board of Trade on the Sweating System in Leeds, C. 5513, 1888.]

doubtedly it smooths out obstacles. But then I am so planning my life that the work I need it for will be done before I lose it! [MS. diary, 28 March 1888.]

The last days of my active life for some months to come. On the whole I have been very happy – full of interest and blessed with content. I have not felt living alone. My work is now all in all to me. When I am not at work I sit and dream, and chew the cud of all I see and hear; when I am utterly exhausted I am not depressed; only satisfied to wait for returning strength. Prayer is a constant source of strength: to sit in that grand St Paul's, with its still silent spaces; there is a wonderful restfulness in that House of God. And I enjoy the life of the people at the East End; the reality of their efforts and aims; the simplicity of their sorrows and joys; I feel I can realize it and see the tragic and the comic side. To some extent I can grasp the forces which are swaying to and fro, raising and depressing this vast herd of human beings. My painstaking study of detail will help towards the knowledge of the whole, towards which I am constantly striving; I shall leave steps cut in the rock, and from its summit man will eventually map out the conquered land of social life. [MS. diary, 5 May 1888.]

More than half through my paper, with the rest thought out [I record six weeks after my return to The Argoed]. I think it will be a clear, detailed and comprehensive account of the facts of the Tailoring Trade; but it will be too matter-of-fact for the taste of the public – too much of a study of economic life, and not sufficiently flavoured with philanthropy. [MS. diary, 28 June 1888.]

It was during the spring of 1888 that I experimented in the art of investigation, by getting employment as a 'plain trouser-hand' in several workshops, being soon dismissed from the first, but voluntarily leaving the last and (from the standpoint of the worker) lowest of the lot, in order 'to better myself', when I had secured all the information I required. In this brief adventure, besides verifying my second-hand information about the conditions of employment, I obtained the material for my one and only literary 'success' – 'The Pages of a Workgirl's Diary', published in the *Nineteenth Century* (October 1888) – a cheap triumph, seeing that the article was little more than a transcript of the MS. diary, with the facts just enough disguised to avoid recognition and possible actions for libel; and experiences sufficiently expurgated to be 'suited to a female pen'![25] 'Mais oui: vous avez fait un succès ave ce "Pages of a Workgirl's Diary",' observed the brilliant Frenchwoman and candid friend, Marie Souvestre.[26] *'Mais que le public Anglais est bête!'* [MS. diary,

25. Re-published as 'The Diary of an Investigator' in *Problems of Modern Industry*, by S. and B. Webb, 1898. In this essay I omitted the references in my MS. diary to the prevalence of incest in one-room tenements. The fact that some of my workmates – young girls, who were in no way mentally defective, who were, on the contrary, just as keen-witted and generous-hearted as my own circle of friends – could chaff each other about having babies by their fathers and brothers, was a gruesome example of the effect of debased social environment on personal character and family life, and therefore on racial progress. The violation of little children was another not infrequent result. To put it bluntly, sexual promiscuity, and even sexual perversion, are almost unavoidable among men and women of average character and intelligence crowded into the one-room tenement of slum areas, and it is the realization of the moral deterioration involved, more than any physical discomfort, that lends the note of exasperated bitterness characteristic of the working-class representatives of these chronically destitute urban districts.

26. Marie Souvestre, daughter of the Academician Émile Souvestre – 'le philosophe sous les toits' – became the headmistress-proprietor of a fashionable boarding-school, at first at Fontainebleau and then at Wimbledon. She was intimate with the radical and free-thinking set, Morley, Chamberlain, Leslie Stephen, the Frederic Harrisons, Mrs Richard Strachey and Mrs J. R. Green and their large circles of like-minded friends. I give one entry descriptive of her meeting with her intellectual antithesis, Auberon Herbert: 'Auberon Herbert dropped in before lunch yesterday. He was excited with the prospect of converting Mrs Besant to spiritualism; she had written to him about his article in the *Pall Mall* and it will probably end in a visit to the Old House. Strange will be the intimacy between these two natures: Mrs Besant, with her rabid Socialism, embittered, by personal suffering, against the morality and the creed of Christendom; and Auberon Herbert, with his idealistic individualism, a character softened and perhaps even weakened by perpetually dwelling on spiritual influences. While he and I were chatting in a friendly way, enter Mlle Souvestre. The brilliant and irreligious Frenchwoman glanced with cold contempt at the strange figure of a man reclining on a sofa, advancing in his soft weak voice untenable propositions. It ended in a hot controversy in which I hardened into the Frenchwoman's style of quick logical dispute. Auberon Herbert left with a

January 1889.] Smarting under the cold reception given to my elaborate monograph on 'The East End Tailoring Trade' – a painstaking and, I think, thoroughly competent piece of work, appearing in the preceding issue of the *Nineteenth Century* – for which I had received from the editor one guinea per page as against two guineas per page paid for a dramatized version of but a few of the facts – I endorsed her judgement. And if by any chance the book that I am now writing should prove a 'better seller' than the most intellectually distinguished of our works – *Statutory Authorities for Special Purposes, 1689–1835* (which, I regret to say, has had but a small sale) – I shall see rising up before me the striking presence of my old friend, and hear her reiterate in ghostly but sarcastic tones, *'Mais que le public Anglais est bête!'*

Such were the pleasant consequences of my adventure. Now for the unpleasant.

Gave evidence before the Lords Committee [on the Sweating System]. A set of well-meaning men, but not made of stuff fit for investigation. As they had forced me to appear, they treated me kindly, and lunched me in the middle of my examination. A few peeresses came down to stare at me ... [MS. diary, 12 May 1888.]

Four days after, there is another entry:

Disagreeable consequences of appearing in public. Descriptions of my appearance and dress; and offensive remarks by the

pained expression, and with no favourable impression of the clever French schoolmistress, and her influence on his friend. After he had gone, Mlle Souvestre softened into affectionate admiration and loving solicitude. A remarkable woman with a gift of brilliant expression, and the charm of past beauty and present attractiveness. Purely literary in her training, and without personal experience of religious feeling or public spirit, she watches these characteristics in others with an odd combination of suspicion, surprise, and what one might almost call an unappreciative admiration. You feel that every idea is brought under a sort of hammering logic, and broken into pieces unless it be very sound metal. If the idea belongs to the religious sphere and is proof against ridicule, it is laid carefully on one side for some future hostile analysis.' [MS. diary, 10 March 1889.]

*Pall Mall Gazette*. The economic side of the question is an unattractive one, and attracts abuse of all kinds from the least scrupulous class of men. [MS. diary, 16 May 1888.]

In another ten days I am still more distressed:

Detestable misstatement of my evidence brings down unpleasant imputations; all the harder to bear as I was pressed into giving evidence, and was unwilling to speak of my personal experience of a workshop. [MS. diary, 25 May 1888.]

The 'detestable misstatement' was, as far as I remember, an accusation that my evidence before the Select Committee of the House of Lords was, in substance, mendacious; that in the shops in which I had worked as a trouser-hand I was known and exceptionally treated; and that, accordingly, my statement of the workers' conditions was misleading. My accuser, the A. B. to whom I have already referred, said that he knew the workshop in which I had thus pretended to work. This was a misunderstanding which I was able easily to clear up by a letter to the newspapers; it was plain that A. B. had confused my first friendly interviews, at the workshop to which I had been introduced as an inquirer (described in the foregoing pages), with the transient engagements as a trouser-hand that I subsequently got for myself at other workshops. But there was a fly in the ointment. In my hasty answers to the Lords' cross-examination, I had exaggerated the number of weeks during which I thus 'worked'; and it was this exaggeration that got widely reported. When I received the proof of my evidence, my conscience was sorely tried by the appended notice that no mistake was to be corrected other than any made by the shorthand-writer or compositor. Was I to leave my own hasty exaggeration uncorrected? I disobeyed the injunction, and scrupulously reduced the number of weeks to less than the truth. This double sin of saying what was not true, and then altering it in what seemed a sly way, caused me many sleepless nights. To this day I do not know whether witnesses are at liberty to correct their own statements as distinguished from misstatements of their evidence by the reporter. (The Other One tells me that I might have put the correction in a footnote;

but how was I to know that? Moreover, that would have meant an admission of my inaccuracy!) Considering the difficulty, to the ordinary untrained man or woman, of answering unexpected questions with accuracy under the novel and disconcerting experience of being cross-examined, it seems desirable that witnesses should be permitted to correct, after quiet consideration, their own statements of fact and opinion, even if these have been correctly taken down by the shorthand-writer. What happens now is that the cautious and experienced witness refuses to be led beyond a reiteration of the contents of his 'statement of evidence' deliberately prepared for circulation, whilst the flustered novice says what is not true, and, in nearly all cases, exactly what the more skilled of his examiners, intend him to say! I remember an episode at an official inquiry, years afterwards, in which I took part. 'I object to Mrs Webb's unfair cross-examination,' complained one of my colleagues. The room was cleared. 'Now, Mr—,' said I in my blandest tone, 'I have listened to you cross-examining a series of witnesses on the abstruse point of the effect on tenement occupiers of compounding for rates; and however ignorant of the whole subject-matter these witnesses may be, they invariably come out at your conclusion. So long as you pursue this policy I shall continue to make each successive witness say the exact contrary of what he has said to you.' In the interests of national economy – for I pointed out that the travelling expenses and the shorthand report of each day's evidence cost at least one hundred pounds – he and I silently agreed to abandon our malpractice.

I skip eighteen months, in order to give the last scenes of my relation to the House of Lords Committee on the Sweating System:

Dined with Lord Thring to meet Lord Monkswell to discuss the Dunraven draft report, and help to draft an opposition. Lord Thring is a dried-up little lawyer, upper-middle-class in origin, made a peer for many years' faithful service as head of the Parliamentary Drafting Office. His views are strictly economic; biased against sensationalism, against State interference; in fact, the high and dry orthodoxy of 1850. The 'sweating business' he regards as so much 'gas'. But with the present combustible state of public opinion a safety-valve must be provided. Hence in the Opposition Report he will deny all Dunraven's sensational premises, but declare that there *are evils* to be remedied (which he does not believe). The remedies he suggests are utterly insufficient to cure the evils – if they did exist – *and he knows it*. His attitude is typical of the time; he dare not *dare* public sentiment; so he suggests remedies which are absurdly roundabout, and bound to fail. 'Of course we must pat trade unions on the back,' said he, 'but I will die on the floor of the House before I see trade unions made absolute by driving all workers into factories where they have unlimited opportunities for combination. Dunraven is playing the card of Tory democracy; representing the middle class as the tyrants of society; and himself, representing the Tory aristocracy, as the only guardians of the interests of the poor. That is why it won't suit us to be quite frank,' he adds with cynical candour. 'We must go in for the evils as strongly as he does. But we must cut the ground from under his remedies.'

After dinner, when we three were reading over and recasting Lord Thring's notes, I managed, 'in cutting the ground from under Dunraven's remedies', to prepare the ground for my special erection, which will appear as a review of the two reports in the *Nineteenth Century*. If I can make them retain my proposal to transfer the factory inspectors to the Labour Department of the Board of Trade, or to the Local Government Board, I shall have laid the foundation for a thoroughly efficient Labour Bureau. The enforced publicity of all business accounts will be one step further. That done, we shall be on the right road to transforming all property-holders into voluntary officials of the State; paid by results instead of by salaries; and compelled by self-interest to inspect each other's work, the landlord the employer, the employer the landlord. Though I am suspected of Socialism, my anti-sensationalism gives me a footing among the sternest school of *laissez-faire* economists. This position must be guarded jealously, if I am to be of some little use as a reforming agency. [MS. diary, 9 February 1890.]

Uncomfortable dinner with Lord Thring and Mr Vallance here [Devonshire House Hotel] – the Assessment Clerk to the Whitechapel Union. Lord Thring was as obstinate as an old dried-up lawyer of seventy could possibly be; would not listen to

my conscientious official, but snubbed him severely. And to
make matters worse, the church bells began to ring wildly so that
our voices were drowned in spite of my determined shoutings.
Poor old man; he came to chat with a good-looking woman, and
found an enthusiastic reformer possessed by one idea, to make
him accept a suggestion which he did not agree with. All the
same, I think I shall get in to the Lords' Report the thin edge of
the wedge as to owners' [of the finished product; that is, the
*original* 'giver out' of the material to be made up] responsibility.
His report, which he showed me, is three pages to Dunraven's
seventy: it begins with my definition of sweating as certain conditions of employment; expressly omitting all reference to sub-
contract, subdivision of labour, machinery, foreign immigration,
to which Dunraven has devoted some twenty pages; it lays stress
on the defencelessness of female labour, the badness of general
sanitation. With regard to remedies, he proposes to repeal certain
clauses of the Factory Act which disallow the entry of the factory
inspector into dwellings without a warrant from the magistrates;
he adopts my idea of the transference of the Factory Department
to the Board of Trade or Local Government Board, and lays
stress on the advantages of publicity. Altogether, though it is
utterly ineffective, the report is sound so far as it goes, and will
serve as a foundation for my own proposals. [MS. diary, 15 February 1890.]

## An Encouraging Discovery

The outcome of these studies in East End life, more particularly the examination of the manufacture of slop-
clothing in the homes and workshops of the East End, was
an attempt, and I think a successful attempt, to diagnose
specific social disease, and to suggest how it could be mitigated, and probably overcome.

All those who had hitherto interested themselves in the
evils of the so-called 'sweating system' had been obsessed
with the sinister figure of the 'sweater', or rather of an
endless series of middlemen or sweaters, between the actual
producer of slop-clothing or cheap furniture, and the citizen
who eventually bought the article for his own use. Closely
associated with the presence of his middleman, or these
middlemen, was the practice of subdividing labour, so that

the coat or the cabinet was the product, not of one skilled craftsman, but of a group of poverty-stricken employees, sometimes at work in the back premises of the sweater himself, and sometimes individually toiling night and day in their own one-roomed tenements. It was adding insult to injury in the eyes of patriotic British citizens that the evil ways of these 'grinders of the face of the poor' were made easy by the inrush of Polish or Russian and German Jews, whose desperate plight compelled them to accept work at wages below the subsistence level of English workers. The following extracts from the evidence of the best-known explorers of the sweating system will illustrate the state of informed public opinion at the time that I began my investigations.

'How do you define the Sweating System?' inquired a member of the House of Lords Committee of the then great authority on the subject – Arnold White, afterwards a Conservative M.P. 'I think it is impossible to give a scientific definition of the term,' he answered, 'but it involves three ideas, which are sufficiently distinct. The broadest definition that I can give of a sweater is, one who grinds the face of the poor; the second is that of a man who contributes neither capital, skill, nor speculation, and yet gets profit; and the third is the middleman.' [Question 404.]

'Any person who employs others to extract from them surplus labour without compensation is a sweater,' exclaimed Lewis Lyons, a notorious socialist agitator. 'A middleman sweater is a person who acts as a contractor for labour for another man. . . . A sweater is a person who practises a subdivision of labour for his own private ends. Now, my Lords, you will find that this definition speaks of a sweater as subdividing labour. The subdivisions of labour in the tailoring trade would be about twenty-five, and I would just proceed to explain. [Etc.]' [Question 1772.]

'As an illustration of what I mean,' stated William Parnell, the secretary of the Cabinetmakers' Trade Union, 'I will say that if a firm gets an order to supply furniture to a customer, and the firm which gets that order does not itself manufacture the furniture, but gives it out to a sub-contractor, that is the first step in sweating. When these steps go from one to two, three, four, or five degrees, it is quite evident, and every man will admit, that that is sweating; but I think that the first step is as much sweating as the last. The real effect of it is to reduce both the quality of the article and the wages of the workman. I know of a case in which work has been obtained by a large firm and given out to a sub-contractor, who has given it out to another sub-contractor, who has given it out again to a man supposed to be his foreman, and the foreman has then given it out as piecework to the workmen. I will leave your Lordships to judge whether, if that had been made by the firm who obtained the order, the customer would not have received a better article, and also whether the man who made it would not have received better wages.' [Question 2862.]

'Under any circumstances, this condition of affairs would have been fraught with misery for most of those engaged in such work,' states John Burnett, the Labour Correspondent of the Board of Trade in September 1887, 'but matters have been rendered infinitely worse to the native workers during the last few years by the enormous influx of pauper foreigners from other European nations. These aliens have been chiefly German and Russian Jews, and there can be no doubt that the result has been to flood the labour market of the east end of London with cheap labour to such an extent as to reduce thousands of native workers to the verge of destitution. But for this special cause there would be no demand for inquiry on the subject. The evil, however, is becoming so intense as to raise a cry for its special treatment. The previous conditions of life of the unhappy foreigners who are thus driven, or come here of their own accord, are such that they can live on much less than our English workers. They arrive here in a state of utter destitution, and are compelled by the very necessity of their position to accept the work most easily obtained at the lowest rate of wages. In this way has grown up in our midst a system so bad in itself and so surrounded by adherent evils as to have caused, not only among the workers themselves, great suffering and misery, but in the minds of others grave apprehensions of public danger.[27]

Now, it was this conception of the sweating system and its causes that was embodied in the draft report of Lord Dunraven, the first chairman of the House of Lords Committee on the Sweating System; a draft which was rejected by the

27. Report to the Board of Trade on the Sweating System at the East End of London by the Labour Correspondent of the Board, 12 September 1887, p. 4. [H.C. 331 of 1889.]

majority of the committee under the chairmanship of Lord Derby and the leadership of Lord Thring. Lord Derby and his colleagues finally decided that sweating was no particular method of remuneration, no peculiar form of industrial organization, but certain conditions of employment; *'earnings barely sufficient to sustain existence; hours of labour such as to make the lives of the workers periods of almost ceaseless toil; and sanitary conditions which are not only injurious to the health of the persons employed but dangerous to the public'.*[28] When any one of these conditions existed in extreme and exaggerated form – for instance, if a woman sewing neckties in her own home strained every nerve to earn only a halfpenny an hour – still more, when these conditions were combined, as in the cellar dwellings in which the Jewish boot-finishers worked sixteen or seventeen hours a day for a wage of 12s. per week – then the House of Lords Committee said that the labour was sweated, and that the unfortunates were working under the sweating system.

What were the causes of these evil conditions of employment? Had these causes been correctly described by the most prominent witnesses before the House of Lords Committee and in the official reports of Government Departments?

There was a measure of truth in John Burnett's statement that the evil conditions of sweating in some departments of industry had been initiated, or at any rate aggravated, by the inrush of poverty-stricken Jews. The ease with which the untiring and thrifty Jew became a master was proverbial in the East End. His living-room became his workshop, his landlord or his butcher his surety; round the corner he found a brother Israelite whose trade was to supply pattern garments to take as samples of work to the wholesale house; with a small deposit he secured, on the hire system, both sewing-machine and presser's table. Altogether, it was estimated that with £1 in his pocket, any man might rise to the dignity of a sweater. And, when one Jew had risen to the position of

28. Fifth Report from the Select Committee of the House of Lords on the Sweating System, 1888–9: Conclusions and Recommendations, pp. xlii and xliii.

entrepreneur, there were always, not only the members of his own family, but also hundreds of newcomers ready to become subordinates, many of whom were destined, in due time, to become his competitors. But the Jews had, at any rate, the merit that at the East End of London they 'kept themselves to themselves'; for instance, they monopolized the slop-coat trade and boot-finishing; they seldom intruded into the manufacture of vests and trousers, or into the factories in which the machining of the work was done; and if the investigator surveyed all the industries in which the evil conditions of sweating prevailed, whether in the metropolis or in the provinces, the Jewish workers were found to be but a fraction of the whole body of workers, and also, to a large extent, a non-competing group, confined to the manufacture of certain commodities, in many instances commodities which had not been produced in the locality before. In short, if every foreign Jew resident in England had been sent back to his birthplace, the bulk of the sweated workers would not have been affected, whether for better or for worse.

But though the immigrant Jews served as raw material for the sweating system, no one suggested that they alone were responsible for what was deemed to be a particular type of industrial organization. The real sinner, according to current public opinion, was the unnecessary middleman or middlemen, whether British or foreign, each middleman taking toll, like the medieval baron, from all those who passed under his jurisdiction. Now what my observations and inquiries (verified by Charles Booth's statistics) had proved was that there were actually fewer middlemen between the producer and the consumer, and, be it added, far less subdivision of labour, than in the contrasted machine industry of the characteristic factory system, as seen not only in such staple industries as textiles or engineering, but also in the machine production of 'ready-made' garments, or boots and shoes, in the well-equipped factories of Leeds or Leicester.

I pass now to my own explanation of the causes of the misery and degradation laid bare by the House of Lords Committee on the Sweating System.

'How would you define the Sweating System?' I was asked by a member of the Committee.

'An inquiry into the Sweating System is practically an inquiry into all labour employed in manufacture which has escaped the regulation of the Factory Act and trade unions,' I answered. (Question 3248.)

At this point I will quote from a paper that I read at the Co-operative Congress held at Rochdale, June 1892, supplemented by a quotation from the review in the *Nineteenth Century* for June 1890, on the Report from the Select Committee of the House of Lords on the Sweating System, 1888–9.

Some persons maintain that sweating is restricted to industries in which sub-contract prevails [I tell the Co-operative Congress of 1892]; that, in fact, it is the middleman who is the sweater; that this man grinds the face of the poor, and takes from them the fruits of their labour. You will remember a cartoon that appeared in *Punch* about the time of the House of Lords inquiry, in which the middleman was represented as a bloated man-spider sucking the life-blood out of men and women who were working around him. Now, before I studied the facts of East London industries for myself I really believed that this horrible creature existed. But I soon found out that either he was a myth, or that the times had been too hard for him, and that he had been squeezed out of existence by some bigger monster. For I discovered that in the coat trade, and in the low-class boot trade – which are exclusively in the hands of the Jews – where the work is still taken out by small contractors, these middlemen, far from being bloated idlers, work as hard, if not harder, than their sweated hands, and frequently earn less than the machinist or presser to whom they pay wages. On the other hand, in those trades in which English women are employed – such as the manufacture of shirts, ties, umbrellas, juvenile suits, etc. – the middleman is fast disappearing. It is true that formerly the much-abused sub-contract system prevailed in these trades – that is to say, some man or woman would contract with the wholesale manufacturer to make and deliver so many dozen garments for a certain sum. He would then distribute these garments one by one in the homes of the women, or perhaps he would engage women to make them in his own house. He might receive a shilling for the making of each garment, but he would give only tenpence to the actual workers, pocketing twopence in return for his trouble and risk. But of late years the more enterprising wholesale manufacturers have thought it most unjust that the middleman should pocket the twopence. To remedy this injustice they have opened shops all over the East End of London, where they give out work just as the middleman used to do, first to be machined and then to be finished. But, strangely enough, they still pay tenpence to their workers, the only difference being that instead of the middleman getting the balance they pocket the twopence themselves. Nor do they trouble themselves in the very least where these garments are made. The women who support themselves and perhaps their families by this class of work live in cellars or in garrets, sometimes two or three families in one room. This does not concern the wholesale manufacturer. No doubt he would tell you that the middleman was the sweater and that he had destroyed him. But, unfortunately, he did not destroy, or even diminish, what the practical observer means by sweating. The actual worker gains absolutely nothing by the disappearance of the sub-contractor, middleman, or so-called sweater. In East London the change has been, so far as the workers are concerned, from out of the frying-pan into the fire.

And if we leave the clothing trade and pass to the lower grades of the furniture trades, in which all the evils of sweating exist, we may watch the poverty-stricken maker of tables and chairs hawking his wares along the Curtain Road, selling direct to the export merchant, or to the retail tradesman – or perchance, to the private customer. In the manufacture of cheap boots in London, of common cutlery at Sheffield, of indifferent nails at Halesowen, we meet with this same sorrowful figure – the small master or out-worker buying his material on credit, and selling his product to meet the necessities of the hour; in all instances underselling his competitors, great and small. Respectable employers, interested in a high standard of production, trade unionists, keen for a high standard of wage, agree in attributing to this pitiful personage the worst evils of the sweating system. Here, not only do we fail to discover the existence of sub-contract, but even the element of contract itself disappears, and the elaborate organization of modern industry is replaced by a near approach to that primitive higgling of the market between the actual producer of an article and the actual consumer – to that primeval struggle and trial of endurance in which the weakest and most necessitous invariably suffers.

I do not wish you to imagine that I deny the existence of the sweater in the sweated industries. But I deny that the sweater is necessarily or even usually the sub-contractor or employing middleman. The sweater is, in fact, the whole nation. The mass of struggling men and women whose sufferings have lately been laid bare are oppressed and defrauded in every relation of life; by the man who sells or gives out the material on which they labour; by the shopkeeper who sells them provisions on credit, or forces them under the truck system; by the landlord who exacts, in return for the four walls of a bedroom, or for the unpaved and undrained backyard, the double rent of workshop and dwelling; and, lastly, by every man, woman and child who consumes the product of their labour. In the front rank of this, the most numerous class of sweaters, we find the oppressed workers themselves. The middleman where he exists is not the oppressor, but merely one of the instruments of oppression. And we cannot agree with *Punch*'s representation of him as a spider devouring healthy flies. If we must describe him as a noxious insect we should picture him much more truly as the maggot that appears in meat after decay has set in. He is not the cause, but one of the occasional results of the evil. He takes advantage of the disorganized state of the substance which surrounds him, and lives on it; if he does not do so, some other creature will devour both him and his food. What we have to discover, therefore, is the origin of the disorganization itself.

Now, in all the manufacturing industries in which 'sweating' extensively prevails we discover one common feature. The great mass of the production is carried on, not in large factories but either by small masters in hidden workshops or by workers in their own dwellings. And, as a natural consequence of this significant fact, the employer – whether he be the profit-making middleman, wholesale trader, or even the consumer himself – is relieved from all responsibility for the conditions under which the work is done. The workers, on the other hand, incapacitated for combination by the isolation of their lives, excluded by special clauses from the protection of the Factory Acts, are delivered over body and soul to the spirit of unrestrained competition, arising from the ever-increasing demand for cheap articles in the great markets of the world. If we compare this state of things with the industries in which sweating does not exist, we see at once that in the case of the engineer, the cotton-spinner or the miner the men work together in large establishments, and the employer becomes responsible for the conditions of their employment. The mill-owner, coal-owner or large iron-master is forced to assume, to some slight extent, the guardianship of his workers. He is compelled by the State to provide healthy accommodation, to regulate the hours of labour of women and young persons, to see to the education of children, to guard against and insure all workers against accident. Trade unions, arising from the massing of men under the factory system, insist on a recognized rate of wages. Public opinion, whether social or political, observes the actions of a responsible employer in the open light of day. Willingly or unwillingly, he must interpose his brains and his capital between groups of workers on the one hand, and the great mass of conscienceless consumers on the other. These are the services exacted from him by the community in return for the profits he makes. He is, in fact, the first link between the private individual intent on his own gain, and the ideal official of the Socialist State administering the instruments of production in trust for the people. It is the absence of this typical figure of nineteenth-century industry which is the distinguishing feature of the sweating system.[29]

It is obvious [I write in my review of the Report from the Select Committee of the House of Lords on the Sweating System], if we wish to determine whether the presence of middlemen, machinery and subdivision of labour are at once the cause and the essence of the evils of sweating, we must take a wider survey of industrial facts than that afforded us by the four volumes of evidence published by the Committee. We must use the comparative method; we must lay side by side with the organization of production in the sweated trades the organization of production in those industries admittedly free from the grosser evils of sweating. In short, to discover what constitutes disease, we must compare the diseased body with the relatively healthy organism ...

In the staple manufactures of the kingdom – in the cotton, woollen and manufactured metal trades – we find, as a general fact, three profit-making capitalist middlemen between the manual worker and the consumer: (1) the master of the factory or workshop; (2) the wholesale trader, supplying foreign agents and English shopkeepers; (3) the large or small retailer in direct

29. A paper read at the twenty-fourth annual congress of Co-operative Societies, held at Rochdale, June 1892, by Beatrice Potter; see *Problems of Modern Industry*, by S. and B. Webb, 1898, pp. 140–45.

contact with the consumer. At the present time [1890] this may be considered the typical organization of English industry. In the manufacture of slop-clothing, the three profit-making middle-men, typical of English industry – the manufacturer, the whole-sale trader and the retail tradesman – are not multiplied; on the contrary, they are in many instances reduced to one or two hybrid figures – the small master who works as hard as, if not harder than, those he employs (and may be therefore considered, in many instances, as a manual worker), and the wholesale or retail tradesman, manufacturing to some extent on his own premises, and giving work out, not only to large and small masters, but direct into the homes of the people . . .

Alike from the obligations and the expenses of the factory owner, the sweater is free. Meanwhile the slum landlord is receiv-ing, for his cellars and attics, the double rent of workshop and dwelling without incurring the expensive sanitary obligations of the mill-owner. In short, it is home work which creates all the difficulties of our problem. For it is home work which, with its isolation, renders trade combination impracticable; which enables the manufacturer to use as a potent instrument, for the degradation of all, the necessity of the widow or the greed of the Jew. And more important still, it is home work which, by with-drawing the workers from the beneficent protection of the Fac-tory Acts, destroys all legal responsibility on the part of the employer and the landlord for the conditions of employment . . .

In this labyrinth of technical detail I have been led by the insinuating logic of facts again and again to the one central idea, round which gather scientific description and practical sugges-tion – an idea which has loomed larger and larger with a closer and more personal study of the suffering and degradation of the workers – an idea which I conceive to be embodied in all the labour legislation of this century: the direct responsibility, under a capitalist system of private property, of all employers for the welfare of their workers, of all property owners for the use of their property. From the denial of this personal service, in return for profits and rent, arise the dire evils of sweating – evils de-scribed in simple but touching words in the Lords' Report: 'earn-ings barely sufficient to sustain existence; hours of labour such as to make the lives of the workers periods of almost ceaseless toil, hard and unlovely to the last degree; sanitary conditions in-jurious to the health of the persons employed, and dangerous to the public'. It will be through awakening the sense of this responsibility, through insisting on the performance of this duty, by legislative enactment, by the pressure of public opinion and by all forms of voluntary combination, that we can alone root out and destroy those hideous social evils known as the Sweating System.[30]

30. 'The Lords and the Sweating System', the *Nineteenth Century*, June 1890. I must not burden the reader with the subsequent history of this problem. But the student may find help in some brief references. The idea of the sub-contractor, the middleman, the alien or the Jew being the 'cause' of sweating disappeared. Home work (more strictly 'out work') was generally recognized as the evil. Only very slowly and very imperfectly did the suggestion get adopted of imposing on someone as employer a definite responsibility for the conditions under which the sweated home worker performed his or her task. The first stage was by way of what is known as the 'particulars clause'. The Factory Act of 1891, which quite failed to incorporate what I desired, did at least put upon the factory employer in the textile industries the obligation to supply all his weavers, and (in cotton) also winders and reelers, with written 'particulars' of the terms on which they were working; and the amending Act of 1895 not only extended this to all textile workers but also enabled the Home Secretary to apply it to pieceworkers in non-textile factories or workshops. The 'particulars clause' was accordingly so applied in 1897 to the manufacture of handkerchiefs, aprons, pinafores and blouses, and to that of chains, anchors and locks. (*Industrial Democracy*, by S. and B. Webb, 1897, pp. 310–11.) By subsequent orders in 1898 and 1900 it was applied to felt hat makers, to all textile workshops, to pen makers and, in this connection most important of all, to the wholesale tailoring trade.

The next stage was the obligation imposed upon all persons who gave out work to be done at home, to keep a register, open to inspection, of the names and addresses of these out workers, whose homes could thus be visited by the sanitary inspectors of the Local Health Authority. This was effected by the Factory Act of 1901, which not only re-enacted the above provisions but also (by section 116) authorized their extension to out workers in any trades required to keep registers of out workers. In 1903 the existing orders applying to felt hat making and the wholesale tailoring trade were extended to out workers; and in 1909 a comprehensive order was made applicable to the out workers in all the wearing apparel trades.

But although all this went in the direction of putting responsibility on the 'giver out' of work, it amounted to little. We owe to the unwearied persistence of Sir Charles Dilke, M.P., and to Lady Dilke, in 1908 a House of Commons Select Committee on Home Work, under the chairmanship of Sir Thomas Whittaker, M.P., whose report (H.C. No. 246 of 1908), backed by renewed public agitation, led to the Trade Boards Act of 1909 (9 Edward VII., c. 22), which enabled the Board of

To state my 'discovery' dogmatically: it seemed to me that, unless 'the capitalist system' was to destroy the body and soul of great masses of the wage-earners, it was imperative that 'free competition' should be controlled, not exceptionally or spasmodically, but universally, so as to ensure to everyone a prescribed National Minimum of Civilized Life. This, in fact, was the meaning that Factory Acts, Public Education, Public Health and Trade Unionism had been empirically and imperfectly expressing.

---

Trade to apply, to any trade in which wages were exceptionally low, provisions permitting a joint board, representative of employers, workers and the public, to fix minimum rates of wages for definite working hours, employment below which was made an offence. Incidentally (by section 9) this Act brought in the shopkeeper, dealer or trader who made any arrangement express or implied with any worker', enacting that this 'giver out of work' should be 'deemed to be the employer', so as to become liable if the rates that he paid to his sub-contractor 'after allowing for his necessary expenditure in connection with the work' were less than the legally fixed minimum rates.

This Act was amended, after nine years' experience, by the Trade Boards Act of 1918 (8 and 9 George V., c. 32), and has done much to raise the level of earnings, to lessen the excessive hours of labour, and to protect the worker from cheating and oppression throughout nearly the whole range of what used to be known as the sweated trades. The apparent tendency of all this legislation has been to drive the work into large factories, in which improved machinery and more efficient organization reduce the cost of production so as to enable the better wages to be paid. (See *The Establishment of Minimum Rates in the Tailoring Industry*, by R. H. Tawney, 1915; *Minimum Rates in the Chain-making Industry*, by the same, 1914.)

A critical Departmental Committee appointed by the Ministry of Labour reported in 1922 (Cmd. 1645 of 1922) somewhat unsympathetically upon some of the details of the Trade Boards Acts, but no further legislation has ensued. What, in my opinion, now (1926) needs doing, in order to sweep away the remnants of the 'Sweating System', is to carry into law my suggestion; and to make thus responsible, for the conditions of employment of all persons working on the job (by whomsoever engaged), the original 'giver out of work', the owner both of the material given out and of the finished article eventually returned to him, who is ultimately the real employer, and who ought to accept all the responsibilities of the factory occupier.

340

*A Science of Society*

My participation in Charles Booth's grand inquest into the life and labour of the people in London served as a training in the art of a social investigator and confirmed my faith in the application of the scientific method to social organization.

In the course of this inquiry I had learnt the relation between personal observation and statistics. However accurate and comprehensive might be the description of technical detail, however vivid the picture of what was happening at the dock gates or in the sweated workshops, I was always confronted by Charles Booth's sceptical glance and critical questions: 'How many individuals are affected by the conditions you describe; are they increasing or diminishing in number?' 'What proportion do they bear to those working and living under worse or better conditions?' 'Does this so-called sweating system play any considerable part in the industrial organization of the four million inhabitants of London?' Thus, though I never acquired the statistical instrument because I had not the requisite arithmetic, I became aware that every conclusion derived from observation or experiment had to be qualified as well as verified by the relevant statistics. Meanwhile, in another part of the technique of sociology – the gentle art of interviewing – I think I may say that I became an adept. But, as I quickly discovered, this way of extracting facts from another person's mind has but a limited use; in many cases it has no value at all except as an introduction to opportunities for direct personal observation. Even direct observation has varying degrees of value according to the nature of the opportunity. For instance, I discovered more about dock labourers as a rent-collector than I did either by touring the docks along with officials or by my subsequent visits to dockers' homes as an investigator. Observation is, in fact, vitiated *if the persons observed know that they are being observed*; and it was in order to avoid any such hampering consciousness that I decided to try my luck in getting work in a series of sweaters' shops. Moreover, as a mere observer, having no position in the organization, it is impossible to experiment. As the managers of Katherine Buildings, my colleague and I could select our tenants according to any principle or prejudice; we could, with the consent of the directors, raise or lower rents, permit arrears or ruthlessly put in the broker; and, having chosen a policy, we could watch its results on the number and character of the applicants, the conduct of the tenants, or the profit and loss account of the buildings. 'Experimenting in the lives of other people, how cold-blooded!' I hear some reader object. Is it necessary to explain that such 'experimenting' cannot be avoided; that all administration, whether from the motive of profit-making or from that of public service, whether of the factory or the mine, of the elementary school or the post office, of the cooperative society or the trade union – unless it is to be reduced by precedent and red tape to a mindless routine – necessarily amounts to nothing less than 'experimenting in the lives of other people'. What is required to safeguard the community against callousness or carelessness about the human beings concerned is *that the administrator should be effectively responsible, for all the results of his administration, to the consumers and producers of the commodities and services concerned and to the community at large.* And it is essential, if we are to learn from such 'experiments', that the effect on other persons' lives should be observed and recorded. Further, though it is perhaps a counsel of perfection, it is desirable (as Bismarck pointed out) that the administrator should learn not only from his own mistakes – which is expensive – but also from those of other persons. In short, there can be no sound administration, even for profit-making, without the use, consciously or not, of observation, inference and verification; that is to say, of the scientific method. The irony is that those persons who, as participators in an organization, and wielding authority in its direction, have the most valuable opportunities for the use of the scientific method, usually lack the requisite training, if not also the leisure and the desire for this intellectual effort.

And here I must recall a queer, deep-rooted fallacy lying at the very base of Herbert Spencer's administrative nihilism; an error in reasoning pervading the capitalist world in which I was brought up. Herbert Spencer asserted, and every capitalist assumed, that the system of profit-making enterprise with which we were all familiar, belonged to 'the natural order of things', whereas any activity on the part of the State or the municipality, or even of the trade union, such as factory acts, public health administration, compulsory schooling and standard rates of wages, were 'artificial' contrivances; or, to use the philosopher's own words, 'clumsy mechanisms devised by political schemers to supersede the great laws of existence', and therefore bound – because they were 'against nature' – to be social failures. For instance, a rate of wages determined by unrestricted individual competition was a 'natural rate of wages'; a rate of wages determined by combination or by law was an 'artificial wage', and therefore injurious to the commonweal.

Today it is difficult to understand from whence came this curious fallacy; probably it arose, like so many other fallacies, from a muddle-headed use of words. For when we talk about things being natural, on the one hand, and artificial on the other; when we say, for instance, that a waterfall or a lake is natural or that it is artificial, we attach to these two adjectives definite meanings: in the one case the lake or the waterfall happens without the intervention of man; in the other case it is due to human artifice. But there is no such thing as social structure apart from human beings, or independent of their activity. Thus, strictly speaking, every development of social structure and function, from the family to a police force, from the institution of personal property to the provision of public parks and libraries, from the primitive taboo to the most complicated Act of Parliament, is alike 'artificial', that is to say, the product of human intervention, the outcome of human activities. The plain truth is that to apply the antithesis of 'natural' and 'artificial' to social action is sheer nonsense. Anything that exists or happens to human nature in society, whether war or peace, the custom of marriage or the growth of empire, the prevention of disease or the wholesale slaughter of battle, and 'civilization' itself, is equally 'natural'; its very happening makes it so. Moreover, if antiquity or ubiquity be taken as a test of what is in conformity with a hypothetical 'nature of man', governmental intervention and also vocational organization (from the ancient castes of priests and warriors to the modern labour union) are not only far older in human history than the form of industrial organization known as the capitalist system, with its divorce of the worker from the ownership of the instruments of production, but are also – when we remember the vast uncounted populations of Asia and Africa – actually more widely prevalent among the inhabitants of the earth today.

It is, indeed, obvious that every social transformation, every development of human society, necessarily amounts, whether we like it or not, to an experiment in the conduct of life. In the days of my capitalist bias I denounced, as interferences with the natural order of things, 'these gigantic experiments, State education, State intervention in other matters which are now being inaugurated' (see p. 202). Why? Not, as I then thought, because these 'interventions' were 'against nature', but, as I now realize, because these particular experiments were at the cost of my class for the assumed benefit of another class. A study of British Blue Books, illuminated by my own investigations into the chronic poverty of our great cities, opened my eyes to the workers' side of the picture. To the working class of Great Britain in the latter half of the eighteenth and first half of the nineteenth century – that is, to four fifths of the entire population – the 'industrial revolution', with its wholesale adoption of power-driven machinery and the factory system, its breaking up of the family as an industrial unit, and its summary abrogation of immemorial customs sanctioned by both religion and law (to which ruthless revolution, I may observe, my family owed its position of wealth – an explanation but not an excuse for my regarding it as peculiarly in 'the natural order of things'!), must have appeared not only as artificial and unnatural, but also as a gigantic and cruel experiment which, in so far as it was affecting their homes, their health, their subsistence and their pleasure, was proving a calamitous failure.

My reaction from this fallacy was an ever-deepening conviction of the supreme value, in all social activity, of the scientific method.

'This ceaseless questioning of social facts', the Ego that denies was always insisting, 'seems an interesting way of passing the time, but does it lead anywhere?'

The Ego that affirms could now answer with confidence:

'Seeing that society is one vast laboratory in which experiments in human relationship, conscious or unconscious, careless or deliberate, are continuously being carried on, those races will survive and prosper which are equipped with the knowledge of how things happen. And this knowledge can only be acquired by persistent research into the past and present behaviour of man.'

'How things happen!' mocks the Ego that denies, 'but that does not settle what *ought* to happen.'

'I thought I told you long ago', calmly answers the Ego that affirms, 'that with regard to the purpose of life, science is, and must remain, bankrupt; and the men of science of today know it. The goal towards which we strive, the state of mind in ourselves and in the community that we wish to bring about, depends on a human scale of values, a scale of values which alters from race to race, from generation to generation, and from individual to individual. How each of us determines our scale of values no one knows. For my own part, I find it best to live "as if" the soul of man were in communion with a superhuman force which makes for righteousness. Like our understanding of nature through observation and reasoning, this communion with the spirit of love at work in the universe will be intermittent and incomplete and it will frequently fail us. But a failure to know, and the fall from grace, is the way of all flesh.'

# CHAPTER 7

*Why I Became a Socialist*
1888–92

WHILST serving my apprenticeship under Charles Booth, I had reached a tentative conclusion about the most far-reaching 'experiment in the lives of other people' that the world had then witnessed; though it has since been equalled in ruthlessness, and excelled in speed and violence, but not, I think, in thoroughness and permanence, by the Russian Revolution that began in 1917.

The industrial revolution in Britain, which had its most intense phase in the latter end of the eighteenth and the beginning of the nineteenth century, cast out of our rural and urban life the yeoman cultivator and the copyholder, the domestic manufacturer and the independent handicraftsman, all of whom owned the instruments by which they earned their livelihood; and gradually substituted for them a relatively small body of capitalist *entrepreneurs* employing at wages an always multiplying mass of propertyless men, women and children, struggling, like rats in a bag, for the right to live. This bold venture in economic reconstruction had now been proved to have been, so it seemed to me, at one and the same time, a stupendous success and a tragic failure. The accepted purpose of the pioneers of the new power-driven machine industry was the making of pecuniary profit; a purpose which had been fulfilled, as Dr Johnson observed about his friend Thrale's brewery, 'beyond the dreams of avarice'. Commodities of all sorts and kinds rolled out from the new factories at an always accelerating speed with ever falling costs of production, thereby promoting what Adam Smith had idealized as *The Wealth of Nations*. The outstanding success of this new system of industry was enabling Great Britain, through becoming the workshop of the world, to survive the twenty years' ordeal of the Napoleonic Wars intact, and not even invaded, whilst her ruling oligarchy emerged in 1815 as the richest and most powerful government of the time.

On the other hand, that same revolution had deprived the manual workers – that is, four-fifths of the people of England – of their opportunity for spontaneity and freedom of initiative in production. It had transformed such of them as had been independent producers into hirelings and servants of another social class; and, as the East End of London in my time only too vividly demonstrated, it had thrust hundreds of thousands of families into the physical horrors and moral debasement of chronic destitution in crowded tenements in the midst of mean streets. There were, however, for the manual working class as a whole, certain compensations. The new organization of industry had the merit of training the wage-earners in the art of team-work in manufacture, transport and trading. Even the oppressions and frauds of the capitalist profit-maker had their uses in that they drove the proletariat of hired men, which capitalism had made ubiquitous, to combine in trade unions and cooperative societies; and thus to develop their instinct of fellowship, and their capacity for representative institutions, alike in politics and in industry. Moreover, the contrast between the sweated workers of East London and the Lancashire textile operatives made me realize how the very concentration of wage-earners in the factory, the ironworks and the mine had made possible, in their cases, what the sweater's workshop, the independent craftsman's forge and the out-worker's home had evaded, namely, a collective regulation of the conditions of employment, which, in the Factory Acts and Mines Regulation Acts on the one hand, and in the standard rates of wages and the normal working day of the trade unions on the other, had, during the latter part of the nineteenth century, wrought so great an improvement in the status of this regulated section of the world of labour. It was, in fact, exactly this collective regulation of the conditions of employment, whether by legislative enactment or by collective bargaining, that had raised the cotton operatives, the coal-miners and the workers of the iron trades into an effective democracy; or, at least, into one which, in comparison with the entirely unorganized workers of East London, was eager for political enfranchisement and education; and which, as the chapels, the cooperative societies and the trade unions had demonstrated, was capable of self-government. I wished to probe further this contrast between the wage-earners who had enjoyed the advantages of collective regulation and voluntary combinations, and those who had been abandoned to the rigours of unrestrained individual competition. But I wanted also to discover whether there was any practicable alternative to the dictatorship of the capitalist in industry, and his reduction of all the other participants in production to the position of subordinate 'hands'. For it was persistently asserted that there was such an alternative. In this quest I did not turn to the socialists. *Fabian Essays* were still unwritten and unpublished; and such socialists as I had happened to meet in the East End belonged to the Social Democratic Federation, and were at that time preaching what seemed to me nothing but a catastrophic overturning of the existing order, by forces of whose existence I saw no sign, in order to substitute what appeared to me the vaguest of incomprehensible utopias.

There was, however, another alternative lauded by idealists of all classes: by leading trade unionists and the more benevolent employers, by revolutionary socialists and by Liberal and Conservative philanthropists: an experiment in industrial organization actually, so it was reported, being brought into operation on a small scale by enthusiastic working men themselves. This was the ideal of 'self-employment', and the peaceful elimination from industry of the capitalist *entrepreneur*; to be secured by the manual workers themselves acquiring the ownership, or at any rate the use, of the capital, and managing the industry by which they gained their livelihood. It was this ideal, so I was told, that animated the Co-operative Movement in the North of England and the Lowlands of Scotland – a movement barely represented in the London that I knew.

There were, however, drawbacks to such a scheme of inquiry. It entailed breaking away from my fellow-workers in London, thus sacrificing skilled guidance and stimulating companionship. Further, I doubted whether I had the capacity and training to undertake, unaided, an inquiry into what was, after all, a particular form of business enterprise. Would it not be wiser to follow up one of the many questions opened out by Charles Booth's skilfully planned and statistically framed exploration of industrial London? For instance, he had suggested to me that I should take up the problem of the woman worker, with her relatively low standard of personal expenditure, her reputed willingness to accept wages below subsistence rates in aid of her husband's bare subsistence earnings, and even to work for mere pocket-money; whilst there was always haunting the dreary days of the sweated female worker the alluring alternative of the gains of casual love-making, too often ending in professional prostitution. The following entries in my diary reveal my hesitation. I also give the frankly expressed opinion of the greatest living economist that I was unfit for the larger and more independent task; though whether this authoritative condemnation of my proposed inquiry into the Co-operative Movement diminished my desire or increased my determination to do what I had a mind to do is an open question!

In trouble – perplexed about my work [I write while I am still collecting facts for the chapter on the Jewish community]. Charlie wants me to do *Woman's Work at the East End*, and have it ready by March; it means sacrificing part of February [my spring holiday] to writing – at least a fortnight. Unless I could make it a part of a bigger subject, would cut into my free time without occupying the whole of it. It would unfortunately postpone Co-operation. On the other hand, female labour is a subject of growing importance: one which for practical purposes is more important than Co-operation. ... Then the work is needed to complete Charles Booth's. I have already a mass of material in my head which could be used for it, and it would be doing work which lieth to my hand instead of seeking far afield for it. [MS. diary, 3 November 1888.]

Delightful visit to the Creightons[1] at Cambridge [I record six months later]. Interesting talk with Professor Marshall, first at dinner at the Creightons', and afterwards at lunch at his own house. It opened with chaff about men and women: he holding that woman was a subordinate being, and that, if she ceased to be subordinate, there would be no object for a man to marry. That marriage was a sacrifice of masculine freedom, and would only be tolerated by male creatures so long as it meant the devotion, body and soul, of the female to the male. Hence the woman must not develop her faculties in a way unpleasant to the man: that strength, courage, independence were not attractive in women; that rivalry in men's pursuits was positively unpleasant. Hence masculine strength and masculine ability in women must be firmly trampled on and boycotted by men. *Contrast* was the essence of the matrimonial relation: feminine weakness contrasted with masculine strength: masculine egotism with feminine self-devotion.

'If you compete with us we shan't marry you,' he summed up with a laugh.

I maintained the opposite argument: that there was an ideal of character in which strength, courage, sympathy, self-devotion, persistent purpose were united to a clear and far-seeing intellect; that the ideal was common to the man and to the woman; that these qualities might manifest themselves in different ways in the man's and the woman's life; that what you needed was not different qualities and different defects but the same virtues working in different directions, and dedicated to the service of the community in different ways.

1. In the autumn of 1888 I had been introduced to the Creightons by our common friend, Marie Souvestre. From that time onward I enjoyed their friendship, a privilege extended to The Other One when, four years later, he appeared as my betrothed. I often wonder how many of the young intellectuals of the eighties and nineties have, in later life, looked back on the days spent in this delightful family circle at Worcester or Cambridge, at Peterborough or Fulham, as one of the inspiring influences of their lives. In my memory Mandell Creighton appears as the subtlest, broadest-based and, I must add, the most elusive intellect, as well as one of the most lovable characters that I have come across in my journey through life. (See *The Life and Letters of Bishop Creighton*, by Louise Creighton.)

At lunch at his house our discussion was more practical. He said that he had heard that I was about to undertake a history of Co-operation.

'Do you think I am equal to it?' I said.

'Now, Miss Potter, I am going to be perfectly frank: of course I think you are equal to a history of Co-operation: but it is not what you can do best. There is one thing that *you* and only you can do – an inquiry into the unknown field of female labour. You have, unlike most women, a fairly trained intellect, and the courage and capacity for original work; and you have a woman's insight into a woman's life. There is no man in England who could undertake with any prospect of success an inquiry into female labour. There are any number of men who could write a history of Co-operation, and would bring to this study of a purely economic question far greater strength and knowledge than you possess. For instance, your views on the relative amount of profit in the different trades, and the reason of the success of Co-operation in cotton and its failure in the woollen industry, might interest me; but I should read what you said with grave doubt as to whether you had really probed the matter. On the other hand, if you described the factors enabling combinations of women in one trade and destroying all chance of it in the other, I should take what you said as the opinion of the best authority on the subject. I should think to myself, well, if Miss Potter has not succeeded in sifting these facts no one else will do so, so I may as well take her conclusion as the final one. To sum up with perfect frankness: if you devote yourself to the study of your own sex as an industrial factor, your name will be a household word two hundred years hence: if you write a history of Co-operation it will be superseded and ignored in a year or two. In the one case you will be using unique qualities which no one else possesses, and in the other you will be using faculties which are common to most men, and given to a great many among them in a much higher degree. *A book by you on the Co-operative Movement I may get my wife to read to me in the evening to while away the time, but I shan't pay any attention to it*,' he added with shrill emphasis.[2]

2. I confess to a certain *Schadenfreude* in reading the following extract from an obituary appreciation of Professor Marshall by Professor C. R. Fay, a favourite pupil, now the well-known economist and writer on Co-operation, as proving that, ten years after publication, my little book still interested him!

Of course I disputed the point, and tried to make him realize that I wanted this study in industrial administration as an education for economic science. The little professor, with bright eyes, shrugged his shoulders and became satirical on the subject of a woman dealing with scientific generalizations: not unkindly satirical, but chaffingly so. He stuck to his point and heaped on flattery to compensate for depreciation.

'Here you are a beginner – a one-year-old in economic study, and yet you have outstripped men like myself and Foxwell (who have devoted all the years of our life to economic questions) on the *one* subject of woman's labour. You have made a great success because you have a talent for a special kind of investigation. And yet you insist on ignoring your own talent and taking to work for which, pardon my absolute frankness, you have no more ability than the ordinary undergraduate who comes to my class. Naturally enough I feel strongly about it. I stand to you in the relation of a consumer to the producer. I am, in fact, one of your principal customers; and yet, though I am willing to lavish gratitude on you if you will only produce what I want, you insist on trying to produce what you cannot make successfully, and when you have made it will be practically useless.'

I confess, after all this contempt sugared over with an absurdly kind appreciation of my talent for one particular type of investigation, I was relieved to find that in his forthcoming work on political economy the dear little professor had quoted my generalization about the division of labour being characteristic neither of the best nor of the worst type of production, but of the medium kind. That generalization, at any rate, is a purely intellectual one, unconnected with the special insight of a woman into the woman's life.

I came away liking the man, and with gratitude for the kindly way in which he had stated his view; refreshed by his appreciation, and inclined to agree with him as to the slightness of my

'Gradually I arrived at my subject – Co-operation,' recalls Professor Fay. 'I was under a bond with him to write down, on a separate page in my notebook, the proposed title, altering it each week till it fitted my ambition. At last it became 'Co-operation at Home and Abroad, an analysis and description'. *His only fear was that I should be over-influenced by a pernicious book written by Beatrice Potter on this subject.*' (*The Canadian Forum*, p. 147, 1925.)

strength and ability for the work I proposed to undertake. Still, with the disagreeable masculine characteristic of persistent and well-defined purpose, I shall stick to my own way of climbing my own little tree. Female labour I may take up some day or other, but the Co-operative Movement comes first. [MS. diary, 8 March 1889.]

## A False Step

What finally determined me to select as my next field of inquiry the Co-operative Movement was the very fact that I suspect lay at the bottom of Professor Marshall's high opinion of my unique qualifications for the alternative question of woman's labour, namely, that I was at that time known to be an anti-feminist. In the spring of 1889 I took what afterwards seemed to me a false step in joining with others in signing the then notorious manifesto, drafted by Mrs Humphry Ward and some other distinguished ladies, against the political enfranchisement of women, thereby arousing the hostility of ardent women brain-workers, and, in the eyes of the general public, undermining my reputation as an impartial investigator of women's questions. When pressed by Frederic Harrison and James Knowles to write a reasoned answer to Mrs Fawcett's indignant retort to this reactionary document, I realized my mistake. Though I delayed my public recantation for nearly twenty years, I immediately and resolutely withdrew from that particular controversy.[3] Why I was at that time an anti-feminist in feel-

3. The anti-suffrage 'appeal' was published in the *Nineteenth Century* for June 1889, and the replies mentioned in the following letter from Frederic Harrison appear in the same review for July 1889:

'The papers of Mrs Fawcett and of Mrs Ashton Dilke, though the latter is far better in tone, are manifestly beneath the dignity and force of the Appeal (Frederic Harrison writes to me on 7 July 1889). Mr Knowles [the Editor of the *Nineteenth Century*] and I are cordially agreed in this, that you are the woman most fitted, on every ground most fitted, to take up the task, and as I have been active in urging your name as the champion, he has begged me to try and induce you to undertake it. There was needed something more full, more sympathetic and more definite than the Appeal. I really think it is a duty you

ing is easy to explain, though impossible to justify. Conservative by temperament, and anti-democratic through social environment, I had reacted against my father's over-valuation of women relatively to men; and the narrow outlook and exasperated tone of some of the pioneers of woman's suffrage had intensified this reaction. I remember at a luncheon given by an American lady to American suffragists (who had not given me a cigarette to soothe my distaste for the perpetual reiteration of the rights of women) venting this irritation by declaring provocatively – 'I have never met a man, however inferior, whom I do not consider to be my superior!' My dislike of the current Parliamentary politics of the Tory and Whig 'ins' and 'outs' seemed a sort of argument against the immersion of women in this atmosphere. But at the root of my anti-feminism lay the fact that I had never myself suffered the disabilities assumed to arise from my sex. Quite the contrary; if I had been a man, self-respect, family pressure and the public opinion of my class would have pushed me into a money-making profession; as a mere woman I could carve out a career of disinterested research. Moreover, in the craft I had chosen a woman was privileged. As an investigator she aroused less suspicion than a man, and, through making the proceedings more agreeable to the persons concerned, she gained better information. Further, in those days, a competent female writer on economic questions had, to an enterprising editor, actually a scarcity value. Thus she secured immediate publication and, to judge by my

owe to the public. It is criminal to bury your talent in a napkin in Monmouthshire. I do most earnestly implore you as a social obligation to speak out what you think and to make it a reply in fact, if not in form, to the dry democratic formulas of Mrs Fawcett.'

The following entry in the MS. diary probably expresses the tenor of my refusal to comply with this request:

'At present I am anxious to keep out of the controversy. I have as yet accomplished no work which gives me a right to speak as representative of the class Mrs Fawcett would enfranchise: celibate women. And to be frank, I am not sure of my ground; I am not certain whether the strong prejudice I have against political life and political methods does not influence my judgement on the question of enfranchising women.' [MS. diary, 7 July 1889.]

own experience, was paid a higher rate than that obtained by male competitors of equal standing.

## The Co-operative Movement

I was already sufficiently versed in the technique of investigation to realize that it would be useless, and indeed impertinent, to interview the directors and officials, employees and members of the Co-operative Movement, without first preparing my own mind. From my friend Benjamin Jones, the General Manager of the London Branch of the Co-operative Wholesale Society, I borrowed a collection of Congress Reports, 1869–88, and twenty years' files of the leading co-operative journal; and during the following year (1889) I used the months spent with my father to work steadily through this arid mass of print – an irksome task – rendered still more tedious by the lack of any proper system of note-taking. How well I remember the mental weariness, and even physical nausea, with which, after some hours' toil, I would turn over yet another page of the small and faint letterpress of these interminable volumes!

Just ten days reading at co-operative periodicals [I record midway in one of these spells of reading]. Tiresome work: with apparently little result, except a gathering of disjointed facts, none of which I can at present verify. It is peculiarly tiresome because I have no clear idea of the exact facts I am searching for; no settled plan of the scope of my work. Two conclusions I have reached: (1) that the Co-operative Movement means an association of working men to secure a large share of the profits from the middleman, the trader and the manufacturer, but that it fails entirely to check the fall of prices, and consequently of wages, brought about by competition for the custom of the consumer; (2) that the notion that the present Co-operative Movement arose out of the sentimental propaganda of gentlemen idealists is not true: it grew up on the basis of self-interest, and the idealism was grafted on to it. I am still in doubt as to whether this idealism has done much good? The one use of the 'gentlemen' connected with the movement has been promoting legislation to legalize co-operative societies. Also, profit-sharing was not considered a *sine qua non* in the earlier phases of the successful movement begun by the Rochdale Pioneers. [MS. diary, 29 June 1889.]

Struggling with the *Co-op. News* and enduring all the miseries of want of training in methods of work [I write some weeks later]. Midway I discover that my notes are slovenly, and under wrong headings, and I have to go through some ten weeks' work again! Up at 6.30 and working 5 hours a day, sometimes 6. Weary but not discouraged. [MS. diary, 26 July 1889.]

A grind, and no mistake! Six hours a day reading and note-taking from those endless volumes of the *Co-operative News*. A treadmill of disjointed facts, in themselves utterly uninteresting and appallingly dry, and not complete enough to be satisfactory. And there is the perpetual exercise of judgement – Is it worth while reading this paper or that speech? the unsatisfactoriness of the decision either way. If one does *not* read on, the fear that one has missed a suggestion or a fact of importance; if one persists with aching eyes, the dreary sense of time and effort wasted, if the material turns out to be useless theorizing, dreamy idealism, or ill-considered and patently inaccurate description. A grim determination to finish with it makes me sit at the work longer than is good for body or mind. So I feel sick and irritable, and in my off times I am desperately cross. However, it is satisfactory to feel that one will never be beaten for lack of industry. . . . 'Genius is given by God; but talent can be attained by any straight-forward intellect bent on doing its best.' So says Flaubert, and I console myself in my despondent hours with the thought that talent for excellent work may be mine . . . [MS. diary, 20 August 1889.]

This arduous and continuous acquisition of peculiarly indigestible material proved worth while. Not that I gained from these accounts and reports of innumerable societies, from the papers and discussions at conferences and congresses, from reminiscences of aged Owenites, from the bitter controversies raging round about the cooperative faith between the group of distinguished Christian Socialists on the one hand and the working-class officials and committee-men on the other, any explanation of the successes and failures of the Movement. What I secured was a 'bunch of keys': key events, key societies, key technical terms and key personalities, by the use of which I could gain the confidence of the person I interviewed, unlock the hidden stores of experience in their minds, and secure opportunities for actually observing and recording the working constitution and divers activities of the different types of organization within the Co-operative Movement.

Meanwhile, whenever I was free from attendance on my father, I wandered through the Midlands, the Northern Counties of England and the Lowlands of Scotland, attending sectional conferences and members' meetings, and settling down for days or weeks at such centres as Leeds, Newcastle, Glasgow and Manchester, in order to interview every type of cooperator. In my current diary I note visits to the stores of large towns and of small, as well as to practically all the 'self-governing workshops' and hybrid co-partnerships then known as cooperative productive societies. A few sample entries from the pages of my diary for the spring and summer of 1889 will enable the student to follow the course and manner of these adventures. Let me say, in passing, that the investigator should make a point of recording 'first impressions' of scenes, events and personages. These first impressions correspond with the hasty snapshots of the Kodak: they are proof that some such event happened, but they are seldom portraits, and frequently caricatures; they must never be taken as considered and verified statements of fact. The value of these rapid sketches is that they may afford clues to puzzle-questions – hypotheses that can be subsequently disproved or verified – unexpected glimpses of the behaviour of men under particular circumstances, when they are unaware of being observed; and as such they are a useful supplement to the mechanical and dry record of sociological detail contained in analytic notes and statistical tables. For obvious reasons I disguise the identity of some of the persons whom I describe, or whose words are quoted.

Three days at Hebden Bridge staying with the widow of an iron-founder. [I had come to Hebden Bridge to attend a conference summoned by the Hebden Bridge Fustian Society, at that time the most successful of the co-operative productive societies, but afterwards absorbed in the Co-operative Wholesale Society.] Three daughters and a son of twenty. Lower middle class just risen out of the working class. Mother a shrewd, warm-hearted body: true Yorkshire straightforwardness and cordiality. Daughters 'genteel' but pleasant girls. One does the house-keeping and is paid for it; another is the accountant of the family business, and the third is an assistant schoolmistress; whilst the son works at the business. They all talk broad Yorkshire. They have few sympathies or interests outside the life of gentility except the working-class mother, who is a vigorous politician of the Gladstonian type. But though their interests are not public, the family life is charming, and they are good friends with every-one. Indeed, Hebden Bridge resembles Bacup in its fusion of the middle and working class. Upper class it has none. My interest was in the vigorous cooperative life of the place; I saw many cooperators and attended their meetings. Young Oxford men are down here; and they and the cooperators form a mutual admiration society between intellectual young Oxford and cooperative working class. Cooperative working man: common con-demnation of the capitalist class and money-making brain-workers: a condemnation the form of which bordered perilously on cant, and was clearly the outcome of ignorance.

Back to Manchester by afternoon train. [MS. diary, 21 March 1889.]

Mitchell,[4] chairman of the C.W.S., is one of the leading per-

---

4. J. T. W. Mitchell (1828–95), the most remarkable personality that the British Co-operative Movement has thrown up, was the illegitimate son of 'a man in good position, but of ungoverned character'. Mitchell himself, so we are told by his biographer (*John T. W. Mitchell*, by Percy Redfern, p. 12), 'felt that he owed small moral benefit to this side of his parentage'. The mother 'lived only for the boy'; and, 'although hard pressed, she would not allow her child from her side'. Apparently she gained her livelihood by keeping a tiny beerhouse in a working-class street, supplemented by letting lodgings to working men. From ten years old, when Mitchell began as a piecer in a cotton mill, he earned his livelihood in the textile industry, until he retired at the age of about forty-five, without means, to devote his whole energies to the development of the Co-operative Wholesale Society, of which he was re-elected chairman, quarter by quarter, for twenty-one years, 1874–95. Throughout these twenty-one years of complete absorption in building up the most varied if not the largest business enterprise in the world at that time, Mitchell lived on the minute fees, never ex-ceeding £150 a year, that this vast enterprise then allowed to its

sonalities in the Co-operative Movement ... he is an enthusiast
for the consumers' interests; a sort of embodiment of the working-
man customer, intent on getting the whole profit of production, out of the hands of the manufacturer and trader, for the
consumer. ... As the representative of the Wholesale he is inspired by one idea – the enlargement and increased power of the
organization of which he is the head. He supports himself on the
part proceeds of a small woollen business, and draws perhaps 30s.
a week from the Wholesale to which he devotes his whole
energies. With few wants (for he is an old bachelor), he lives in a
small lodging, eats copiously of heavy food and drinks freely of
tea: no spirits and no tobacco. Corpulent, with a slow, bumptious
pronunciation of long phrases, melting now and again into a
boyish bonhomie. ... He is a good fellow, and in his inflated way
a patriotic citizen, according to his own ideal, the consumers'
welfare. His Board of Directors are entirely subordinate to him:
they are corpulent, heavy eaters, but for the most part they are
neither more nor less than simple tradesmen. They strike one as
an honest set of men, above corruption and proud of their position as directors of the central organization of working-class
capitalists.

Three or four times I have dined with the Central Board. A
higgledy-piggledy dinner; good materials served up coarsely,
and shovelled down by the partakers in a way that is not

chairman, in a small lodging at Rochdale, his total estate on death
amounting to the magnificent sum of £350 : 17 : 8. He never married,
and was romantically attached to his mother. Soon after her death in
1874 he compassionately took to live with him a neighbour – Thomas
Butterworth – who had been imprisoned for theft and found it impossible to get employment, and who became first his devoted servant,
and, inheriting small house property, his devoted landlord and habitual companion till death parted them. Throughout this long, al-
truistic business career Mitchell remained an ardent advocate of
temperance and an assiduous teacher of the Sunday School at the
Rochdale Chapel, to which he made a point of returning, Sunday after
Sunday, from the longest business journeys, even if this involved
travelling (third class) all night. In his Presidential Address to the
Rochdale Congress, 1892, he summed up his faith: 'The three great
forces for the improvement of mankind are religion, temperance, and
co-operation; and as a commercial force, supported and sustained by
the other two, co-operation is the grandest, noblest, and most likely to
be successful in the redemption of the industrial classes' (p. 89 of
*John T. W. Mitchell*, 1913, by Percy Redfern).

appetizing. But during dinner I get a lot of stray information, mostly through chaff and rapid discussion. Occasionally I am chaffed in a not agreeable way about matrimony and husbands, and the propriety of a match between me and Mitchell. But it is all good-natured, and I take it kindly. After dinner, in spite of the Chairman's disapproval, we smoke cigarettes, and our conversation becomes more that of business camaraderie.

If the Central Board of the Wholesale supplies me with food, the Central Board of the Co-operative Union supplies me with office room. I shall describe hereafter the different functions of these two organizations. But in this daily record I wish to outline personalities. Gray[5] is working secretary of the Co-operative Union (Neale[6] is too old to be a living force). He is a nice young

5. J. C. Gray (1854–1912) was the son of a Baptist Minister at Hebden Bridge, and was trained as a clerk in the Audit Office of the Lancashire and Yorkshire Railway Co. Owing to his co-operative sympathies and work, he was made General Secretary of the Hebden Bridge Fustian Society in 1874; Assistant Secretary to the Central Board of the Co-operative Union in 1883; becoming, on the death of E. Vansittart Neale, General Secretary of the Co-operative Union in 1891, a post he retained until disabled by ill-health in 1910. His sympathies were from the first with associations of producers rather than with the Consumers' Co-operative Movement; and in 1886, at the Plymouth Congress, he read an able paper on Co-operative Production, outlining a scheme for the formation of self-governing productive societies linked up with the Co-operative Wholesale Society. The scheme was unanimously adopted by the Plymouth Congress, the Directors of the Co-operative Wholesale Society remaining silent. But there the matter ended. In after years, in order to prevent the obstinate evil of overlapping between the various separate consumers' societies, then becoming thick on the ground, he sketched out a striking proposal for their amalgamation into a single national society with local branches. (See *The Consumers' Co-operative Movement*, 1921, by S. and B. Webb, pp. 307–9.)

6. E. Vansittart Neale (1810—92), a grandson of Mr Vansittart of Bisham Abbey, M.P. for Berkshire during Pitt's Administration and a lineal descendant of Oliver Cromwell, was educated at Rugby and Oriel College, Oxford; practised as Chancery barrister, and was, in 1849, one of the founders of the Society for promoting Working Men's Associations. I believe that in all the annals of British philanthropy no more honourable example can be found of a life devoted from first to last to the disinterested and self-denying service of the wage-earning class. Possessed of considerable means, he lavished money on the associations of producers started by the Christian Socialists and their successors, until in 1855, owing to the repeated failures of the

man: that is the first impression: scrupulously turned out in co-operative cloth made by a cooperative tailor. He is an idealist: looking at cooperation not as a huge organized consumers' interest, but as a true and equitable cooperation between capital and labour. He is not a self-seeker; he is a refined and modest-natured man, though, in his inmost soul, he has flights of ambition towards a seat in the County Council or perhaps even in Parliament. He lacks the energetic push of Mitchell, and his weary expression seems to betoken that he feels he is fighting a lost cause. In spare moments at the office he and I have many a cigarette together, and talks on philosophy, religion and politics as well as cooperation. [MS. diary, 28 March 1889.]

Here is a typical day among cooperators [I note a few days later]. Dined at one o'clock with the buyers at the Wholesale. Head of our table, manager of drapery department: strong able man, straightforward and business-like; to my right, Odgers, Secretary of Co-operative Insurance Company; to my left, Head of Boot and Shoe Department; in front, A. B., Chairman of the X and Y Co-operative Society, and C., cashier to the same society. Odgers is a positivist, an enthusiast who gave up a salary of £200

enterprises, he had become a comparatively poor man. From 1869 onward he organized the Annual Co-operative Congress, becoming the unpaid General Secretary of the Co-operative Union from 1873 to 1891. His greatest service to the Co-operative Movement was acting as its legal adviser, drafting not only all its rules and reports but also practically all the legislation concerned with this form of industrial association. In the last year of his life he recognized and deplored the permeation of the Co-operative Movement by Fabian economics. 'There seems' (he wrote to Hughes in 1892) 'to be a growing disposition to seek the solution of social questions through municipal action, imbued with wholesale production for the sole benefit of the consumer, rather than through the growth and federation of true co-operative societies which will benefit the consumer by raising up his position as a worker. If this conception is to be served, I think we must oppose to this consumers' flood such strength as can be got out of union for the express promotion of cooperative production, with the ultimate hope of getting the consumers' societies to see that the spheres of production and consumption, though they should be closely allied, must be kept distinct, if the permanent welfare of the working population is to be secured by cooperation' (*Memorial of Edward Vansittart Neale*, compiled by Henry Pitman, 1894, p. 9). After his death, without any recognition by the public of his prolonger social service, a memorial tablet was placed in St Paul's Cathedral at the expense of the Co-operative Movement.

a year to become a cooperative employee at £1 a week, inspired by J. S. Mill's chapter on Co-operation. He is without humour, and without push or striking ability. But he is one of those men who make the backbone of great movements through steadfastness and integrity of character. 'Where shall we find the moral impulse wherewith to inspire the Co-operative Movement? profit-sharing is played out', is his constant meditation. The conversation at dinner naturally turned on profit-sharing. Pearson and the other Wholesale employees were dead against it. It had been tried at the Wholesale, and it was found impossible to work out equitably. A. B., a large, fair-haired man who has recently taken a considerable place in the Movement through his pleasant manner, gift of the gab, and imposing presence (somewhat of a sham), talked in favour of some ideal form of profit-sharing which he could not define or explain, but which would be free of all the shortcomings of other forms. Odgers maintained that each man should have a fair wage (what is a fair wage?), and that profit was a selfish thing and a taste for it not to be cultivated. Then came coffee and cigarettes, and the conversation broadened out into the discussion of man's general nature and the character of his motives; and then narrowed down into an interesting description of the difficulties experienced by the Wholesale at their Leicester works, with the Boot and Shoe Trade Union. 'If you can get at the officials of the Unions they are sensible enough; but the men themselves are simply childish, and they frequently refuse to follow the advice of their own officials.' Eccles Manufacturing Society was mentioned as one successful instance of profit-sharing.

At five o'clock set out for Burnley to attend meeting of shareholders of the Self-Help.[7] This is one of the six weaving sheds

7. For an account of this society from 1886 see *Co-operative Production*, by Benjamin Jones, vol. i. pp. 315–22. Further details will be found in a more laudatory article by Thomas Blandford in *Labour Co-partnership* for December 1894; see also *New Statesman* Supplement on Co-operative Production and Profit-sharing, 14 February 1914, p. 21. The society still (1925) exists; but how far it has continued to stand on its original basis that all workers should be shareholders and all shareholders workers in the Society's mill is not clear to me. In 1914 I see it noted that the whole enterprise had been leased to the manager for ten years. In 1924 it was reported to have 289 members (shareholders) with a share capital of £12,034, making sales during the year of £30,008, and a profit of £1053, after paying 'salaries and wages' of £1029 to six 'employees'. How many of the 289 'members' are employed as weavers in the mill is not stated.

belonging to the workers themselves, who are responsible for profit, loss and management. Each weaver must take shares to cover cost of looms and room, and other workers in proportion. They hire their room and power, and frequently their machinery. Two of these societies have already come to grief; the one I visited has been in low water; the workers paying sixpence per loom back out of their wages to cover losses. The manager walked from the station with me. Big, burly man; neither he nor the secretary looked up to the mark of other managers and secretaries; and though that was only the third quarter they were the second instalment of managerial brains in the concern. He was full of complaint against those who were both his masters and his workers. It was impossible to keep discipline amongst them. They wanted first-class yarn to work and then expected him to compete in the market with masters who were making up yarn at half the price. They insisted on full Trade Union prices, whereas small masters were paying $7\frac{1}{2}$ per cent less.

'They wants an aisy place; just to look at the machine and never so much as tie a bit o' yarn; they wants list prices and a bit over, and a couple of hours more holiday in the week into the bargain. And then they cries and grumbles if there is no divi. at the end of the quarter. The like of these places will never stand until they trust a man and not heckle him out of his life with one thing or another!'

The meeting was dramatic. A long, low warehouse, wooden, banded with iron, with here and there a wheel or belt peering through the ceiling from the upper chamber filled with machinery. Long wooden tables down the centre, upon which and upon the floor were heaps of printers' cloth ready for packing, whilst scattered about were tin twist-holders. When I entered with one of the directors these tins were being collected to serve as seats. The chairman, one of the weavers, a thin, weak individual, was poring hopelessly over the rules and regulations of the society. Men, and women with shawls thrown over their heads, were groping their way and squatting down one after the other as near as possible to the president's chair; and four jets of gas lit up the central position of the chair, and behind us the long, high wooden table, all the rest of the room being in darkness. The secretary was reclining on a heap of material; the directors were, some of them lying at full length on the table, peering over the minute book, at which the secretary was gazing indifferently. To the right of the chairman some of the elder men were seated. To the left a band of youths were bent on obstruction and rebellion. There was a loud muttering amongst these youths and men, but the women shareholders were gossiping and laughing. Bits of paper were pinned up on the beams supporting the wall with the agenda of the meeting scribbled on them.

Minutes of the last meeting read; obstruction of weak but noisy youth on some point of order which neither he nor the poor worried chairman understood. Then the question of the committee's fees. This was received in silence and hastily dropped by the chairman.

Next a personal explanation from a resigning director. This man was a slow but respectable person; his long, rambling speech, frequently obstructed by the small knot of boy shareholders, consisted of a complaint against the want of loyalty among the directors to each other. Everything said in committee, and many things not said, were repeated by one or more of the directors to the general body of shareholding workers.

'I might say this,' ended up the injured man, 'there is not one of your committee as never opens 'is mouth; but no sooner 'as 'e left the committee-room than 'e begins to ferment bad feeling. I will just give you, gentlemen and ladies, an instance. We 'ad our committee night and discussion as to lowering wages: it was adjourned as we could not agree. But before noon next day 'alf the hands in the shop came to me and insulted me because they said I wanted to lower wages, when I know who put them up to it, too.'

'Mr Chairman, I think 'e's out of order,' shrieked an evil-looking youth.

'You needn't 'ave put the cap on if it didn't fit,' growled the director. 'Next question,' shouted out the mass of the members, not inclined to take one side or the other.

'Election of new directors,' drawled the secretary, and then proceeded to deal out slips of paper. The names of the candidates were written upon the agenda paper, but no one could see it, and general confusion resulted. At length after a passing to and fro of persons, an unpinning of the paper in one place and pinning it up in another, the hundred or so members present were supposed to have mastered the names. Voting was by ballot: each member writing down the name of his candidate and throwing it into the teller's hat.

'Now for the stocktakers,' cried the chairman. 'Now, gentlemen and ladies, you will have to look to the front of you in this.

We must get a man who is a practical man and knows the business straight through. Will anyone move and second any gentleman as he thinks fit?'

'John Ashworth'; 'seconded'. 'I decline to stand: I did it last time, to the best of my ability, and you weren't satisfied. You can find another man this time.'

'John Ardley'; 'seconded'. 'My son won't stand,' said a quiet old man; 'he doesn't know the business.' The son looked sheepish. He wanted the post and had put up two companions to propose and second him; but he dare not dispute his father's view of his capacity.

'I propose,' says the evil-looking youth who is standing for the directorate, 'that there be three stocktakers, and not two.'

The chairman looks helpless; they have not got one yet, and he cannot quite see how having to get three will make it easier. But he accepts the suggestion and asks for three nominees. Someone who is not present is nominated, seconded and carried. The chairman accepts another for the second position. But the third? The secretary whispers to the chairman that the motion for a third was not seconded. 'Aye,' says the chairman with a sigh of relief. 'Gentlemen, the motion for the third stocktaker was not seconded, so it falls to the ground.'

And now the real business of the evening. A suggestion from a leading member that they should make up better stuff and reduce the cost by lowering wages. Why should they attend to the Trade Union regulation: they were so many small masters each working for himself, and they could work for what wage they pleased, and so on. Then followed a rambling discussion, led off the point on to all sorts of general principles and details. A knock at the outer door startled the meeting. Was it the trade union official come to see what they were up to? No, it was, alas! my cab, come to fetch me to catch the last train to Manchester. As I drive rapidly down the steep streets of Burnley I meditate on the mingled ignorance, suspicion and fine aspirations of this small body of working-class capitalists doomed to failure. [MS. diary, April 1889.]

Two months later I am attending the Annual Co-operative Congress; my second congress, as I had been at the Dewsbury Congress, Whitsun 1888. In those days of the Co-operative Movement these gatherings were more informal, more intimate, and also more amateur and quarrelsome, than the expert, self-respectful and politically important Co-operative Congress of today. Judging by the length of the entry in my diary, the Congress at Ipswich in June 1889 seems to have been a happy hunting-ground for the social investigator. Here is a portion of my rapid presentation of the personalities of this congress:

Whirled down to Ipswich in a crowded excursion train. Arrived at the White Horse Inn with Burnett, and Fielding, Manager of the Tea Department. At the door my old friends of the Wholesale, including Mitchell, welcomed me warmly. In the commercial room I find other cooperators; an American professor and his wife. The next four days a strange procession of men of all grades and conditions, the majority belonging to the working and lower middle class, but sprinkled with upper-class inquirers and sympathizers – a politician, two Toynbee young men, an Irish peer's son who has started a store on his father's estate, the unassuming wives of the more distinguished working men, and a few exceptional women, glorified spinsters like myself. A rapid and somewhat unconsequential presentation of economic, social and political theories, of industrial, financial and economic facts, takes place in these conversations. Forty of us are installed in the romantic 'Pickwick' Inn, with its rambling passages and covered courtyard; and here other leading cooperators congregate, drink whisky and smoke tobacco. At the Cooperative Congress there is an absolute equality: all live together on the freest of terms; excursions and business are conducted under the democratic co-operative system . . .

It is Sunday evening and we are all assembled in the long coffee-room – scattered up and down in knots round a long table, some devouring cold beef and tea, others chatting together. In one of these parties, behold the hero of this year's Congress: the distinguished man whom working-men cooperators have elected to give the inaugural address, Professor Marshall of Cambridge. He looks every inch a professor. A small slight man with bushy moustache and long hair, nervous movements, sensitive and unhealthily pallid complexion, and preternaturally keen and apprehending eyes, the professor has the youthfulness of physical delicacy. In spite of the intellectuality of his face, he seems to lack the human experience of everyday life. . . . Tonight, however, his desire to gain information outweighs his nervous fear of a sleepless night, and he is listening with mingled interest and impatience to the modicum of facts dealt out in the inflated and involved phrases of Mitchell, the Chairman of the Manchester Wholesale. As I approach I am greeted by my old friend.

'Now, Miss Potter, come and join me in a cup of tea. I was just telling the Professor my view of the true nature and real use of the great Co-operative Movement. What we wants to do is to make the purchasing power of a man's wage, whether received from us or from other employers – and mind you' (continues Mitchell, tapping me confidentially on the arm and lowering his voice), 'at present – I do not say what may happen in the future – at present the men we employ is a mere handful to those employed by private firms – well, what I was saying was' (raising his voice so that all might hear) 'that our great object was to increase the purchasing power of all men's wages by returning the profits of trading and manufacturing into the consumers' pocket. Now look you here; some people who don't understand say we are not just to Labour. But I will take an actual case. We have made a profit of £50,000 on our productive works. Now who should that profit go to? To the thousand working men and working women who are already paid fair wages, and many of whom spend these very wages at private shops, or to the million working men and women who belong to our Movement and who have given the capital and paid for the brains which have made these manufactures grow up around us? It seems to me,' concluded Mitchell, raising his sonorous voice and thundering on the table with his fat fist, 'it seems to me, and I am moreover prepared to maintain it on religious, social and political grounds, that the Wholesale's method of organizing production, combining as it does economy of capital, efficiency of administration and regularity of demand, is the best possible system of cooperation for the working man: and that if it is loyally supported and indefinitely extended it will solve all social problems, destroy poverty, eradicate crime and secure the greatest happiness to the greatest number.'

Mitchell having delivered himself of his usual tea-party peroration and finding no one to dispute his points (the Professor was busily engaged on the £50,000 profit, combining that statement with some other fact he had heard, and calculating from the two some result withheld from him), relapsed into the enjoyment of highly sugared tea and much-buttered toast; his huge corpulent form, shiny bald head, clean-shaven face, exhibiting a full, good-tempered mouth, largely developed jaw and determined chin, so completely affirmed the force of his argument in favour of organized consumption, that it seemed useless to draw from him further verbal expressions of it. A tall, slim and hungry-looking youth, a delegate from some small but independent productive society, appeared on the point of disputing it, but doubtless remembering that the Wholesale was their best customer, thought better of his intention.

I turned to the group on the other side, including Benjamin Jones, astride a chair, Burnett leaning back with stately dignity, and Dent with his head half buried between his brawny arms and large, powerfully made, workman's hands.[8] Dent and Jones were disputing vigorously; Burnett was listening with the weighty responsible silence of a Government official. These three men are typical and representative of the three great working-class movements: Jones of associations for trading purposes, Burnett of trade unions, and Dent of workmen's clubs and of the self-governing workshop side of cooperation. Benjamin Jones is a combination of a high-minded grocer, a public-spirited administrator and a wire-puller. Within the Co-operative Movement he is all three. Burnett has the dignity of a skilled mechanic; the self-restraint of a great organizer; the massive power of a leader of great strikes based on broad claims. Dent[9] is a much younger

8. These three men, John Burnett, Benjamin Jones and J. J. Dent, had acted as my sponsors in the World of Labour, and here is an entry descriptive of two of them:

'Seen something during my London stay of Burnett, Benjamin Jones and J. J. Dent, the three most intimate of my working-men friends. My friendship with the two former is becoming a close one and likely to endure, as future work will bring us together. For Burnett I have a strong admiration; he is singularly disinterested, with a reserve of thought and feeling and a dignity of manner which makes him attractive. Jones is on a lower plane; but he, also, is an enthusiast for the service of humanity; a pushing, fighting soldier in the great army, ready to sacrifice himself personally, but thinking any means good enough to fight the enemy; tolerating all things true and false, good or evil, so long as they seem to work in his direction. He strives night and day in order that mankind should enjoy the "results of goodness", but forgets that the fruit cannot exist without the tree. An enlightened selfishness in men and women cannot bring about the peace of an unconscious self-devotion to the public good.' [MS. diary, 6 March 1889.]

9. J. J. Dent, born 1856; a highly skilled bricklayer, who was in 1883 elected Secretary of the Working Men's Club and Institute Union (a

man, clear-headed and sympathetic, but an enthusiast for abstract theories and perfect justice, still feeling his way as to the best method of social reform. At present his square forehead is contracted with thought, and in his dark grey eyes there is an expression of worried perplexity.

'Now look you here, Dent,' says Ben Jones in his confident cheery manner; 'I am simply going to state facts on Wednesday [Ben Jones is President of that day]. I am going to give the older men their due; they have done for the working class with their joint stock companies[10] what we have failed to do with our attempt at profit-sharing; but it is no use making it into a shibboleth when it is simply one method of reaching our common aim. If you want to go to Japan you can go to the west or to the east;

---

post he resigned when appointed in 1893 as Co-operative Correspondent to the Labour Department of the Board of Trade, remaining a member of the Executive and Vice-President of the Working Men's Club and Institute Union until 1922, retired from the Government service in 1919, after being made C.M.G. for service in Emigrants' Information Office of Colonial Office. Throughout his life he has been closely connected with the Co-operative Movement, having already attended forty-one Annual Co-operative Congresses, and assisted in the formation of many societies. He has also been associated with the Workers' Educational Association and the Working Men's College, and other educational organizations.

10. Benjamin Jones was here referring to some eighty cotton-spinning and cotton-weaving factories in Lancashire, then known as 'Working Class Limiteds'. These cotton mills had been started and were being managed by working men, the original capital having been contributed either by the members of local co-operative stores, as in the case of the Rochdale Manufacturing Company started by the Rochdale Pioneers in 1854 (see note on p. 379), or by other groups of artisans. Some of these establishments began by sharing profits with the workers, but by 1886 they had all dropped this method of remuneration, and were, in constitution and activities, in no respect different from ordinary capitalist establishments, being governed, not by the representatives of the consumers or by the representatives of the workers concerned, but by the shareholders, with voting power according to the number of shares held. These limited liability companies, formed principally by men of the wage-earning class, and governed by boards of directors mainly drawn from the same class, were on this account often alluded to by economists and others as being 'co-operative'; and, for historical reasons, they were, up to about 1890, regarded as part of the Co-operative Movement, though they were not at any time admitted to direct representation in the Co-operative Congress.

you can go ways that seem absolutely opposite, but eventually they meet. It is the same with these two methods of association; and all we can say is that the store method has arrived at better results than the so-called cooperative productive method.'

'Well, if you are going to say that,' replied Dent, 'I don't see what is the good of praising up profit-sharing. If the East way is also the best way, we might as well give up the idea of the other.'

'No, look you here! Profit-sharing *is* the best if we can work it out: it is better for the men employed. I am not going to deny that, else why should I be interested in the Co-operative Aid Society[11] and spend my time and money on that? What I want is that both systems should have fair play and no favour. But if you go and put up the back of the Wholesale Board by this constant abuse you will just make them shut the door to the other principle, and then it will have no chance. Tom Hughes by

11. The Co-operative Aid Society was an organization for helping groups of working men to start self-governing workshops, and was in those days of muddled thinking mildly patronized by some of the leading officials of the C.W.S. Here is an entry relating to it, dated 19 November 1889:

'Attended Committee meeting of Co-operative Aid Association in Board Room of London C.W.S.; Dent in the chair.

'Deputations from productive societies or would-be societies. Ignorant but well-meaning young man, boot and leather examiner, who wished to start West-end boot factory. "The hand-sewn trade", he told us, "is dying a natural death: every person takes machine-made boots because of their cheapness." And yet it was in the hand-sewn trade that he wanted to start a society! After a lengthy dissertation on the foot being the most important member of the body, he produced a written statement of wages, cost of raw material, prices given by customers: a statement which showed the respectable profit of 30 per cent. The small matter of management was of course left unconsidered: the existence of a market was assumed.

' "To whom will you sell your boots?" asks one of the Committee with a puzzled expression.

' "Oh that's easy enough," says the young man; "the public will see the advantage of our manufacture: they will know that our principle is to do honest work; our wish to give satisfaction. I have not the slightest doubt of our success"; and then follows another muddled oration on co-operative ideals. At last the young man is dismissed with a letter to David Schloss, an expert on the boot trade. More deputations; and at 7.45 Vaughan, Nash and I adjourned to Canito's for supper.'

his dogmatism and violence has thrown the whole question of profit-sharing back for at least ten years, and X. has absolutely stamped it out of the Wholesale organization, merely because he would not let it grow up from a small beginning.'

'I am not going to defend X. He is a schemer and has feathered his own nest with his fine theories. But Tom Hughes has lost money in the Movement, and you had better not have a hit at him in your address. The Southern Section look upon him as their leader. I confess I am glad he is not here. We do not want a split between the North and the South; X is doing his best to start one.'

'Not much chance of that while *we* hold the purse-strings,' retorted the said Jones with a chuckle; 'and after all we satisfy both parties. At Congress we pass resolutions in favour of profit-sharing, and during the year we ignore them.'

'The danger of the Movement,' interposed Burnett, 'is that consumption is becoming so highly organized that these independent productive societies will have no chance.'

'Yes,' said Dent, 'I do not feel much inclined to help the store movement. Every store that is started lessens the chance of Productive Co-operation with profits given to the producer. No sooner has the working man touched his "divi" and his one cry is more.'

'He is much the same as other men,' replies the matter-of-fact Jones. 'The sooner we get out of our head that the cooperator is the most unselfish of men, the better. It is all cant and twaddle. The cooperator is not one whit less selfish than other men, only he goes about it in a more sensible manner and gets more return for his selfishness. If we cannot prove that, by giving a share of profits to the worker we make him work better, we shall never convert even ten per cent of cooperators to profit-sharing. Now what I want to do is to clear all this humbug out of the way; to look facts in the face and start fair. And here is Miss Potter, who is going to study the question and show us the way out of the difficulty. Come, Miss Potter, leave Mitchell to his tea, and come and help me to make Dent understand our view of the question.'

'There is another question Miss Potter has to explain to us, one for which she is far more responsible' – Dent remarks in a grave tone but with a kindly light in his grey eyes – 'why she lent her influence to that appeal against the suffrage. I believe it is just this: she is satisfied with her own position because she is rich and strong; she does not see that other women need the power to help themselves which would be given by the vote.'

This I feel to be an unpleasant accusation, especially as Dent and I are old friends and he speaks seriously. But before I have time to advance any sober proposition or arguments the little Professor, in tones of nervous irritability, intervenes.

'Miss Potter sees what the women suffrage people do not see; that if women attempt to equal men and be independent of their guidance and control, the strong woman will be ignored and the weak woman simply starved. It is not likely that men will go on marrying if they are to have competitors for wives. *Contrast* is the only basis of marriage, and if that is destroyed we shall not think it worth our while to shackle ourselves in life with a companion whom we must support and must consider.'

There are two sides to that question, think I, and the celibate condition of the human race can be brought about by either party to the matrimonial contract. However, I laughingly reply:

'Mr Marshall, I pity you deeply. You are obliged to come to the rescue of a woman who is the personification of emancipation in all ways; who clings to her cigarette if she does not clutch at her vote. Why don't you leave me to my fate? Convicted of hopeless inconsistency, I might even give up smoking, hoping thereby to protect myself against my rights.'

'That's just it,' whispers Jones. 'That's why these women are so bitter against you. It is pure perversity on your side to say one thing and act another.'

'Surely, Mr Jones, I am simply taking a hint from your admirable method of controlling the Co-operative Movement; signing resolutions in favour of one policy, and acting according to another.'

'She's got you there, Jones.' But the smile which played across Dent's face gives way to a perplexed expression as he adds, 'I believe you are in earnest with your views; I should like some day to have it out with you; a clever, strong woman like you must have some reasons to give. I cannot say I think much of those in the protest. Will you come down into the courtyard?' he adds. 'Maxwell is there and some of the Scottish delegates: you might like to ask them some questions.'

'I will go anywhere for a cigarette.'

The company disappears; the Marshalls retire to their room, I to the smoking-room, where I spend the rest of a late evening in telling fortunes from hands, and in a stray search for facts in the chaff of a smoking-room conversation . . .

On the whole the Ipswich Congress has been unsatisfactory to me personally. . . . The little clique of exceptional women, with their correct behaviour and political aspirations, give me most decidedly the cold shoulder – this in a company of men annoys me more than it should do. But the supreme discouragement of the Congress is the growing consciousness that I am unfit for the work I have undertaken, and that I am only at the beginning of my study of the Co-operative Movement. The little Professor frightens me by asking in sinister tones whether I have considered the effect of the appreciation of gold in the years 1871–4 on the productive societies then started! and tells me quite frankly that I have got the wrong end of the stick. Still, I got a good deal out of him in my long interview in his Cambridge study; and, though disheartened, I came away more than ever determined to grasp my subject firmly. [MS. diary, June 1889.]

When in the country with my father, I ponder over my study of cooperative theory and my observations of cooperative practice; and I see visions of a more equitable distribution of wealth and a higher standard alike of knowledge and brotherhood than had proved to be practicable in profit-making enterprise.

How inexpressibly ugly are the manners and ways of a typical middle-class man, brought up in the atmosphere of small profitmaking; securing profit by 'driving other chaps', a phrase which represents in H.-C.'s mind the great world of invention and enterprise; for the small manufacturing and retail tradesman's business is a matter of driving and 'doing' workers and customers. Experience of this class makes me wonder whether profit is not on the whole a demoralizing force? Whether a system of standard salaries and standard wages, such as is being gradually evolved by trade unionism and cooperative enterprise, is not a higher form of industrial organization? Should not the use of a man's faculties after he has received his maintenance be dedicated to society? Is not profit-making the sharing of unlawful gain? And are not the forces of public opinion and the natural evolution of industry tending in that way?

Some such conclusion I am coming to in my study of the Co-operative Movement. It seems to me to have been essentially a movement *not* towards the sharing of profits by workers, but towards an unconscious realization of the socialist ideal of officially managed business on the basis of voluntary association; the difference between the Co-operative Movement and mere joint stock association lying in the fact that the religious element of work for humanity has entered into it as a vivifying force. Moreover, embodied in its creed are the ethics of industry: purity of goods; equal payment and care for the workers. And yet I am slow to accept this theory as it is contrary to the whole idealism of the actual leaders [of the Co-operative Movement]. [MS. diary, October 1889.]

Now, I do not reproduce these diary entries as affording any vision of my investigation into the Co-operative Movement. They do but indicate the nature of the 'contacts' that I made, in order to gain the necessary opportunities to examine the extensive and somewhat amorphous piece of social tissue that I had undertaken to study. So as not to repeat the book that I eventually wrote, I confine the statement of my conclusions to the baldest summaries.

My first discovery had really some resemblance to that of the child in Hans Andersen's story, who looked at the king when all the courtiers were admiring his regal robes, and declared that the monarch was, in fact, naked! The cooperators who, with the assent of their intellectual supporters and admirers, kept on asserting that the object of their movement was the abolition of the wage system and the organization of industry in the interest of the manual working producers, had, in fact, by 1889, built up a great industrial organization of a hierarchial character exclusively in the interest of working-class consumers. Far from abolishing the wage system, all they had done was to extend it to the brain-worker. What they had abolished was the profit-making entrepreneur! In one sense, as I shall presently show, they had abolished profits. Yet at congress after congress the cooperators resolutely refused to witness the transfiguration of their own movement. All I did was to point out this transformation, whilst at the same time I explained and justified it.

Within the Co-operative Movement of the eighties there were two diametrically opposed schemes of industrial organization: on the one hand, government by the producers of the commodities and services concerned, and on the other, government by the consumers thereof. Control by the workers was professed, control by the consumers was practised. My study of industrial history of the first half of the nineteenth century enabled me to trace how the practice of the cooperators had worked out differently from the idea with which they had started.

Let us first consider the origin of that 'charmer' within 'the order of thought' but 'gay deceiver' within 'the order of things', the idea of the 'self-governing workshop'.

What seemed clear, alike to the wage-earner himself and to the intellectuals concerned about the chronic penury and insecurity of the manual worker's lot in the midst of riches, was that all the misery had arisen from the divorce which the industrial revolution had brought about between the manual worker and the ownership, alike of the instruments of production and the product itself. Why, it was asked, should not this evil be undone, and the land given back to the peasant cultivator and the tools again placed in the hands of the craftsman and his apprentice?

Some such vision seems to have appeared to William Cobbett in the rare intervals when his mind passed from asserting political rights to considering the conditions of economic freedom. But anyone born and bred in a manufacturing district, whether employer or employed, was aware that, under the circumstance of modern machine industry, with its large establishments and subdivision of labour, this act of restitution could not be made to the individual worker; it had necessarily to be made to all the workers in a particular workshop, factory or mine, for them in concert to carry on their industry. Hence the conception of the 'self-governing workshop' – an ideal of surpassing attractiveness. To the workman it gave the feeling that he would be his own master; to the Conservative it seemed a reversion to the healthier conditions of a former time; to the Christian it seemed to substitute in industry the spirit of fellowship and mutual assistance for that of competitive selfishness. Even to the mid-Victorian orthodox political economist, with his apotheosis of pecuniary self-interest and his unbending faith in the struggle for existence, the self-governing workshop seemed the only practicable way of extending to all those who were cooperating in production the blessed incentive of 'profit on price', and thus broadening the basis and strengthening the defences of an acquisitive society.

Now it was this fascinating conception of the self-governing workshop that was wrapped round and round the Co-operative Movement when I first began studying it. To read the reports of the Annual Co-operative Congresses between 1869 and 1887, one would imagine that it was this conception of industrial self-government that was the universally accepted goal of those who professed the cooperative faith. All the lecturers and writers on cooperation from the little group of talented Christian Socialists led by F. D. Maurice, Charles Kingsley, J. M. Ludlow, Tom Hughes and Edward Vansittart Neale, to distinguished political economists – John Stuart Mill, John Elliot Cairnes and Alfred Marshall – held aloft, with more or less enthusiasm, the banner of self-employment by groups of working men, owning alike the instruments and the product of their labour, as the desirable and the only practicable alternative to the dictatorship of the capitalist. Nor was this notion confined to middle-class intellectuals. Had not the short-lived revolutionary movement of 1833–4, embodied in the 'Grand National Consolidated Trades Union', proclaimed its intention of transforming each trade union into a national company, the agricultural union to take over the land, the miners the mines, the textile unions the factories? The Builders' Guild actually started on the erection of a guildhall at Birmingham and was inviting orders for houses. This syndicalist trade unionism crashed to the ground within a few months of its initiation.[12] For another decade the pendulum swung in favour of political revolution. But in 1848 the collapse of the Chartist Movement led to a revival of the plan of self-employment. Under

12. See *History of Trade Unionism*, by S. and B. Webb, chapter iii, 'The Revolutionary Period, 1829–42'.

the inspiration of F. D. Maurice and the direction of J. M. Ludlow, a whole litter of little self governing work-shops were started within the Metropolitan area, to be followed a few years later by a larger experiment in self-employment by the Amalgamated Society of Engineers.[13] From that time onward there appeared at Co-operative Congresses the representatives of a succession of cooperative productive societies cropping up and dying down with disconcerting suddenness. After a succession of disastrous experiments by some of the richer and more powerful unions, trade union officials, whilst urging the cooperators to put in practice the faith they professed, politely refused to use their societies' funds for the employment of their own members. For in spite of all the allurements of the self-governing workshop, whether it was deemed to be promoting the spirit of Christian fellowship among the workers or stimulating their pecuniary self-interest, the ideal of the control of industry by the workers concerned had the supreme demerit *that*

13. For information about British Christian Socialism and its leaders see *Christian Socialism, 1848–54*, by Charles E. Raven, an admirable account of the founders of Christian Socialism, though, I think, an over-enthusiastic description of their advocacy of the ideal of the self-governing workshop. F. D. Maurice and his friends, who started with no experience of British business enterprise, seem to have thought that because they themselves, as promoters and financial guarantors, were inspired by benevolence, they could transfer, with their capital, this emotion of service to the little group of craftsmen they set up as profit-makers. As a matter of fact, they were appealing to the self-interest of the workers, as F. D. Maurice's friend, F. J. A. Hort, pointed out to his fellow-ecclesiastic:

'Just then I heard of the forthcoming Socialist Tracts, and added a postscript wishing him success, but protesting against the cant of praising the meritoriousness and benevolence of those who joined an association. ...

'Nor is selfishness a whit removed; *he* [the working member of the Co-operative Productive Society] seeks "*our* interest", "the interest of that of which *I* am a part", instead of "*my* interest"; and I own I do not see what is gained by the change. Of course he may be unselfish under such circumstances, but not more so than under a state of competition' (*Life and Letters of Fenton John Anthony Hort*, by his son Arthur Fenton Hort, vol. i., 1896, p. 152 and pp. 141–2).

*it would not work.*[14] Either the cooperative productive society failed, after no very lengthy endurance, or it ceased, in one way or another, to be self-governing. At best, the concern was taken over by the Co-operative Wholesale Society, or by a group of local consumers' cooperative societies; at worst, it petered out as an employer's profit-sharing scheme, with the workers excluded from any effective share in the management of the establishment in which they worked, whilst their trade union had been undermined; or it degenerated into the lowest type of modern industry, the small master system, with its inevitable 'sweating' of subordinate workers, who were actually excluded from membership.

To one who had been bred in a stronghold of capitalism, the Consumers Co-operative Movement seemed a unique romance in the industrial history of the world. For this closely knit organization of hundreds of retail shops, grouped into two colossal trading and manufacturing federations, was being administered by men of the manual working class, at salaries which at that time did not exceed, and frequently fell below, the earnings of a skilled compositor or a foreman engineer. How could I explain, by the canons of capitalist economics, the continuous growth of a great business enterprise, which was not making the private fortune of any man or group of men, but was increasing the individual incomes, the accumulated wealth and also the economic freedom of a whole self-governing community, today comprising a quarter or even a third of all the families of Great Britain; wielding a working capital approaching a hundred million pounds; doing a trade of nearly two hundred millions sterling annually; and still, as at all times, effectively open to any newcomer to join and participate in its benefits on equal terms with the original promoters?

I found enlightenment, curiously enough, in a develop-

14. For the cause of this failure of Associations of Producers, I must refer the student to *Co-operative Production*, by Benjamin Jones, 1894, and my own *Co-operative Movement in Great Britain*, 1891, to which may be added *The New Statesman* Supplement of 14 February 1914, on Co-operative Production and Profit-sharing, by S. and B. Webb.

ment of the Theory of Value – implicit in my own hypothesis, to which I have already referred, of the emergence of exchange value in the *correspondence* of economic faculty with economic desire. The self-governing workshop was rooted in the commonly held theory, which Karl Marx had accepted from David Ricardo, William Thompson and Thomas Hodgskin, that 'Labour is the source of Value'. But this 'did not work'! What the Rochdale Pioneers had unwittingly discovered, by the method of trial and error, was that the essential element in the successful conduct of production is the *correspondence* of the application of labour with some actually felt specific desire.

Throughout my study of the Co-operative Movement during 1889, I had in fact been watching the very process of trial and error by which this community of working men was establishing a 'New Social Order'. The eight-and-twenty flannel weavers at Rochdale started, in 1844, to sell groceries to themselves, partly to free themselves from the toils of 'truck', but also with the idea of accumulating a capital fund with which they might realize their ideal of self-employment in flannel weaving[15] – very much as the congregation of a chapel organizes a bazaar to raise money for buying an organ. In order to attract purchasers to their store, they pressed each new customer to become a member of their society, and, as such, entitled to share in its management and accumulate capital. In order to secure continuous membership, they invented the device of 'dividend on purchase', whereby the margin between the cost of the article and the retail selling price was returned to the purchaser himself, as

15. In 1854 the members of the Rochdale Pioneers' Society attempted to carry out their ideal of a self-governing workshop; and a number of them started the Rochdale Co-operative Manufacturing Society. Until 1860 they divided profits on an equal ratio of pence for every sovereign of capital invested or wages paid. Presently the fourteen hundred shareholders, of whom only three hundred worked in the mill, objected to this division of the profit; and in 1862 the bonus to labour was finally dropped out of the rules by a three to one majority, the concern becoming a mere joint stock company. (See *John T. W. Mitchell*, by Percy Redfern, 1923, pp. 27–9.)

a sort of deferred rebate or discount on his purchases a sum of money which each purchasing member found automatically put to his credit in the books of the society until this credit amounted to the one pound qualifying share. From the use of one room in a member's house, in which tea and other groceries were served out by enthusiastic members without remuneration, the 'Rochdale Pioneers' became a steadily growing department store, employing clerks and shop assistants, who, though usually sons or daughters of members, were merely engaged at current wages. In those early days there was no thought of profit-sharing with the employees, for the very good reason that it seemed that there were no 'profits' to divide, the so-called 'dividend on purchase' being merely a device for returning to the consumer the whole of what proved to have been charged in excess of the cost of production, and of carrying on and developing the common services rendered by the society to its members. In this indirect way the Rochdale Pioneers fulfilled Robert Owen's principle of eliminating profit and extinguishing the profit-maker.

Now, the device of dividing the margin between cost and price among customer-members, according to their purchases, has many direct and indirect advantages. One peculiar and possibly unforeseen result was that it established the Co-operative Movement on the broad foundation of human democracy, in which each member, whatever his holding, had one vote and one only. But it was a democracy of the customers of the store, and thus of the consumers, not of the producers of the commodities and services concerned, a democracy which was by its very nature bound to be, as it has in effect proved to be, perpetually open to newcomers, without limitation of class or sex, for the simple reason that the larger the number of customers, the greater the financial prosperity. It was, however, not merely a new constitution for industrial organization that the Rochdale Pioneers had discovered. What was ultimately more important is that they had tumbled, in a fit of characteristically British absentmindedness, to an essential factor of exchange value years before the professional political economists had realized either its nature or its importance. They were, in fact, Jevonians before Stanley Jevons, in discovering *that it was in recognized 'utility', or specific demand, that lay the dominating and delimiting factor of exchange value.* Unlike the self-governing workshops and industrial partnerships, the eleven hundred cooperative stores, and their two great federations, the English and Scottish Wholesale Societies, produce, and cannot help recognizing that they produce, for a known market. One of my experiences in the spring of 1889 was to watch how the quarterly meetings of the delegates from the managing committees of the stores, and the periodical buyers' conferences with the expert officials of the Wholesale Societies, brought together in conference, on the one hand, those who reported the wants of the customers, and, on the other, the directors and managers of the trading and productive departments which were undertaking to supply these wants. What interested me was the unself-consciousness of these cooperators, whether members or officials, about the nature of their activity. The self-governing workshop was born of a theory, or was it a sentiment? and the whole movement of the associations of producers has been, in one country after another, nursed and dandled by successive generations of intellectual philanthropists and world reformers, and even by capitalist governments. The Co-operative Movement of Great Britain, manifested in the local store and the national Wholesale Society, perhaps because it was genuinely of working-class origin, achieved without intending; grew, indeed, to maturity before there was any accurate formulation of the theory on which it was based. To organize industry from the consumption end, and to place it, from the start, upon the basis of 'production for use' instead of 'production for profit', under the control and direction not of the workers as producers, but of themselves as consumers, was the outstanding discovery and practical achievement of the Rochdale Pioneers.

The question arises, why was it that, from 1869 to 1889, the cooperators in congress assembled had never recognized

shop and the wholesale warehouse were so radically different from those of the workshop and the factory, the mine and the farm, that it was both practicable and desirable to adopt an entirely different basis of government, and an entirely different method of remuneration, for shopkeeping, warehousing and cartage on the one hand, and for manufacturing, mining and agriculture on the other. Not even the most enthusiastic believer in cooperative production suggested that the retail store should be managed by the counter-men, the packers or the carmen, or their elected representatives. On the contrary, the model rules of the Cooperative Union, drafted by the leading exponent of the ideal of the self-governing workshop, Edward Vansittart Neale himself, expressly disqualified the employees of the store, *just because they were employees, not merely for election on the committee of management, but even for participation, as ordinary customer-members of the society, in voting for the committee!* Nevertheless, it was held by all the middle-class theorists and, in a muddle-headed way, also by nearly all the working-class cooperators who troubled to think about it, that the ideal government in any manufacturing process was government by the workers in that process; and that it was these men and women, and not the consumers of their products, who ought to absorb any surplus that (after defraying incidental expenses) might prove to remain out of the margin necessarily existing between the bare cost of production in the factory and the retail price paid over the counter by the customer. The practical administrators who were at that time refusing to transform the manufacturing departments of the larger stores, and those of the Wholesale Societies, into self-governing workshops, and were even declining to adopt profit-sharing, did so only on the plea 'that time was not ripe for it'. I never heard them dispute the ideal justice or ultimate expediency of associations of producers. Alone among cooperators John Mitchell, the business genius who had built up the English Co-operative Wholesale Society, stood out as the advocate of government by the consumers in the interests of the consumers, not only in retail and wholesale trading, but in manufacturing and mining, farming and shipowning, insurance and banking. Unfortunately he was not only intellectually inarticulate, but also a megalomaniac about his subject; he failed to see the limitation of government by *voluntary* associations of consumers to industries in which the day-by-day consumers constitute both a practical and a desirable unit of association.[17] This condition is obviously unfulfilled among the users of roads and railways, or in such common services as main drainage and hospitals, schools and police, and much else that is necessary to the well-being of the whole community over a long period of time, needing inevitably to be paid for otherwise than item by item, over the counter, by the individual consumers as such. This all-important limitation, I may note in passing, had not occurred to me during my own investigations of 1889; it was revealed to me, as I shall presently tell, in the course of the development of 'My Apprenticeship' into 'Our Partnership'. What was more directly relevant to the controversy raging in the Co-operative Movement as I knew it in the eighties was Mitchell's in-

17. John Mitchell seldom spoke at the Co-operative Congress. But at the Carlisle Congress in 1887, stung by a violent attack by Tom Hughes on the policy of the Co-operative Wholesale Society in starting manufacturing departments, he asserted that 'There was no higher form of cooperative production upon the face of the earth than the Wholesale Society manifested in its cooperative works. . . . He would start productive works, when they would pay, in every centre in the United Kingdom; and would never be satisfied until the Wholesale manufactured everything that its members wore. . . . If cooperation was to be permanently successful, we should have to finally settle this question – To whom does profit and the increment of value belong? He held that, as it was created by the industrious classes, it belonged to them. Profit was made by the consumption of the people, and the consumers ought to have the profit. . . . He advised cooperators never to be satisfied until they got control of the entire producing, banking, shipping, and every other interest in the country. The Wholesale had £100,000 in Consols, and in course of time cooperators might possess the whole of the National Debt of this country. If cooperators saved their money they might in time possess the railways and canals, besides finding employment for themselves' (*Report of Nineteenth Annual Co-operative Congress*, 1887, pp. 6–7).

ability to perceive that consumers' cooperation, unless tempered by the intervention of the political State through Factory Acts, and by due participation in the management of each enterprise by powerful trade unions, might become an effective coadjutor of the co-existing capitalist employer in the exploitation of the worker.

My second discovery was that democracies of consumers, if they are to be a desirable as well as a practicable alternative to private profit-making, must be complemented by democracies of workers by hand and by brain, that is, by Trade Unions and professional societies. In attending the committee meetings of local stores or lunching with the directors of the Co-operative Wholesale Society, I noticed that they were completely absorbed either in discussing what their members were buying and would in future buy, or in discovering how the commodities or services could be produced at a lower cost and of a better quality. Unless the manager of the store reported the dishonesty or incapacity of a shop assistant, or unless a threat of strike disturbed the equanimity of the Board of the Wholesale Society, they were *absentminded* about the conditions of employment of the rapidly increasing staff of the local stores and manufacturing departments. A subordinate official would normally select whatever additional staff was required, at whatever wages he found it necessary to pay, under conditions not differing essentially from those of neighbouring shopkeepers or manufacturers. The natural bias of the committees of management, like that of all administrators, was to 'maintain discipline and keep down cost of production. They inevitably tended to ignore the way this maintenance of discipline and lowering the cost of production might affect the daily life of the employees. Though the cooperative society meant to be a 'good employer' (and did, in fact, sometimes lead profit-making enterprise in such boons as the weekly half-holiday), it never occurred to cooperative committees to allow the workers concerned any 'rights' beyond what was customary in profit-making establishments. The position was rendered more serious by the fact that in the eighties and nineties all commercial employees, and more especially the shop assistants, were among the lowest paid, the hardest worked and the most arbitrarily treated of the wage-earning class;[18] whilst the managers of the manufacturing departments of the stores and the Wholesale Societies found themselves in direct competition with the notorious sweated industries of cheap clothing and cheap furniture.

For these and other reasons it became clear to me that the existence of strong trade unions, enforcing standard rates and the normal working day, and protecting the individual from arbitrary fines and capricious dismissal, was as essential to the economic welfare and sense of personal freedom of the worker within the consumers' Co-operative Movement as it was in profit-making industry. Thus, 'government from above' had to be supplemented by 'government from below'.

Once again, therefore, [I told the cooperators in 1891] by a conjunction of cooperative and trade union organization, we must bring the producer and consumer face to face. I do not mean that the bootmaker can sell his boots to the weaver, while the weaver disposes of his cloth to the farmer's wife; this personal relationship is no longer possible in a commercial system trans-

18. In 1893 Mr (now Sir) William Maxwell, then Chairman of the Scottish Co-operative Wholesale Society, created great consternation in the Movement by reading a paper at the Bristol Co-operative Congress, in which he described what seemed to him the excessive hours of labour exacted from cooperative employees. Taking only the hours during which the stores were open, which understated the actual day of the assistants by something like 5 or 10 per cent, he showed that 93.5 of the societies were open for business for more than 60 hours per week; 43.4 per cent of them were open for more than 66 hours per week; whilst 163 societies, or 13.5 per cent of those making returns, were open from 70 to no less than 85 hours per week. Slowly and gradually did improvement take place. In 1909, sixteen years later, there were still 40 societies in the last category, 123 in the last but one, whilst 947, or 76.7 of the total, were still open for more than 60 hours per week (*The Working Life of Shop Assistants*, by J. Hallsworth and R. J. Davies, 1913, pp. 78–80; quoted in *The Consumers' Co-operative Movement*, by S. and B. Webb, 1921, p. 189). For a description of the relations of the Co-operative Movement to cooperative employees up to 1920 see chapter iii. of that book.

formed by the industrial revolution. Barter between individuals must be superseded by negotiations, through authorized representatives, between groups of workers and groups of consumers. Individualist exchange must follow individualist production, and give place to collective bargaining.

To gain a clear conception of the collective bargain – of the social relation which will supersede the individual relation – let us imagine therefore, that this industrial democracy were fully developed and that industry were organized by associations of consumers (whether voluntary or compulsory, the Store, the Wholesale Societies, the Municipality and the State), while all workers were united in trade unions. Then the official of the Weavers' Union would debate questions of wages and technical training with the official of the Store or the Municipality; the college of surgeons or physicians would, as at present, determine the standard and subjects of examination for the medical student and fix fees for medical attendance, subject perhaps to the democratic control of a Minister of Health. The official of the trade union and the official of the community would, it is true, represent the rival interests of different sections of the community. But as members of one State the interests of their constituents are ultimately identical. For under a democratic organization of industry it will be recognized that the well-being of each individual will be indissolubly bound up in a high standard of capacity among the whole body of citizens.

Nor is it difficult to discover the practical basis for a compromise between the immediately conflicting interests of the consumer and producer of special commodities or services, supposing that these different groups of citizens should persistently refuse to recognize the 'larger expediency' of efficient citizenship among all classes of the community. Fleeming Jenkin, in his Essay on Trade Unions, has expressed it with admirable conciseness:

'But while the wants of men determine their pay, it is the demand for men of that class which determines how many shall be employed at that pay. This is a corrective to discontent. If their wants are great, few or no men of the given class may get any pay at all. It is the seller of labour who determines the price, but it is the buyer who determines the number of transactions. Capital' (or the community) 'settles how many men are wanted at given wages, but labour settles what wages the men shall have.'

It is noteworthy [I add in a note to the above paragraph] that this determination by a trade union or Association of Professionals of the price at which they will work, or the educational qualifications upon which they will insist, is not demurred to by the capitalist class in professions such as the Law and Medicine, of which they have practically the monopoly. But the limited and broken authority of working-class Unions, the attempt on their part to secure a full subsistence wage for their members, is bitterly resented as an interference with individual liberty.[19]

## The Successive Stages in Socialist Evolution

Can I describe in a few sentences the successive steps in my progress towards socialism?

My studies in East End life had revealed the physical misery and moral debasement following in the track of the rack-renting landlord and capitalist profit-maker in the swarming populations of the great centres of nineteenth-century commerce and industry. It is true that some of these evils – for instance, the low wages, long hours and insanitary conditions of the sweated industries, and the chronic under-employment at the docks – could, I thought, be mitigated, perhaps altogether prevented, by appropriate legislative enactment and trade-union pressure. By these methods it might be possible to secure to the manual workers, so long as they were actually at work, what might be regarded from the physiological standpoint as a sufficient livelihood. Thus, the first stage in the journey – in itself a considerable departure from early Victorian individualism –, was an all-

19. I believe that this was the first use of exactly the phrase 'Collective Bargaining' as a process for settling wages. See *The Co-operative Movement of Great Britain*, by Beatrice Potter, 1891, pp. 216–18. This little book has had a remarkable career, especially in foreign parts, having been translated into about a dozen languages, the earliest being a German translation by Professor Brentano, published in 1892, and the latest to be authorized, in 1925, being a Finnish version. Its largest circulation is said to have been in Russia, in the early years of this century, when it was used as a text-book in starting the Russian Co-operative Movement. It has never been revised, or brought down to date; and it has now been superseded by *The Consumers' Co-operative Movement*, by S. and B. Webb, 1921.

pervading control, in the interest of the community, of the economic activities of the landlord and the capitalist.

But however ubiquitous and skilful this state regulation and trade-union intervention might become, I could see no way out of the recurrent periods of inflation and depression – meaning, for the vast majority of the nation, alternate spells of overwork and unemployment – intensified, if not actually brought about, by the speculative finance, manufacture and trading that was inspired by the mad rush to secure the maximum profit for the minority who owned the instruments of production. Moreover, 'man does not live by bread alone'; and without some 'socialism' – for instance, public education and public health, public parks and public provision for the aged and infirm, open to all and paid for out of rates and taxes, with the addition of some form of 'work or maintenance' for the involuntarily unemployed – even capitalist governments were reluctantly recognizing, though hardly fast enough to prevent race-deterioration, that the regime of private property could not withstand revolution. This 'national minimum' of civilized existence, to be legally ensured for every citizen, was the second stage in my progress towards socialism.

There remained to be considered the psychological evils of a community permanently divided into a nation of the rich and a nation of the poor, into a minority always giving orders and a vast majority always obeying. For the example of the United States showed that a rise in wages and an improvement in technique, far from promoting economic equality, might, through increasing efficiency, and the consequently augmented yield of rent and interest, produce even greater inequalities in wealth and personal power between one citizen and another than prevailed in less favoured capitalist countries. 'Choose equality and flee greed,' said Menander; for, as Matthew Arnold had explained to an unheeding generation, 'our inequality materializes our upper class, vulgarizes our middle class, brutalizes our lower'.[20] At this

20. See the essay on 'Equality' in *Mixed Essays*, by Matthew Arnold, p. 92.

point I remained for some time, because I could see no alternative to the authority of the profit-making employer.

Now it was in the constitution and activities of the consumers' cooperative movement, as developed by the British working class, with its production for use, and its elimination of the profit-maker, that I perceived a possible alternative to modern business enterprise, and one which would, at the same time, increase the security of livelihood and equalize the opportunity for self-development among the whole people. It was, in fact, by the recognition that the essential feature in the cooperative movement was not the advantages that it brought in the way of economical housekeeping and the thrifty accumulation of continual small savings, but the invention of a new type of industrial organization – the government of industry by the community of consumers, for their common benefit as consumers – that my difficulties were removed.

To this organization of commerce and industry by democracies of consumers, I added the complementary organization of democracies of workers by hand and by brain, organized in trade unions or in professional societies, in order to protect personal dignity and individual freedom by giving to the community of workers in each vocation such participation in the administration of their service as might prove to be practicable and desirable. It was, indeed, with a view to discovering the exact sphere of vocational organization in the government of industries and services that I decided, early in 1889, to make the British trade union movement my next field of inquiry, and I actually attended, in September of that year, the Annual Trades Union Congress that was meeting at Dundee during the critical week of the epoch-making strike of the London dock labourers.

In the ensuing year, whilst I was writing my little book, I got some further illumination in discussions with a leading member of the Fabian Society, out of which emerged (among other and more personally significant transformations!) the recognition that the municipality, and even the state itself, in so far as they undertook the provision of commodities and services for their citizens, were, from the economic standpoint, also associations of consumers, based upon an obligatory instead of upon a voluntary membership. Thus, the conception of the organization of 'production, distribution and exchange' by the consumers, not for individual profit but for the common good, could be extended from merely voluntary groupings, associated for the purchase of household requisites, to the obligatory association of all the residents of a city, for every civic purpose; and I saw a new meaning in the steady growth of municipal enterprise and other forms of Local Government. I may note, in passing, that this analogy between the consumers' cooperative movement and modern municipal socialism was further strengthened when we discovered, in the course of our investigation into the local government of the eighteenth century, that the characteristic functions of the modern municipality had their origin, not in the ancient municipal corporation based on vocational organization, but in *voluntary associations of consumers* which had come into existence spontaneously for the very purpose of meeting new needs and providing new services.[21] Further study of the constantly developing consumers' cooperative movement in all the European countries opened a vista of the eventual supersession of the export trade by a system of deliberately arranged reciprocal imports, organized by communities of consumers, whether states, municipalities or cooperative societies; each importing country thus obtaining from other countries *merely what it found it desirable to order* – thus avoiding all questions of protective tariffs or 'dumping'. Today we can see this system of reciprocal imports actually begun among the Co-operative Wholesale Societies of the various European countries, without any toll of profit to the capitalist trader or banker,

21. For a description of these voluntary associations of consumers becoming, through Local Acts, Local Government Authorities, see *English Local Government: Statutory Authorities for Special Purposes*, by S. and B. Webb, 1922; especially chapter vii., on the emergence of the new principles of government, pp. 397–486.

and without any occasion for either booms or depressions of trade, or for loss or profit in the mercantile sense.[22]

It was this vision of a gradually emerging new social order, to be based on the deliberate adjustment of economic faculty and economic desire, and to be embodied in an interlocking dual organization of democracies of consumers and democracies of producers – voluntary as well as obligatory, and international as well as national – that seemed to me to afford a practicable framework for the future cooperative commonwealth.

## The Passage from Life

The inquiry into the Co-operative Movement was carried out under the deepening gloom of my father's last illness; and at times I despaired of completing my task. In the pages of my diary, during the autumn of 1889, I watch myself falling back for encouragement on a growing faith in the possibility of reorganizing society by the application of the scientific method directed by the religious spirit.

Unfit for work: alone with poor dear father and his shadowlike mind and irresponsible character. Depressed, I take up a volume of Matthew Arnold's poems and read these words as the expression of the ideal life towards which I constantly strive:

> Of toil unsevered from tranquillity!
> Of labour, that in lasting fruit outgrows
> Far noisier schemes, accomplished in repose
> Too great for haste, too high for rivalry!

This state of toil unsevered fron tranquillity I sometimes feel I have attained. Still, one is troubled (alas, too often troubled) with the foolish dreams of personal success and with a deep depression of personal failure. I love my work; that is my salvation; I delight in this slow stepping towards truth. Search after truth by the careful measurement of facts is the enthusiasm of my life. And of late this has been combined with a realization of the common

22. *The Consumers' Co-operative Movement*, by S. and B. Webb, 1921, p. 289.

aim of the great army of truth-seekers: the ennobling of human life. It has been enriched by the consciousness of the supreme unity of science, art, morality; the eternal trinity of the good, the beautiful and the true; knit together in the ideal towards which humanity is constantly striving, knowingly or unknowingly, with failure or success according to the ebb and flow of pure motive and honest purpose. [MS. diary, 17 August 1889.]

Constantly during the last week, as I have eagerly read every detail of the Strike [the famous Dock Strike of August 1889] I have been depressed by my own powerlessness to suggest any way out of the difficulty; I have been disheartened by a consciousness that my little mite of knowledge is not of much avail – that the great instinctive movements of the mass are perhaps, after all, more likely to effect than the carefully reasoned judgements of the scientific (or pseudo-scientific?) observer.... Then I have realized that if we are to get a basis for action through knowledge of facts, that knowledge must be far more complete and exhaustive than it is ever likely to be in my time; certainly than it is likely to be in my case. For instance, the little knowledge I gained of the London Docks is practically useless. In order to offer an opinion of any value, one would need to thoroughly master the facts about trade at the docks; to realize exactly the methods of management; to compare these with other methods of management so as to discover deficiencies and possibilties. Is that kind of exhaustive knowledge, even granting the opportunity and the ability and the strength to acquire it, open to a mere observer? Is it not the exclusive opportunity of the great organizer? On the other hand, this realization of the extent of the knowledge required shows me that in my desire to master commercial and financial facts as a key to the labour problem I was guided by a true instinct; that on my capacity to master these facts will rest my power to influence for good the condition of my people.

Finished up my work for the summer, and leave for a fortnight's change tomorrow [this was the visit to the Trades Union Congress at Dundee]. The summer has passed quickly away with the content of a fully occupied life. The work has been hard and to a great extent mechanical, and in my spare time I have usually been too tired to enjoy beauty, so that my existence has been for the most part a mere routine of sleep, work, food and exercise. Poor dear father, his companionship is saddening, inexpressibly depressing in its soullessness. And yet, now and again there are glimpses of calm reason and warm feeling which make me wonder whether the general habit of the family of cajoling and flattering him, of ignoring all responsible thought or action in him, is right and sound? If there be an immortal principle in him, are we degrading it? But the assumption is that he is a creature whose effectual life is gone but that love and duty bid us make him physically easy and mentally content; that there is no room for moral progress or retrogression; that morally he is dead. Sometimes I think that the repulsiveness of the conclusion must mean untruth in the premises. At other times I see in our method of treatment simply a logical view of the facts of human life; a realization of the inevitable. [MS. diary, 31 August 1889.]

It was a hard week, scarcely a holiday [I write in my diary after a lively description of the Trades Union Congress and its personalities, which I reserve for some future account of our investigation into trade unionism]. When I arrived early on Sunday morning at Auberon Herbert's little cottage on the banks of Loch Awe I was thoroughly exhausted, with a bad cold in the head into the bargain. A somewhat dreary little plastered cottage, with none of the charm of 'Old House', supplemented by two wooden shanties; low brushwood and unkempt grass surrounding it. In front the Loch, behind the moor, mountains rising in the distance, not wild or grand, not exactly beautiful; pretty conventional lake scenery, nothing more. Inside, no fires, and constant open windows; comfortless furniture. The children (the boy this time at home) most attractive; the elderly idealist interesting and becoming an intimate friend. But with his nature, distance lends enchantment to the view! There is restfulness in his gentle courtesy and idealistic aloofness from the passions which move mankind. But both courtesy and idealism cover subtle egotism and a waywardness of nature, a persistent determination to follow his own caprices of thought and feeling, which make him impracticable and inconsiderate in all the relations of life. (Is this fair? He is charming with his children.) His little fads about his health are ludicrous; no sound is to be heard before he is called in the morning; no window to be shut in his presence; he cannot take exercise but needs air, and nothing must interfere with his afternoon sailing. What between vegetarianism and valetudinarianism, he is rapidly sinking into old age, though he is a healthy man of fifty.

I enjoyed my days there. Between us we started a novel, *Looking Forward* – an answer to *Looking Backward* – for which I supplied the plot and the characters, while he is to work out a reformed world on individualist lines. He told me during the long evenings, looking on to the moonlit lake, the story of his life . . .

A solitary day at Stirling, feeling unutterably sad – a long night journey – the exquisite beauty of the early morning spread over the Monmouth valley as I drive up to our mountain home; the faithful Neale with all things prepared; the breakfast table with a family party of Playnes; cordial welcome; long gossip. The darling old father is delighted to see 'my little Bee'; in one word – 'Home'. And now for work. [MS. diary, 22 September 1889.]


This last month or so I have been haunted by a longing to create characters and to move them to and fro among fictitious circumstances. To put the matter plainly – by the vulgar wish to write a novel. In the early morning hours when one's half-awakened brain seems so strangely fruitful, I see before me persons and scenes; I weave plots and clothe persons, scenes and plots in my own philosophy. There is intense attractiveness in the comparative ease of descriptive writing. Compare it with work in which movements of commodities, percentages, depreciations, averages, and all the ugly horrors of commercial facts are in the dominant place, and must remain so if the work is to be worthful. . . . The whole multitude of novels I have read pass before me; the genius, the talent, the clever mechanism or the popularity-hunting of mediocrities – what have the whole lot of them, from the work of genius to the penny-a-liner, accomplished for the advancement of society on the one and only basis that can bring with it virtue and happiness – the scientific method? This supreme ambition to present some clear and helpful idea of the forces we must subdue and the forces we must liberate in order to bring about reformation may be absurdly out of proportion to my ability. But it alone is the faith, the enthusiasm of my life, the work which I feel called upon to do.

Still, I have in my mind some more dramatic representation of facts than can be given in statistical tables or in the letterpress that explains them; some way of bringing home to rich and poor those truths about social organization that I may discover, illustrations of social laws in the terms of personal suffering, personal development and personal sin. But these must be delayed until I have discovered my laws! And as yet I am only on the threshold of my inquiries, far enough off, alas, from any general and definite conclusions. [MS. diary, 30 September, 1889.]

The very demon of melancholy gripping me, my imagination fastening on Amy Levy's story, a brilliant young authoress of seven-and-twenty, in the hey-day of success, who has chosen to die rather than stand up longer to live. We talk of courage to meet death; alas, in these terrible days of mental pressure it is courage to *live* that we most lack, not courage to die. It is the supreme courage of fighting a battle for an unknown leader, for an unknown cause, that fails us now and again. Poor Amy Levy! If there be no other faith for humanity but to eat, drink and be merry, for tomorrow we die, she has done well and wisely in choosing death, for to our natures such contentment, such merriment, is not possible; we are the 'unfit', and the sooner we leave our room to others, the better. But if this be only a passage to other things, a pilgrimage among other pilgrims whom we may help and cheer on the way, then a brave and struggling life, a life in which suffering measures progress, has the deepest meaning – in truth, embraces the whole and the sole reason for human existence. [MS. diary, 11 October 1889.]

Five months' work here and at last I have got the table of contents of my first book. Now I can let my imagination play at construction instead of restricting all my energies to investigation. My spirits begin to rise as I see the whole subject mapped out before me and know exactly the extent of my discoveries and the boundaries of the ground that must be covered. In a week or so I shall have sketched out each chapter and shall have before me my plan of campaign for the next six months. [MS. diary, November 1889.]

The final entry in the diary for the year 1889 was written during a crisis in my father's illness which we all thought would be the last. It is a long account of his life, the better part being used as material in the first chapter of this book. Here I give the concluding paragraphs as they stand in the MS. diary because they reveal, more vividly than I can from memory, the happy relationship throughout life between the father and his nine daughters.

Companionship with him was a liberal education in human nature and in the affairs of the world; near relationship to him was a tie of extraordinary tenderness and charm owing to the absolute self-devotedness of his character. His own comfort, his own inclinations were unconsidered before the happiness of his wife, the welfare of his children. With him the domestic instinct was a passion to which all else was subordinated . . .

Darling father! How your children have loved you: loving even your weaknesses, smiling over them tenderly like so many mothers. How we have all combined to blind you to the realities of your illness: nine diplomatists sitting round the old diplomatist, hiding things, smoothing things; and you all the while perhaps the most polished diplomatist of the lot; accepting the illusion as pleasanter than the fact: delighting in the diplomacy that you have taught us. With what gentle dignity you have resigned your grasp on life, though not without an internal struggle, but all hidden from view.

'I know you did it for my good, dear child, but it is a little hard.'

These were his only words when, a year after his first stroke, I refused absolutely to post his letter ordering his brokers to buy for speculation. He tried it again, but this time I checkmated him by writing privately to the brokers urging them on their honour to discourage it: I remember the queer expression when he read their letter – the passing look of irritation – then the bright glance at me when he perceived my move – the affectionate tone in which he next addressed me on some indifferent matter: the silent acknowledgement of my good intention, the inward chuckle over the smartness of his offspring; and from that moment the absolute and entire resignation of his affairs into Daniel's hands; betaking himself exclusively to the contracted routine of a shadow-like existence. His content would have been painful if one had not felt that it was reasoned out on his large unselfish philosophy of life; an idealized Epicureanism: the happiness of the world (i.e. of those around you) and of yourself as a unit of the world.

And now that he lies helpless, the vitality flickering to extinction: his limbs motionless, his breathing laboured, the last pleasure in his sleep, food and cigarette gone, he still brightens up to welcome his 'bright-eyed daughter'; to compliment a middle-aged married woman on her good looks; to inquire how each husband is doing; to ask how much he will leave to his children. In the long hours of restlessness he broods over the success of his children, and finds reason for peace and satisfaction. 'I want one more son-in-law' (a proof that he feels near his end, as he has discouraged the idea of matrimony for me, put it off as something I could easily attain), 'a woman is happier married; I should like to see my little Bee married to a good strong fellow', and the darling old father dreams of the 'little Bee' of long ago; he does not realize that she has passed away, leaving the strong form and determined features of the 'glorified spinster' bending over him as a mother bends over her sick child. [MS. diary, 26 November 1889.]

## 'The Other One'

My father lingered on for another two years, barely conscious of his surroundings. But within a few weeks of his call for 'one more son-in-law' there came 'The Other One'!

This culminating event of my life – for did it not lead to the rapid transformation of 'My Apprenticeship' into 'Our Partnership', and therefore to the ending of this book? – clearly deserves a preface. And this preface shall consist in a recollection of a mysterious penumbra, making me aware of a new and significant Presence in my environment at least a year before I was introduced to the little figure with a big head who was to become the man of my destiny, the source of unhoped-for happiness; and, be it added, the predominant partner of the firm of Webb.

It was, I think, in the spring of 1888 that my friend J. J. Dent, at that time General Secretary of the (working men's) Club and Institute Union, talked to me, in tones of mingled admiration and suspicion, about a group of clever young men who, with astonishing energy and audacity, were haranguing the London Radical clubs; contributing innumerable articles and paragraphs, signed or unsigned, to the *Star* and the *Daily Chronicle*, and distributing, far and wide, 'Facts for Socialists', and other subversively plausible pamphlets. One result of these activities was a stream of resolutions to Liberal Headquarters and Liberal leaders, passed by Radical clubs and trade-union branches, in favour of the legal eight hours day; of municipal ownership and administration of water, gas, tramways and docks for the profit of the ratepayers; of an unlimited extension of free educational and health services; and, in order to meet the cost, of stiff taxation of wealth by increased and steeply graduated income taxes and death duties. 'There are among them', said he, 'some very clever speakers, but the man who organizes the whole business, drafts the resolutions and writes the tracts, is Sidney Webb.' Other stray reports reached me to like effect, the gist of which I find expressed, a few years later, in the report of Bernard Shaw to the Fabian Conference of 1893.

In 1888 [he told the Conference] we had not been found out even by the *Star*. The Liberal party was too much preoccupied over Mr O'Brien's breeches and the Parnell Commission with its dramatic climax in the suicide of the forger Pigott, to suspect that the liveliness of the extreme left of the Radical wing in London meant anything but the usual humbug about working-class interests. We now adopted a policy which snapped the last tie between our methods and the sectarianism of the [Social Democratic] Federation. We urged our members to join the Liberal and Radical Associations of their districts, or, if they preferred it, the Conservative Associations. We told them to become members of the nearest Radical Club and Co-operative Store, and to get delegated to the Metropolitan Radical Federation, and the Liberal and Radical Union if possible. On these bodies we made speeches and moved resolutions, or, better still, got the Parliamentary candidate for the constituency to move them, and secured reports and encouraging little articles for him in the *Star*. We permeated the party organizations and pulled all the wires we could lay our hands on with our utmost adroitness and energy; and we succeeded so far that in 1889 we gained the solid advantage of a Progressive majority, full of ideas that would never have come into their heads had not the Fabian put them there, on the first London County Council. The generalship of this movement was undertaken chiefly by Sidney Webb, who played such bewildering conjuring tricks with the Liberal thimbles and the Fabian peas, that to this day both the Liberals and the sectarian socialists stand aghast at him. It was exciting while it lasted, all this 'permeation of the Liberal party,' as it was called; and no person with the smallest political intelligence is likely to deny that it made a foothold for us in the press, and pushed forward Socialism in municipal politics to an extent which can only be appreciated by those who remember how things stood before our campaign.[23]

It was certainly surprising that, given all these activities of the Fabian Society during 1888–9, and absorbed as I was in political and economic problems, I failed to become known to any of the future Fabian essayists (apart from a slight acquaintance with Mrs Annie Besant, then at the zenith of her power as a great popular orator) until January 1890. The explanation is, that I had entered the field of controversy from the standpoint of big enterprise, party politics and metropolitan philanthropy, and was biased against socialist solutions of political and economic problems; whilst the Fabians entered this same field as Radicals and rebels, drawn, by a vision of a new social order, from every vocation and many parts of the country. Further, my craft being that of an investigator, I was seeking enlightenment, not from socialist lecturers and theoretical pamphlets, but from an objective study of the Co-operative Movement and of trade unionism, the leaders of which were at that time contemptuous of the socialism that they knew. The great Dock Strike of August 1889, led, as it was, by three socialist workmen – John Burns, Tom Mann and Ben Tillett – together with the emergence of the 'New Unionism', with its reliance on political changes, altered the orientation of the Labour Movement itself. Meanwhile, I had realized, as already described, that the working-class Co-operative Movement, as distinguished from the middle-class projects of self-governing workshops, industrial partnerships and schemes of profit-sharing, was essentially 'collectivist' in character and aims, having for its object the elimination from industry of profit

23. Fabian Tract No. 41, *The Fabian Society: Its Early History*, by G. Bernard Shaw, 1892; also *History of Fabian Society*, by Edward Pease, 1925.

and the profit-maker, by the substitution of an open democracy, managing by the instrumentality of salaried officials the services that it desired. Hence when, in October 1889, a friend forwarded to me the recently published *Fabian Essays* as the true gospel of distinctively British socialism, I read this daintily-turned-out volume from cover to cover. In passing it on to J. C. Gray of the Co-operative Union, I find that I incidentally remarked (in a letter which he afterwards returned to me) that 'by far the most significant and interesting essay is the one by Sidney Webb; *he has the historic sense*'. Those interested in tracing 'affinities' may find amusement if not instruction in the fact that, in an appreciative review of Charles Booth's first volume published in the *Star* in the preceding spring, 'The Other One' had observed that 'the only contributor with any literary talent is Miss Beatrice Potter'!

What interested me in this particular Fabian essay was an early presentation of 'the inevitability of gradualness'.

Owing mainly to the efforts of Comte, Darwin, and Herbert Spencer [writes the Fabian essayist in 1889] we can no longer think of the ideal society as an unchanging State. The social ideal from being static has become dynamic. The necessity of the constant growth and development of the social organism has become axiomatic. No philosopher now looks for anything but the gradual evolution of the new order from the old, without breath of continuity or abrupt change of the entire social tissue at any point during the process. The new becomes itself old, often before it is consciously recognized as new; and history shows us no example of the sudden substitutions of Utopian and revolutionary romance.

Further on in the essay the same thought is elaborated.

Advocates of social reconstruction [he tells his readers] have learnt the lesson of democracy, and know that it is through the slow and gradual turning of the popular mind to new principles that social reorganization bit by bit comes. All students of society who are abreast of their time, Socialists as well as Individualists, realize that important organic changes can only be (1) democratic, and thus acceptable to a majority of the people, and prepared for in the minds of all; (2) gradual, and thus causing no dislocation, however rapid may be the rate of progress; (3) not regarded as immoral by the mass of the people, and thus not subjectively demoralizing to them; and (4), in this country at any rate, constitutional and peaceful. Socialists may therefore be quite at one with Radicals in their political methods. Radicals, on the other hand, are perforce realizing that mere political levelling is insufficient to save a State from anarchy and despair. Both sections have been driven to recognize that the root of the difficulty is economic; and there is every day a wider consensus that the inevitable outcome of democracy is the control by the people themselves, not only of their own political organization, but, through that, also of the main instruments of wealth production; the gradual substitution of organized cooperation for the anarchy of the competitive struggle; and the consequent recovery, in the only possible way, of what John Stuart Mill calls 'the enormous share which the possessors of the instruments of industry are able to take from the produce'. The economic side of the democratic ideal is, in fact, socialism itself.[24]

The reason for our meeting in the first days of January 1890 was in itself a presage of our future comradeship in work. The critical phase of my father's illness having once again passed away, my sister Kate begged me to return with her husband to London for a week's rest and recreation, a welcome opportunity to get material I urgently needed for the first chapter of my forthcoming book. For whilst planning out my analysis of the Co-operative Movement of that day, I became aware that I lacked historical background. As was my wont, I applied for help to the best available authority: in this case to a London acquaintance, the distinguished historian of the eighteenth century, W. E. H. Lecky. 'Why was there no working-class association in these years of turmoil and change?' I innocently and ignorantly asked. The answer to this incorrect assertion, disguised as a question, was a courteous, kindly and lengthy explanation of the

24. *Fabian Essays in Socialism*, 1889, pp. 31 and 34–5. This original edition should be compared with the latest reprint of 1920, with its elaborate introduction; and with a fuller exposition of the same thesis in vol. xii of the *Cambridge Modern History*, republished by the Fabian Society under the title *Towards Social Democracy?*

'reason why', meant to be helpful. But seeing that my mistaken assumption was apparently accepted as the starting-point of the answer, the professional historian led me nowhere. Not satisfied, I was on the look-out for another guide. 'Sidney Webb, one of the Fabian Essayists, is your man,' casually remarked a friendly woman journalist. 'He knows everything: when you go out for a walk with him he literally pours out information.' An interview was arranged during my short stay in London. A list of sources, accessible at the British Museum, including the then little known Place manuscripts, various State trials, old Chartist periodicals, and autobiographies of working-class agitators, was swiftly drafted, then and there, in a faultless handwriting, and handed to me. A few days later brought the first token of personal regard in the shape of a newly published pamphlet by the Fabian on the Rate of Interest, thus opening up a regular correspondence.

I give a few from many entries from the MS. diary revealing the new ferment at work.

Already one month of the New Year past. Father lying in a half-conscious, motionless state, recognizing his children but not realizing ideas or feelings; his life a flickering shadow which at times seems to disappear, then to gather substance, and for a while you imagine that it is the dear familiar spirit lighting up the worn-out frame.

I am, in the meantime, so long as life lasts, chained to his side; all my plans for this six months of the year indefinitely postponed. . . . Sometimes I feel discouraged. Not only am I baulked in carrying out my work, but with the lack of all accomplishment I begin to doubt my ability to do it. Continuous reading makes me feel a mere learner, entangled in my own growth, helpless before this ever-accumulating mass of facts, which must be carved into some intelligible shape indicative of its main characteristics. At present, the facts are heaped up around me, oppressing me with their weight.

I feel, too, exiled from the world of thought and action of other men and women. London is in a ferment: strikes are the order of the day; the new trade unionism, with its magnificent conquest of the docks, is striding along with an arrogance rousing employers to a keen sense of danger, and to a determination to strike against strikes. The socialists, led by a small set of able young men (Fabian Society) are manipulating London radicals, ready, at the first checkmate of trade unionism, to voice a growing desire for state action; and I, from the peculiarity of my social position, should be in the midst of all parties, sympathetic with all, allied with none, in a true vantage ground for impartial observation of the forces at work. Burnett and the older trade unionists on the one side; Tom Mann, Tillett and Burns on the other; round about me cooperators of all schools, together with new acquaintances among the leading socialists. And as a background, all those respectable and highly successful men, my brothers-in-law, typical of the old reign of private property and self-interested action. ... And then I turn from the luxurious homes of these picked men of the individualist system, and struggle through an East End crowd of the wrecks, the waifs and strays of this civilization; or I enter a debating society of working men, and listen to the ever-increasing cry of active brains, doomed to the treadmill of manual labour, for a career in which intellectual initiative tells: the bitter cry of the nineteenth-century working man and the nineteenth-century woman. And the whole seems a whirl of contending actions, aspirations and aims, out of which I dimly see the tendency towards a socialist community, in which there will be individual freedom and public property, instead of class slavery and private possession of the means of subsistence of the whole people. At last I am a socialist! [MS. diary, 1 February 1890.]

Sidney Webb, the socialist, dined here [Devonshire House Hotel] to meet the Booths. A remarkable little man with a huge head and a tiny body, a breadth of forehead quite sufficient to account for the encyclopaedic character of his knowledge. A Jewish nose, prominent eyes and mouth, black hair, somewhat unkempt, spectacles and a most bourgeois black coat shiny with wear. But I like the man. There is a directness of speech, an open-mindedness, an imaginative warm-heartedness which will carry him far. He has the self-assurance of one who is always thinking faster than his neighbours; who is untroubled by doubts, and to whom the acquisition of facts is as easy as the grasping of things; but he has no vanity and is totally unselfconscious. Hence his absence of consciousness as to treading on his neighbours' corns. Above all, he is utterly disinterested, and is, I believe, genuine in his faith that collective control and collective administration will diminish, if not abolish, poverty. [MS. diary, 14 February 1890.]

Every day my social views take a more decidedly socialist turn, every hour reveals fresh instances of the curse of gain without labour; the endless perplexities of the rich, the never-failing miseries of the poor. In this household [there are] ten persons living on the fat of the land in order to minister to the supposed comfort of one poor old man. All this faculty expended to satisfy the assumed desires of a being wellnigh bereft of desire. The whole thing is a vicious circle as irrational as it is sorrowful. We feed our servants well, keep them in luxurious slavery, because we hate to see discomfort around us. But they and we are consuming the labour of others and giving nothing in return, except useless service to a dying life past serving. Here are thirteen dependents consuming riches and making none, and no one the better for it. [MS. diary, 22 April 1890.]

Glasgow Co-operative Congress. Exquisite Whitsun weather. A long journey up in third-class saloon, I, in one of the two comfortable seats of the carriage, with S. W. squatted on a portmanteau by my side, and relays of working-men friends lying at my feet, discussing earnestly trade unionism, cooperation and socialism. S. W.'s appearance among them surprises, and, on the whole, pleases them.

'He is humbler than I have ever seen him before,' says Vaughan Nash;[25] 'quite a different tone.'

'Let us all work together as far as we can go; by the time we have got there, depend on it, we Cooperators will be willing to go further,' declares emphatically Hey, a member of the Central Board, and Secretary to the Ironmoulders' trade union.

In the evening S. W. and I wandered through the Glasgow streets. A critical twenty-four hours, followed by another long walk by glorious sunset through the crowded streets, knocking up against drunken Scots. With glory in the sky and hideous

25. Vaughan Nash, C.B., C.V.O., born 1861, a lifelong student of trade unionism and cooperation, was at that time a journalist. He became for seven years the confidential private secretary of two successive Prime Ministers, 1905–12; and then Vice-Chairman of the Development Commission. With Hubert (afterwards Sir Hubert) Llewellyn Smith he wrote *The Story of the Dockers' Strike*, 1890; and, after visiting India during the famine of 1900, *The Great Famine*, 1901.

bestiality on the earth, two socialists came to a working compact.

'You understand you promise me to realize that the chances are a hundred to one that nothing follows but friendship ...' [Glasgow, MS. diary, Whitsun 1890.]

A day out in Epping Forest: 'When I left you yesterday [said he] (we had travelled up from Haslemere, where I had stayed at the Frederic Harrisons, and he with the Pearsall Smiths) I went straight home; found two urgent letters, one from O'Brien begging me to write the London articles for the *Speaker*; the other from Massingham telling me I must review Marshall's new book for the *Star*. I went straight to the Club and read right through Marshall's six hundred pages – got up, staggering under it. It is a great book, nothing new – showing the way, not following it. For all that, it is a great book, it will supersede Mill. But it will not make an epoch in Economics. Economics has still to be re-made. Who is to do it? Either you must help me to do it; or I must help you ...' We talked economics, politics, the possibility of inspiring socialism with faith leading to works. He read me poetry, as we lay in the Forest, Keats and Rossetti, and we parted. [MS. diary, 27 July 1890.]

Throughout the remaining months of 1890 we saw little of each other. When not in attendance on my father, I was staying in Glasgow, Manchester, Leeds, Leicester and other big industrial centres, completing the cooperative inquiry and starting the investigation into trade unionism. But letters in the faultless handwriting followed me wherever I went, suggesting new sources of information, or telling me of the doings of the Fabians. Occasionally he would forget the 'inevitability of gradualness', and there would be a hitch. But he was soon forgiven after due penitence! In the spring of 1891 I sent my newly-found counsellor proofs of my forthcoming book on the Co-operative Movement. 'I am disappointed,' he wrote with commendable sincerity; 'this book ought to have taken six weeks to write, not seven months. Why not let me help you in the investigation into trade unionism? Whilst you interview officials and attend trade-union meetings, I can rush through reports and MS. minutes at the trade-union offices.'

'I am a piece of steel,' I warn my friend. 'One and one

placed close together, in a sufficiently integrated relationship, make not two but eleven,' he answered unconcernedly.

I recall another episode. In April 1891 I went to stay with that most loyal of friends – Mrs J. R. Green – to give a course of lectures (my first experience of this kind) at University Hall on the Co-operative Movement. The day before my first lecture, just as I was leaving my home for London, the post brought me a letter from the editor of *The Times*, asking for an advance report of my first lecture. 'How can I write a report of a lecture which I have not yet given?' said I helplessly to the little lady who acted as housekeeper and secretary. 'Why not ask Mr Webb to do it?' was her startling suggestion, made demurely. 'Not half a bad idea,' said I, in my coldest tone. 'Write out a telegram and I will send it,' she urged. On arrival, I found The Other One chatting with Mrs Green, whose friendship he had already won. Said he, when we were left alone in the little study, 'Give me your syllabus, and just tell me what else you are going to say.' An admirable statement of my argument, far more lucid than the lecture itself, duly appeared in *The Times* the next day.

The Lincoln Co-operative Congress of 1891 found us journeying down together. 'I cannot tell how things will settle themselves,' I write in my diary; 'I think probably in his way. His resolute, patient affection, his constant care for my welfare – helping and correcting me – a growing distrust of a self-absorbed life and the egotism of successful work, done on easy terms and reaping more admiration than it deserves – all these feelings are making for our eventual union. Meanwhile father lingers on, and while he lives, nothing can be decided.' [MS. diary, May 1891.] In the course of the summer The Other One and I became definitely but secretly betrothed, my father's state making disclosure, even to my own family, undesirable. Here are a few entries about my new outlook on life.

We had a queer party at Alice Green's towards the end of my stay: five of the young Radicals – Asquith, Haldane, Grey, Buxton and Acland – to meet five Fabians – Massingham,

407

Clarke, Olivier, Shaw and S. W., with Alice and myself. It was not successful; though not quite a failure, since all were pleasant and cordial. Asquith spoilt it. He was the ablest of the lot, and determined that it *should not go*. Haldane made himself most pleasant, and is really playing up; but the *machine* of the Liberal Party is slow to move.[26] [MS. diary, 31 May 1891.]

We are both of us [I write in my diary, 7 July] second-rate minds; but we are curiously combined. I am the investigator and he the executant; between us we have a wide and varied experience of men and affairs. We have also an unearned salary. These are unique circumstances. A considerable work should be the result if we use our combined talents with a deliberate and persistent purpose.

Since the hurry-scurry of that week [at the Newcastle Trades Union Congress] [I write in the first days of my autumn holiday] I have drudged in offices on records or trudged to interview after interview. The work is stupendous, and as yet, the material does not shape itself. I do little but work and sleep and then work again. My fingers, cramped with hours of note-taking, threaten revolt, and my brain whirls with constitutions, executives, general councils, delegate meetings, district delegates, branches, lodges, socials, with objections to piece-work and 'subbing', demarcation disputes – until all the organs of my body and faculties of my mind threaten to form into one federated trade union and Strike against the despotism of the will! Meanwhile there is one bright moment: the clearly written letter precipitated every morning; one half-hour of willing obedience of the cramped fingers when I turn aside from my work and talk with him. And in five days he will be here working by my side. [25 September 1891.]

I get so sick of these ugly details of time-work and piece-work, overtime and shop-rent, and the squalid misfortunes of de-

26. All the five 'young Radicals' became Liberal Cabinet Ministers, and one of them (H. H. Asquith) was for eight critical years Prime Minister; two of the Fabians (Sydney Olivier and Sidney Webb) and one of the Liberals (R. B. Haldane) were members of the first British Labour Cabinet, and Alice Stopford Green is on the roll of the first Senate of the Irish Free State. In the world of today the outshining one of this star company is Bernard Shaw, socialist and dramatist. Only two members of the party are dead (1926) – H. W. Massingham and William Clarke – both of whom achieved distinction in journalism.

faulting branch officers or heckling by unreasonable members [I write to my Beloved]. Who would choose to imprison the intellect in this smelly kitchen of social life if it were not for the ever-present 'thirty per cent' [Charles Booth's statistics of those who were below the line of poverty], with the background of the terrible East End streets? The memory of the low, cunning, brutal faces of the loafers and cadgers who hang about the Mint haunts me when I feel inclined to put down the trade union reports and take up a bit of good literature.

'You are not fit to write this big book alone [is his answer]; you would never get through it. When I really get to work on it, you will find me not only a help instead of a hindrance – but also *the* indispensable help which will turn a good project into a big book.'

A blessed time! He found me utterly worked out with a combination of hard clerk's work and the insufficient food of a pitman's cottage in a miners' village, whither I had gone for *physiognomie*. He took over all the accumulated work, and while I have been lying on a sofa he has been busily abstracting and extracting, amply rewarded, he says, by a few brief intervals of confidential talk over the cigarette and the afternoon cup of tea. With our usual coolness, I have taken a private sitting-room (he staying at another hotel); and he spends the day with me in the capacity of private secretary. The queer little knot of hotel residents are so impressed with the bulk of my correspondence and the long hours of work that I do not think they suspect the intervals of 'human nature'; they no doubt think that I keep my amanuensis hard at it all the hours of the day! And now that I am fairly well again, we are driving through the mass of reports fast and well with the blessedness of companionship. Without his help I doubt whether I could get through this bulk of material; I have too little staying power for the bigness of my aims. [MS. diary, 10 October 1891.]

The last evening of the blessed fortnight, and I have sent him ruthlessly to interview the 'Good Intent Coopers'! Yesterday evening we spent at a public-house in Newcastle interviewing plumbers; and today we have been hard at work on rules and reports. The danger I see ahead is of one-idea'dness, an absorption in this somewhat ugly side of humanity, an absorption which will be made even more absolute by our companionship. It is hard to steer clear between one-idea'dness and futile mental

# Further Reading

*My Apprenticeship* is followed by:

> *Our Partnership*, Longmans, 1948.
> *Diaries, 1912–24*, ed. Margaret Cole, Longmans, 1952.
> *Diaries, 1924–32*, ed. Margaret Cole, Longmans, 1956.

Beatrice Webb died before *Our Partnership* was finally ready for the press, and Sidney Webb asked Margaret Cole and Barbara Drake to see it through. In doing so, they omitted a chapter dealing with the Webbs's visit to America and Australia, as they said it had 'little or no bearing on the main concerns of the present volume'. Not surprisingly, Americans, Australians and New Zealanders have taken a different view, and the material has been published in:

> *Beatrice Webb's American Diary*, ed. D. A. Shannon, University of Wisconsin, 1963.
> *Visit to New Zealand in 1889: Beatrice Webb's Diary with entries by Sidney Webb*, Price, Milburn, 1959.
> *The Webbs' Australian Diary*, ed. A. E. Austin, Pitman, Melbourne, 1965.

To complete the picture, one might also look up Sidney Webb's *Reminiscences* in the *St Martin's Review* for 1929.

*Their Work and Worlds:*

*Beatrice Webb* by Margaret Cole, Longmans, 1945, 'the greatest woman I have ever known, set down by one who had the privilege of being her friend and her fellow-worker within the Fabian Society'.

*The Webbs and their Work*, Margaret Cole, Longmans, 1949.

*Beatrice and Sidney Webb*, Margaret Cole, preface by Clement Attlee, Fabian Society, 1955.

*Sidney and Beatrice Webb*, M. A. Hamilton, Sampson Low, 1933.

*Beatrice Webb*, R. H. Tawney, British Academy, 1943.

*Beatrice Webb: A Life*, Kitty Muggeridge and Ruth Adam, Secker & Warburg, 1967.
An anecdotal, not wholly sympathetic memoir, which tells more fully than elsewhere the story of Beatrice's passion for Joseph Chamberlain.

*The Pursuit of Certainty: Studies in Hume, Bentham, Mill, and Beatrice Webb*, S. R. Letwin, Cambridge, 1965.

*Father Figures*, Kingsley Martin, Hutchinson, 1966; Penguin Books, 1969.

*Sowing*, Hogarth, 1960; *Growing*, Hogarth, 1961; *Beginning Again*, Hogarth, 1964; *Downhill all the Way*, Hogarth, 1967 by Leonard Woolf.
An autobiography through which many of the same figures move, and one which recreates, often very differently, the intellectual and social climate of the Webbs.

*Sidney Webb and East Africa*, R. E. Gregory, University of California, 1962.

'The Educational Influence of the Webbs' by A. V. Judges in *British Journal of Educational Studies*, vol X, No. 1, November 1961.

*Hidden Portraits:*

in *The New Machiavelli*, H. G. Wells, Harper, 1909; Penguin Books, 1966, 1970.

in *The Millionairess*, G. B. Shaw, Constable, 1936.

*The Fabians: 'intelligence officers without an army':*
*Fabian Essays*, ed. G. B. Shaw. Jubilee edition, Allen & Unwin, 1948.

*This Little Band of Prophets*, Ann Freemantle, Allen & Unwin, 1959.

*History of the Fabian Society*, E. R. Pease, Allen & Unwin, 1924.

*The Story of Fabian Socialism*, Margaret Cole, Heinemann, 1961.

*On Pioneer Research:*
*Origins of British Sociology, 1834–1914*, ed. P. Abrams, Chicago, 1968.

*Charles Booth, Social Scientist*, T. S. and M. B. Simey, Oxford, 1960.

*A Study of the Work of Seebohm Rowntree*, Asa Briggs, Longmans, 1961.

*Power and Influence, an Autobiography*, William Beveridge, Hodder & Stoughton, 1960.

*Intellectual Background:*

*Mill on Bentham and Coleridge*, ed. F. R. Leavis, Chatto & Windus, 1950. The most coherent and compact of nineteenth-century reading lists.

*Autobiography*, John Stuart Mill (1873).

*Praeterita* – outlines of scenes and thoughts perhaps worthy of memory of my past life by John Ruskin (1885–9).

*Autobiography*, Herbert Spencer (1904).

*Culture and Anarchy*, Matthew Arnold (1869).

*Social Background:*

*England in the Nineteenth Century*, David Thomson, Penguin Books, 1950.

*The Making of the English Working Class*, E. P. Thompson, Gollancz, 1963; Penguin Books, 1969.

*Victorian England*, G. M. Young, Oxford University Press, 1936.

*Victorian Cities*, Asa Briggs, Odhams, London, 1963; Penguin Books, 1968.

*The Coming of the Welfare State (1560–1960)*, Maurice Bruce, Batsford, 1961.

*Their Writings:*

Surprisingly, a complete list of the Webbs' main writings is hard to come by, and the following, compiled from the catalogue of the University Library at Cambridge, may even so not be complete. But at a glance it indicates their marvellous energy, and wide range of interest: their readiness to spend a decade on a research project and yet their rapidity in pamphlet warfare – above all through the platform they built themselves: the Fabian Society.

# FURTHER READING

## BY BEATRICE WEBB:

'The Docks' and 'The Tailoring Trade' in Charles Booth, *Life and Labour of the People in London*, vol. 1 (1892).
*The Co-operative Movement in Great Britain* (1891).
*Women and the Factory Acts*, Fabian Society, 1896.
*The Case for the Factory Acts* (1901).
*The Case for the National Minimum* (1913).
*The Abolition of the Poor Law*, Fabian Society, 1918.
*My Apprenticeship* (1926).
*The English Poor Law; will it endure?*, Sidney Ball Lecture, 1927, Barnett House Papers, 1928.
*Life under the Soviets*, by Alexander Wicksteed with an introduction by B. Webb (1928).
*A New Reform Bill*, Fabian Society, 1931.
*Nine women, drawn from the epoch of the French Revolution*, by Halina Sokolnikova, with an introduction by B. Webb.
*The Modern State*, by L. Woolf, Lord E. Percy, B. Webb, ed. by M. Adams (1933).
*Our Partnership*, ed. by B. Drake, Margaret Cole (1948).
*Diaries 1912–24*, ed. by Margaret Cole, with an introduction by Lord Beveridge (1952).
*Diaries 1924–32*, ed. and with an introduction by M. Cole (1956).
*Visit to New Zealand in 1898: Beatrice Webb's Diary with entries by Sidney Webb* (1959).
*Beatrice Webb's American Diary*, ed. D. A. Shannon (1963).
*The Webbs' Australian Diary*, ed. A. E. Austin (1965).

## BY SIDNEY WEBB:

*Fabian Essays in Socialism*, Bernard Shaw, Sidney Webb, Graham Wallas, 1889; Jubilee edition, Allen & Unwin, 1948.
*Socialism in England*, Baltimore, 1889.
*English Progress towards Social Democracy*, Fabian Society, 1890.
*The London Programme* (1891).
*Socialism: true and false*, Fabian Society, 1894.
*The Difficulties of Individualism*, Fabian Society, 1896.
*Labour in the Longest Reign 1837–97*, Fabian Society, 1897.
*Twentieth Century Politics*, Fabian Society, 1901.
*London Education* (1904).

*Decline in the Birth Rate*, Fabian Society, 1907.

*Paupers and Old Age Pensions*, Fabian Society, 1908.

*Socialism and Individualism*, S. Webb, B. Shaw, S. Ball and Sir O. Lodge, Fabian Society, 1908.

*The Basis and Policy of Socialism*, by S. Webb and the Fabian Society, 1908.

*Grants in Aid* (1911).

*The Necessary Basis of Society*, Fabian Society, 1911.

*Seasonal Trades*, ed. S. Webb and A. Freeman (1912).

*What about the Rates?*, Fabian Society, 1913.

*The War and the Workers*, a handbook of some immediate measures to prevent unemployment and relieve distress, Fabian Society, 1914.

*The Anya Samaj*, Lajpat Rai, preface by S. Webb (1915).

*How to pay for the War*, ed. S. Webb, Fabian Society, 1916.

*When Peace Comes* – the way of industrial reconstruction, Fabian Society, 1916.

*Great Britain after the War*, S. Webb and A. Freeman (1916).

*The Works Manager Today* (1917).

*The Reform of the House of Lords*, Fabian Society, 1917.

*The Restoration of trade union conditions* (1917).

*The Teacher in Politics*, Fabian Society, 1918.

*National Finance and a Levy on Capital*, Fabian Society, 1919.

*The Root of Labour Unrest*, Fabian Society, 1920.

*Wages, Prices and Profits* – a report from the Labour Research Department, preface by Sidney Webb (1922).

*The Constitutional Problems of a Co-operative Society*, Fabian Society, 1923.

*The Labour Party on the threshold*, Fabian Society, 1923.

*The Co-operative Movement in Japan*, by Keyoshi Ogata, preface by S. Webb (1923).

*The need for federal reorganization in the Co-operative Movement*, Fabian Society, 1923.

*A History of Factory Legislation*, by B. L. Hutching and A. Harrison, preface by S. Webb, 1926.

*The Local Government Act 1929 – how to make the best of it*, Fabian Society, 1929.

*Co-operative Banking*, by N. I. Barou, introduction by S. Webb (1932).

*What happened in 1931 – a record*, Fabian Society, 1932.

*Constitution of the Union of Socialist Soviet Republics*, annotated by P. Sloan, introduction by S. Webb (1936).

BY BEATRICE AND SIDNEY WEBB:

*The History of Trade Unionism* (1894).

*Industrial Democracy* (2 vols., 1897).

*Problems of Modern Industry* (includes 'Pages from a Work-girl's Diary' [1888]) (1898).

*Bibliography of road making and maintenance in Great Britain* (1906).

*English Local Government from the Revolution to the Municipal Corporations Act: The Parish and the County* (1906).

*English Local Government: The Manor and the Borough* (2 vols., 1908).

*The Break-up of the Poor Law* (part 1 of the Minority Report of the Poor Law Commission, ed. with an introduction by S. and B. Webb, 1909).

*The Public Organization of the Labour Market* (part II of the Minority Report of the Poor Law Commission, ed. with an introduction by S. and B. Webb, 1909).

*The State and the Doctor* (1910).

*English Poor Law Policy* (1910).

*The Prevention of Destitution* (1911).

*Grants in Aid* (1911).

*English Local Government: The Story of the King's Highway* (1913).

*The Consumers' Co-operative Movement* (1921).

*English Local Government: English Prisons under Local Government* (1922).

*English Local Government: Statutory Authorities* (1922).

*The Decay of Capitalist Civilization* (1923).

*English Poor Law History: The Old Poor Law* (1927).

*English Poor Law History: The Last Hundred Years* (2 vols., 1929).

*Methods of Social Survey* (1932).

*Soviet Communism: a new civilization?* (1935).

*The Truth about Soviet Russia*, preface by G. B. Shaw (1942).

*List of books mentioned in* My Apprenticeship

This list of books mentioned in *My Apprenticeship* may be useful for reference, but it also suggests the temper, curiosity and climate of the author's mind.

*From Ploughshare to Parliament*, Georgina Meinertzhagen.

*A Bremen Family*, Georgina Meinertzhagen.
*Many Memories of Many People*, M. C. M. Simpson.
*Notes on England*, H. Taine.
*Ancien Régime*, H. Taine.
*Early Memories*, J. B. Yeats.
*Autobiography*, Herbert Spencer.
*Man versus the State*, Herbert Spencer.
*First Principles*, Herbert Spencer.
*Social Statics*, Herbert Spencer.
*Sociology*, Herbert Spencer.
*Synthetic Philosophy*, Herbert Spencer.
*System of Philosophy*, Herbert Spencer.
*Lord Randolph Churchill*, Winston Churchill.
*Life of Canon Barnett*, Henrietta Barnett.
*Life of Macaulay*, G. M. Trevelyan.
*Life and Letters of Sir Joseph Dalton Hooker*, Leonard Huxley.
*Life and Letters of Charles Darwin*, Francis Darwin.
*My Reminiscences*, Rabindranath Tagore.
*History of Philosophy*, G. H. Lewes.
*Words and Idioms*, Logan Pearsall Smith.
*Inquiry into Human Faculty*, Francis Galton.
*The Martyrdom of Man*, Winwood Reade.
*Life of Francis Galton*, Karl Pearson.
*Adenoid Diseases of the Rectum*, W. H. C. Cripps.
*Lectures on the English Poets*, William Hazlitt.
*Autobiography*, John Stuart Mill.
*System of Logic*, John Stuart Mill.
*Principles of Political Economy*, John Stuart Mill.
*History of Civilization in England*, H. T. Buckle.
*An Appeal to Caesar*, Margaret Hobhouse.
*English Prisons Today*, Stephen Hobhouse and Fenner Brockway.
*Past and Present*, Thomas Carlyle.
*Life of William Ewart Gladstone*, by John Morley.
*Life of Lord Goschen*, A. D. Elliot.
*Progress and Poverty*, Henry George.
*A Summary of the Principles of Socialism*, H. M. Hyndman and William Morris.
*The Rights of Labour*, Cardinal Manning.
*Life of Cardinal Manning*, Edmund Sheridan Purcell.
*A Politician in Trouble with his Soul*, Auberon Herbert.

*Life of Octavia Hill*, C. E. Maurice.

*Charity and Social Life*, Charles Stewart Loch.

*Christian Charity in the Ancient Church*, E. Uhlhorn.

*Social Work in London*, Helen Bosanquet.

*Essentials of Scientific Method*, A. Wolf.

*Poverty*, Seebohm Rowntree.

*Livelihood and Poverty*, A. L. Bowley and A. R. Burnett Hurst.

*Life and Labour of the People in London*, Charles Booth.

*The Aged Poor in England and Wales*, Charles Booth.

*Charles Booth: a memoir*, Mrs Charles Booth.

*Changes and Chances*, H. W. Nevison.

*Philosophies*, Sir Ronald Ross.

*English Diaries from the XVIth to the XXth Century*, Arthur Ponsonby.

*Co-operative Production*, Benjamin Jones.

*Working Men Co-operators*, Benjamin Jones and Arthur Dyke Acland.

*A Short History of National Science*, Arabella Buckley.

*My Years of Exile*, Edouard Bernstein.

*Lord Hobhouse: a Memoir*, L. T. Hobhouse and J. L. Hammond.

*A Defence of Philosophic Doubt*, A. J. Balfour.

*The Foundations of Belief*, A. J. Balfour.

*The Establishment of Minimum Rates in the Tailoring Industry*, R. H. Tawney.

*Minimum Rates in the Chain-Making Industry*, R. H. Tawney.

*The Wealth of Nations*, Adam Smith.

*Fabian Essays*, ed. G. B. Shaw.

*Life and Letters of Bishop Creighton*, Louise Creighton.

*John T. W. Mitchell*, Percy Redfern.

*Memorial of Edward Vansittart Neale*, ed. Henry Pitman.

*Christian Socialism 1848–1854*, Charles E. Raven.

*The Working Life of Shop Assistants*, J. Hallsworth and R. J. Davies.

*Mixed Essays*, Matthew Arnold.

*Fabian Society: its early history*, G. B. Shaw.

*History of the Fabian Society*, Edward Pease.

*The Story of the Dockers' Strike*, Vaughan Nash and Hubert Llewellyn Smith.

*The Great Famine*, Vaughan Nash.

*Daniel Deronda*, George Eliot.

418

*The Victorian Novel: 'I have been haunted by a longing to create characters and to move them to and fro among fictitious circumstances.'*

Beatrice Webb remained perpetually uncertain about her sense of the greatness of the Victorian novel, and her doubts about its usefulness. Yet the most elusive and delicate insights into the age in which she lived are probably to be found in the work of the novelists. Dickens is the most prolific: *Little Dorrit* universalizing the dilemma of the human spirit in an acquisitive society; *Our Mutual Friend* giving as part of a greater canvas a sense of the poor law at work, even more remarkable than that in the earlier *Oliver Twist*. And with *Hard Times* Dickens takes the reader to the point that Beatrice Webb was at before her visit to Bacup: conscious that the great organized upsurge of the working class movement was going to change society, but fearful of what this might mean. Mrs Gaskell's *North and South* offers a contrasting, more sympathetic report. Trollope and Disraeli in their political novels present in a less searching vein many of the social and political concerns that lodge themselves in Beatrice Webb's Journals. But in temper and passion, the novelist who stands nearest to her remains George Eliot, both the earlier writer of *Mill on the Floss* but more especially the later artist of *Middlemarch* and *Daniel Deronda*.

# Index

Acland, Rt Hon. Sir Arthur Dyke, 407
Administrative Nihilism, 61, 142, 179–80, 191, 195–205, 313n., 329–40, 342–3
Aked family, the, 168–70, 177, 179, 181–2, 184
Allen, Grant, 57
Anti-Corn Law League, 28, 46
Arnold, Dr, 85
Arnold, Matthew, 389, 392
Asquith, Rt Hon. H. H., see Oxford and Asquith, Earl of
Asquith, Mrs M., see Oxford and Asquith, Countess of
Aves, Ernest, 262

Bacup, working-class cousins at, 12, 44, 167–85
Balfour, Earl of, 190, 307
Barnett, Canon and Dame Henrietta, 12, 101n., 188, 192, 207, 208, 209, 210, 216n., 217–24, 261, 266n., 269, 270, 278, 279, 281, 284, 292, 315
Baylis, Lilian, 272n.
Beaconsfield, Earl of, 34, 84
Beesly, E. S., 228, 298n.
Beringer, Oscar, 97–8n.
Bernstein, Édouard, 306n.
Besant, Annie, 324n., 400
Beveridge, Sir William, 22
birth control, 306; relation of, to destitution, 256
Blandford, Thomas, 362n.
Bond, Edward, 270, 277, 280
Booth, Rt Hon. Charles, 12,

14–15, 17, 42, 188, 218, 226–39, 241, 242–3, 245, 247–9, 250, 252–5, 257, 258, 260–63, 264, 291–2, 293, 298n., 300, 310n., 313–14, 315, 316, 319–20, 333, 341, 346, 349, 401, 404, 409
Booth, Mary, 188, 227, 228, 230n., 231, 262, 274, 298n., 300, 404
Bowley, A. L., 255n.
Bradlaugh, Charles, 129, 147, 189, 191, 306n.
Brassey, Thomas, 31
Brentano, Luigi, 388n.
Bright, Rt Hon. John, 28, 35, 38, 142, 191
Brockway, Fenner, 163n.
Burnett, John, 318—19n., 322n., 331, 332, 366, 368, 371, 404
Burns, Rt Hon. John, 400, 404
Buxton, Rt Hon. Sydney (afterwards Earl Buxton), 407

Cairnes, John Elliott, 376
Capitalist enterprise: my father's connection with, 10, 29–32; ethics of, 32–3; attitude of Charles Booth to, 229–30; relation of, to poverty, 232–3, 244–5, 251–2; the sweating system and, 313–40 description of, 301–40
Carlyle, Thomas, 35, 48, 187, 191, 193
Census, use of, by Charles Booth, 234

## MORE ABOUT PENGUINS

*Penguinews,* which appears every month, contains details of all the new books issued by Penguins as they are published. From time to time it is supplemented by *Penguins in Print,* which is a complete list of all books published by Penguins which are in print. (There are well over three thousand of these).

A specimen copy of *Penguinews* will be sent to you free on request, and you can become a subscriber for the price of the postage. For a year's issues (including the complete lists) please send 30p if you live in the United Kingdom, or 60p if you live elsewhere. Just write to Dept EP, Penguin Books Ltd, Harmondsworth, Middlesex, enclosing a cheque or postal order, and your name will be added to the mailing list.

Some other books published by Penguins are described on the following pages.

Note: *Penguinews* and *Penguins in Print* are not available in the U.S.A. or Canada

## Charles Booth's London

Albert Fried and Richard Elman,
with a foreword by Raymond Williams

'No. 34 is occupied by the widow of a boatman. He committed suicide and left her with eleven children . . . She makes sailor jackets, but is nearly blind . . . there are also living in this house, in one room, Coleman and his wife, and two children. Coleman was a porter but does nothing, preferring to smoke his pipe . . . A third room is occupied by Owen, a labourer, often out of work, with wife and three children. They are nearly starving.'

No. 34 Carver Street was one of the households Charles Booth investigated in the 1880s for his classic study of the poor in an industrial environment, *Life and Labour of the People in London*. This is a selection from a work originally published in seventeen volumes, which is astonishing for its detail and objectivity, and was a forerunner of every modern social inquiry.

*A History of British Trade Unionism*

Henry Pelling

'A genuine and worthwhile addition to the growing literature on trade unionism' – George Woodcock in the *Sunday Times*

Today trade unionism plays a more important part in the nation's economy than ever before, and its problems of internal reform and its relations with the government and the public are constantly under discussion. But its present structure can only be understood in relation to its long history.

Henry Pelling, a Fellow of St John's College, Cambridge, and author of *The Origins of the Labour Party,* leads the reader through a vivid story of struggle and development covering more than four centuries: from the medieval guilds and early craftsmen's and labourers' associations to the dramatic growth of trade unionism in Britain in the nineteenth and twentieth centuries.

He shows how powerful personalities such as Robert Applegarth, Henry Broadhurst, Tom Mann, Ernest Bevin, and Walter Citrine have helped to shape the pattern of present-day unionism; and also how the problems of today's leaders stem from the need to adapt attitudes and structure moulded in the conflicts of earlier generations.

'Readable and intelligent' – *The Times Educational Supplement*

ROBERT OWEN

## Report to the County of Lanark
## A New View of Society

Robert Owen, the New Lanark mill-owner and social philosopher, was one of the first to stress the influence of environment upon character. His rationalistic belief in human perfectibility, and his unbounded faith in education to bring about a new moral order without class conflict led the Fabians to revere him as the father of English socialism. But his influence, V.A.C. Gatrell argues, was even wider: for although 'Owenism' as a cooperative movement soon dated, his belief in a harmonious organic community in contrast to unrestrained capitalism also inspired a Tory tradition. Owen's ideas and practice have entered our cultural bloodstream through many different channels.

## KINGSLEY MARTIN

### Father Figures

Among Kingsley Martin's father figures were George Bernard
Shaw and Lowes Dickinson, and his friends and acquaintances also included the Webbs, Maynard Keynes, Leonard
and Virginia Woolf, R. H. Tawney, Harold Laski, C. P. Scott
and Lord Reith. They all appear in this scrupulously honest
record of Kingsley Martin's youth, in which he brings to life
a dissenting background, both moralistic and unconventional,
a war spent in a pacifist ambulance unit, a controversial university career at Cambridge, Princeton and the L.S.E. – and
a training in journalism on the *Manchester Guardian* which
fitted him for his true role as editor of the *New Statesman*
and perhaps the greatest moulder of English intellectual
opinion in the thirties.

### Editor

As the forceful editor of the *New Statesman*, Kingsley Martin
was at the centre of all the acute intellectual and moral conflicts of the thirties, from the slump, the breakdown of social
democracy and the rise of fascism to the Stalinist purges, the
Spanish Civil War and the Second World War. In this sequel
to *Father Figures*, his first volume of autobiography, he writes
with the same ruthlessly honest self-scrutiny, and includes
equally shrewd pen-portraits of contemporary politicians and
writers. This superb autobiography is a unique evocation of
the state of mind of the English progressive community in the
years up to the end of the Second World War.
As we enter a new age of ideology, there is much in it to
learn and enjoy.